2nd edition September 2004

Original edition printed May 2001

Published by AA Publishing (a trading name of Automobile Association Developments Limited, whose registered office is Millstream, Maidenhead Road, Windsor, Berkshire SL4 5GD. Registered number 1878835).

Mapping produced by the Cartography Department of The Automobile Association. A2087

Key to map pages ii-iii

Key to map symbols iv–1

Enlarged map pages 2-9

Main map pages 10-137

Index – towns & villages 138

Index – streets 140-184

Index – featured places 185-193

Acknowledgements 193

A CIP Catalogue record for this book is available from the British Library.

Printed by GRAFIASA S.A., Porto, Portugal

Ref: MN069z

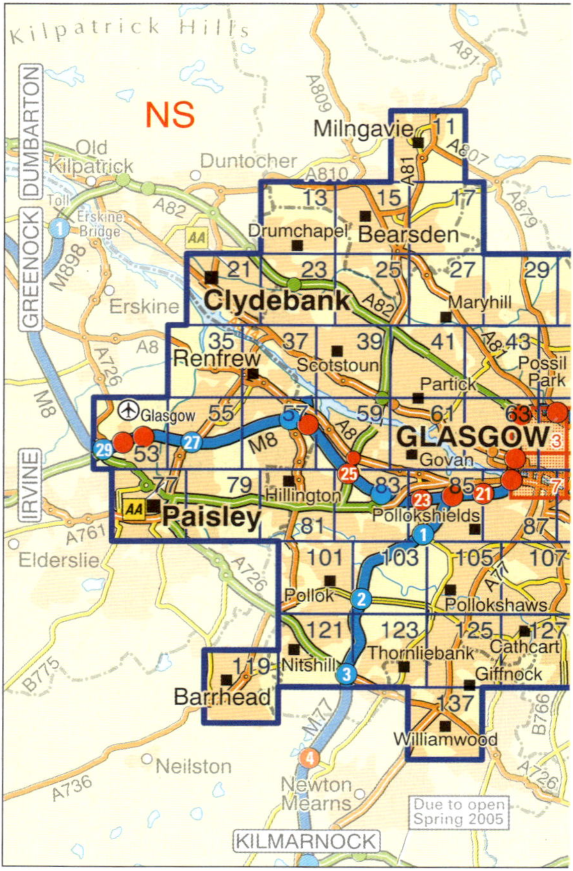

Kilpatrick Hills
NS
DUMBARTON
GREENOCK
IRVINE
KILMARNOCK
Milngavie
Old Kilpatrick
Duntocher
Toll
Erskine Bridge
Erskine
Drumchapel
Bearsden
Clydebank
Maryhill
Renfrew
Scotstoun
Partick
Possil Park
Glasgow
GLASGOW
Govan
Paisley
Hillington
Pollokshields
Elderslie
Pollok
Pollokshaws
Nitshill
Thornliebank
Cathcart
Giffnock
Barrhead
Williamwood
Neilston
Newton Mearns
Due to open Spring 2005
A81 A809 A807 A810 A879 A82 A8 A726 M8 M898 A761 A77 M77 B775 A736 B766

11 13 15 17 21 23 25 27 29 35 37 39 41 43 53 55 57 59 61 63 77 79 81 83 85 87 101 103 105 107 119 121 123 125 127 137

Scale of enlarged map pages 1:10,000 **6.3 inches to 1 mile**

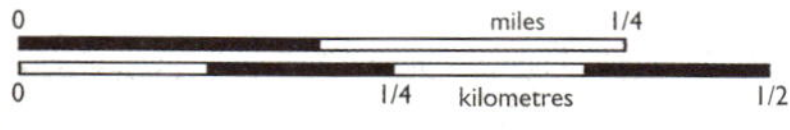

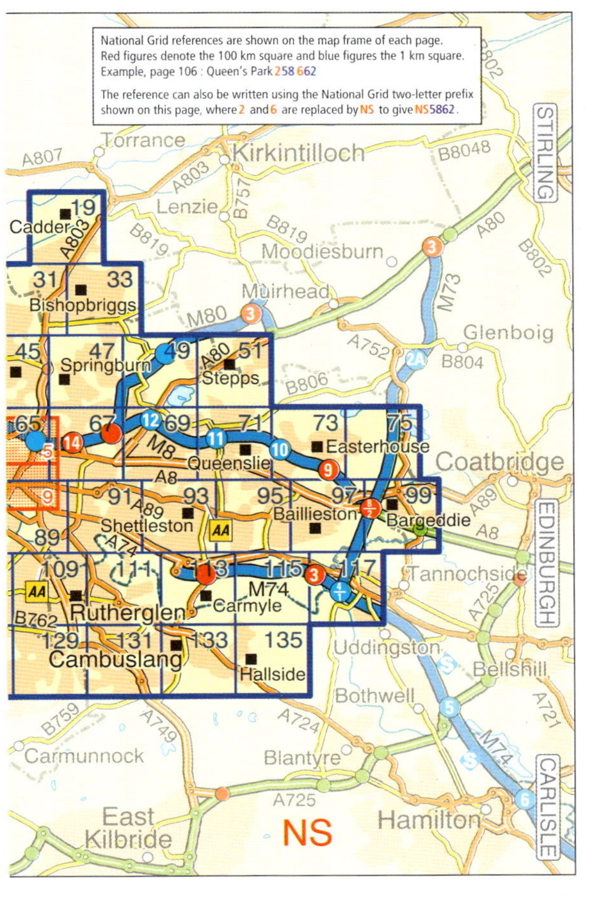

4.2 inches to 1 mile

Scale of main map pages **1:15,000**

0 1/4 miles 1/2

0 1/4 1/2 kilometres 3/4 1

Junction 9 — Motorway & junction

Services — Motorway service area

Primary road single/ dual carriageway

Services — Primary road service area

A road single/dual carriageway

B road single/dual carriageway

Other road single/dual carriageway

Minor/private road, access may be restricted

One-way street

Pedestrian area

Track or footpath

Road under construction

Road tunnel

AA — AA Service Centre

P — Parking

P+ — Park & Ride

Bus/coach station

Railway & main railway station

Railway & minor railway station

Underground station

Light railway & station

Preserved private railway

LC — Level crossing

Tramway

Ferry route

Airport runway

County, administrative boundary

Mounds

93 — Page continuation 1:15,000

7 — Page continuation to enlarged scale 1:10,000

River/canal, lake

Aqueduct, lock, weir

465 Winter Hill — Peak (with height in metres)

Beach

Woodland

Park

Cemetery

Built-up area

Featured building

City wall

Map Symbols

A&E	Hospital with 24-hour A&E department
PO	Post Office
	Public library
	Tourist Information Centre
	Seasonal Tourist Information Centre
	Petrol station, 24 hour Major suppliers only
	Church/chapel
	Public toilets
	Toilet with disabled facilities
PH	Public house AA recommended
	Restaurant AA inspected
Madeira Hotel	Hotel AA inspected
	Theatre or performing arts centre
	Cinema
	Golf course
	Camping AA inspected
	Caravan site AA inspected
	Camping & caravan site AA inspected
	Theme park
	Abbey, cathedral or priory
	Castle
	Historic house or building
Dirleton Castle NTS	National Trust for Scotland property
	Museum or art gallery
	Roman antiquity
	Ancient site, battlefield or monument
	Industrial interest
	Garden
	Garden Centre Garden Centre Association Member
	Arboretum
	Farm or animal centre
	Zoological or wildlife collection
	Bird collection
	Nature reserve
	Aquarium
V	Visitor or heritage centre
	Country park
	Cave
	Windmill
	Distillery, brewery or vineyard

2
63
58
6
Junction 17
Junction 18
Junction 19
GREAT WESTERN ROAD
ST GEORGE'S RD
M8
St Georges Cross Station
North Woodside Swimming Pool
Oakgrove Primary School
Islamic Mosque
Glasgow Gaelic School
St Georges Medical Cen
Douglas Inch Centre
Tenement House
Royal Highland Fusiliers Museum
Stow College
Preparatory School
Garnetbank Primary School
School of Art
St Aloysius College
Dental Hosp
Kings Theatre
Mitchell Thtr & Lib
Charing Cross Stn
Premier Lodge
Police Station
Malmaison Hotel
Novotel
Ibis Hotel
William Street Clinic
St Patricks Primary School
Scottish Enterprises
Holiday Inn
Glasgow Marriott Hotel
1 grid square represents 250 metres

Port Dundas
Farnell St
Burns St
Raglan St
Raglan Street
Sawmillfield St
Barratt Trading Est
Edington St
Manresa Pl
Braid Sq
Abercorn School
Corn Street
Civic St
ROAD
A879
High St
North Canal Bank Street
Dundashill
CRAIGHALL ROAD
Payne Street
Townsend St
Mid-Wharf St
A804
Dobbie's Loan
Dundas Business Cen
Police Stn
Stewart St
Maitland St
Dunblane Street
Port Dundas Road
Renton Street
Tyndrum Street
New City Rd
School of Art
Garscube Rd
Cowcaddens Stn
Glenmavis St
Fire Station
Milton Street
DOBBIE'S
Cowcaddens Road
Scottish Ambulance HQ
Larbert St
Dunblane St
McPhater St
National Piping Centre
Travelodge
Theatre Royal
Cambridge St
RSAMD
Express by Holiday Inn
Renfrew St
Film Theatre
Scottish TV
Renfield St
Port Dundas Pl
Sauchiehall Street
The Pav Theatre
UGC Cinema
Langs Hotel
Killermont Street
Caledonian University
Sauchiehall La
Bath Street
Cncl Bldg
Sauchiehall Lane
E Bath La
Royal Concert Hall
Buchanan Galleries & Shopping Centre
Bath La
W Regent Street
West Regent Lane
West George Lane
Odeon Cinema
Buchanan Street Stn
Cncl Bldg
Bath St
Coll of Building & Printing
Queen Street Station
Hope St
Renfield St
W George La
Nile St
Nelson
W George St
George Square
Millennium Hotel
St Vincent Street
St Mary's La
St Vincent La
Renfield Lane
Drury St
West Nile St
Gordon Street
North Ct
Anchor La
George St
Wellington St
Waterloo La
Campbell Lane
Cowcaddens Rd
Buchanan Bus Station
Cathedral St
Harvey St
PO
P
D
E
F
64
59
7
1
2
3
4
5

4
Harvey Street
Broadford Street
65
A
B
C
Pinkston Road
Fountainwell Dr
North Canal Bank
Street
Mid-Wharf St
Street
Townsend St
G4
Junction 16
M8
Canal St
Swan St
DOBBIE'S LOAN
A804
Calgary St
Stafford Street
Kyle St
N Wallace St
A804 BAIRD STREET
Post Office Sorting Office
KYLE STREET
Couper Street
N Wallace St
Lister St
Black St
Glebe St
Kennedy St
Dobbie's Loan
Glasgow Caledonian University
3
Kennedy St
Dobbie's Pl
Dobbie's Loan
Council Building
Glebe Ct
St Mungo Av
St Mungo Pl
McAslin Ct
Cowcaddens Road
Buchanan Bus Station
Townhead
St Mungo Avenue
St Mungo Av
Hanover St
North St
Grafton Pl
Taylor Pl
International Christian College
St James Road
Hanover Ct
Coll of Food & Technology
Central College of Commerce
University of Strathclyde
Stirling Rd
College of Building & Printing
Cathedral Street
Cathedral Street
Provand's Lordship
University of Strathclyde
Rottenrow
Royal Maternity Hospital
University of Strathclyde
Martha St
Frederick St
Cncl Bldg
Taylor St
Weaver St
N Portland St
Richmond St
8
John St
Square
George
Millennium Hotel
GLASGOW
George
PO
I grid square represents 250 metres

Sighthill
Royston
St Kevins Special School
St Stephen's Primary School
Police Station
Pinkston
Drive
SPRINGBURN ROAD
A803
Charles Street
Royston Sq
Royston Road
Provanhill Street
Royston Primary School
ROYSTON ROAD
St Rochs Secondary School
Council Building
Rhymer St
Glenbarr St
Gadshill St
CASTLE ST
Junction 15
Roystonhill
James Nisbet St
M8
ALEXANDRA PARADE
McAslin St
Glasgow Royal Infirmary
Townhead Health Centre
Warnock St
Wishart Street
Firpark Street
A8
GLEBE ST
A&E
Glasgow Cathedral
Cemetery
Golfhill Primary School
St Mungo Mus of Religious Life & Art
Macleod St
Rottenrow
Cathedral Square
Cathedral Sq
Drygate
Glasgow Necropolis
Firpark Ter
Ark La
Broompark
Circus
Hanson St
The Young People's Theatre
Fountainwell Sq
Huntingdon Square
Huntingdon Rd
Road
65
66
9
D
E
F
60

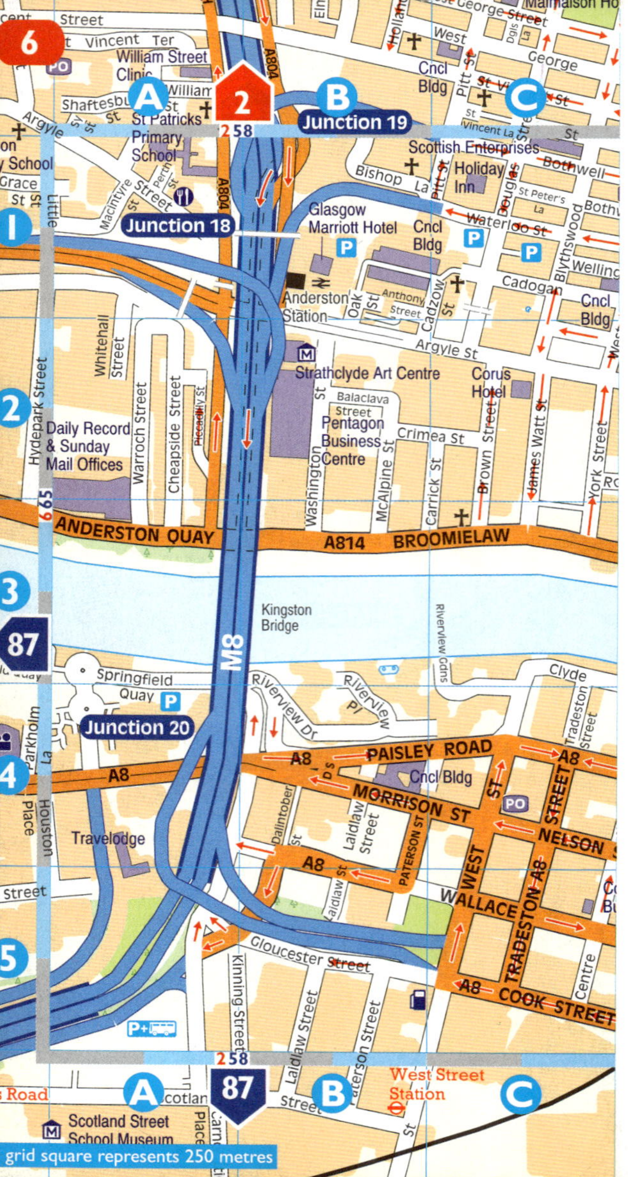
6
2
Junction 19
Junction 18
Junction 20
A
B
C
1
2
3
4
5
87
258
665
William Street Clinic
St Patricks Primary School
Scottish Enterprises
Holiday Inn
Glasgow Marriott Hotel
Cncl Bldg
Anderston Station
Strathclyde Art Centre
Corus Hotel
Pentagon Business Centre
Daily Record & Sunday Mail Offices
ANDERSTON QUAY
A814
BROOMIELAW
Kingston Bridge
M8
A804
Springfield Quay
PAISLEY ROAD
MORRISON ST
NELSON ST
WEST ST
TRADESTON A8
WALLACE ST
COOK STREET
A8
Travelodge
Gloucester Street
Kinning Street
West Street Station
Scotland Street School Museum
Argyle St
Waterloo St
Bothwell St
Cadogan
Hydepark Street
Whitehall Street
Warroch Street
Cheapside Street
Washington St
McAlpine St
Carrick St
Brown Street
James Watt St
York Street
Riverview Dr
Riverview Pl
Riverview Gdns
Clyde
Tradeston Street
Laidlaw Street
Paterson St
Houston Pl
Parkholm La
1 grid square represents 250 metres

Regent
West Regent
West George
Bath La
St Vincent Street
St Vincent La
Renfield Lane
Gordon Street
Drury St
W George La
St Mary's La
Stock Exchange
Queen Street Station
W George Street
Citizen La
St Vincent Pl
North Ct
Millennium Hotel
George Sq
Mandela Pl
Scottish Youth Thtr
Royal Ex Sq
Gallery of Modern Art
Royal Ex Ct
S Ex Ct
Stirling's Lib
Virginia
Cncl Bldg
Thames Open College
Quality Hotel
Glasgow Central Station
Union Pl
Union St
Mitchell St
Mtchll La
Holm Street
Police Station
Argyle Street
Radisson SAS Glasgow
The Lighthouse
Prince's Sq Shop Ctr
Buchanan St
Queen Street
Argyle Indoor Market
Virginia Ct
St Enoch Stn
Police Station
Maxwell St
Midland St
Arches Theatre
Robertson Street
Oswald Street
Jamaica St
Adams Ct La
St Enoch Bus Cen
St Enoch Shopping Centre
Osborne St
Dunlop St
Argyle Street Station
Howard St
University
Dixon St
Fox St
Stockwell Pl
BROOMIELAW
George V Bridge
COMMERCE ST A77
BRIDGE ST
Glasgow Bridge
A814 CLYDE STREET
St Andrews Cathedral
Ropework La
Metropole La
Goosedubbs
River Clyde
Place
Centre Street
Carlton Place
Carlton Court
Portland St
KINGSTON ST
OXFORD ST A8
Oxford St
Nicholson St
Sheriff Court
A8 GORBALS STREET
Victoria Bridge
Adelphi St
Central Mosque
Mosque Avenue
Coburg St
S PORTLAND ST
Oxford La
Nicholson St
NORFOLK ST
A8 BALLATER ST
Council Building
Bridge Street Stn
St Johns Primary Sch
Cncl Bldg
Norfolk Ct
Coburg Street
S Portland Street
Portugal St
Bedford Street
Kilbarchan Street
Eglinton Court
Cleland La
Tulip Inn
St Lukes Ter
Thistle Street
A728
Old Rutherglen
Ninian St
CALEDONIAN ROAD
259
87
65
D
E
F
G2
G1
1
2
3
4
5
8

8
4
A
B
C
Coll of Food & Technology
Central College of Commerce
University of Strathclyde
College of Building & Printing
Cathedral Street
Provand's Lordship
Martha St
Rottenrow
Royal Maternity Hospital
University of Strathclyde
N Portland St
Taylor St
Weaver St
Cncl Bldg
Register Office
N Frederick St
John St
Richmond St
Rottenrow E
Millennium Hotel
GLASGOW
Travel Inn
City Chambers
George Sq
George Street
Cochrane St
Newspaper Offices
Ramshorn Thtr
Montrose St
Albion St
Nicholas St
Shuttle Street
College La
College St
HIGH STREET
A8
High St Station
of Modern Art
Hanover St
S Frederick St
Italian Cen
Hutchesons' Hall
Cncl Bldg
Stirling's Lib
Virginia Pl
Ingram Street
Garth St
Albion Ga
G1
PH
PO
Wilson Street
Blackfriars St
City Halls
Argyle Indoor Market
Virginia Street
Glassford St
Hutcheson Street
Brunswick Street
Bell St
Walls St
Parsonage Rw
Parsonage Sq
Brunswick La
Mlvl Ct
Candleriggs
Cncl Bldg
Tontine La
Cncl Bldg
Tolbooth Steeple
Bell Street
Watson Street
Argyle Street Station
Trongate
Cncl Bldg
Brenda Temple
Old Wynd
New Wynd
Tron Steeple
Tron Thtr
Glasgow Cross
A89
Molendinar St
Little Dovehill
Great Dovehill
Spmth
GALLOWGATE
MOIR ST
Gallowgate Mkt
Charlotte St
Ross St
Suff St
Stockwell St
Express by Holiday Inn
Goosedubbs
King St
St Andrew's La
St Andrew's St
James Morrison St
Cncl Bldg
BRIDGE-GATE
A8
Mart St
Open Air Mkt Stall
Jocelyn Sq
SALTMARKET
Steel St
Turnbull St
Dyer's La
St Andrew's Square
Monteith Rw
Mcht La
High Ct & Ct of Justiciary
Victoria Bridge
Greendyke Street
Charlotte St
Council Building
Glasgow College of Nautical Studies
A8
Albert Bridge
Florence Street Clinic
Gorbals Leisure Centre
Glasgow Green
CROWN STREET
Thistle Street
Florence St
BALLATER ST
A728
Ninian Ter
Commercial Road
Adelphi
1
2
3
4
5
7
88
grid square represents 250 metres

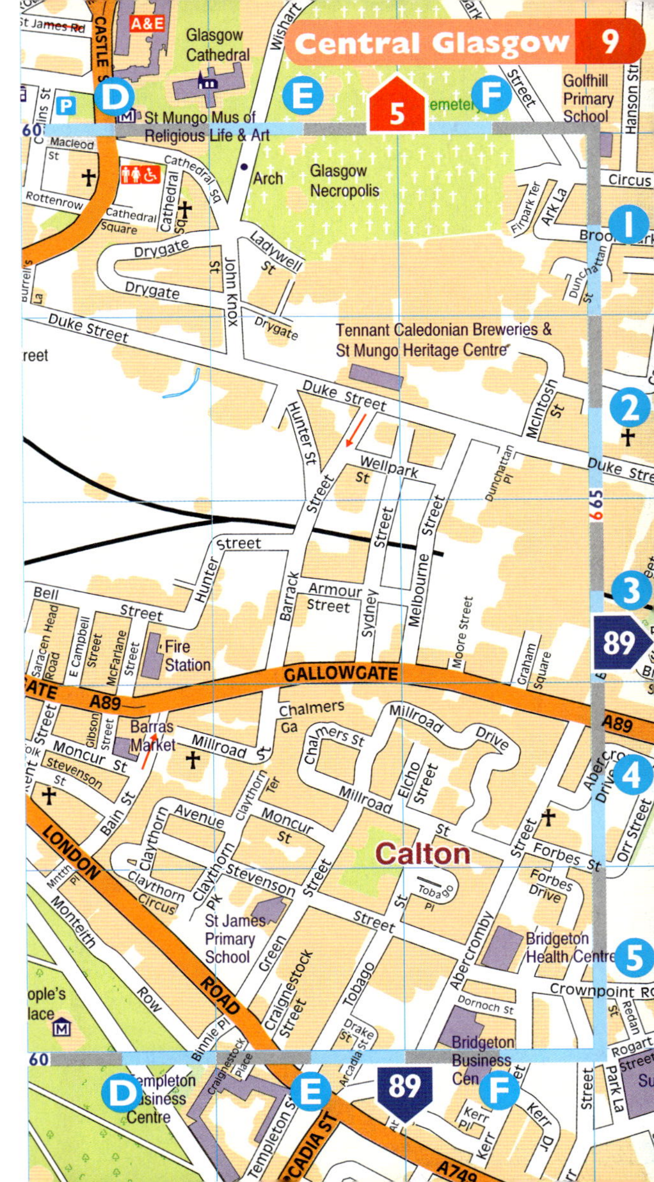

Glasgow Cathedral
St Mungo Mus of Religious Life & Art
Glasgow Necropolis
Golfhill Primary School
Tennant Caledonian Breweries & St Mungo Heritage Centre
Fire Station
Barras Market
GALLOWGATE
Calton
St James Primary School
Bridgeton Health Centre
Bridgeton Business Cen
Templeton Business Centre
LONDON ROAD
Duke Street
Drygate
John Knox St
Wellpark St
Melbourne Street
Armour Street
Millroad Drive
Abercromby Street
Crownpoint Rd
Forbes St
Moncur St
Stevenson Street
Claythorn Avenue
Monteith Row
A89
A749
89
5

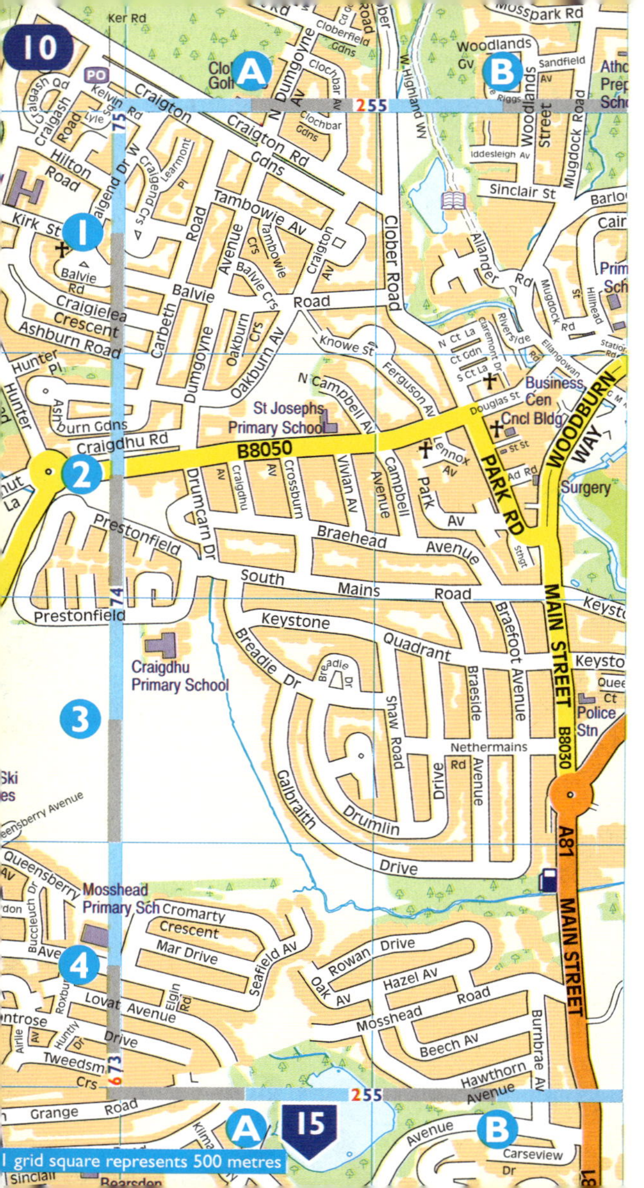

10
Ker Rd
Craigton Rd
Craigton Rd
Craigton Gdns
Tambowie Av
Balvie Road
Balvie Crs
Kirk St
Hilton Road
Craigleea Crescent
Ashburn Road
Hunter Pl
Ashburn Gdns
Craigdhu Rd
B8050
Prestonfield
South Mains Road
Keystone Quadrant
Breadie Dr
Craigdhu Primary School
St Josephs Primary School
Clober Road
Mosspark Rd
Woodlands Gv
Sandfield Av
Woodlands Street
Mugdock Road
Iddesleigh Av
Sinclair St
Allander Rd
Knowe St
N Campbell Av
Ferguson Av
Campbell Avenue
Vivian Av
Crossburn Av
Drumcarn Dr
Braehead Avenue
Park Av
Lennox Av
PARK RD
Douglas St
Business Cen
Cncl Bldg
WOODBURN WAY
Surgery
MAIN STREET
B8030
Braefoot Avenue
Braeside Avenue
Nethermains Rd
Shaw Road
Drumlin Drive
Galbraith Drive
Police Stn
A81
Mosshead Primary Sch
Cromarty Crescent
Mar Drive
Seafield Av
Queensberry Av
Lovat Avenue
Tweedsmuir Crs
Rowan Drive
Oak Av
Hazel Av
Mosshead Road
Beech Av
Hawthorn Avenue
Burnbrae Av
Grange Road
Carseview Dr
Dumgoyne Av
Oakburn Av
Carbeth Road
Craigend Dr W
Learmont Pl
Clochbar Gdns
Cloberfield Gdns
W Highland Wy
Mugdock Rd
Riverside Rd
Ellangowan Rd
Claremont Dr
Hillhead St
Buccleuch Dr
Elgin Rd
Huntly Dr
Roxburgh
A B
1 2 3 4
255
15
1 grid square represents 500 metres

MILNGAVIE
STRATHBLANE
Blane Drive
Roselea Drive
Campsie Drive
Middleton Dr
Lynn Dr
Tower Pl
Ln Dr
Moor Rd
Buchanan St
Kersland Dr
Craigmillar
Tannoch
Cncl Bldg
Grange Av
Surg
Town Hall
STATION RD
Garwhitter Dr
Barloch Rd
Balfleurs St
Briarwell La
Briarwell Rd
Connell Crs
S Glassford St
Dougalston Avenue
Dougalston Gdns N
Dougalston Crs
Dougalston Gdns S
Fulton Rd
Vr Pl
Milngavie Station
Crssvggt
A81
GLASGOW ROAD
A807
AUCHENHOWIE
Finlay Ri
Finlay Rise
Mitchell Dr
Lawn Pk
Ewing Wk
Achncrv
Brdggt
Oswald Wlk
Virginia Grdns
Dunmore Dr
Mrdch Dr
Dougalston Loch
Golf Cour
Esporta, Do
Allandar Sports Centre
Milngavie & Bearsden Sports Club
Boclair
56
75
74
73
6
1
2
3
4
C
D
17

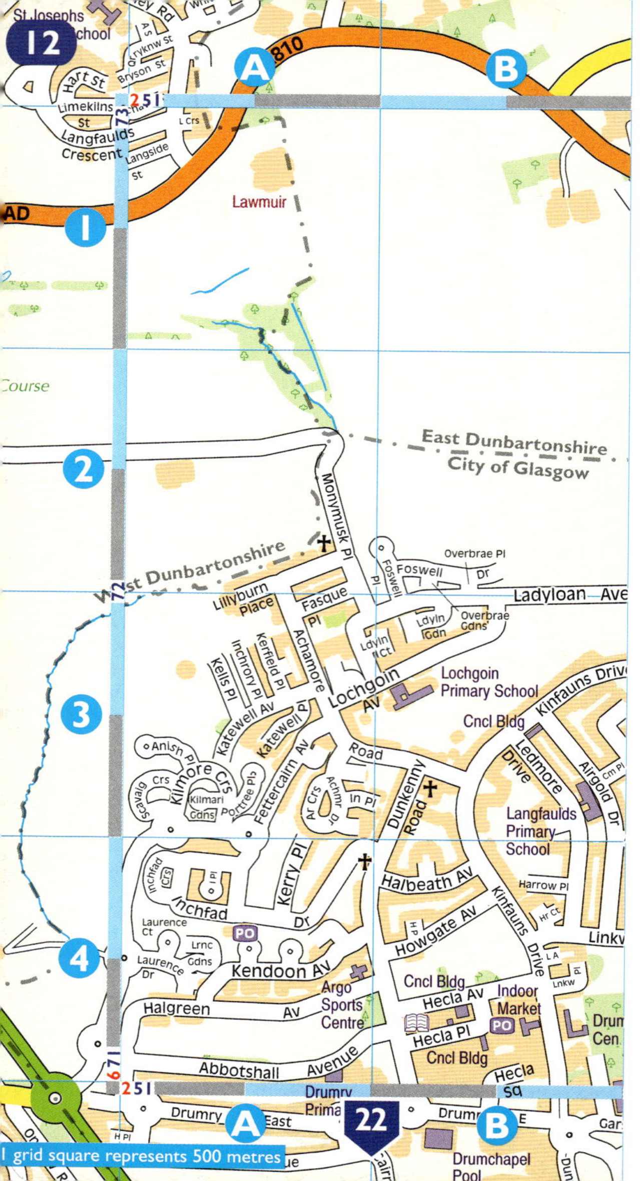

12
St Josephs School
Hart St
Bryson St
Limekilns St
Langfaulds Crescent
Langside St
L Crs
A810
A
B
1
2
3
4
Lawmuir
Course
East Dunbartonshire
City of Glasgow
West Dunbartonshire
Monymusk Pl
Foswell Pl
Foswell Dr
Overbrae Pl
Ladyloan Ave
Overbrae Gdns
Ldyln Gdn
Ldyln Ct
Lillyburn Place
Fasque Pl
Achamore Rd
Kerfield Pl
Inchrory Pl
Kells Pl
Katewell Av
Katewell Pl
Lochgoin Av
Lochgoin Primary School
Kinfauns Drive
Cncl Bldg
Ledmore Drive
Airgold Dr
Cm Pl
Langfaulds Primary School
Anish Pl
Kilmore Crs
Kilmari Gdns
Portree Pl
Scavaig Crs
Fettercairn Av
Ar Crs
Achmr Dr
In Pl
Road
Dunkenny Road
Kerry Pl
Inchfad Crs
Inchfad Dr
Halbeath Av
Howgate Av
Harrow Pl
Hr Ct
Linkw
Laurence Ct
Lrnc Gdns
Laurence Dr
PO
Kendoon Av
Argo Sports Centre
Cncl Bldg
Hecla Av
Indoor Market
Hecla Pl
Cncl Bldg
Hecla Sq
Lnkw
Drum Cen
Halgreen Av
Abbotshall Avenue
Drumry Prima
Drumry East
22
H Pl
Drumchapel Pool
Gar
251
73
72
71
67
1 grid square represents 500 metres

DUNTOCHER ROAD
A810
Castlehill Primary School
Summerhill Primary School
St Clare's Prim Sch
Police Station
St Pius Primary School
Drumchapel High School
Pinewood Primary School
Bearsden Golf Club
Golf Course
Drumchapel
G15
Donald Dewar Leisure Centre
Linkwood Gardens
Peel Glen Road
Kilcloy Av
Summerhill Rd
Drummore Rd
Kinfauns Drive
Southdeen Avenue
Carolside Drive
Tallant Road
Fairway
Golfview
Southview
Antonine Rd
Eagle Crs
Abbotsford
Bonnaughton Rd
Tinto Road
Cairngorm Crs
Belsyde Av
Cloan Avenue
14
23

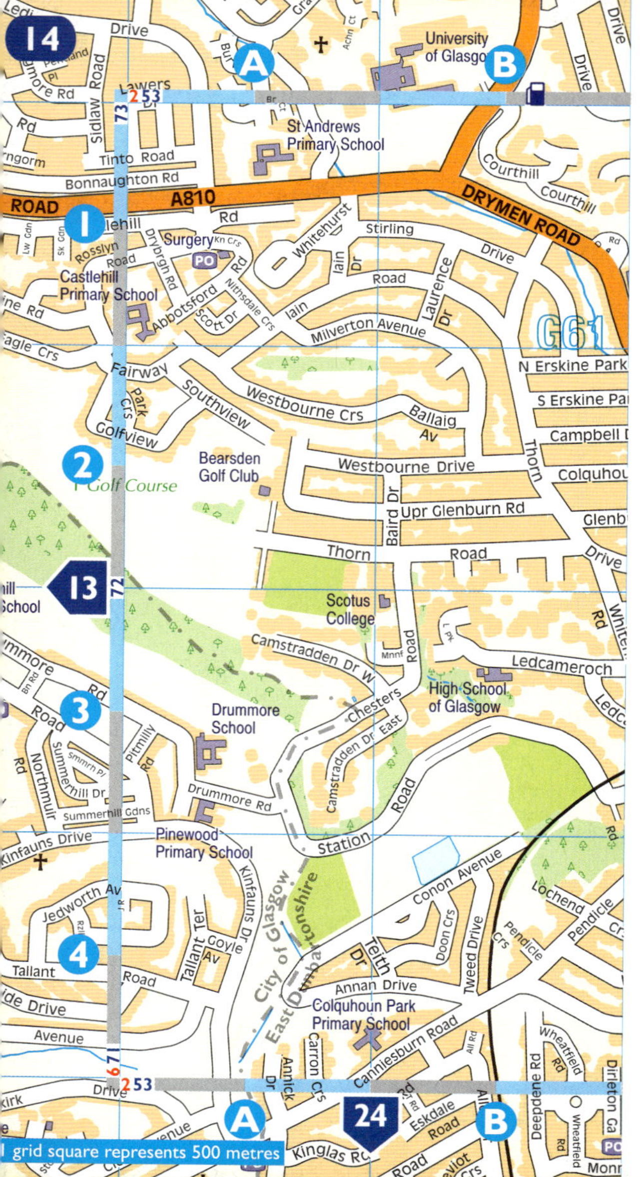
14
13
24
A
B
1
2
3
4
2 53
73
72
67
University of Glasgow
St Andrews Primary School
Castlehill Primary School
Surgery
PO
Bearsden Golf Club
Golf Course
Scotus College
High School of Glasgow
Drummore School
Pinewood Primary School
Colquhoun Park Primary School
A810
ROAD
DRYMEN ROAD
G61
Drive
Lawers
Sidlaw Road
Tinto Road
Bonnaughton Rd
Stirling Road
Whitehurst
Iain Dr
Iain Road
Laurence Dr
Milverton Avenue
Abbotsford
Nithsdale Crs
Scott Dr
Drybrgh Rd
Rosslyn Road
Fairway
Park Crs
Southview
Golfview
Westbourne Crs
Ballaig Av
Westbourne Drive
Baird Dr
Upr Glenburn Rd
Thorn Road
Thorn Drive
N Erskine Park
Campbell
Colquhou
Courthill
Camstradden Dr W
Camstradden Dr East
Chesters Road
Ledcameroch
Drummore Rd
Station Road
Summerhill Dr
Summerhill Gdns
Northmuir Rd
Pitmilly Rd
Kinfauns Drive
Kinfauns Dr
Jedworth Av
Tallant Road
Tallant Ter
Goyle Av
City of Glasgow
East Dunbartonshire
Conon Avenue
Doon Crs
Tweed Drive
Teith Dr
Annan Drive
Carron Crs
Annick Dr
Canniesburn Road
Lochend Rd
Pendicle Crs
Wheatfield Rd
Deepdene Rd
Eskdale Road
Kinglas Rd
Avenue
Drive
1 grid square represents 500 metres

BEARSDEN
Bearsden Academy
Bearsden Primary School
Bearsden Station
Cannieshurn Hospital
North Grange Road
Morven Road
Sinclair Avenue
Edgehill Road
Gartconnell Road
Gartconnell Dr
Elm Walk
Russell Dr
Russell Drive
Ralston Road
Manse Road
Grange Rd
Grange Road
Kilmardinny Dr
Kilmardinny Gv
Kilmardinny Av
Kilmardinny Crescent
Thomson Dr
Hillfoot Dr
Hillside Av
Hillneuk Av
ROMAN RD
ROMAN DR
A808
A809
A81
DRYMEN ROAD
MILNGAVIE ROAD
Collylinn Rd
Rosevale Rd
Jubilee Gdns
W Chapelton Crs
West Chapelton Dr
West Chapelton Avenue
Chapelton Avenue
Chapelton Gdns
Douglas Gdns
Boclair Av
Station Road
Ellergreen Rd
St Germains
Hillcrest Rd
Endrick Dr
Ferguston Road
Leven Dr
Carrickarden Rd
Rubislaw Drive
Lochend Road
Lochend Dr
Whistlefield Ct
Norwood
Cannieshurn Road
Fernlea
Elderbank
Gray Dr
Moore Dr
Macfarlane Road
Buchanan
Kessington
Borland
Pollock Road
Second Avenue
First Avenue
Kilmermont
MARYHILL
Hollymount
Cluny Dr
Birch Vw
Montrose
Lovat Avenue
Tweedsmuir Crs
Kirk Rd
Roman Ct
Surg
Surgery
PO
Cncl Bldg
Tweedsmuir
Drive
Crs
10
16
25
54
55
C
D
1
2
3
4

16
10
15
26
A
B
1
2
3
4
255
73
72
671
Mosshead Road
Beech Av
Hawthorn Avenue
Centre
Carseview Dr
A81
Cncl Bldg
Kilmardinny Crescent
Douglas Park Crs
Reid Av
ROAD
Golf Course
Thomson Dr
Hillneuk Av
Hillneuk Dr
Hillside Dr
Hillfoot Dr
MILNGAVIE
Burnmouth Pl
Cemetery
Douglas Park Golf Club
Hillfoot Station
Birch Vw
ROMAN DR
BOCLAIR ROAD
B8049
Antonine Wall: Bearsden Bath-house
Aviemore Gdns
Kinnaird Crs
Durness Avenue
Methven Av
Birnam Crs
Killermont Primary Sch
Cncl Bldg
Boclair Av
Boclair Crescent
Glenfarg Crs
Dunkeld Dr
Inveroran
Rannoch Drive
Glendaruel Av
Drive
Avenue
Surgery
Buchanan
PO
Greenwood Dr
Hillcrest Rd
Ferguston Road
Leven Dr
Kessington
Drive
Brora Dr
Etive Av
Earn Av
Avon Av
Drive
Rannoch Dr
Oronsay Crs
Clathic Av
Carrickarden Rd
MILNGAVIE ROAD
Borland
Road
Afton Crs
Kessington Rd
Kessington Sq
Macfarlane Road
Pollock Road
Cameron Dr
Speirs
Gray Dr
Second Avenue
Road
Albert Drive
Arisaig Dr
First Avenue
Morar Dr
Schaber Rd
Killermont
Rd
Woodvale
Cluny Av
1 grid square represents 500 metres

C
11
56
57
East Dunbartonshire
City of Glasgow
73
Boclair
BOCLAIR
1
Garden
Centre
Millichen
Road
Road
2
72
Millichen
3
Boclair
Academy
Kessington
Kelvin
4
Golf Course
Av
Dr
71
56
57
C
27
D
East Dun
shire
City of Glasgow
Glasgow
Blackhill

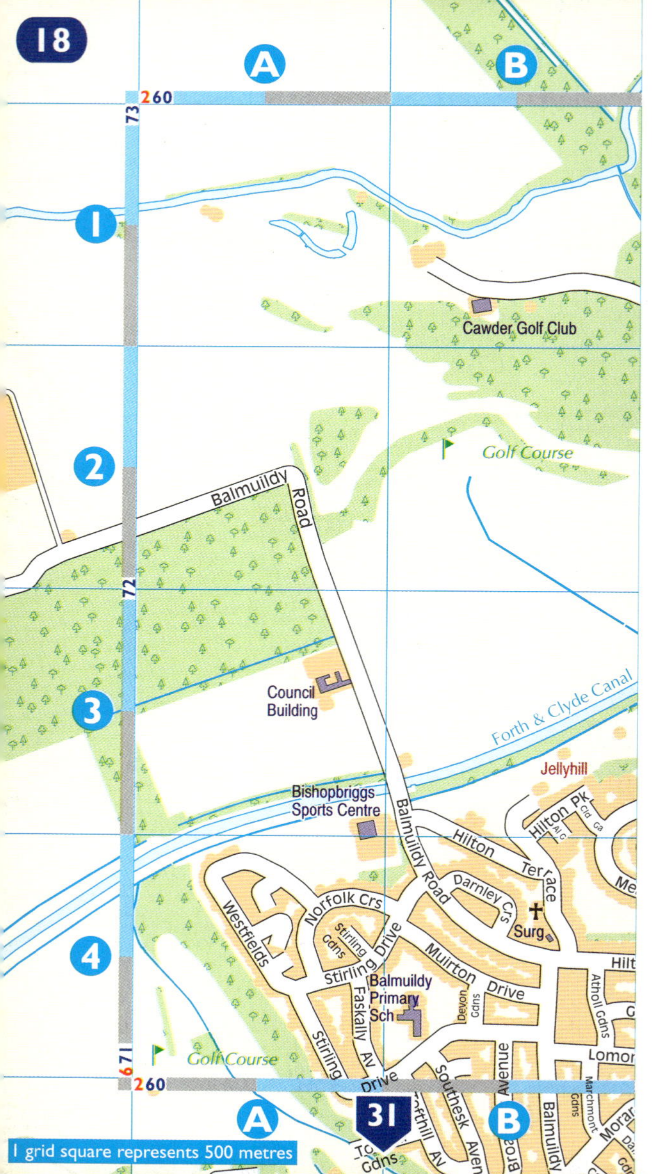
A
B
260
73
1
Cawder Golf Club
2
Golf Course
Balmuildy Road
72
3
Council Building
Forth & Clyde Canal
Jellyhill
Bishopbriggs Sports Centre
Hilton Pk
Hilton Terrace
Balmuildy Road
Darnley Crs
Norfolk Crs
Westfields
Stirling Gdns
Stirling Drive
4
Surg
Muirton Drive
Balmuildy Primary Sch
Faskally Av
Devon Gdns
Atholl Gdns
Stirling Drive
Southesk Avenue
Avenue
Golf Course
671
260
A
31
B
Balmuildy
1 grid square represents 500 metres

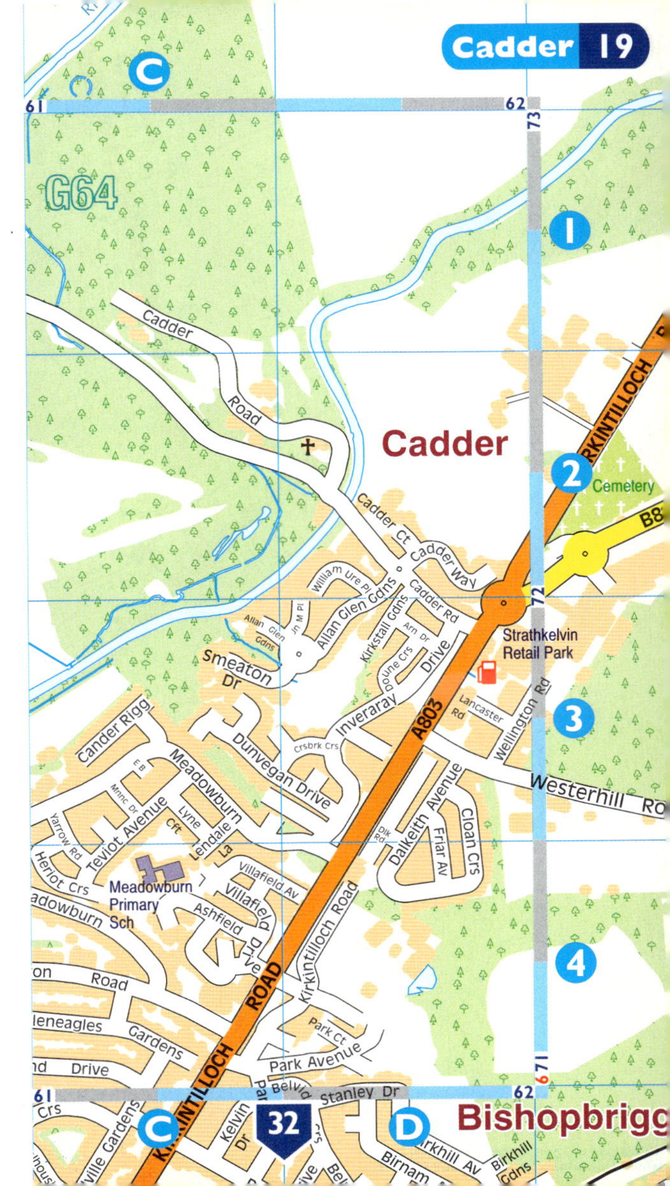
C
61
62
73
G64
1
Cadder Road
Cadder
2
Cemetery
B8
Cadder Ct
Cadder Way
William Ure Pl
Allan Glen Gdns
Kirkstall Gdns
Cadder Rd
Arn Dr
Jn M Pl
Allan Glen Gdns
Smeaton Dr
Doune Crs
Drive
72
Strathkelvin Retail Park
Wellington Rd
Lancaster Rd
3
Inveraray
A803
Crsbrk Crs
Dunvegan Drive
Cander Rigg
EB
Meadowburn
Westerhill Ro
Mnnc Dr
Lyne Cft
Teviot Avenue
Yarrow Rd
Lendale La
Dalkeith Avenue
Cloan Crs
Friar Av
Dlk Rd
Heriot Crs
Meadowburn Primary Sch
Villafield Av
Villafield Drive
Ashfield
adowburn
Kirkintilloch Road
4
on Road
leneagles Gardens
nd Drive
ROAD
KIRKINTILLOCH
Park Ct
Park Avenue
71
61
62
Belvid
Stanley Dr
Crs
C
32
D
Bishopbrigg
Kelvin Dr
Birnam
Birkhill Av
Birkhill Gdns

1 grid square represents 500 metres

Clydebank 21
Drumry
Whitecrook
Robert
Armour
Kirkoswald Drive
Burns
Av
Abbots
DRUMRY ROAD
B8055
Drumry Road
Heathcot
Melfort Av
St Eunans Primary School
Montrose
Police Station
Arran Pl
Kilbowie Retail Park
Kilbowie Cemetery
Braidfield High School
Qu Mary Av
Hood Street
Vanguard St
Onslow Road
Alsatian Av
Bedford Av
York St
Drumry Station
Forth Rd
Argyll Road
Onslow Road
GREAT
AA
Service Centre
Megabowl
Cripps Av
Greenwood Qd
Livingstone Street
Livingstone St
Kirkwood
Morrison Qd
McNeil Av
Bevin Av
Attlee Avenue
Dalton Avenue
Whitecrook Business Cen
Forth & Clyde Canal
Shinwell Av
Silkin Av
Linnvale Primary School
Jowitt Av
Westwood Quadrant
Argyll Rd
Stanford St
Whitecrook Primary School
Cunard Primary School
Cncl Bldg
Braes Avenue
Braes Av
Richmond St
Barns St
Whitecrook Street
Forth St
Taylor St
Cochno St
Dean St
Dunmore St
King St
Boyle St
Meldrum St
Gran St
Davidson
22
Barns St
Aberconway St
Andrew Dr
Elgin St
Fleming Av
PO
Lappin St
McCreery St
Longden St
Avenue
Angus St
Henderson St
Cameron Court
St Andrews High School
Street
N Elgin St
McDonald Crescent
Johnstone
E Barns Street
Abbott Crs
Sinclair St
Low Crs
Millburn Av
Dalgarroch
Brackla Av
Clydebank Business Cen
N Bank St
N Bank Pl
John Knox St
McGregor Street
White Street
Edward St
Yoker
DUMBARTON ROAD A814
Clyde St
S Elgin Pl
S Elgin St
N Elgin Pl
Napier St
John Knox St
Hamilton St
Hamilton Ter
Bell Street
Our Holy Redeemers Primary Sch
Yoker Station
Mill Road
Yokerburn Terrace
Glen Crs
Hawick St
Dock St
Cooperage Ct
Coldingham Av
Tweedvale Av
50
51
71
70
69
1
2
3
4
C
D
36

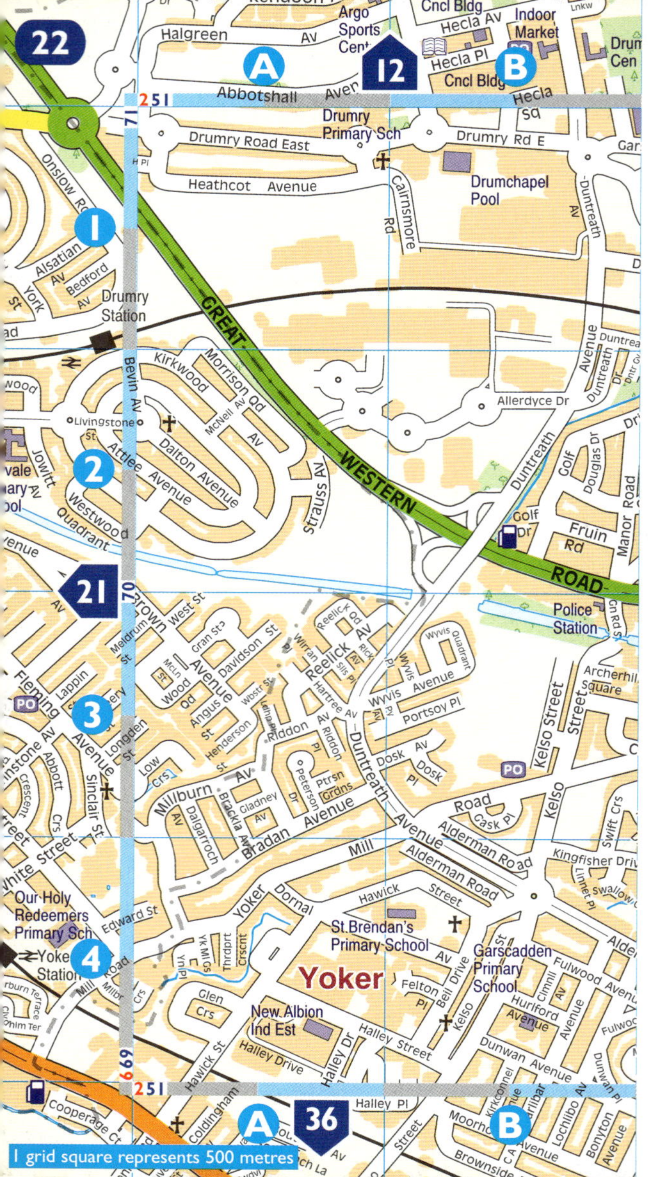
22
Halgreen
Av
Argo
Sports
Cent
12
Cncl Bldg
Hecla Av
Indoor
Market
Hecla Pl
Cncl Bldg
Hecla
Sq
Abbotshall
Avenue
Drumry
Primary Sch
Drumry Road East
Drumry Rd E
Heathcot Avenue
Cairnsmore
Rd
Drumchapel
Pool
Duntreath
Av
Onslow Rd
Alsatian
Av
Bedford
Av
York
St
Drumry
Station
GREAT
WESTERN
ROAD
Kirkwood
Morrison Qd
McNeill Av
Av
Bevin Av
Livingstone
St.
Attlee Avenue
Dalton Avenue
Strauss Av
Allerdyce Dr
Duntreath
Avenue
Golf
Dr
Douglas Dr
Fruin
Rd
Manor
Road
Jowitt
Av
Westwood
Quadrant
21
Police
Station
Brown
West St
Meldrum
St
Gran St
Davidson St
Wirran
Reelick
Reelick Qd
Av
Wyvis
Quadrant
Wyvis
Avenue
Archerhill
Square
Kelso Street
Street
Fleming
Lappin
PO
3
Avenue
Wood
Qd
Angus
St
Henderson
St
Riddon
Hartree Av
Riddon
Pl
Duntreath
Portsoy Pl
Dosk
Av
Dosk
Pl
PO
Kelso
Abbott
Crescent
Crs
Sinclair St
Longden
St
Low
Crs
Millburn
Av
Dalgarroch
Brackla Av
Gladney
Av
Dr
Peterson
Ptrsn
Grdns
Avenue
Bradan
Road
Cask Pl
Swift Crs
Alderman Road
Alderman Road
Kingfisher Drive
Linnet Pl
White Street
Mill
Street
Our Holy
Redeemers
Primary Sch
Edward St
Yoker
Dornal
Hawick
Street
St.Brendan's
Primary School
Av
Beil Drive
Garscadden
Primary
School
Fulwood Avenue
4
Yoker
Station
Mill Road
Glen
Crs
Yoker
Felton
Pl
Kelso
Hurlford
Avenue
Avenue
New Albion
Ind Est
Halley Drive
Halley Dr
Halley Street
Dunwan Avenue
Dunwan Pl
Hawick St
Coldingham
Halley Pl
A
36
B
Street
Brownside
Kirkconnel
Avenue
Lochlibo Av
Bonyton
Avenue
Cooperage Ct
1 grid square represents 500 metres

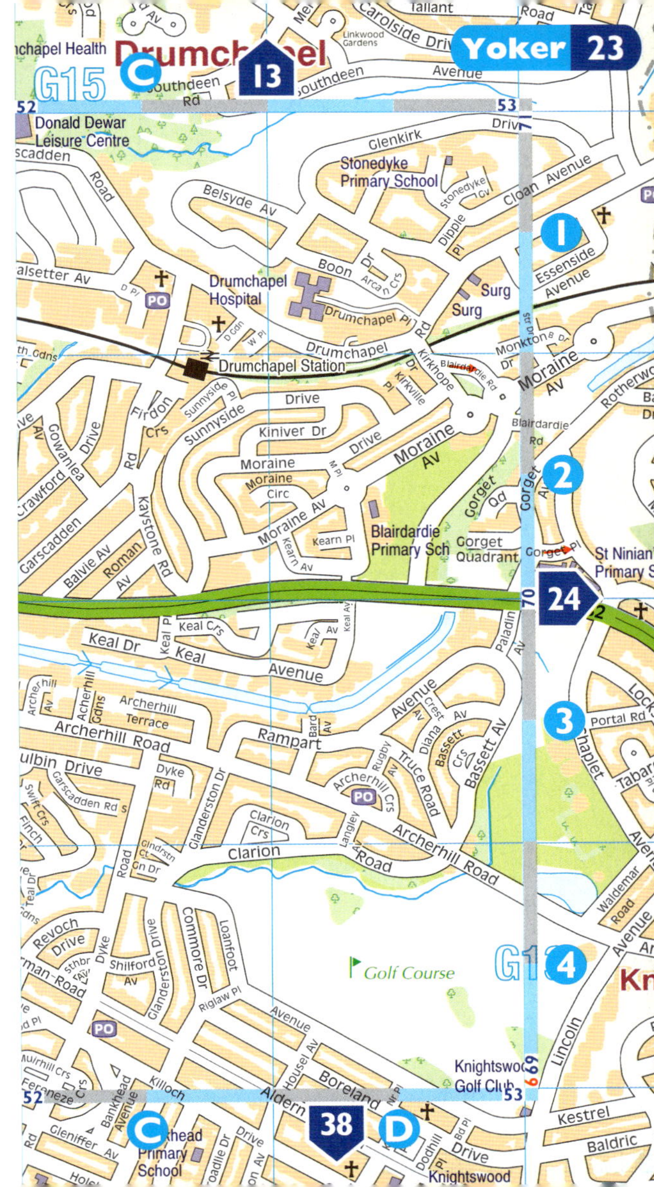

Yoker 23
Drumchapel
13
G15
Linkwood Gardens
Carolside Drive
Southdeen Rd
Southdeen Avenue
Donald Dewar Leisure Centre
Glenkirk Drive
Stonedyke Primary School
Stonedyke Gv
Cloan Avenue
Belsyde Av
Dipple Pl
Boon Dr
Arcan Crs
Essenside Avenue
Drumchapel Hospital
Drumchapel Pl
Drumchapel Rd
Surg
Surg
Monkton Dr
Drumchapel Station
Kirkhope Dr
Kirkville Pl
Blairdardie Rd
Moraine Av
Sunnyside Pl
Sunnyside Drive
Firdon Crs
Kiniver Dr
Moraine Drive
Moraine Circ
Moraine Av
Kearn Pl
Kearn Av
Blairdardie Primary Sch
Gorget Quadrant
Gorget Av
Gorget Pl
St Ninian's Primary S
Gowanlea Drive
Crawford
Garscadden
Balvie Av
Roman Av
Kaystone Rd
Rotherwood
24
Keal Dr
Keal Pl
Keal Crs
Keal Avenue
Keal Av
Paladin Av
Archerhill Av
Acherhill Gdns
Archerhill Terrace
Archerhill Road
Rampart Avenue
Bard Av
Crest Av
Diana Av
Bassett Crs
Bassett Av
Rugby Av
Truce Road
Portal Rd
Chaplet
Tabard
Culbin Drive
Garscadden Rd S
Dyke Rd
Glanderston Dr
Clarion Crs
Clarion Road
Langley Av
Archerhill Crs
PO
Archerhill Road
Waldemar Road
Avenue
Revoch Drive
Sthbr Av
Dyke
Shilford Av
Glanderston Drive
Commore Dr
Loanfoot
Riglaw Pl
Avenue
Housel Av
Boreland
Golf Course
Knightswood Golf Club
G13
Lincoln
Kestrel
Baldric
Muirhill Crs
Ferguson Crs
Bankhead Avenue
Killoch
Aldern
38
Gleniffer Av
Bankhead Primary School
Drive
Dodhill Pl
Drive
Knightswood
Kn
52
53
52
53
71
70
69

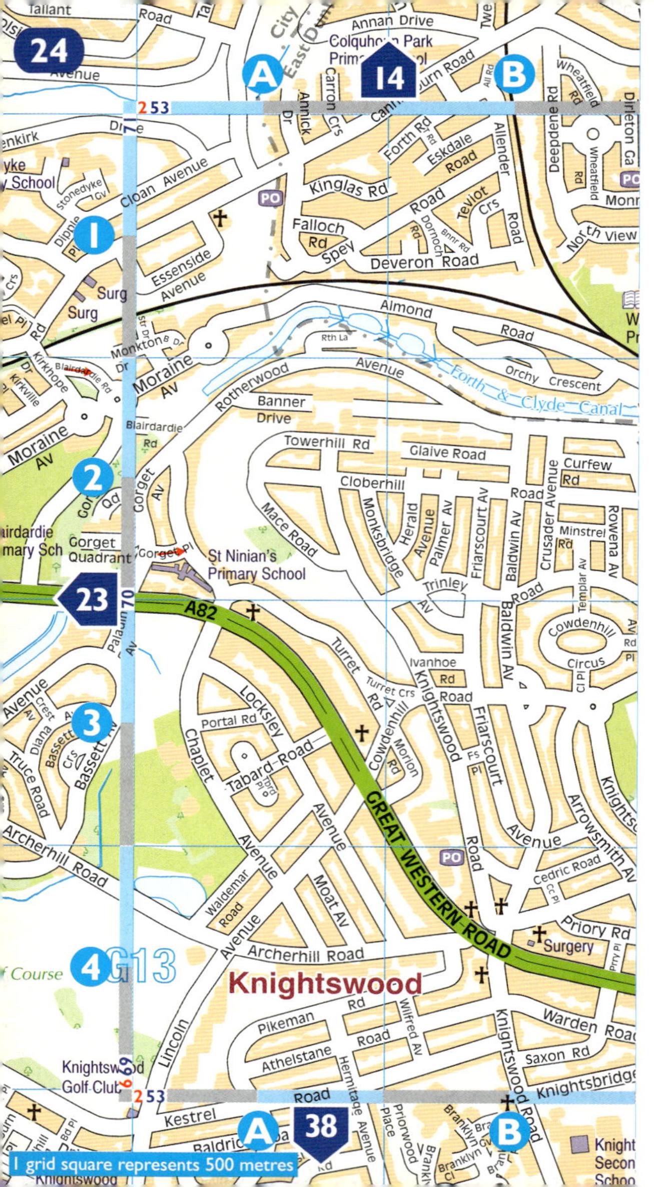
24
14
23
38
A
B
1
2
3
4
253
71
70
69
G13
Annan Drive
Colquhoun Park
Primary School
City East Dr
Carron Crs
Annick Dr
Road
Tallant
Avenue
Canniesburn Road
Wheatfield Rd
Deepdene Rd
Dirleton Ga
Allender
Forth Rd
Eskdale Road
Kinglas Rd
Falloch Rd
Spey Rd
Deveron Road
Teviot Crs
Dornoch Rd
Bnnr Rd
North View
Monr
Cloan Avenue
Stonedyke Gv
Dipple Pl
Surg
Essenside Avenue
Almond Road
Rth La
Monkton Dr
Moraine Av
Moraine Dr
Blairdardie Rd
Kirkhope Dr
Kirkville
Rotherwood Avenue
Forth & Clyde Canal
Orchy Crescent
Banner Drive
Towerhill Rd
Glaive Road
Curfew Rd
Cloberhill Road
Monksbridge Av
Herald Avenue
Palmer Av
Friarscourt Av
Baldwin Av
Crusader Avenue
Minstrel Rd
Rowena Av
Templar Av
Mace Road
Gorget Av
Gorget Pl
Gorget Quadrant
Gorget Qd
St Ninian's
Primary School
Blairdardie
Primary Sch
A82
Trinley Av
Cowdenhill Circus
Cl Pl
Ivanhoe Rd
Knightswood Road
Turret Rd
Turret Crs
Cowdenhill Rd
Morion Rd
Friarscourt Avenue
Fs Pl
Arrowsmith Av
Palacerigg Av
Locksley Avenue
Portal Rd
Chaplet Avenue
Tabard Road
Tbrd Pl
Bassett Crs
Bassett Av
Diana Av
Crest Avenue
Truce Road
Archerhill Road
GREAT WESTERN ROAD
Moat Av
Waldemar Road
PO
Cedric Road
CC Pl
Priory Rd
Surgery
Prry Pl
Knightswood
Golf Course
Knightswood
Golf Club
Lincoln Avenue
Pikeman Rd
Athelstane Road
Wilfred Av
Hermitage Avenue
Warden Road
Saxon Rd
Knightsbridge
Kestrel Road
Baldric
Priorwood Place
Branklyn Cl
Branklyn Gv
Knightswood
Secondary
School
1 grid square represents 500 metres

Canniesburn Road
Fernlea
Elderbank
15
Gray Dr
Killermont
First Avenue
Canniesburn Hospital
Henderland Dr
Hollymount
MARYHILL
Cluny Dr
Braemar Crs
Birkhall Dr
Ballater
Coronation Wy
Balmoral Dr
Drive
Lomond Rd
Ravelston Road
Bute Crs
Ascog Road
Kelvin Crs
Switchback Rd
A739
Keith Av
Maxwell Av
Stirling Av
Westfield Dr
W Crs
Henderland Rd
Westerton Primary School
Crarae Av
Westerton Station
Murrayfield Dr
Cairnhill Rd
Somerford Road
Larchfield Rd
SWITCHBACK ROAD
East Dunbartonshire
City of Glasgow
Glendinning Road
Henderland Road
Wardlaw Rd
Kinellan Rd
Wyvil Av
Ashby Crs
Avenel Rd
Henderland Rd
Maxwell Av
26
Rotherwood
Wamba Av
Wilverton Road
Westerton Avenue
University of Glasgow
Shafton Road
Shafton Pl
Anniesland Industrial Estate
Strathblane Gdns
Anniesland Industrial Estate
Ilay Ct
Netherton Rd
Boclair St
Tambowie St
Netherton Rd
Netherton Road
Hwth Ter
Howth Dr
Netherton Av
University of Glasgow
Netherton Rd
Knightswood Primary School
Woodhouse St
Hilton Ter
Hilton Gdns
Fulton St
Roselea Gdns
Spencer St
Temple Primary Sch
Ochiltree Av
Temple
Blackwood St
Rosewood St
Grywd St
Hemlock St
Willow St
Succoth St
Linden St
PO
Crow Road
Waldo St
Tl Ls Pl
Strathcona Gdns
Strathcona Dr
Eider
A82
Sutcliffe Road
Scliff Ct
Glencoe Pl
Glencoe St
Sf Rd
Sn St
Munro Business Centre
Munro Pl
Gl St
Ck Vs
Ck Ct
Cstlbnk Gdns
40
Chr Bldg
Surg
Anniesland Station
Murchison Avenue
Dunlin
PO
54
55
71
70
69

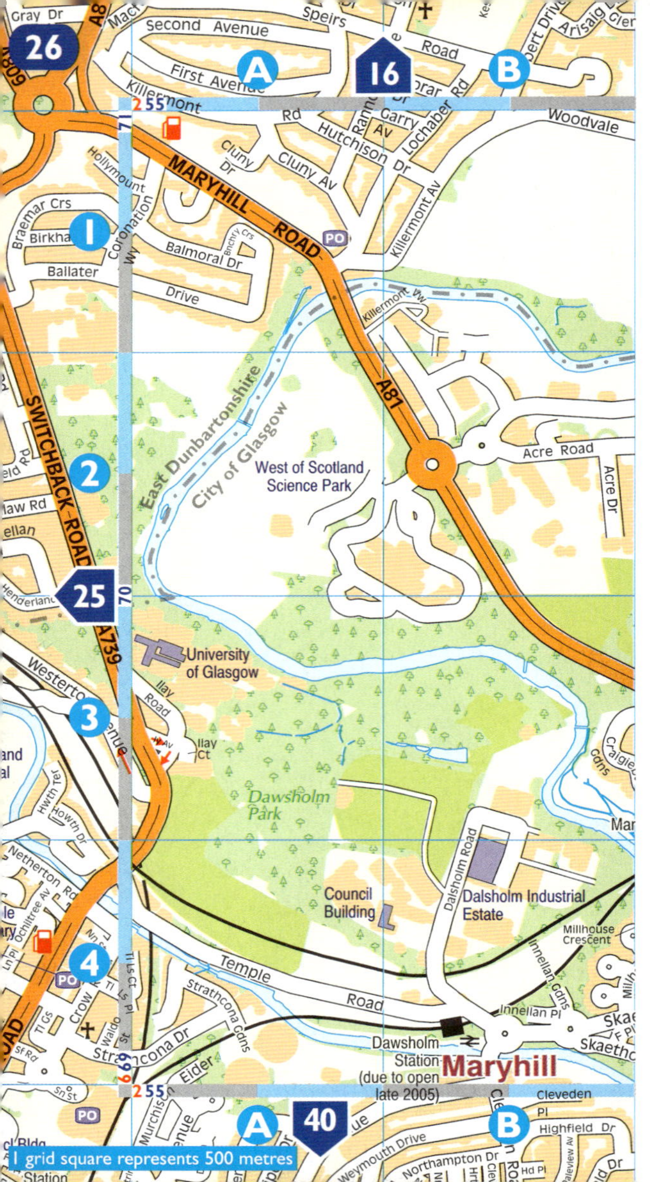
26
16
25
40
A
B
1
2
3
4
Second Avenue
First Avenue
Speirs
Road
Woodvale
Hutchison Dr
Lochaber Rd
Cluny Dr
Cluny Av
Killermont Av
MARYHILL ROAD
Hollymount
Braemar Crs
Ballater
Balmoral Dr
Drive
Coronation Wy
SWITCHBACK ROAD
A739
A81
Killermont Vw
East Dunbartonshire
City of Glasgow
West of Scotland Science Park
Acre Road
Acre Dr
University of Glasgow
Ilay Road
Ilay Ct
Westerton Avenue
Dawsholm Park
Council Building
Dalsholm Road
Dalsholm Industrial Estate
Millhouse Crescent
Innellan Gdns
Innellan Pl
Temple Road
Strathcona Dr
Strathcona Gdns
Netherton Rd
Ochiltree Av
Howth Dr
Dawsholm Station (due to open late 2005)
Maryhill
Cleveden Pl
Highfield Dr
Weymouth Drive
Northampton Dr
PO
1 grid square represents 500 metres

Course
17
56
57
71
East Dunbartonshire
City of Glasgow
Glasgow Golf Club
Blackhill
Cawder Cuilt
Duich Gdns
Shielbridge Gdns
Harburn Pl
Staffin
Foxhills
Hoylake
Calderchuilt Primary Sch
Milovaig St
Milovaig Av
Road
Torrin Rd
Torgyle St
Invershiel
Balmartin Rd
Elphin St
Harris Rd
John Paul Academy
Arrochar Street
Geary St
Calderchuilt Road
Drumlaken St
Drmlkn Av
Drmlkn St
Drmlkn Ct
Chatton St
Arrochar Dr
Arrochar Street
St Blanes Primary Sch
Fs St
Tolsta St
Gallan Av
Crsspnt
Lytham Dr
Muirfield Crs
Rothes Pl
Littleton St
Mllrdch St
Craigbo St
Craigbo Rd
Cb Av
Formby Dr
Hollinwell Rd
28
70
Spence St
Prince of Wales Gdns
Whitton St
Ferndale Gdns
Ferndale Dr
Rothes Dr
Ferndale Pl
Corstan St
Parkview Primary School
Fairhaven Rd
Sunningdale Rd
Ws Pl
Pk Dr
Broughton
Crosbie St
Barra St
Rsdl Gdns
Dalsholm Rd
Crosbie La
Falcon Ter La
Ferndale Ct
PO
Summerston Station
Arrochar Street
A81
Falcon Ter
Shiskine Drive
Ledgowan Pl
Lyndale Rd
Barrisdale Rd
Kirn St
Maryhill Station
Duart St
Shiskine St
Shskn Pl
Kilmun St
Glenavon Road
Gilshochill Station
Knowetap Street
Glenburn Street
Celtic St
River Kelvin
MARYHILL ROAD
St Marys (Maryhill) Primary School
Fearnmore Rd
Duncruin Ter
Maryhill Primary Sch
Thornton St
Thornton Lane
Gy St
Whitelaw St
Lochgilp St
Cowal St
Duncruin St
Cumlodden Drive
Fingal St
Cranbrooke Drive
Duncombe St
Cncl Bldg
Cottar St
Gilhill St
McLaren Crs
Dunure St
Viewmount Drive
Campbell St
Cowal Road
Blairbuie Dr
Bantaskin Street
Sandbank Ter
Sandbank St
Sandbank Dr
Drive
69
Collina Street
Burnhouse St
Niven Street
42
Sandbank Crs
Council Building
Maryhill FC
A81

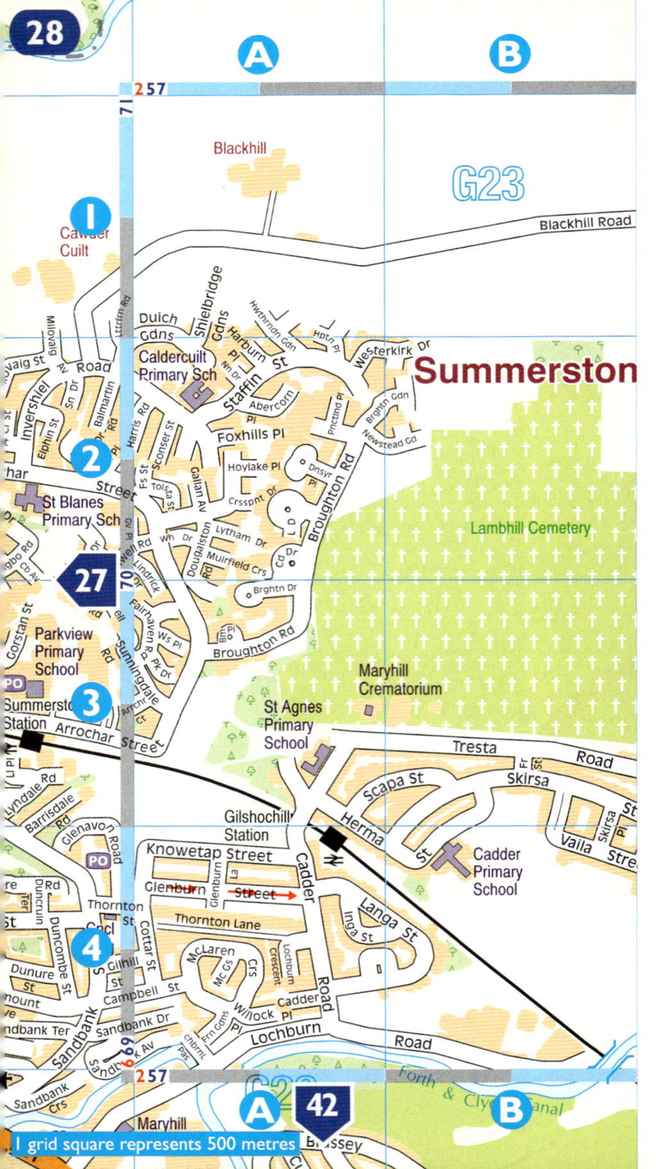
A
B
257
71
Blackhill
G23
Blackhill Road
1
Cawder Cuilt
Summerston
Caldercuilt Primary Sch
Duich Gdns
Shielbridge Gdns
Harburn Pl
Staffin St
Westerkirk Dr
Abercorn Pl
Foxhills Pl
Hoylake Pl
Broughton Rd
Lambhill Cemetery
2
St Blanes Primary Sch
Street
Gallan Av
Lytham Dr
Muirfield Crs
Dougalston Rd
Brghtn Dr
27
70
Parkview Primary School
PO
3
Summerston Station
Arrochar Street
Sunningdale
Maryhill Crematorium
St Agnes Primary School
Tresta Road
Skirsa
Scapa St
Vaila Street
Cadder Primary School
Herma St
Gilshochill Station
Knowetap Street
Glenburn Street
Cadder Road
Thornton Lane
Langa St
Inga St
Thornton St
Cottar St
McLaren Crs
Lochburn Crescent
Willock Pl
Lochburn Road
Campbell St
Sandbank Dr
Sandbank
Duncombe St
Dunure St
4
Glenavon Road
Barrisdale Rd
Lyndale Rd
Forth & Clyde Canal
669
257
42
Maryhill
1 grid square represents 500 metres

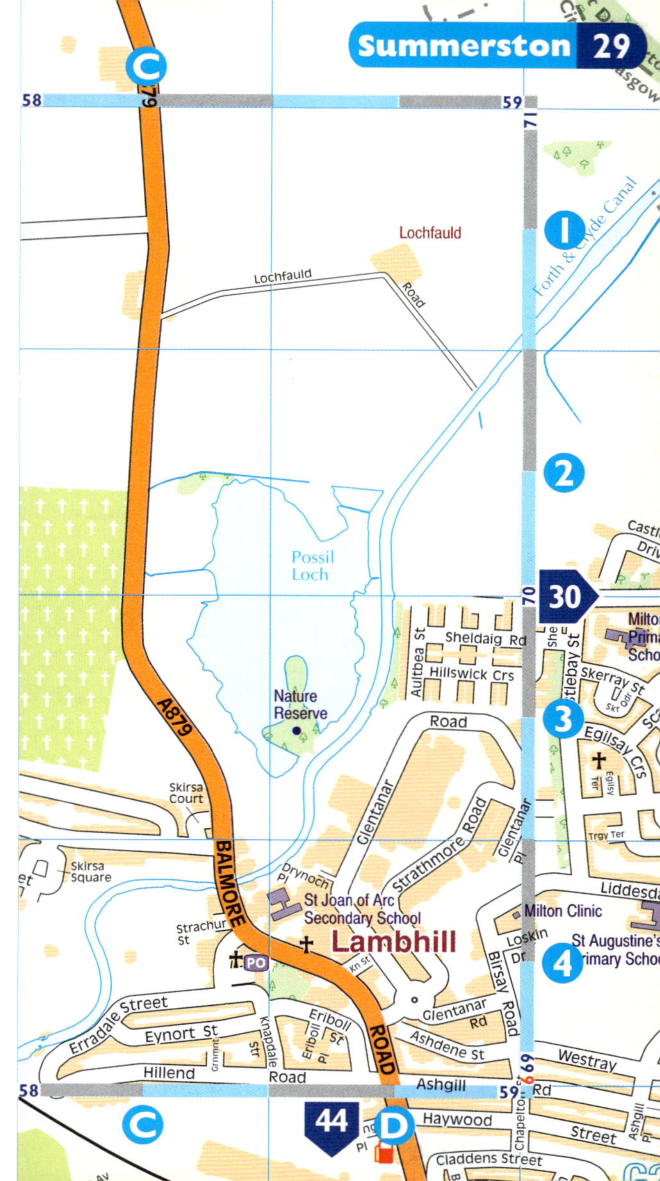

Lochfauld
Lochfauld Road
Forth & Clyde Canal
A879
BALMORE ROAD
Possil Loch
Nature Reserve
Skirsa Court
Skirsa Square
Strachur St
Drynoch Pl
St Joan of Arc Secondary School
Lambhill
Glentanar Road
Strathmore Road
Glentanar Pl
Aultbea St
Sheldaig Rd
Hillswick Crs
Skerray St
Egilsay Crs
Milton Clinic
St Augustine's Primary School
Loskin Dr
Birsay Road
Glentanar Rd
Ashdene St
Kn St
Erradale Street
Eynort St
Hillend Road
Knapdale Str
Eriboll St
Eriboll Pl
Ashgill Rd
Westray
Haywood Street
Claddens Street
Chapelton St
Liddesdale
Trgy Ter
Castle Drive

30
44

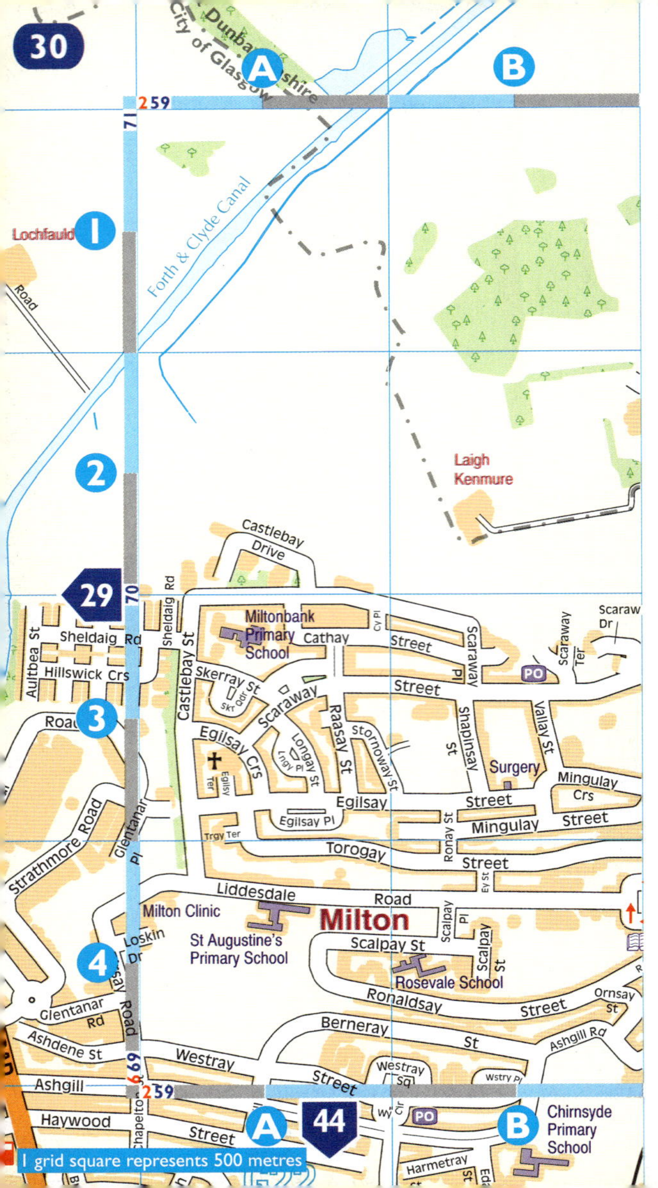

30
A
B
Dunbartonshire
City of Glasgow
259
71
Forth & Clyde Canal
Lochfauld
1
Road
2
Laigh Kenmure
Castlebay Drive
29
70
Miltonbank Primary School
Cathay
Street
Scaraway Pl
Scaraway Ter
Scaraw Dr
PO
Sheldaig Rd
Aultbea St
Hillswick Crs
Castlebay St
Skerray St
Skr Qdr
Scaraway
Raasay St
Stornoway St
Shapinsay St
Vallay St
Surgery
Mingulay Crs
3
Road
Egilsay Crs
Egilsy Ter
Longay St
Lngy Pl
Egilsay
Street
Egilsay Pl
Ronay St
Mingulay
Street
Strathmore Road
Glentanar Pl
Trgy Ter
Torogay
Street
Ey St
Liddesdale
Road
Milton Clinic
Milton
Scalpay Pl
Loskin Dr
St Augustine's Primary School
Scalpay St
Scalpay St
4
Rosevale School
Ronaldsay
Street
Ornsay St
Glentanar Rd
Road
Ashdene St
Berneray
St
Ashgill Rd
Westray
Westray Sq
Wstry Pl
Street
69
Ashgill
259
Haywood
Street
A
44
B
PO
Chirnsyde Primary School
Harmetray St
1 grid square represents 500 metres

Colston 31
18
32
46
Golf Course
Balmuildy Primary
Turnbull High Sch
Bishopbriggs Golf Club
Council Building
St Mary's Kenmure School
The Fort Theatre
PO
Bishopbriggs High School
Bishopbriggs Stn
The Triangle Shopping Centre
Outdoor Recreation Centre
Gask House School
Milton Sch
Colston
Stirling Drive
Lomond Drive
Tofthill Av
Tofthill Gdns
Southesk Avenue
Broadleys Avenue
Balmuildy Road
Keir Dr
Glenburn Gardens
Carrour Gdns
Dalhousie Gdns
Moray Crs
St Andrew's Av
Bishop Gardens
St Mary's Rd
Brackenbrae
Novar Gardens
Eldon Gdns
Beaufort Gardens
Pollok Drive
Kenmure Gardens
Kenmure Avenue
Brackenbrae Road
Brackenbrae Avenue
Kenmure Dr
Kenmure La
Boclair Rd
Boclair Crs
South Crosshill Rd
Clovergate
Heatherbrae
Corsewood
Duncryne Place
Coltmuir Dr
Viewfield Rd
Scaraway St
Torogay St
Mingulay St
Mingulay Place
Kirkintilloch Road
A803
St Mungo St
Springfield
Mavis Bank
Lennox Crs
Crowhill Road
Avon Road
Buchlyvie Gardens
Stuart Dr
Coltpark Av
Colston Gdns
Colston Road
Colston Dr
Colston Rd
Colston Av
Southview Ter
Ashgill Road
Leehill Road
Bishopsgate Rd
Everard Ct
Everard Qd
Everard Drive
Stobhill Road
Springburn Road
Milton
Ldd Ter
Nw Av

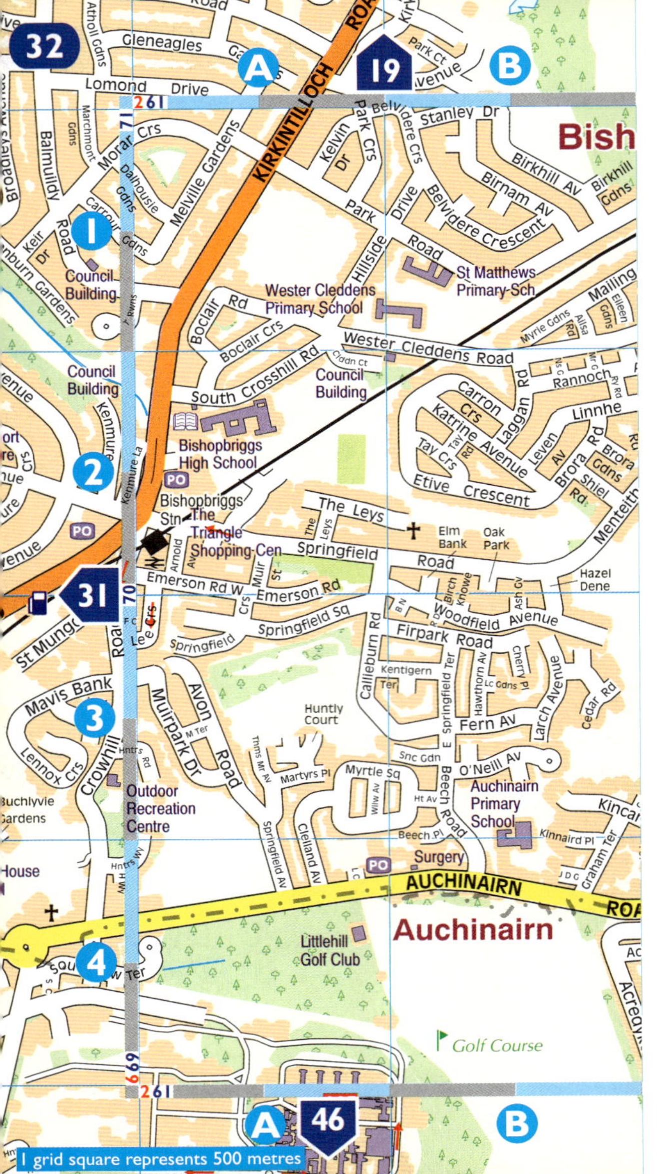
32
19
31
46
A
B
1
2
3
4
Bish
Auchinairn
KIRKINTILLOCH ROAD
AUCHINAIRN ROAD
Gleneagles
Lomond Drive
Stanley Dr
Birkhill Av
Birnam Av
Belvidere Crescent
Wester Cleddens Primary School
St Matthews Primary Sch
Wester Cleddens Road
Council Building
Bishopbriggs High School
Bishopbriggs Stn
The Triangle Shopping Cen
Springfield Road
Emerson Rd
Springfield Sq
Woodfield Avenue
Firpark Road
Mavis Bank
Outdoor Recreation Centre
Auchinairn Primary School
Surgery
Littlehill Golf Club
Golf Course
Huntly Court
Kentigern Ter
Fern Av
O'Neill Av
Myrtle Sq
Martyrs Pl
Etive Crescent
Katrine Avenue
Carron Crs
Laggan Rd
Rannoch
Linnhe
The Leys
Elm Bank
Oak Park
Hazel Dene
Melville Gardens
Boclair Rd
Boclair Crs
South Crosshill Rd
Kelvin Dr
Park Crs
Park Road
Hillside
Muirpark Dr
Avon Road
Crowhill Road
Lennox Crs
St Mungo
Calliebourn Rd
Beech Road
Larch Avenue
Cedar Rd
Kinnaird Pl
Graham Ter
1 grid square represents 500 metres

opbriggs
Ronaldsay Drive
Burra Gdns
Sella Road
Colla Gdns
Solway Road
Monymusk Gdns
St Helens Primary School
Pentland Drive
Lorne Crs
Cromarty Av
Kintessack Pl
Pitmedden Rd
Tweedsmuir
Bemersyde
Abbotsford
Sandra Rd
Flora Gdns
Elspeth Gdns
Avenue
Wester Cleddens Road
Woodhill Primary Sch
Kirriemuir Gdns
Kirriemuir Rd
Thomas Muir High Sch
Dunnottar St
Grainger Rd
Careston Pl
Cortachy Pl
Dunnichen Gdns
Muirhead Way
Westerhill
PO
Thrums Avenue
Ochil Rd
Clair Rd
Torr Road
Mr Av
Nw Pl
M Gdns
Angus Avenue
Sunart Gdns
Sunart Avenue
Woodhill Road
Carnoustie Crescent
Brechin Road
Crr Rd
Crinan Gdns
Gannochy Dr
Moray Pl
Cree Av
Fintry Crs
Falkland Cr
Ceres Gdns
St Cyrus Rd
St Cyrus Gdns
Morven Av
Rossie Crs
Greenhill
Angus Av
Forfar Crs
Edzell Gdns
Lunan Drive
Letham Drive
Hurly Hawkin
Ln Gdns
L Gdns
Falkland Crs
Forgan Gdns
Dairsie Gdns
Fife Wy
Balruddery Pl
Woodhill Road
Wheatley
Loan
Lthm Ov
Glendale Drive
Rth Pl
Bch Dr
Achnrn Rd
T Grvs
Glnd Pl
Montrose
AUCHINAIRN ROAD
B812
HILLHEAD ROAD
B765
W Ga
Brookfield
Strmfld Lea
Strmfld Ga
Tarn Gv
Strmfld Pl
Brkfld Rd
Wtrhgh Gdns
Wtrhgh Gv
B Pl
B Gdns
B Av Ga
S Gdns
Brookfield Avenue
Brookfld Cl
B Gv
Brookfield Av
B Crs
Beckfield Dr
Beckfield Gv
B Gdns
B Cnr
B Ga
B Wk
Dr
East D
Cit
Broomton Road
PO
Nairnside Rd
Auldearn Rd
Knockburn Primary Sch
Geddes Rd
Brodie Rd
Northgate
Fr Pl
Ferness Oval
Ferness Rd
Wallacewell Road
Standburn
Road
B Dr
B Rd
Briarcroft Rd
Briarcroft Dr
Brcft Dr
Brcft Rd
Brrcr Pl
Robroyston Road
Northgate
Acredyke Place
Road
62
63
71
70
69
1
2
3
4
C
D
48

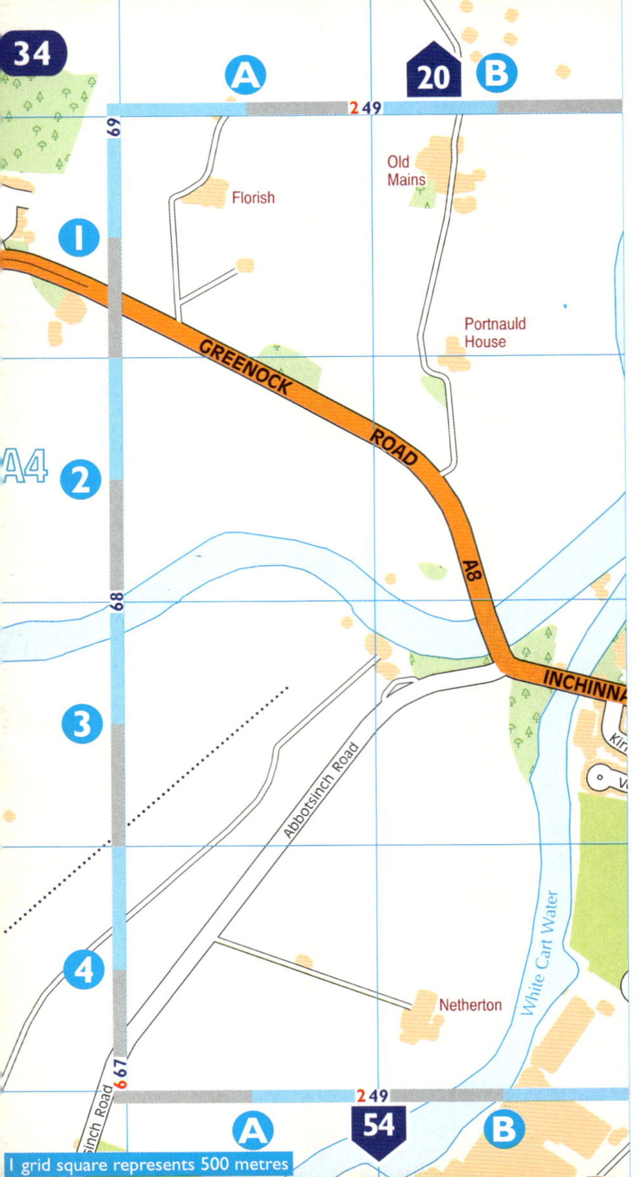

A
20
B
2 49
69
Florish
Old Mains
Portnauld House
GREENOCK ROAD
A8
INCHINNA
68
Abbotsinch Road
White Cart Water
Netherton
67
2 49
A
54
B
A4
1
2
3
4

Golf Course
Blythswood
Meadowside Estate
Meadowside
Renfrew Golf Club
Blythswood Estate
Cryffe Av
Argyll Avenue
West Ldg Rd
North
Elm Avenue
Lodge
Road
Rowan Avenue
Fulbar Avenue
Fulbar Street
Blythswood Avenue
Blythswood Rd
Hamilton Crs
Aranthrue Crs
Rannoch Drive
Craigielea Road
Kirklandneuk Road
Kirklandneuk Rd
Ennacher Road
Ness Rd
Creran Dr
Ard Rd
McClue Av
McClue Rd
Kirklandneuk Primary School
Police Station
Victory Baths
Hairst St
A741
RENFREW
Paisley Road
Fauldshead Road
Haining Road
Lobnitz Av
Oxford Rd
West Av
East Av
Nethergreen Wynd
Porterfield Road
Robertson Av
Brown St
Clark Street
Victoria Dr W
St James's Primary Sch
Albert Rd
St Andrew's Rd
French Street Industrial Estate
Moorpark
Meikle Av
Glendee Road
Road
PO
21
36
55
50
68
69
67
C
D
1
2
3
4

36
Yoker
Station
Yokerburn Terrace
Mill
Milbr
Crs
Glen Crs
New Albion Est
Drive
Halley Dr
Dock St
ROAD A81
A
21
B
251
Hawick St
Cooperage Ct
Greenlaw Rd
Coldingham Av
Bouverie St
Tweedvale Av
Southinch Av
Southinch La
Twdvl Pl
Lasswade Street
Kelso Pl
Kelso
Surg
DUMBAR
YOKER FERRY RD
Bulldale St
69
1
Meadowside Industrial Estate
hswood
PASSENGER ONLY
Meadowside Street
Nell St
Clyde Street
London St
FERRY ROAD A741
City of Glasgow
Renfrewshire
2
Meadow Lane
Simons Crs
Hamilton Crs
Campbell Street
Royal Inch Ter
35
68
Elm
Lodge
Rowan Avenue
Blythswood Avenue
Blythswood Rd
Orchard Street
Castlehill Crs
Ferry Rd
Station
Fulbar Street
Fulbar Avenue
Fibr Crt
Fibr Ln
Renfield St
Houston St
Cncl Bldg
Station Road
Anne Av
3
Bell Vw Ct
Bell St
Anderson Dr
Wilson St
CANAL ST
PO
Manse St
Charles Av
Victory Baths
Police Station
HAIRST ST
A877
Edward Avenue
Ferguson St
Trinity High Sch
Queen St
HIGH STREET
Andrew Avenue
A741
Millburn Rd
Merlinford Avenue
PAISLEY ROAD
4
Fauldshead Road
Ferguson Av
Lobnitz Av
GLEBE STREET
A8
Alexandra Drive
Merlinford Dr
Mrlnfrd Crs
Oxfrd La
West Av
South Av
East Av
Haining
Cowdray Crs
Ross Hall Place
Brora Drive
Findhorn Av
Tay Av
Dee Av
667
Oxford Rd
St Andrew's Rd
Road
251
56
Esk Av
Tweed Crs
Gala Av
Don Avenue
Dean Pa
1 grid square represents 500 metres

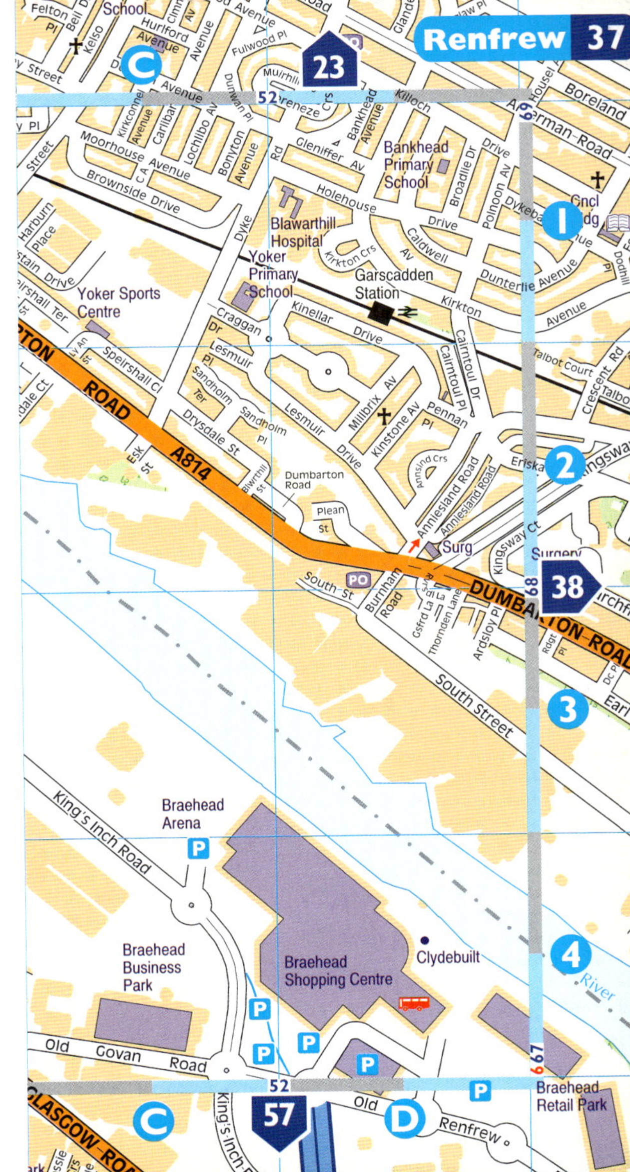

Yoker Sports Centre
Blawarthill Hospital
Yoker Primary School
Bankhead Primary School
Garscadden Station
Dumbarton Road
Braehead Arena
Braehead Business Park
Braehead Shopping Centre
Clydebuilt
Braehead Retail Park
DUMBARTON ROAD
A814
South Street
King's Inch Road
Old Govan Road
GLASGOW ROAD
River

38
23
A
B
Knightswood Golf Club
Boreland
Alderman Road
Kilburn Pl
Dodhill Pl
Drive
Knightswood Community Centre
Thornley Av
Cncl Bldg
Foxbar Dr
Dykebar Avenue
Dunterlie Avenue
Avenue
Kirkton
Cairntoul Dr
Cairntoul Pl
Pennan Pl
Lincoln
Kestrel
Baldric Road
Thane Road
Talisman Rd
Alderman Road
Corpus Christi Primary School
Pikeman Rd
Athelstane Road
Hermitage Avenue
Wykeham Pl
Wykeham Rd
Alderman Pl
Kintillo Drive
Eb Dr
Talbot Court
Talbot Drive
Talbot Terrace
Crescent Rd
Scotstoun
Scotstounhill Station
Kingsway
Eriska Av
Anniesland Rd
Surg
Surgery
Goldberry Av
Danes Drive
Harefield Drive
Larchfield Avenue
Stronvar Drive
Birchfield Drive
Esslemont Av
Victoria Drive
Northland Dr
Northland La
Danes Av
Danes La N
Southbrae Drive
Hallydown Dr
Windydg Crs
Danes Dr
Danes Lane South
Norse La N
Norse Lane South
Verona Av
Verona Lane
Earlbank Av
Earlbank La S
Gleneagles La N
Scotstoun Prim Sch
Duncan Avenue
Ormiston Av
Queen
37
68
DUMBARTON ROAD A814
DUMBARTON ROAD
Raploch Av
Raploch La
Earl Street
Balmoral Street
The Surg
Gleneagles Lane S
Earl St
Earl La
Harland St
Fore St
Methil St
Scotstoun St
Ardsloy
Thornden La
South Street
1
2
3
4
Clydebank
River Clyde
69
67
2 53
Braehead Retail Park
Renfrew
58
G1
Scotstoun
grid square represents 500 metres

25
A82
Warden Road
Saxon Rd
Wilfred Av
Knightsbridge St
54
Munro Business Centre
Munro Pl
Glencoe St
BEARSDEN RD
69
Knightswood Road
Priorwood Place
Branklyn
Branklyn Gv
Branklyn Cl
Branklyn Pl
Branklyn Crs
Knightswood Secondary School
Gl St
Cd Pl
Cstlbnk Gdns
Ck Vs
Ck Ct
Crgnd St
Annniesland
Road
Chmbrln Rd
Surg
Annniesland
Ryvra Rd
Helensburgh Drive
Road
Wilmot
Sggl La
Sggl Rd
GHK RFC
Crow Rd
A739
The High School of Glasgow
Anca
Sackvil
Jordanhill
Drive
Jrdnhill Crscnt
Munro La
Munro
Road
Munro La E
Fern Lane
Skaterigg La
Chmbrln La
Austen Rd
Austen La
Borden Rd
Brdn La
Surgery
University of Strathclyde
Jordanhill School
Chamberlain Road
Jordanhill La
Woodend Drive
Woodend La
CROW RD
Whttnghm La
Slbrn Pl La
Selborne Rd
Mlnr La
Mlnr Rd
Kg Ed La
Kg Ed Rd
Crw La
Southbrae La
Surgery
Surgery
Jordanhill
Drive
40
68
Southbrae Drive
Southbrae
Wstbr Dr
4
Scotstoun Stadium
Drive
Jordan
St Thomas Aquinas RC Secondary School
Cluny Gdns
Av
Abbey
Drive
Clinic
Scotstoun Leisure Centre
Westland
Mtr Ln W
Mitre Lane
Mitre
St Kilda Dr
Av
Eastcote
Manor Rd
Road
Randolph
Elmwood La
Angle Gate
Vr La
LLW
Brsfrd Av
Essex
Essex
Arthry La
Airthrey
Varna Rd
Varna La
Orleans Avenue
Orleans Lane
Balshagray Av
Mitre Rd
Lnnx Gdns
Victoria Pk Cnr
Victoria
Drive
Lane
Park
Bro
Victoria Pk
Lennox Avenue
Lennox La
East
Westland Dr
Tdr Rd
Tdr L S
Drive
N
Victoria Park
Victoria Pk Gdns
Victoria Pk La S
VICTORIA PK DRIVE S
4
Marlborough Av
Nrby Rd
Bowling Gn La
Bg Gn Rd
Lime St
Elm St
Haldane La
Vct Pk St
Surg
Dumbarton Rd
Haldane St
Whiteinch Primary School
Balshagray Dr
Balshagray La
67
Pm Pl
Edzll Pl
St Pauls Prim Sch
Surgery
Surg
Medwyn St
Ladywell St
54
59
Medwyn St
Glndr St
D
Bl P
Broomhill Ter
Bro Sch
C
C
Edzell Ct
Jordan St
Smith St
Dumbarton Rd
Whiteinch

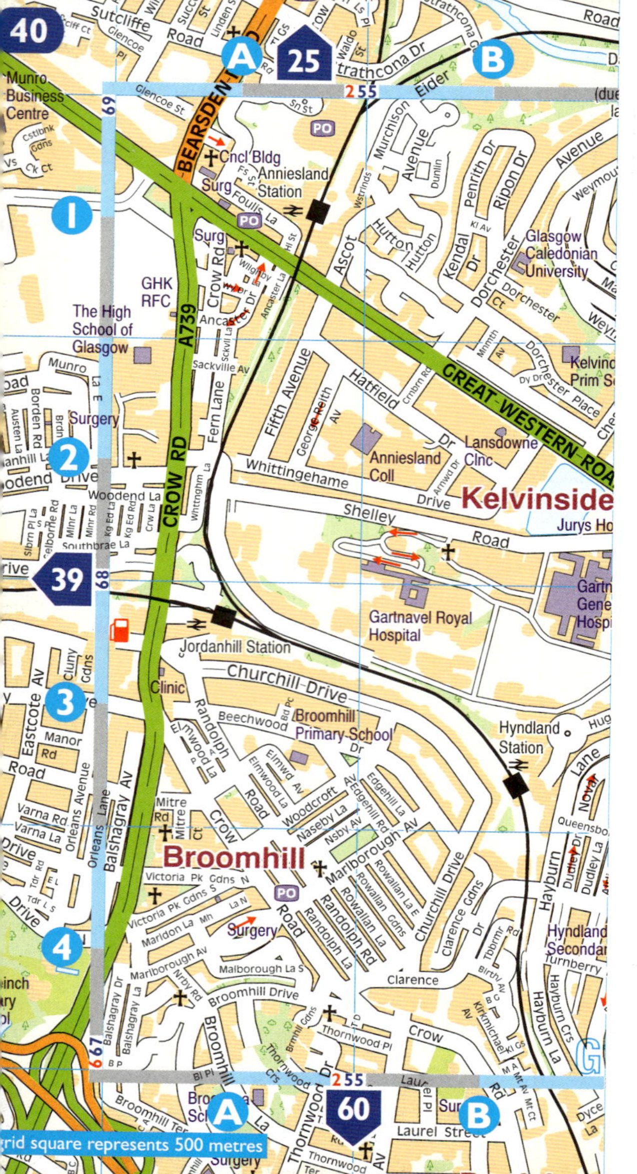
40
25
A
B
255
Sutcliffe
Road
Glencoe Pl
Glencoe St
Linden St
Strathcona Dr
Road
Munro Business Centre
Cstlbnk Gdns
BEARSDEN
Cncl Bldg
Anniesland Station
Surg
PO
Foulis La
Murchison
Avenue
Dunlin
Penrith Dr
Ripon Dr
Avenue
Eider
Weymouth
I
Ascot
Hutton
Kendal Dr
Dorchester
Dorchester Ct
Glasgow Caledonian University
GHK RFC
The High School of Glasgow
A739
Crow Rd
Ancaster Dr
Ancaster La
Sackville Av
Fern Lane
Fifth Avenue
George Reith Av
Hatfield Dr
GREAT WESTERN ROAD
Dorchester Place
Kelvindale Prim Sch
Munro
Borden Rd
Austen La
Surgery
2
Woodend Drive
Woodend La
CROW RD
Whittingehame Drive
Anniesland Coll
Lansdowne Clnc
Kelvinside
Jurys Ho
Shelley Road
Southbrae La
39
68
69
Gartnavel Royal Hospital
Jordanhill Station
Churchill Drive
Clinic
3
Cluny Gdns
Eastcote Av
Manor Rd
Road
Beechwood
Broomhill Primary School
Randolph
Elmwood La
Hyndland Station
Lane
Varna Rd
Varna La
Orleans Avenue
Orleans Lane
Balshagray Av
Mitre Rd
Mitre Ct
Crow
Woodcroft Av
Naseby La
Edgehill Rd
Marlborough Av
Queensborough
Broomhill
Victoria Pk Gdns N
Victoria Pk Gdns S
Maridon La
Marlborough Av
Surgery
PO
Road
Randolph La
Rowallan La
Rowallan Gdns
Churchill Drive
Clarence Gdns
Hyndland Secondary
Turnberry
Hayburn Crs
Hayburn La
Dudley Dr
Dudley La
4
Drive
Malborough La S
Broomhill Drive
Clarence
Crow
Thornwood Pl
Balshagray Dr
Balshagray La
Kirkmichael Av
67
255
A
60
B
Broomhill Ter
Laurel Street
Thornwood Ter
Dyce La
Grid square represents 500 metres
Surgery

Maryhill
Kelvindale
Dowanhill
G12
27
42
61
56
69
68
67
Council Building
Cleveden Secondary School
Glasgow Nuffield Hospital
One Devonshire Gardens Hotel
Hillhead RFC
Wyndford Primary School
St Gregory Primary School
Notre Dame High Sch
University
Primary Sch
The Clnc
Surgery
Uni
Hillhead Stn
Dowanhill Primary School
Hyndland Primary School
St Peter's Primary School
MARYHILL RD
GT WESTERN RD
BYRES RD
A82
Kelvindale Road
Cleveden Road
Cleveden Drive
Cleveden Gdns
Winton Drive
Bellshaugh Lane
Ashburton Road
Winchester Dr
Chelmsford Dr
Leicester Av
Devonshire Ter
Beaconsfield Road
Westbourne Gdns
Kensington Rd
Highburgh Road
Crown Ter
Clarence Lane
Turnberry Rd
Partickhill
Collina Street
Burnhouse St
Niven Street
Stirrat St
Fortingall Pl
Granduly Dr
Hyndland

42
27
41
62
A
B
1
2
3
4
G20
257
69
68
67
Maryhill Rd
A81
Maryhill Road
Maryhill FC
Maryhill Health Centre
Chapel Street Industrial Estate
Cncl Bldg
East Park Home School
Wyndford Primary School
St Gregorys Primary School
Wyndford Recreation Centre
The Kelvinside Academy
Kelbourne School
Secondary School
Glasgow Botanic Gardens
Surg
Gt Western Rd
A82
Qu Margaret Dr
B808
Hillhead Stn
Hillhead Prim Sch
Clinics for Children
High Sch
Dowanhill Primary
University
Temple
Kelvinbridge Stn
Byres Rd
Collina Street
Burnhouse St
Niven Street
Guthrie Street
Balfour St
Sandbank Crs
Brassey
Curzon
Currie St
Shuna Place
Ruchill
Clouston Street
Botanic Crs
Kelvin Drive
Garriochmill Road
Oban Drive
Oban Lane
Kelvinside Gardens
Wilton St
Doune Gdns Lane
Hamilton Drive
Ruskin La
Belmont Street
Observatory Rd
Cranworth St
Kersland Street
Cecil St
Dowanside Road
Caledon St
grid square represents 500 metres

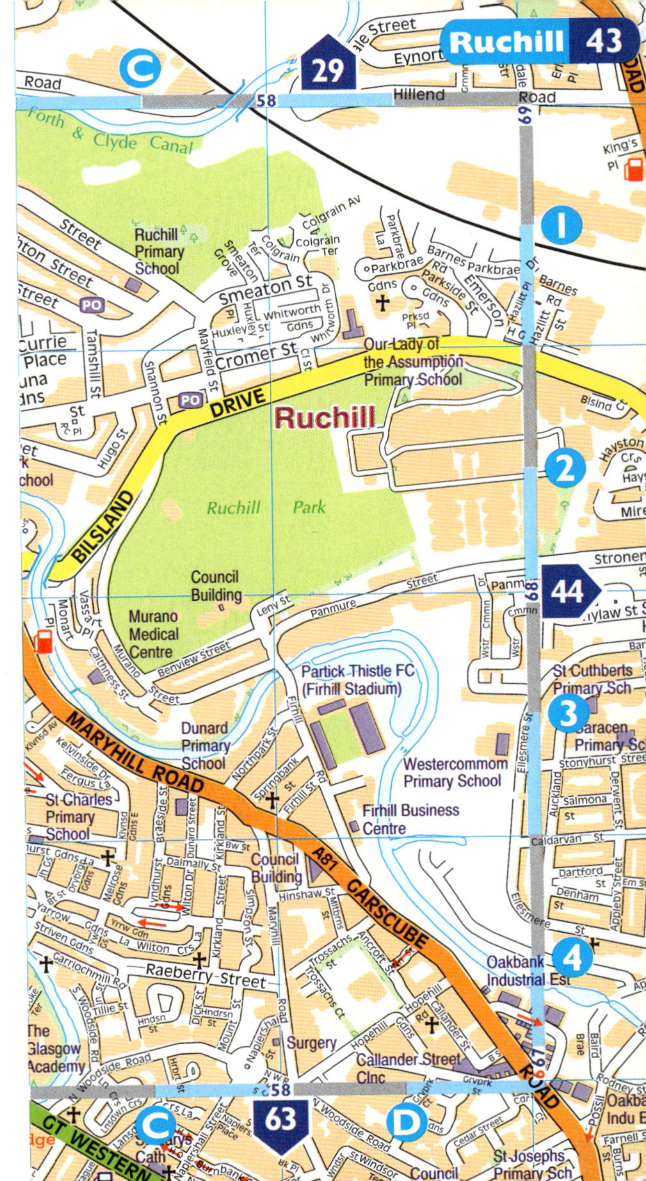
Forth & Clyde Canal
Hillend Road
Ruchill Primary School
Smeaton St
Colgrain Av
Parkbrae
Barnes Rd
Emerson St
Cromer St
Our Lady of the Assumption Primary School
Ruchill
BILSLAND DRIVE
Ruchill Park
Council Building
Murano Medical Centre
Benview Street
Panmure Street
Partick Thistle FC (Firhill Stadium)
Dunard Primary School
MARYHILL ROAD
St Charles Primary School
Westercommon Primary School
Firhill Business Centre
St Cuthberts Primary Sch
Saracen Primary Sch
Stonyhurst Street
Council Building
A81 GARSCUBE ROAD
Raeberry Street
Oakbank Industrial Est
The Glasgow Academy
Surgery
Callander Street Clnc
N Woodside Road
Cedar Street
St Josephs Primary Sch
Council
Stronend St
Caldarvan St
Dartford St
Denham St
Ellesmere St
Hayston Crs
King's Pl
Rodney St
GT WESTERN
29
44
63

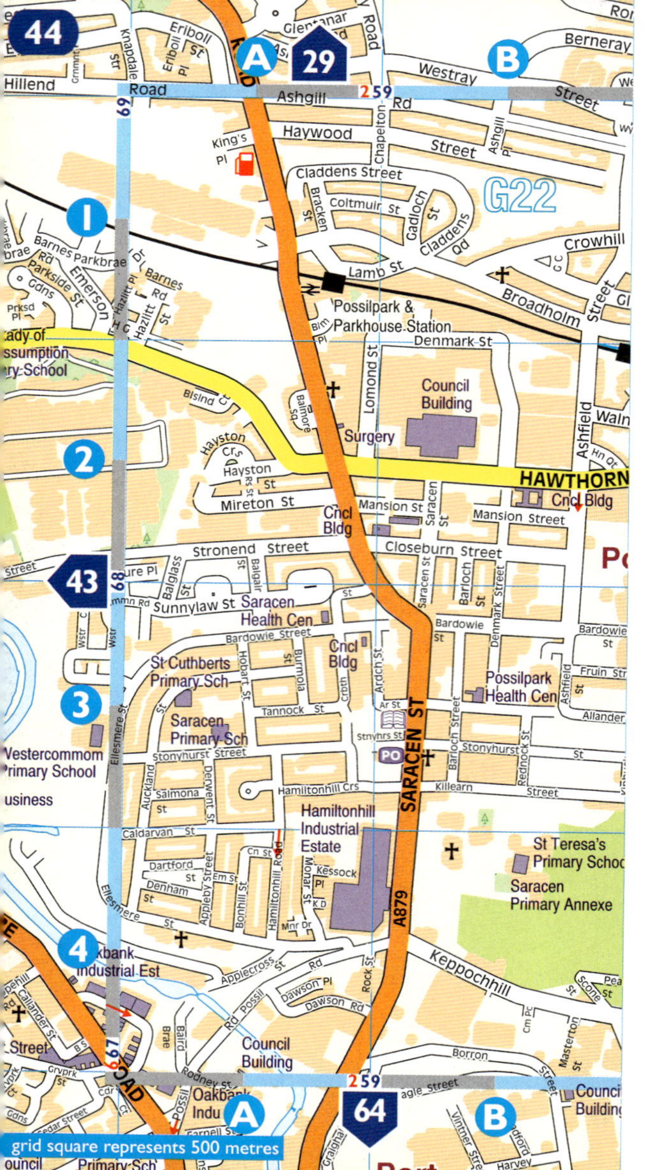

44
29
43
64
A
B
1
2
3
4
G22
259
69
68
67
Hillend Road
Ashgill Rd
Westray Street
Berneray
Eriboll
Eriboll St
Eriboll Pl
Knapdale Str
Glentanar
Haywood Street
Chapelton
Ashgill Pl
King's Pl
Claddens Street
Bracken St
Coltmuir St
Gadloch St
Claddens Qd
Crowhill
Barnes Rd
Parkbrae
Parkside Gdns
Emerson St
Prksd Pl
Hazlitt Pl
Hazlitt St
Barnes Rd
Lamb St
Broadholm Street
Possilpark & Parkhouse Station
Blm Pl
Denmark St
Lady of Assumption Primary School
Blslnd Ct
Balmore Sq
Lomond St
Council Building
Surgery
Ashfield
Hn Qt
Hayston Crs
Hayston St
Mireton St
Cncl Bldg
Mansion St
Saracen St
Mansion Street
HAWTHORN
Stronend Street
Closeburn Street
Balglass St
Balgair St
Sunnylaw St
Saracen Health Cen
Saracen St
Barloch St
Denmark Street
Bardowie St
Bardowie Street
Bardowie St
Fruin Str
Allander
St Cuthberts Primary Sch
Hobart St
Burmola St
Cncl Bldg
Crbth
Ardoch St
Possilpark Health Cen
Ashfield St
Tannock St
Ar St
Saracen Primary Sch
Stnyhrs St
Stonyhurst Street
PO
SARACEN ST
Barloch Street
Stonyhurst St
Rednock St
Westercommon Primary School
Ellesmere St
Auckland St
Derwent St
Salmona St
Hamiltonhill Crs
Killearn Street
Hamiltonhill Industrial Estate
Caldarvan St
Cn St
Hamiltonhill Road
Dartford St
Denham St
Appleby Street
Em St
Bonhill St
Monar St
Kessock Pl
KD
Mnr Dr
A879
St Teresa's Primary School
Saracen Primary Annexe
Ellesmere St
Oakbank Industrial Est
Applecross St
Dawson Pl
Dawson Rd
Rock St
Keppochhill Rd
Scone St
Cm Pc
Masterton St
Callander St
Street
Braid
Baird
Possil Rd
Council Building
Borron Street
Grvprk St
Rodney St
Oakbank Indu
Cedar Street
Eagle Street
Council Building
Vintner Street
Harvey Street
Graighall
Possil
Port
Primary Sch
grid square represents 500 metres

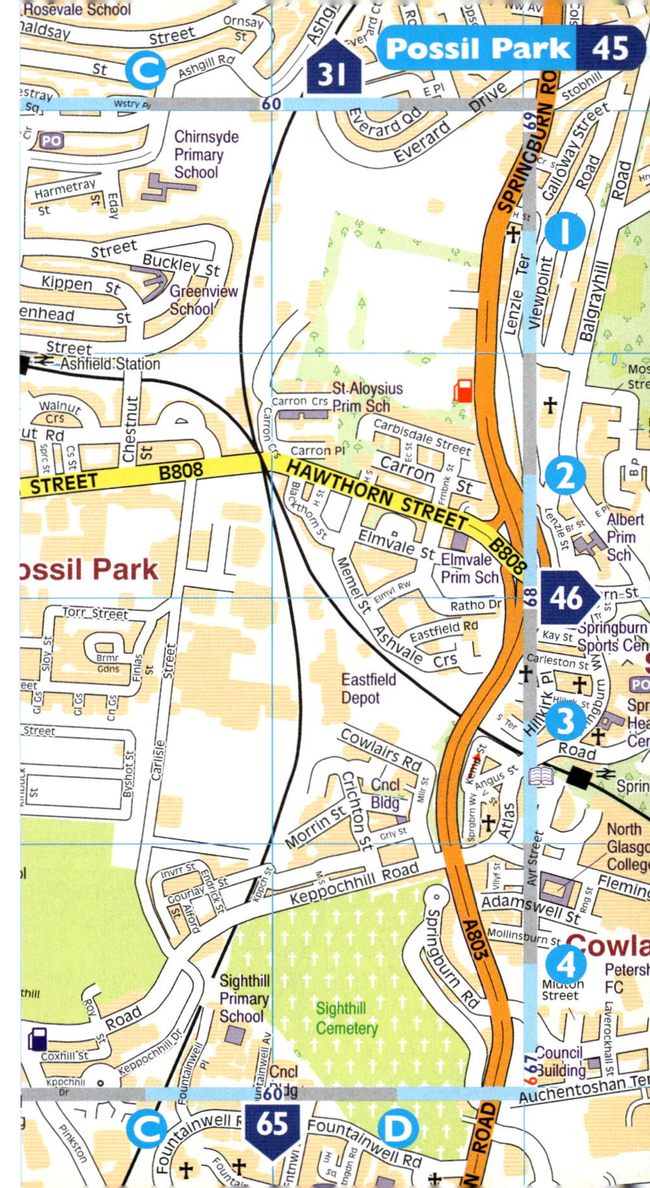

Rosevale School
Ornsay St
Street
Ashgill Rd
Everard Ct
Wstry Pl
E Pl
Everard Qd
Everard Drive
Stobhill
Galloway Street
Road
Road
SPRINGBURN ROAD
Chirnsyde Primary School
PO
Harmetray St
St
Eday
H St
Street
Buckley St
Kippen St
Greenview School
St
Lenzie Ter
Viewpoint
Balgrayhill
Street
Ashfield Station
St Aloysius Prim Sch
Carron Crs
Walnut Crs
Chestnut St
Carron Crs
Carron Pl
Carbisdale Street
Carron St
Frnbnk St
STREET
B808
HAWTHORN STREET
B808
Blackthorn St
Elmvale St
Elmvale Prim Sch
Lenzie St
Br St
E Pl
Albert Prim Sch
ossil Park
Memel St
Elmvl Rw
Ratho Dr
Eastfield Rd
Ashvale Crs
Torr Street
Slov St
Brmr Gdns
Finlas St
Street
Kay St
Springburn Sports Cen
Carleston St
Hillkirk Pl
PO
Eastfield Depot
Street
Carlisle
Byshot St
Cowlairs Rd
Cncl Bldg
Crichton St
Mllr St
Morrin St
Grly St
Angus St
Atlas
Sprgbrn Wy
Road
North Glasgo College
Fleming
Avr Street
Invrr St
Gourlay St
Endrick St
Alford
Kppch St
Keppochhill Road
Adamswell St
Rng St
Mollinsburn St
Cowla
Springburn Rd
A803
Sighthill Primary School
Sighthill Cemetery
Petersh FC
Street
Laverockhall St
Council Building
Road
Coxhill St
Keppochhill Dr
Fountainwell Pl
Fountainwell Av
Cncl Bldg
Kppchhll Dr
Auchentoshan Ter
Fountainwell R
Fountainwell Rd
Pinkston
ROAD

46
31
45
66
A
B
1
2
3
4
Springburn
Cowlairs
Stobhill General Hospital
A&E
Council Building
Springburn Road
Stobhill Road
Colston Av
Everard Drive
Balgrayhill Road
Broomfield Road
Mansel Street
Campsie Street
Springburn Academy
Albert Prim Sch
Springburn Sports Cen
Springburn Health Cen
Springburn Station
North Glasgow College
Barnhill Station
Petershill FC
Petershill Road
Flemington St
Adamswell St
Wellfield St
Cockmuir Street
Broomknowes Road
Balgraybank Street
Edgefauld Rd
Avonspark St
Foresthall Drive
Hawthorn St
Balornock Rd
Mosesfield Street
Bagnell Street
Auchentoshan Ter
B808
G21
1 grid square represents 500 metres

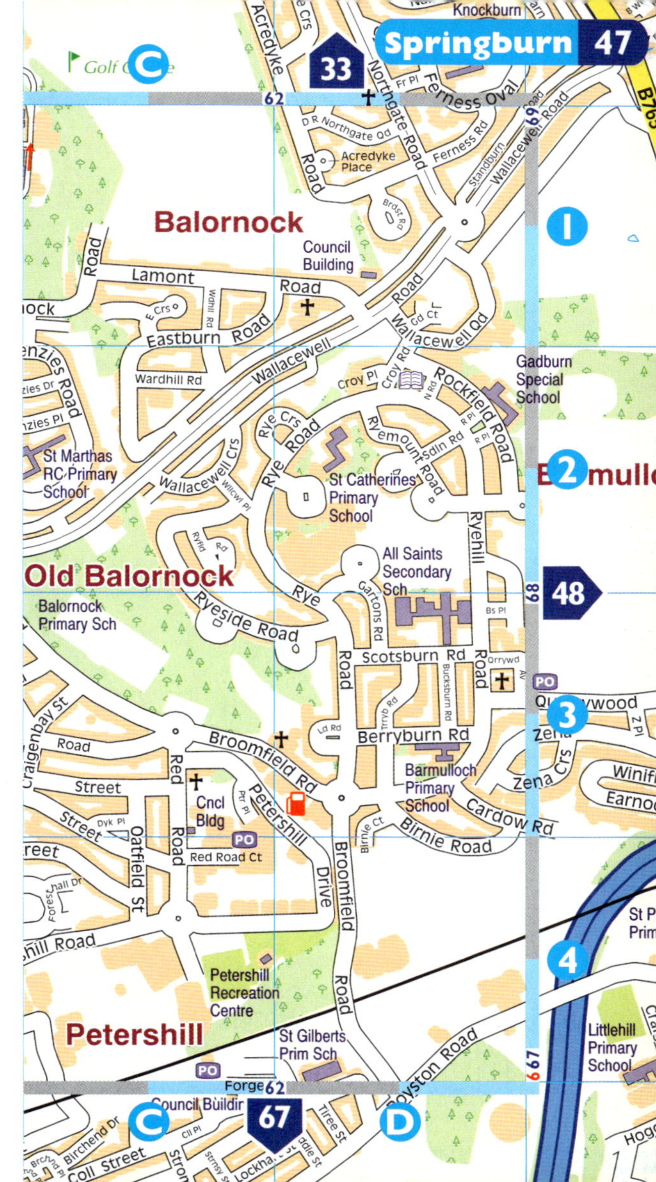
Balornock
Council Building
Lamont Road
Eastburn Road
Wardhill Rd
Wallacewell Road
Wallacewell Crs
Wallacewell Qd
Gadburn Special School
St Marthas RC Primary School
Old Balornock
Balornock Primary Sch
Ryeside Road
Rye Crs
Rye Road
Ryemount Road
Rockfield Road
St Catherines Primary School
All Saints Secondary Sch
Gartons Rd
Ryehill Road
Scotsburn Rd
Berryburn Rd
Bucksburn Rd
Barmulloch Primary School
Cardow Rd
Birnie Road
Birnie Ct
Zena Crs
Broomfield Rd
Broomfield Road
Petershill Drive
Red Road
Red Road Ct
Cncl Bldg
Craigenbay St
Oatfield St
Petershill Recreation Centre
Petershill
St Gilberts Prim Sch
Royston Road
Littlehill Primary School
Acredyke Road
Acredyke Place
Northgate Road
Northgate Qd
Ferness Oval
Ferness Rd
Standburn
Knockburn
Croy Pl
Croy Rd
Golf Course
Birchend Dr
Coll Street
Council Building
Tiree St
Forge
Hogg
Winifr
Earnoc
St P Prim
B765
33
48
67
62
68
69
67

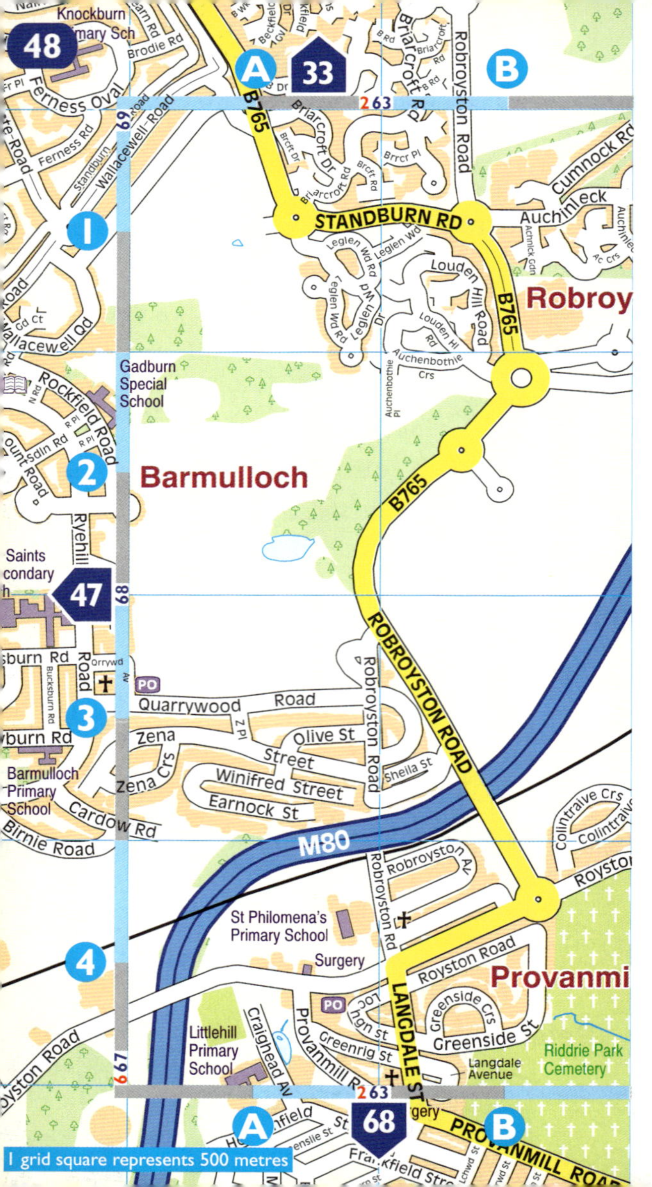

48
33
47
68
A
B
1
2
3
4
263
669
668
667
Knockburn Primary Sch
Brodie Rd
Ferness Oval
Ferness Rd
Standburn Rd
Wallacewell Road
Wallacewell Qd
B765
Briarcroft Dr
Briarcroft Rd
Robroyston Road
Cumnock Rd
Auchinleck
STANDBURN RD
Leglen Wd
Leglen Wd Rd
Louden Hill Road
Louden Hl Rd
Auchenbothie Crs
Auchenbothie Pl
Robroy
Gadburn Special School
Rockfield Road
Barmulloch
Ryehill Road
Saints
condary
PO
Quarrywood Road
Olive St
Zena St
Zena Crs
Winifred Street
Earnock St
Sheila St
ROBROYSTON ROAD
Barmulloch Primary School
Cardow Rd
Birnie Road
M80
Robroyston Av
Robroyston Rd
St Philomena's Primary School
Surgery
Colintraive Crs
Royston Road
Provanmi
Greenside Crs
Greenside St
LANGDALE ST
Langdale Avenue
Riddrie Park Cemetery
Littlehill Primary School
Craighead Av
Provanmill Rd
Greenrig St
PROVANMILL ROAD
Frankfield Street
I grid square represents 500 metres

Auchinleck
C
64
69
Glenbuck Av
Saughs Drive
Av
P Gdn
P Dr
Gingvi Crs
Saughs Ga
Saughs Pl
Kilkerran Drive
Saughs Av
Saughs Road
ston
M80
Saughs Road
Bogside Road
Junction 2
Millersneuk Crescent
Bogside Rd
Station Road
Inglenee
Firth Av
Cochneuk Road
50
Millerston
PO
Mossbank Drive
Avenue
Mossbank Av
Royston Road
A80
Road
Lochview Drive
Lochview Crs
Lochview Gdns
Lochview Pl
Hogganfield Loch
Lethamhill Golf Club
Ashcraig School
Bigton St
Hogganfield
D
1
2
3
4

49
70

1 grid square represents 500 metres

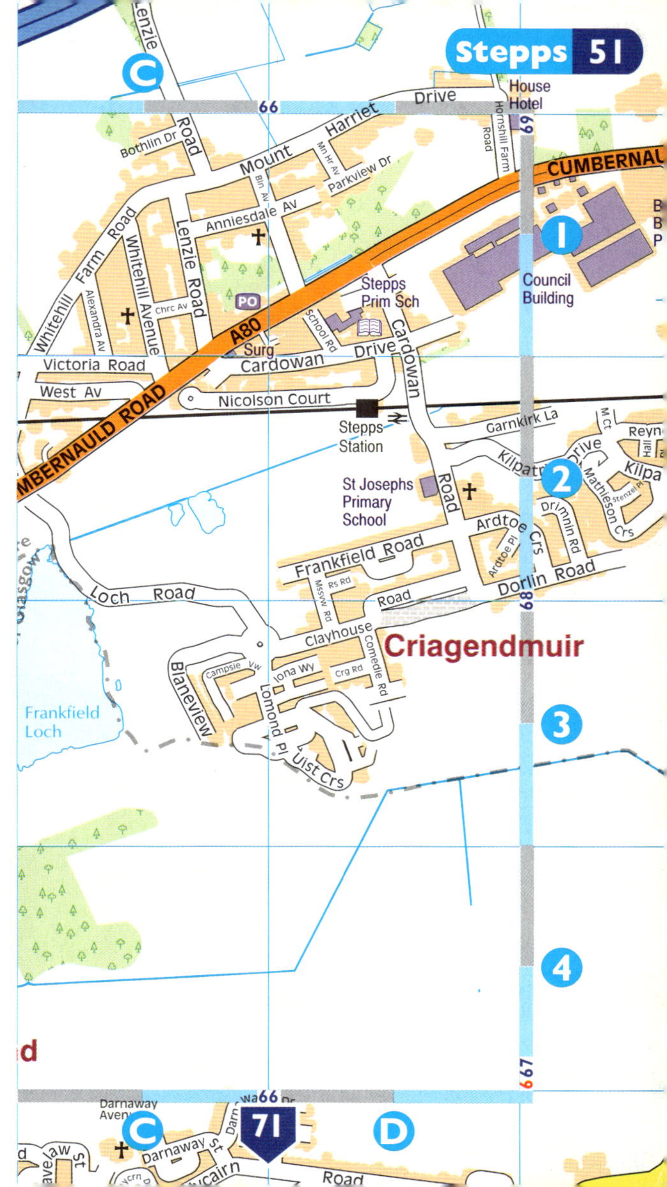
Lenzie Road
Bothlin Dr
Mount Harriet Drive
House Hotel
Hornshill Farm Road
Mn Hr Av
Bln Av
Parkview Dr
Anniesdale Av
CUMBERNAULD ROAD
Council Building
Whitehill Farm Road
Alexandra Av
Whitehill Avenue
Chrc Av
Lenzie Road
PO
A80
Stepps Prim Sch
School Rd
Surg
Cardowan Drive
Cardowan Road
Victoria Road
West Av
Nicolson Court
Stepps Station
Garnkirk La
Kilpatrick Drive
M Ct
Reyn
Hall
Kilpa
Mathieson Crs
Stenzel Pl
St Josephs Primary School
Drimnin Rd
Ardtoe Crs
Ardtoe Pl
Frankfield Road
Rs Rd
Mssvw Rd
Dorlin Road
Loch Road
Glasgow
Clayhouse Road
Criagendmuir
Comedie Rd
Crg Rd
Iona Wy
Campsie Vw
Blaneview
Lomond Pl
Uist Crs
Frankfield Loch
Darnaway Avenue
Darnaway St
Darn
71
Road
66
69
68
67
1
2
3
4
C
D

52
A
B
Walkinshaw Road
ORD ROAD
247
67
1
2
3
4
st Walkinshaw
m
BARNSFORD ROAD
66
ghead
A726
Junction 28a
M8
Junction 29
St James Park (Playing Fields)
Greenock Road
St Andrew's Dr
St Andrew's Crs
Kibb
Edu
Care
Sh
A737
Place
urnside
PA3
St James Av
A726
McFarlane St
Muirdykes Rd
Stirrat St
665
Walkinshaw Crs
Middleton Rd
Middleton Crs
Avenue
76
Clark
Paisley
St James
I grid square represents 500 metres

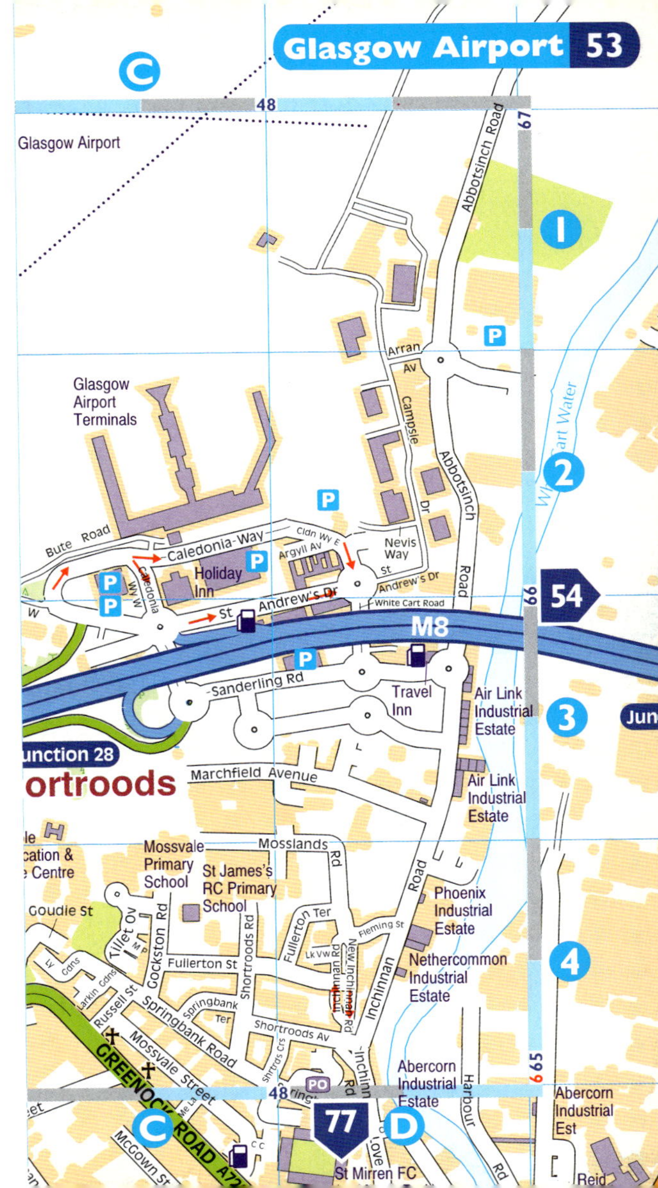

Glasgow Airport
Abbotsinch Road
Arran
Arran Av
Campsie Dr
Abbotsinch Road
White Cart Water
Glasgow Airport Terminals
Bute Road
Caledonia Way
Cldn Wy E
Argyll Av
Nevis Way
St Andrew's Dr
Holiday Inn
Caledonia Wy
White Cart Road
M8
54
Sanderling Rd
Travel Inn
Air Link Industrial Estate
Junction 28
Marchfield Avenue
Air Link Industrial Estate
Mossvale Primary School
Mosslands Rd
St James's RC Primary School
Goudie St
Tillet Ov
Gockston Rd
Shortroods Rd
Fullerton Ter
Fleming St
Phoenix Industrial Estate
Nethercommon Industrial Estate
Fullerton St
Lk Vw Rd
Inchinnan Rd
New Inchinnan Rd
Springbank Ter
Springbank Road
Russell St
Shortroods Av
Shrtrds Crs
Mossvale Street
Greenock Road A726
PO
McGown St
Abercorn Industrial Estate
Abercorn Industrial Est
Harbour Rd
Love St
77
St Mirren FC
Reid

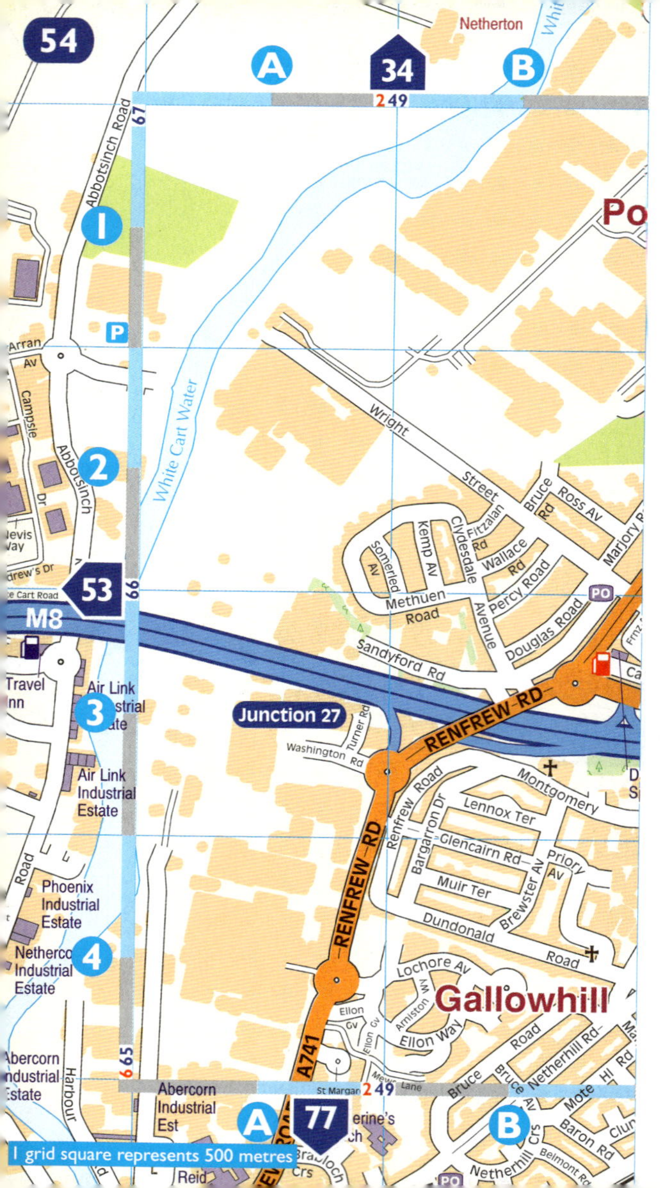

1 grid square represents 500 metres

Porterfield 55
35
50
C
D
79
56
1
2
3
4
French Street Industrial Estate
Moorpark Primary School
Renfrew Health Cen
Cncl Bldg
Newmains Primary Sch
Glynhill Hotel
Gallowhill Primary School
Arkleston
Cemetery
M8
PAISLEY ROAD
B791 COCKELS LOAN
SANDY ROAD
B791
Broadloan
Newmains Road
Cockels Loan
Arkleston Road
Arkleston Rd
Gallowhill Road
Knowe Rd
Montgomery
Merlin Wy
Clyde Rd
Netherhill Rd
Kinloch Road
Gibson Road
Nevis Road
Lomond Av
Paisley Rd
Knockhill Rd
Birmingham Rd
Stewart Av
Tower Dr
Tower Crs
Mitchell Av
Moorpark Sq
St Andrew's Rd
Meikle Av
Windsor Rd
Cambridge Road
Urquhart Crs
Glendee Road
Glendee Gdns
Fifth Avenue
Third Av
Second Av
First Av
Fourth Avenue
Baron St
Beechwood Dr
Cruachan Av
Ochil Rd
Lawers Rd
Viscount Avenue
Mull Avenue
Tiree Av
Staffa Avenue
Barra Av
Colonsay Av
Iona Rd
Holmes Av
Skye Av
Lang Av
Bute Av
Davaar Rd
Arran Rd
Ailsa Rd
Lewis Av
Coll Av
Dean
Arklest Primar
Victory Gardens
Oxford
South
East Av
Albert Rd
Clark Street
Robertson Dr
Brown St
Gleniffer
Kk Dr
Pntlnd Dr
David Lloyd Sports Centre
Motehill Rd
Kilearn Rd
Arkleston Crs
Priory Drive
Porterfield
Green Wynd
Thomson St
Mcgregor Av
Merchn Av
French St
PO

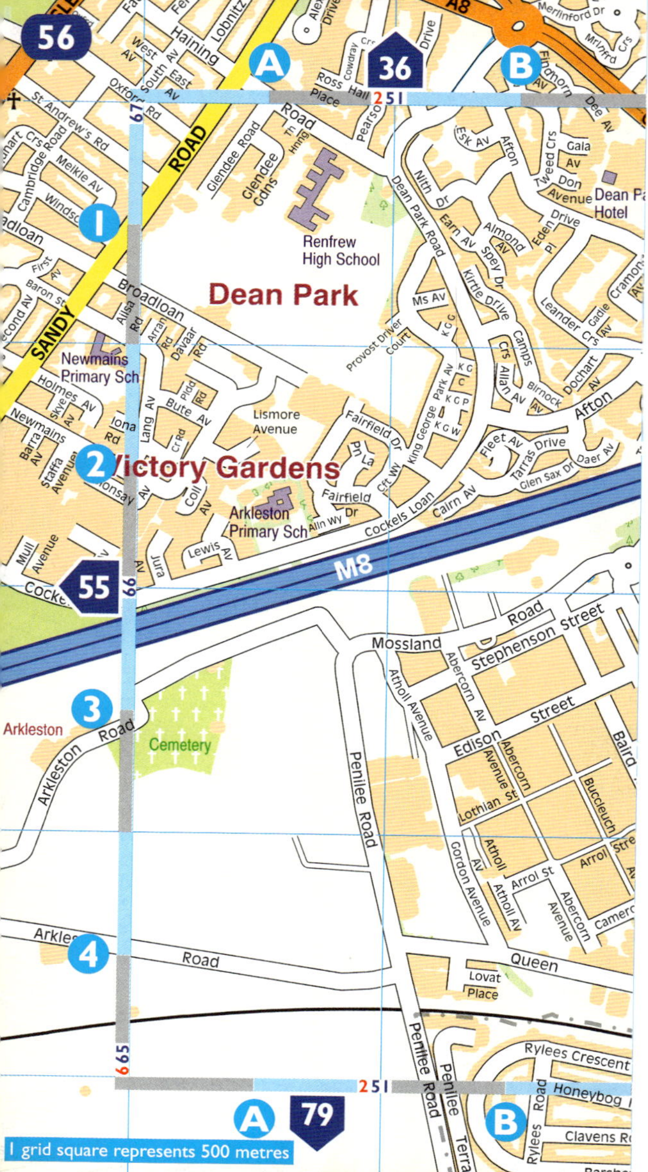

56
36
55
79
A
B
1
2
3
4
A8
M8
SANDY ROAD
Dean Park
Victory Gardens
Renfrew High School
Newmains Primary Sch
Arkleston Primary Sch
Dean Park Hotel
Arkleston
Cemetery
Ross Hall Place
Glendee Road
Glendee Gdns
Dean Park Road
Broadloan
Lismore Avenue
Fairfield Dr
King George Park Av
Provost Driver Court
Cockels Loan
Cairn Av
Mossland Road
Stephenson Street
Edison Street
Abercorn Av
Atholl Avenue
Penilee Road
Gordon Avenue
Lothian St
Arrol St
Buccleuch
Baird
Queen
Lovat Place
Arkleston Road
Rylees Crescent
Honeybog
Clavens Rd
Rylees Road
St Andrew's Rd
Meikle Av
Cambridge Road
Oxford Rd
Haining
Lobnitz
Nith Dr
Afton Drive
Tweed Crs
Almond Av
Kirtle Drive
Leander Crs
Dochart Av
Fleet Av
Tarras Drive
Glen Sax Dr
Daer Av
Lewis Av
Jura
Mull Avenue
Colonsay Av
Coll Av
Bute Av
Iona Rd
Lang Av
Ailsa Rd
Arran Rd
Davaar Rd
Newmains
Holmes Av
Barra Av
Staffa Avenue
1 grid square represents 500 metres

Dean Park 57
37
52
Shopping Centre
Park
Old Govan Road
Braehead Retail Park
Old Renfrew Road
King's Inch Rd
GLASGOW ROAD A8
RENFREW ROAD A8
A736
Junction 26
Junction 25a
58
M8
Hillington Park Retail & Amenities Centre
Renfrewshire
City of Glasgow
Deanside Rd
Napier Road
Kelvin Avenue
Kelvin Av
Carlyle Avenue
Zetland Rd
Scott Rd
Dalziel Road
Montrose Av
Lothian St
Arrol St
Huntly Avenue
Mansfield Road
Earl Haig Rd
Claverhouse Road
Watt Road
Lister Rd
Seaforth Rd N
Seaforth Rd S
Livingstone Av
Carlyle Av
Ainslie Avenue
Ainslie Road
Hillington Rd
HILLINGTON RD
Hillington Road
Ballantine Av
Colquhoun Avenue
Nasmyth Road N
Nasmyth Rd South
Hepburn Road
Hillington Industrial Estate
Jubilee Ct
Buccleuch Av
Elizabeth Avenue
Hillington West Station
Boswell Square
Erskine Sq
Linburn Road
Linburn Special School
Linburn Pl
Deanfield Qd
Kinsail Dr
Moorpark
81
Carnegie Road
Chirnside Pl
Kirkaig Avenue
Lossie Crs
Hallidale Crescent
Cassley Av
Ettrick Av
Tirry Av
Teith Av
Loyne Dr
Lochy Av
Invergis Av
Morriston Crescent
Cnnnghm Rd
Lorne Rd
PO
C
D
1
2
3
4
66
65
67

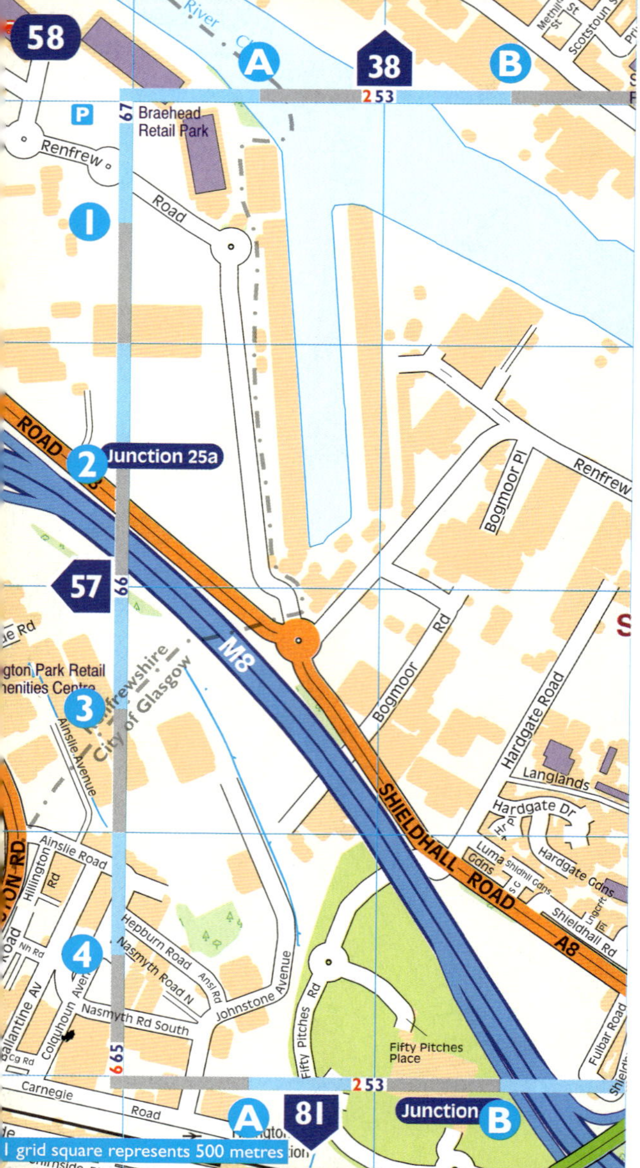

58
River
A
38
B
2 53
Methuen St
St
Scotstoun St
P
67
Braehead
Retail Park
Renfrew
Road
1
ROAD
2
Junction 25a
Bogmoor Pl
Renfrew
57
66
M8
Renfrewshire
City of Glasgow
Park Retail
Centre
3
Ainslie Avenue
Bogmoor
Rd
Hardgate Road
Langlands
Hardgate Dr
Luma Gdns
Shieldhall Gdns
Hardgate Gdns
SHIELDHALL ROAD
A8
Shieldhall Rd
Ainslie Road
Hillington
Rd
Nh Rd
4
Hepburn Road
Nasmyth Road N
Ansl Rd
Johnstone Avenue
Fifty Pitches Rd
Nasmyth Rd South
Colquhoun Ave
Ballantine Av
Cg Rd
665
Fulbar Road
Fifty Pitches
Place
Carnegie
Road
2 53
A
81
Junction
B
1 grid square represents 500 metres

Whiteinch
Shieldhall
Linthouse
Drumoyne
Clyde Tunnel
River Cly
Southern General Hospital
A&E
Govan Road
Govan Rd
Road
HOLMFAULD RD
Holmfauldhead Pl
Linthouse Road
A739
A8
Whiteinch Business Park
Whiteinch Indoor Bowling Stadium
Jordanvale Av
Clydeholm Road
South St
Dumbarton Rd
Northinch St
Curle St
Edzell St
Jordan St
Squire St
Smith St
Dilwara Av
Ferryden St
Broomhill Ter
Byron St
Langlands Road
Langlands School
Elder Park Primary Sch
Govan Health Centre
Govan High School
Elderpark Clinic
St Jerome's Prim Sch
Greenfield Primary School
Drumoyne Primary School
Drumoyne Industrial
Drumoyne Road
Ardshiel Rd
Drumoyne Dr
Balfron Rd
Nimmo
Barnwell Ter
Arngask Rd
Arduthie Rd
Lunan Place
Aberlady Rd
Luss Rd
Mallaig Rd
Muirdrochy Rd
Murroes Rd
Elder Gv Pl
Mountgarrie Rd
Morefield Rd
Langlands Rd
Skipness Dr
Greenloan Av
Greengairs Av
Kennedar Dr
Hutton Dr
Drive Rd
Peninver Dr
Moss Rd
Cressy St
Aboukir St
Carleith Qd
Langcroft Rd
Meiklewood Rd
Daviot St
Kincraig St
Street
Elderpark Street
Craigton
Uist St
Ladywell School
Surgery
Surg
St Pauls Prim Sch
Broomhill School
Colle
39
54
60
66
65
67
83
C
D
1
2
3
4
PO

60
40
59
83
A
B
1
2
3
4
2 55
67
66
65
G51
Whiteinch
Partick
Linthouse
River Clyde
Broomhill Drive
Broomhill Ter
Broomlea School
Surgery
College
Thornwood Primary School
Thornwood Dr
Thornwood Rd
Thornwood Ter
Thornwood Av
Kennoway Dr
Dumbarton Rd
Sorley St
Castlebank Street
Clarence
Crow
Laurel Pl
Laurel Street
Crathie Dr
Kildonan Dr
Apsley St
Apsly La
Ardery Street
Maule Dr
Meadow Rd
Sandy Rd
Rosevale St
Norval St
Beith St
Hayburn Crs
Hayburn La
Dyce La
Castlebank Ct
Meadowside St
PO
Govan Road
St Anthonys Primary School
Garmouth St
Fairfield St
Elder St
Taransay St
Luath St
Howat St
Rathlin St
Wanlock St
Govan Rd
Shaw St
Langlands Rd
Golspie St
Cncl Bldg
Robert St
Helen Street
Harmony Row
Hill's Trust Primary Sch
Harhill St
Greenfield St
Crossloan Ter
Crossloan Rd
Loanbank Quadrant
Elder Park Primary Sch
Govan Health Centre
Elderpark Clinic
St Jerome's Prim Sch
Greenfield Primary School
Elderpark Street
Nimmo Dr
Uist Street
Craigton Road
Arthurlie St
Drive Rd
Hutton Dr
Ardshiel Rd
Arduthie Rd
Aberlady Rd
Kellas St
Dava St
Birkmyre Rd
St Anthonys FC
1 grid square represents 500 metres

Partick 61
41
62
85
Partick Stn
Kelvinhall Stn
BEITH STREET
BYRES RD
B808
A814
POINTHOUSE ROAD
Dumbarton Rd
Highburgh Road
Hyndland Primary School
Middlefield Residential Sch
St Peter's Primary School
Dowanhill Primary School
West of Scotland CC
Byres Road Mkt
Cncl Bldg
Western Infirmary
University of Glasgow
Council Building
Partick Mkt
Museum of Transport
Kelvin Hall International Sports Arena
Royal Hospital for Sick Children and Maternity Hospital
Kelvin Sch
Yorkhill
Glasgow Steiner School
Kelvinhaugh Primary Sch
The Tall Ship at Glasgow Harbour
Govan Station
Govan
Cartvale Sch
St Gerard's Secondary School
Copeland Primary School
St Saviour's Primary School
Glasgow Tower
Prince's Dock
Glasgow Moat House
Glasgow Science Centre and Theatre
Woodville Park Industrial Est

62
42
61
85
A
B
Hillhead Stn
Byres Rd
Dowanhill Primary School
Junior Sch
High Sch
University
Temple Kelvinbridge Stn
Hindu Temple
University Avenue
Western Infirmary
Hunterian Museum
University of Glasgow
University of Glasgow Visitor Centre
Heatherbank Museum of Social Work Trust
Kelvingrove ArtGallery & Museum
Museum of Transport
Kelvin Hall International Sports Arena
River Kelvin
Kelvingrove Park
The Kelvin Park Lorne Hotel
Dumbarton Rd
Argyle Street
Sauchiehall Street
Kelvin Way
Kelvin Sch
Surgery
Glasgow Steiner School
Kelvinhaugh Primary School
Mount Manor Business Park
Exhibition Centre Stn
G3
Scottish Exhibition and Conference Centre
Glasgow Moat House
Clyde Auditorium
Glasgow Tower
Bells Bridge
Prince's Dock
Glasgow Science Centre and IMAX Theatre
Clydeway Business Centre
Finnieston St
A814
Argyle
Lancefield Quay
Congress Road
Stobcross Road
Royal Ter
Royal Crs
Fitzroy Lane
Sandyford
Berkeley
Kent Rd
Finnieston Sq
Eye C
Haugh Road
Minerva Street
257
665
1 grid square represents 500 metres

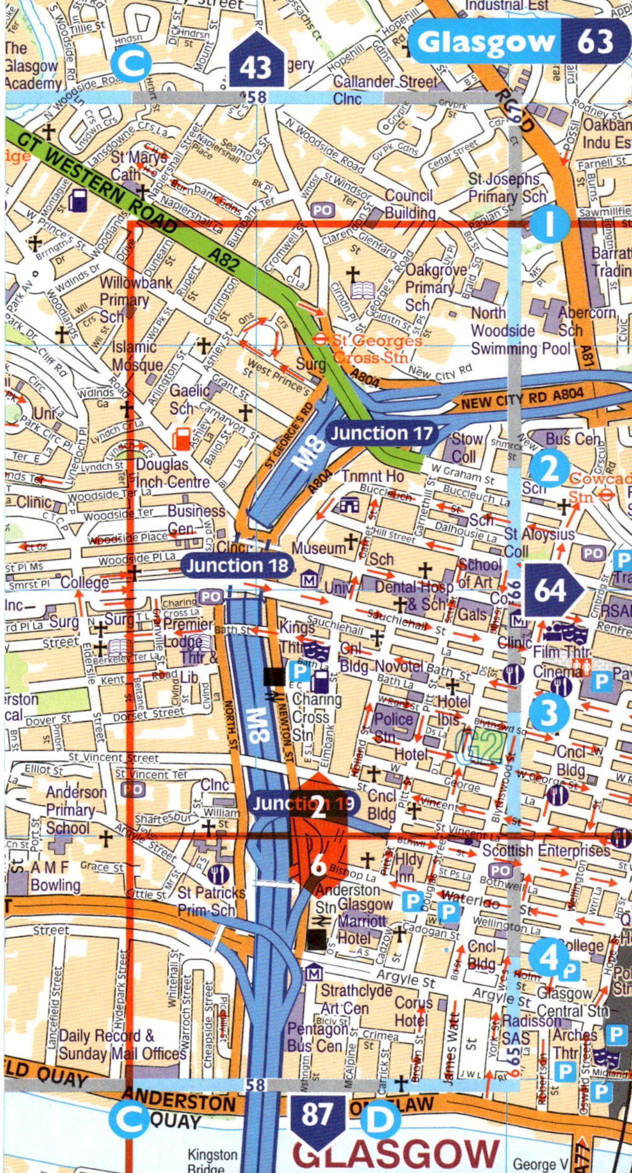

Glasgow 63
43
64
87
Glasgow
GT WESTERN ROAD
A82
The Glasgow Academy
St Marys Cath
Council Building
St Josephs Primary Sch
Oakbank Indu Est
Barratt Trading
Oakgrove Primary Sch
North Woodside Swimming Pool
Abercorn Sch
Willowbank Primary Sch
Islamic Mosque
Gaelic Sch
St Georges Cross Stn
New City Rd
NEW CITY RD A804
Junction 17
Junction 18
Junction 19
M8
Stow Coll
Bus Cen
Cowcaddens Stn
Tnmnt Ho
Douglas Inch Centre
Business Cen
Museum
St Aloysius Coll
School of Art
Dental Hosp & Sch
Univ
College
Premier Lodge
Kings Thtr
Charing Cross Stn
Sauchiehall St
Bath St
Novotel
Film Thtr
Cinema
Police Stn
Hotel Ibis
G2
Cncl Bldg
W George St
St Vincent Street
St Vincent Ter
Anderson Primary School
Argyle Street
AMF Bowling
St Patricks Prim Sch
Scottish Enterprises
Anderston Stn
Glasgow Marriott Hotel
Waterloo St
Wellington La
College
Argyle St
Strathclyde Art Cen
Pentagon Bus Cen
Corus Hotel
Radisson SAS
Glasgow Central Stn
Arches Thtr
Daily Record & Sunday Mail Offices
ANDERSTON QUAY
Kingston Bridge
George V Bridge
James Watt St
Hope St
North St
Newton St
Elmbank St
Pitt St
Douglas St
Blythswood St
Woodside Place
Woodside Ter
Woodlands Rd
Park Circ Pl
St Georges Rd
Callander Street
N Woodside Road
Cedar Street
Possil Rd
Garnethill St
Buccleuch St
Dalhousie La
Hill Street
W Graham St
Renfrew
Pol Stn
Lancefield Street
Hydepark Street
Warroch Street
Cheapside Street
Whitehall St
Carrick St
McAlpine St
Crimea St
Brown St
York St
Robertson St
Oswald Street
Midland St
Bothwell La
Cadogan St
Wellington St
A77
A81
58
65
66
C
D
1
2
3
4

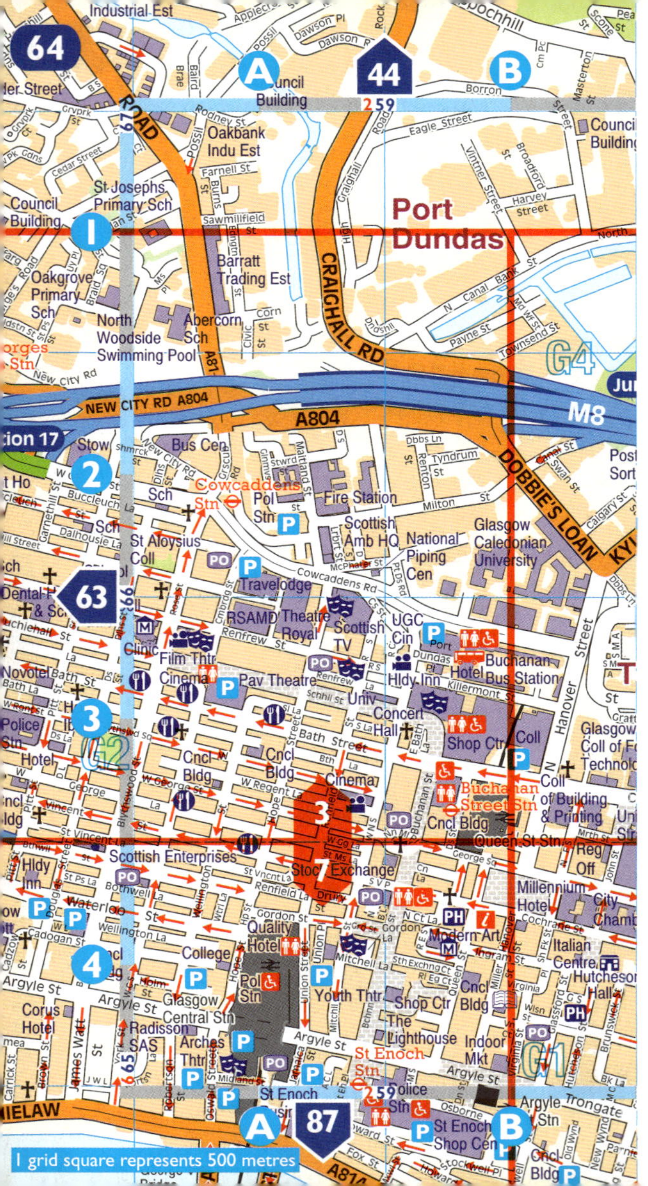
64
44
63
87
A
B
1
2
3
4
259
679
665
Industrial Est
Council Building
Oakbank Indu Est
St Josephs Primary Sch
Council Building
Oakgrove Primary Sch
Barratt Trading Est
North Woodside Swimming Pool
Abercorn Sch
Port Dundas
CRAIGHALL RD
Eagle Street
Borron
Vintner Street
Broadford St
Harvey Street
North
Canal Bank
N Canal Bank St
Payne St
Townsend St
G4
M8
NEW CITY RD A804
A804
A81
New City Rd
Cowcaddens Stn
Pol Stn
Fire Station
Scottish Amb HQ
National Piping Cen
Glasgow Caledonian University
DOBBIE'S LOAN
Milton St
Dalhousie La
Buccleuch St
Garnethill St
St Aloysius Coll
Cowcaddens Rd
Travelodge
RSAMD
Theatre Royal
Scottish TV
UGC Cin
Renfrew St
Buchanan Bus Station
Hotel
Hldy Inn
Killermont St
Hanover Street
Film Thtr
Cinema
Pav Theatre
Concert Hall
Bath Street
Shop Ctr
Coll
Glasgow Coll of Building & Printing
Cncl Bldg
W Regent La
Cinema
Buchanan Street Stn
Queen St Stn
Cncl Bldg
Novotel
Bath St
Police Stn
Hotel
G2
West George St
St Vincent La
Blythswood Sq
Scottish Enterprises
Stock Exchange
Hldy Inn
Bothwell La
Waterloo St
Wellington La
Cadogan St
Argyle St
Corus Hotel
Radisson SAS
Glasgow Central Stn
Quality Hotel
College
Pol Stn
Youth Thtr
Shop Ctr
The Lighthouse
Modern Art
Cncl Bldg
Indoor Mkt
Millennium Hotel
Italian Centre
Hutcheson Hall
City Chambers
Arches Thtr
St Enoch Stn
St Enoch
Police Stn
St Enoch Shop Cen
Argyle St Stn
Trongate
Cncl Bldg
G1
James Watt St
Robertson St
Oswald St
Union Street
Jamaica St
Mitchell La
Gordon St
Ingram St
Virginia St
Glassford St
Cochrane St
George Sq
Renfield St
Hope St
Wellington St
West Nile St
Buchanan St
1 grid square represents 500 metres

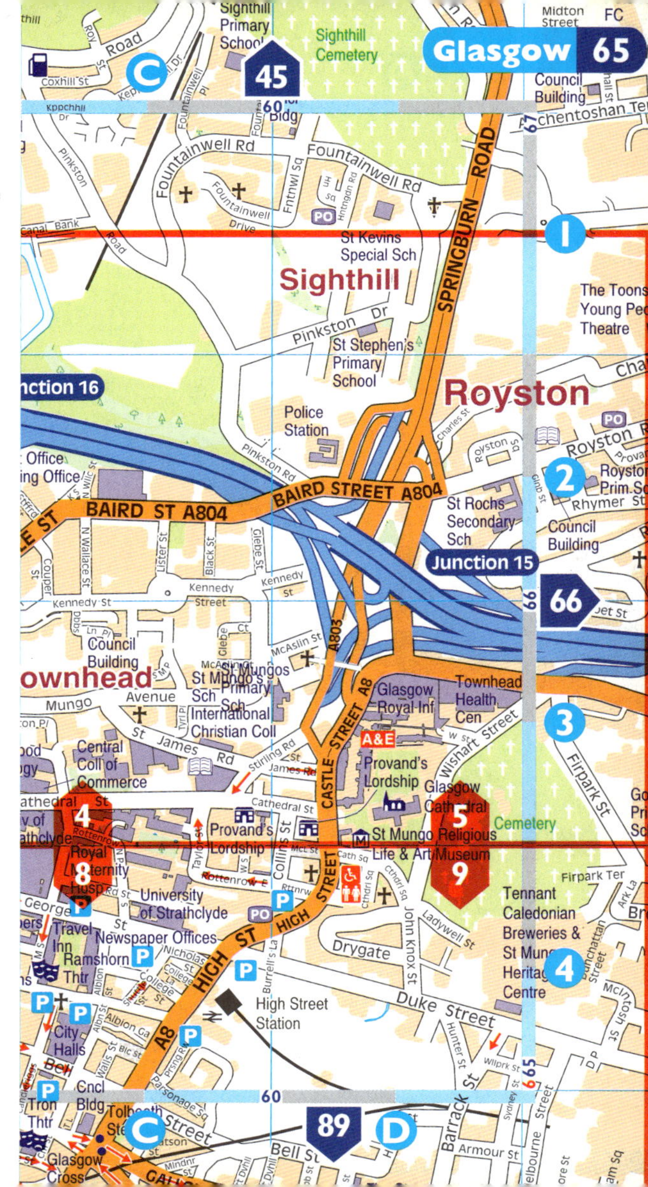
Sighthill Primary School
45
Sighthill Cemetery
Midton Street
FC
Council Building
Roy St
Road
C
Coxhill St
Keppochhill Dr
Fountainwell Pl
Fountainwell Rd
Fntnwl Sq
Hntngdn Rd
PO
Fountainwell Drive
Pinkston Road
Canal Bank
St Kevins Special Sch
Sighthill
SPRINGBURN ROAD
1
The Toons Young Peo Theatre
Pinkston Dr
St Stephen's Primary School
Junction 16
Royston
Police Station
Charles St
Royston Sq
PO
Royston Rd
Provan
Royston Prim Sch
2
Rhymer St
Pinkston Rd
BAIRD STREET A804
BAIRD ST A804
Office
St Rochs Secondary Sch
Council Building
Junction 15
N Wallace St
Lister St
Black St
Glebe St
Kennedy St
Kennedy Street
Couper St
66
Council Building
Glebe Ct
McAslin St
A803
Townhead
St Mungos Primary Sch
St Mungo's Sch
International Christian Coll
Avenue
Mungo
A8
CASTLE STREET
Glasgow Royal Inf
Townhead Health Cen
Wishart Street
3
Firpark St
A&E
St James Rd
Stirling Rd
Central Coll of Commerce
Provand's Lordship
Glasgow Cathedral
Cathedral St
4
5
Cemetery
Provand's Lordship
St Mungo Religious Life & Art Museum
Rottenrow
Royal Maternity Hosp
8
9
Taylor St
Collins St
Cath Sq
Cthdrl Sq
Cthdrl Sq
Firpark Ter
Rottenrow E
University of Strathclyde
George St
PO
P
HIGH STREET
Tennant Caledonian Breweries & St Mungo Heritage Centre
John Knox St
Ladywell St
Travel Inn
Newspaper Offices
Ramshorn Thtr
Nicholas St
College St
HIGH ST
Drygate
Burrell's La
High Street Station
Duke Street
Albion St
Albion Ga
City Halls
Blc St
Walls St
A8
Prsng Rw
Hunter St
Barrack St
Wllprk St
Sydney St
Cncl Bldg
Parsonage Sq
60
Tron Thtr
Tolbooth Steeple
C
Street
89
D
Glasgow Cross
Bell St
Armour St
Street
65
67

66
Midton Street
FC
Council Building
Laverockhall St
A
Petershill Road
46
B
Hobden St
St Gdn
261
Auchentoshan Ter
67
SPRINGBURN ROAD
1
Darnick Street
The Toonspeak Young Peoples Theatre
PO
St Rochs Primary Sch
Charles St
Garnock St
Chrstphr St
B St
C St
Royston Road
Blchrn Rd
Royston
Charles St
Royston Road
Provanhill St
2
A804
Royston Prim Sch
Rhymer St
Tharsis St
Dnlly St
Millburn St
Hollybank St
Sndm St
Clv St
St Rochs Secondary Sch
Council Building
Roystonhill
Frrs St
Crbr St
Kntyr St
Kilberry St
Junction 15
Junction 14
St Joseph's Ct
65
66
James Nisbet St
St Joseph's Vw
Rosemount St
M8
Townmill Road
Townhead Health
3
Wishart Street
ALEXANDRA PARADE
Hanson St
Milnbank St
Whitehill St
Armadale Pl
Armadale St
Blindlch La
Blindl La
Glasgow Cathedral
Cemetery
Firpark St
5
9
Golfhill Prim Sch
Place La
Circus Pl
Brmprk Cir
Lloyd St
PO
Golfhill Drive
Crgl St
Alexandra Parade Prim Sch
Mungo Religious & Art Museum
Firpark Ter
Circus Drive
Craigpark
On Sq
Craigpark
Onslow Drive
Ark La
Brmpr La
Br St
Tennant Caledonian Breweries & St Mungo Heritage Centre
Broompark Drive
Dennistoun
Ladywell St
John Knox St
4
Dunchattan Street
Cardross St
Westercraigs
Cl Ter
Whitehill St
Whitevale St
Ingleby Dr
Garthland
Annfield Medical Cen
Finlay Drive
McIntosh St
Okl Ter
Stn Ter
PO
Duke Street
Hunter St
Wllprk
Rosslea Drive
Annfield Pl
Wh St La
Duke Street
65
66
261
Barrack St
A
89
A Pl
Thompson St
Bellfield St
B
Baungate St
Bluevale St
Reidvale Street
Bellgrove
I grid square represents 500 metres

Dennistoun 67
47
62
Petershill
Recreation
Centre
Germiston
Junction 1/13
68
Alexandra Golf Club
Golf Course
Alexandra Park
Alexandra Parade Station
Kennyhill School
Council Building
Markets
Blochairn Road
Siemens Street
Royston Road
Coll Street
Forge Street
Stroma St
Lockhart St
Dinwiddie St
Tiree St
Birchend Dr
Craigendmuir St
Provan Road
Cumbernauld Road
Viewpark Av
Alexandra Pk St
Sannox Gdns
Roebank St
Coventry Dr
Haghill Primary Sch
Walter Street
Corsock Street
Appin Crs
Appin Road
Aberfoyle St
Ledaig Street
Todd Street
Whitehill Pool
Whitehill Sch
St Denis Prim Sch
Duke Street Station
Duke Street
Paton St
Aitken Street
Haghill Rd
Dunragit St
Bengairn St
Haghill
Cadie St
Gough St
Dinart Street
Hogarth Gdns
Glenpark Industrial
Glendale St
91
C
D

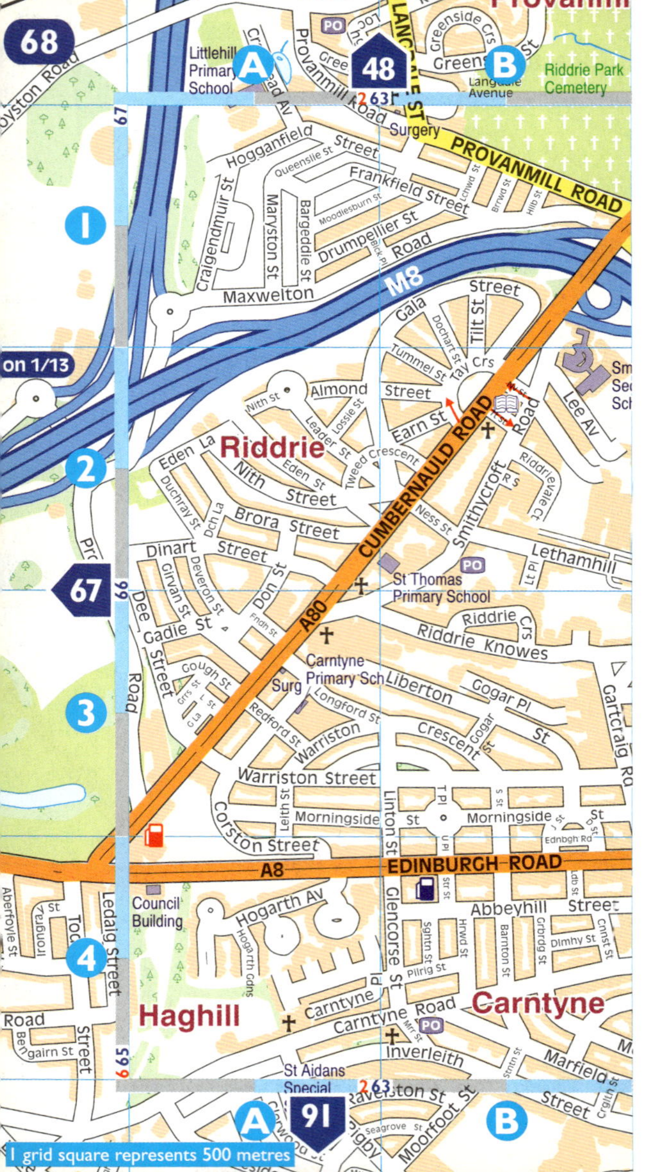
68
Royston Road
Littlehill Primary School
A
48
B
Provanmill
Riddrie Park Cemetery
PO
Greenside Crs
Provanmill Road
Langdale St
Langdale Avenue
Surgery
PROVANMILL ROAD
Hogganfield Street
Queenslie St
Frankfield Street
Moodiesburn St
Drumpellier St
Road
Craigendmuir St
Maryston St
Bargeddie St
Blck Pl
Maxwelton
M8
Street
Gala
Tilt St
Dochart St
Tay Crs
Tummel St
Almond
Street
Nith St
Lossie St
Leader St
Earn St
Lee Av
Riddrie
Eden La
Eden St
Tweed Crescent
Nith Street
CUMBERNAULD ROAD
Smithycroft
Riddrievale Ct
Ness St
Duchray St
Dch La
Brora Street
Dinart Street
Lethamhill
Lt Pl
PO
St Thomas Primary School
Girvan St
Deveron St
Don St
Fndn St
Dee
Gadie St
Street
A80
Riddrie Crs
Riddrie Knowes
Gough St
Carntyne Primary Sch
Surg
Liberton
Gogar Pl
Gartcraig Rd
Longford St
Redford St
Warriston
Crescent
Gogar St
St
Warriston Street
Corston Street
Leith St
Morningside St
Linton St
Morningside St
Ednbgh Rd
A8
EDINBURGH ROAD
Aberfoyle St
Irongray St
Ledaig Street
Council Building
Hogarth Av
Hogarth Gdns
Glencorse St
Str St
Sghtn St
Hrwd St
Abbeyhill Street
Barnton St
Crbrdg St
Dlmhy St
Cnnst St
Pilrig St
Carntyne Pl
Carntyne Road
Carntyne
Haghill
Road
Bengairn St
Street
Mrr St
PO
Inverleith
Marfield Street
Strtn St
St Aidans Special
Ravelston St
Moorfoot St
Seagrove St
91
A
B
on 1/13
67
1
2
3
4
1 grid square represents 500 metres

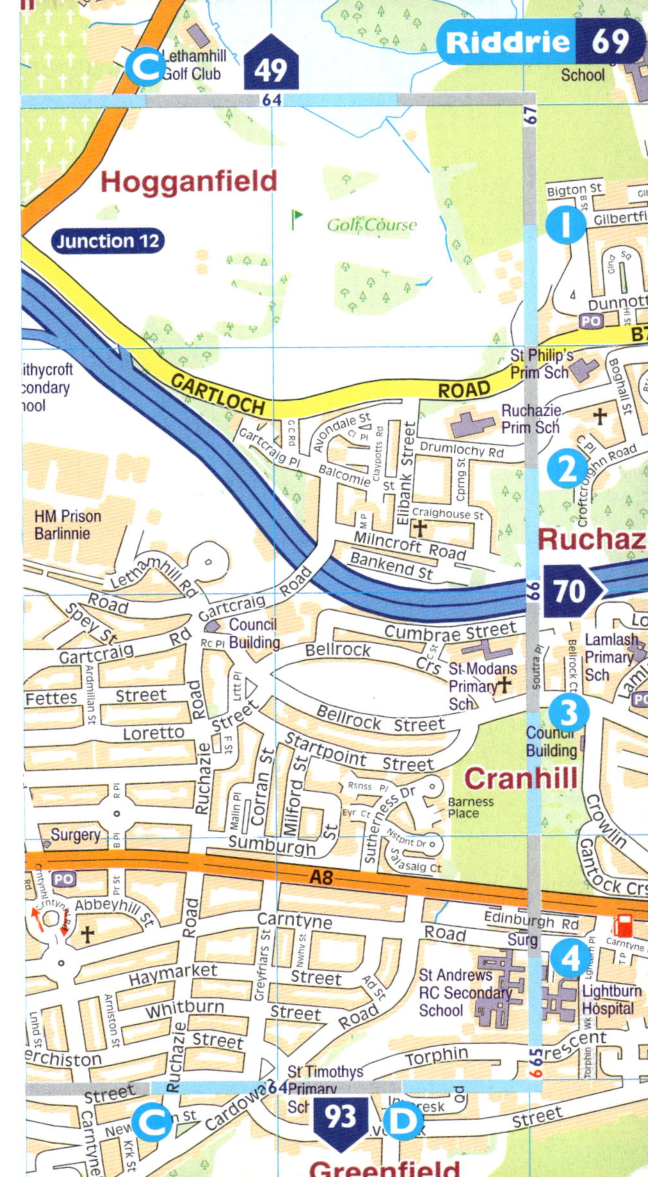

Riddrie 69
49
64
67
Lethamhill Golf Club
School
Hogganfield
Golf Course
Junction 12
Bigton St
Gilbertfield
Dunnottar
PO
B7
Gartloch Road
St Philip's Prim Sch
Boghall St
Ruchazie Prim Sch
Croftcroighn Road
Ruchazie
Garthcraig Pl
Avondale St
Balcomie St
Claypotts Rd
Elibank Street
Drumlochy Rd
Cprng St
Craighouse St
Milncroft Road
Bankend St
HM Prison Barlinnie
Lethamhill Rd
Road
Spey St
Gartcraig Road
Gartcraig Rd
Council Building
Cumbrae Street
Bellrock Crs
St Modans Primary Sch
Soutra Pl
70
66
Lamlash Primary Sch
Fettes Street
Ardmillan St
Loretto Street
Ruchazie Road
Bellrock Street
Startpoint Street
Corran St
Milford St
Malin Pl
Council Building
Cranhill
Barness Place
Sutherness Dr
Crowlin Crs
Gantock Crs
Surgery
Sumburgh St
Salasaig Ct
A8
PO
Abbeyhill St
Road
Carntyne Road
Edinburgh Rd
Surg
Haymarket Street
Greyfriars St
St Andrews RC Secondary School
Lightburn Hospital
Whitburn Street
Arniston St
Ruchazie Street
Merchiston Street
Torphin Crescent
St Timothys Primary Sch
65
64
93
Cardowan Road
Carntyne
Street
Greenfield

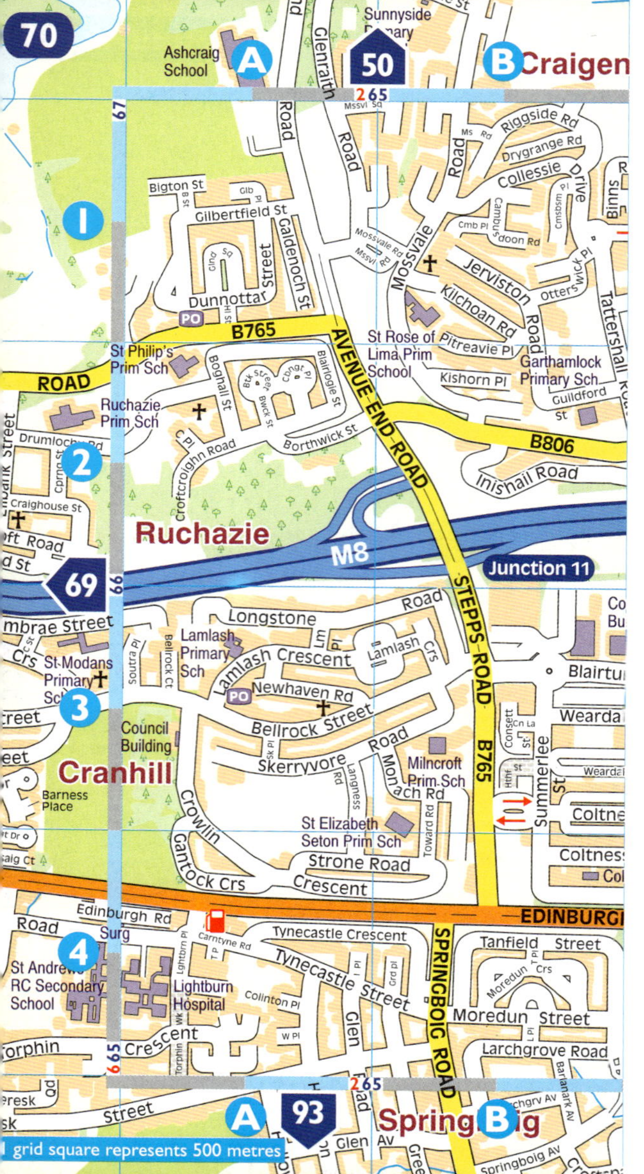

70
Ashcraig School
Sunnyside Primary
50
Craigend
Ruchazie
M8
Junction 11
69
Cranhill
93
Springboig
St Philip's Prim Sch
Ruchazie Prim Sch
St Rose of Lima Prim School
Garthamlock Primary Sch
Lamlash Primary Sch
St Modans Primary Sch
Council Building
Milncroft Prim Sch
St Elizabeth Seton Prim Sch
St Andrews RC Secondary School
Lightburn Hospital
AVENUE END ROAD
STEPPS ROAD
SPRINGBOIG ROAD
EDINBURGH
B765
B806
grid square represents 500 metres

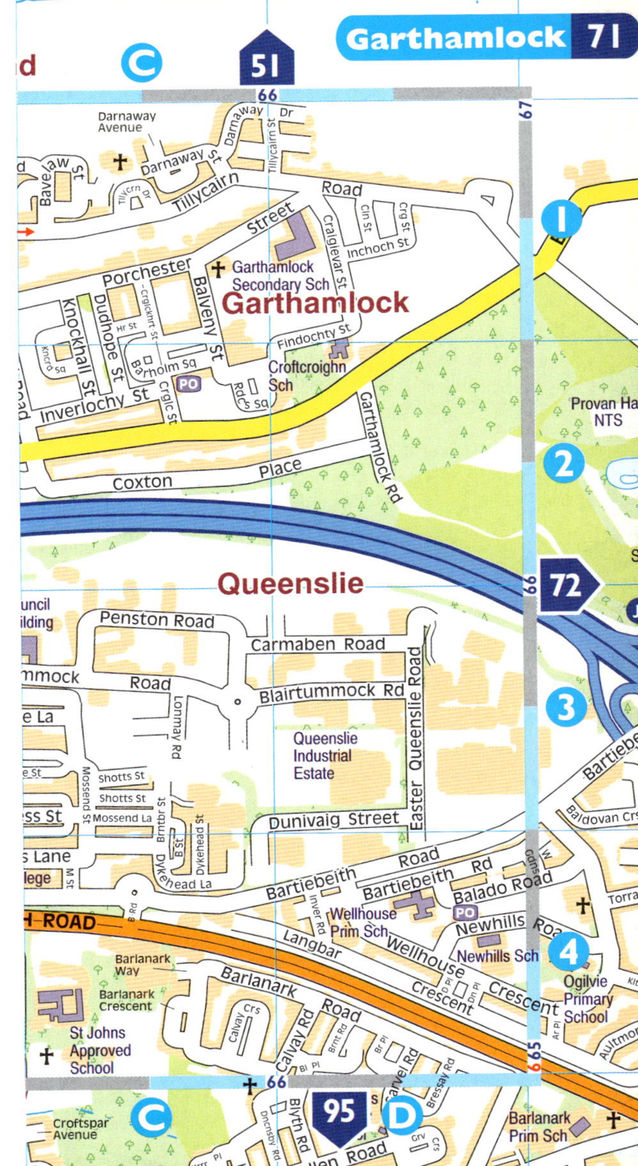

Garthamlock
Queenslie
Darnaway Avenue
Darnaway St
Darnaway Dr
Tillycairn St
Tillycairn Road
Porchester Street
Craigievar St
Inchoch St
Garthamlock Secondary Sch
Balveny St
Knockhall St
Dudhope St
Barholm Sq
Findochty St
Croftcroighn Sch
Inverlochy St
Crgic St
Garthamlock Rd
Coxton Place
Provan Hall NTS
Penston Road
Carmaben Road
Blairtummock Rd
Road
Lonmay Rd
Queenslie Industrial Estate
Easter Queenslie Road
Shotts St
Mossend St
Mossend La
Dykehead St
Dykehead La
Dunivaig Street
Bartiebeith Road
Bartiebeith Rd
Balado Road
Baldovan Crs
Inver Rd
Wellhouse Prim Sch
Langbar
Wellhouse Crescent
Newhills Road
Newhills Sch
Ogilvie Primary School
Barlanark Way
Barlanark Crescent
Barlanark Road
St Johns Approved School
Calvay Rd
Calvay Crs
Bressay Rd
Barlanark Prim Sch
Croftspar Avenue
Blyth Rd
Torran
Aultmore
PO

51
72
95

A
B
GARTLOCH ROAD
B806
Conisborough
Balcurvie Rd
Auchinlea
Balfluig St
Road
Provan Hall NTS
Provanhall Primary School
Duffus St
St Benedict Primary School
Brunstane Rd
Drochil St
Easterhouse Sports Centre
Road
Council Building
Police Stn
Junction 10
Westerhouse
Shandwick St
Bogbain Rd
Arnisdale Road
Easterh Pool
Bartiebeith Road
M8
Kildermorie Road
Baldovan Crs
Wellhouse Road
Trondra Pl
Easthall Primary Sch
Ware Rd
Torran Rd
Balado Road
Newhills Road
Eddlewood Place
Eddlewood Rd
Egerton Pl
Banton Pl
Wardie Road
Ogilvie Primary School
Crescent
Aultmore Rd
Stepford Road
Parkway
Springhill Dr S
Hallhill Rd
Barlanark Prim Sch
95
71
Easter Queenslie Road
1
2
3
4
267
66
67
665

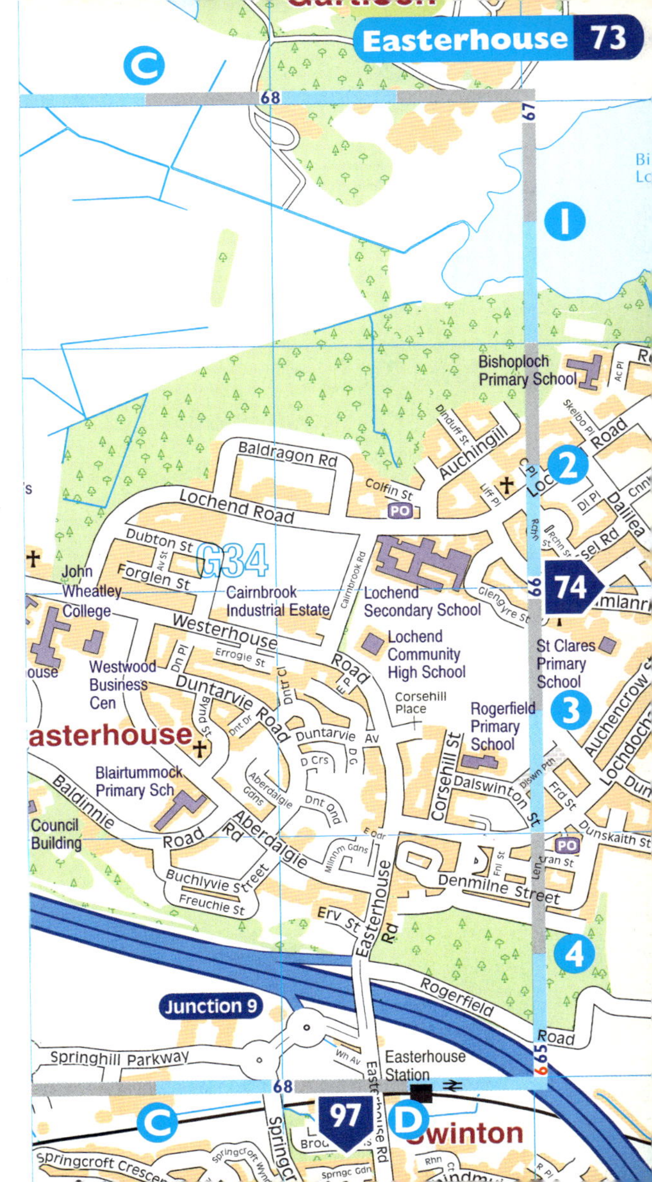
C
68
67
I
Bishoploch
Primary School
Ac Pl
Skelbo Pl
Road
Dinduff St
Auchingill
2
Baldragon Rd
Colfin St
PO
Liff Pl
Dl Pl
Dalilea
Lochend Road
Dubton St
Av St
G34
Cairnbrook Rd
Rchn St
Sel Rd
John
Wheatley
College
Forglen St
Cairnbrook
Industrial Estate
Lochend
Secondary School
Glengyre St
66
74
St Clares
Primary
School
Westerhouse
Errogie St
Road
Lochend
Community
High School
Dn Pl
Westwood
Business
Cen
Duntarvie Road
Dntr Cl
Corsehill
Place
Rogerfield
Primary
School
3
Auchencrow
Bynd St
Dnt Dr
Duntarvie Av
Easterhouse
D Crs
D G
Corsehill St
Dalswinton St
Frd St
Blairtummock
Primary Sch
Baldinnie
Road
Aberdalgie Gdns
Dnt Qnd
Council
Building
Aberdalgie Rd
E Qdr
Milnnm Gdns
Dunskaith St
PO
Fnl St
Denmilne Street
Buchlyvie Street
Freuchie St
Erv St
Easterhouse Rd
4
Junction 9
Rogerfield
Road
Springhill Parkway
Wh Av
Easterhouse
Station
65
68
C
97
D
Swinton
Springcroft Crescent
Springcroft Wynd
Sprngc Gdn
Rhn
Ct
R Pl

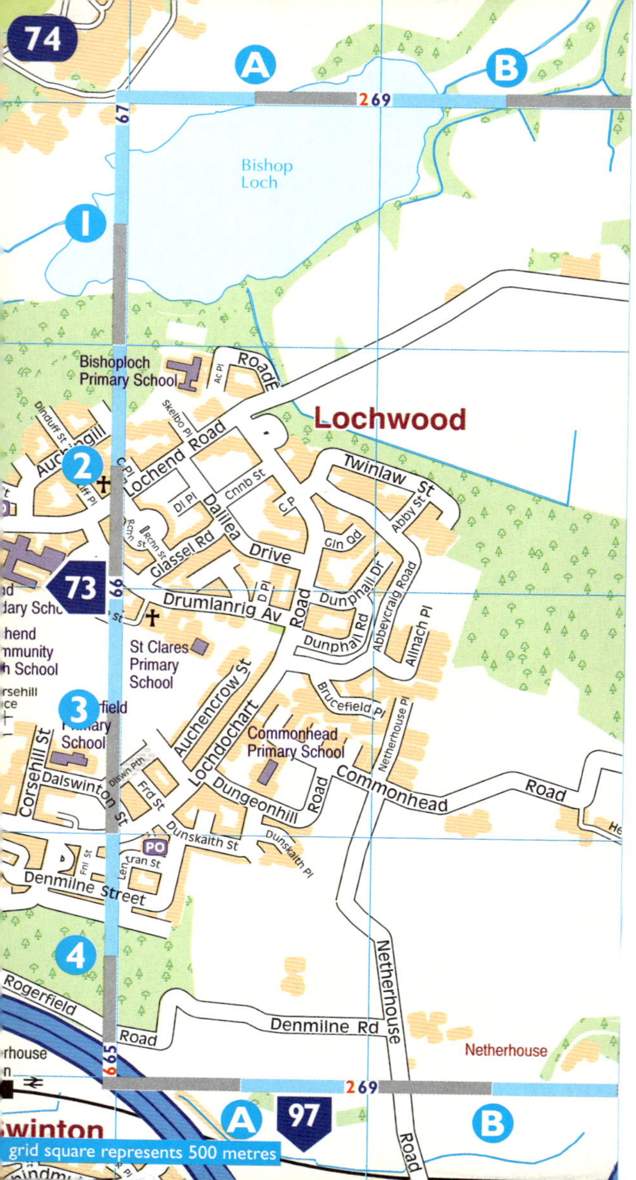

74
A
B
269
67
Bishop Loch
1
Bishopoch Primary School
Lochwood
Twinlaw St
Lochend Road
Dalilea Drive
Glassel Rd
Drumlanrig Av
St Clares Primary School
Auchencrow St
Lochdochart Road
Commonhead Primary School
Commonhead Road
Dungeonhill Road
Dunskaith St
Denmiline Street
Dalswinton St
Corsehill St
Abbeycraig Road
Allnach Pl
Brucefield Pl
Netherhouse Pl
Dunphail Rd
Dunphail Dr
Gln Qd
Abby St
Cnnb St
Skelbo Pl
Ac Pl
2
3
4
73
66
PO
Rogerfield Road
Denmilne Rd
Netherhouse Road
Netherhouse
665
97
grid square represents 500 metres

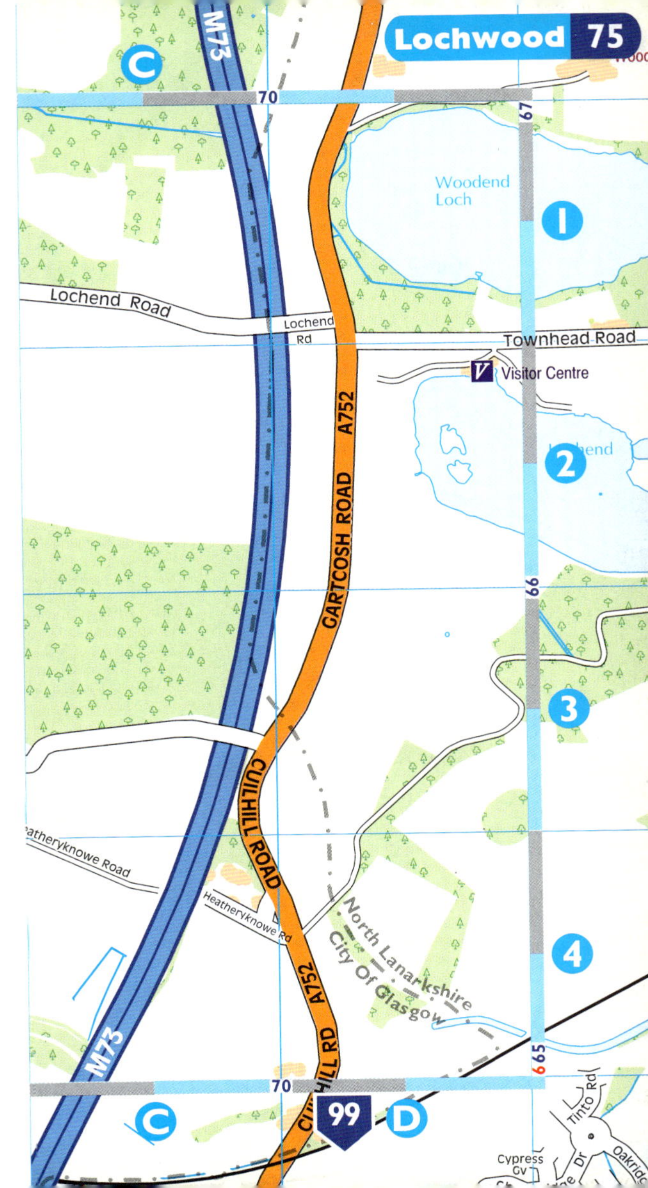
C
M73
70
67
Woodend Loch
1
Lochend Road
Lochend Rd
Townhead Road
Visitor Centre
A752
GARTCOSH ROAD
2
66
3
CUILHILL ROAD
Heatheryknowe Road
Heatheryknowe Rd
North Lanarkshire
City Of Glasgow
A752
4
M73
65
HILL RD
70
99
C
D
Tinto Rd
Cypress Gv

52
A726
GREENOCK ROAD A726
CALEDONIA ST
Paisley St James Station
Clark Street
Murray Street
Macdowall Street
Wellington St
Council Building
UNDERWOOD ROAD B7050
St James St Health C
Brown Street
Blenheim Ct
Coats Observatory
Paisley Crematorium
Cemetery
Ramoy Business Cen
Paisley Museum & Art Galleries
University of Paisley
Glenvale FC
Argyle Street
GEORGE ST
George Street
CANAL STREET
MAXWELLTON ST
B7050
St Fergus Primary Sch
West Primary Sch
St Marys Prim Sch
Castlehead High School
Castlehead
Fergusile CC
Royal Alexandra Hospital
A&E
Riccartsbar Av
Craw Road
Corsebar Way
Low Road
High Rd
Main Road
Camphill
Newton St
Broomlands St
Wellmeadow St
Well St
King St
Douglas St
William St
McKenzie Street
Craigielea Drive
Logan Drive
Greenhill Road
Drums Av
Tannahill Terrace
Park Avenue
Middleton Crs
Blackstoun Oval
Spoolers Rd
The Moorings
Tenters Wy
Weavers Av
Green Road
Kilpatrick
Stranka Av
Glencorse Rd
Mackean St
McCown St
Springbank Road
Russell St
Walker St
Castle St
Lady La
Oakshaw St W
West Brae
Underwood La
Arthur St
Sandholes St
Tower Ter
Sir Michael Pl
Kerr St

54
78
C
D
1
2
3
4
48
49
65
64
63
Abercorn Industrial Estate
Abercorn Industrial Est
Reid Kerr College
Service Centre
St Mirren FC (St Mirren Park)
St Catherine's Prim Sch
X S Superbowl
RENFREW ROAD
A741
A726
NIDDRY ST
ST JAMES' ST
OLD SNEDDON ST
WEIR ST
INCLE ST
GLASGOW
Gilmour Street Stn
University
Paisley Grammar Sch
Police Stn
Cncl Bldg
Town Hall
Paisley Abbey
Renfrew - Paisley Lagoon Ice Rink
MILL ST
A761
GORDON ST
CAUSEYSIDE ST
B774
Abbey Mill Business Cen
PAISLEY
Paisley Canal Station
LONEND
BARRHEAD
Surgery
Surg
Living Waters Christian
Greenlaw Av
Mansionhouse Rd
Netherhill Road
Gallowhill Road
Wallneuk Road
Blackhall Street
Hunterhill Road
Ardgowan St
Saucel Hl Ter
Stockholm Crs
Espedair St
Stevenson St
Gt Hamilton St
Barterholm Rd
Seedhill Rd
Orchard St
Bridge St
Cotton St
Lawn St
Gauze St
Moss St
New St
Storie St
Weighhouse Cl
Sneddon St
Smithhills St
Castle Gait
Stow Brae
Calside
Patrick St
Mavisbank Ter
Millstream Ct
Benn Av
Cochran St
Bank St
Ladyburn St
Violet St
Lang St

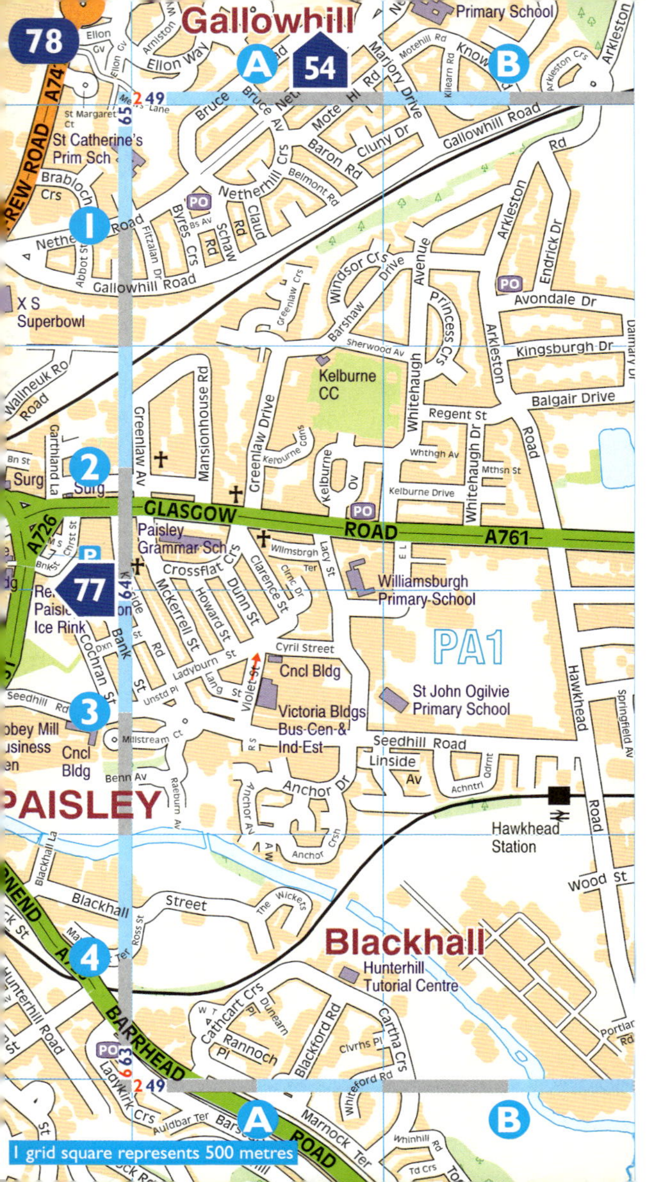
78
54
77
Gallowhill
A
B
1
2
3
4
249
265
264
263
PAISLEY
Blackhall
PA1
Ellon Gv
Ellon Way
Arniston Way
Primary School
Motehill Rd
Kilearn Rd
Arkleston Crs
Arkleston
Marjory Drive
Bruce Rd
Bruce Av
Netherhill Rd
Mote Hl Rd
Cluny Dr
Baron Rd
Belmont Rd
Gallowhill Road
St Margaret Ct
St Catherine's Prim Sch
Brabloch Crs
Netherhill Crs
Netherhill Road
Byres Crs
Bs Av
Schaw Rd
Claud Rd
Fitzalan Dr
Abbot St
X S Superbowl
Greenlaw Crs
Windsor Crs
Barshaw Drive
Avenue
Princess Crs
Arkleston Road
Endrick Dr
Avondale Dr
Kingsburgh Dr
Balgair Drive
Dalmary Dr
Sherwood Av
Kelburne CC
Whitehaugh Av
Regent St
Whthgh Av
Whitehaugh Dr
Mthsn St
Kelburne Drive
Kelburne Gdns
Kelburne Ov
Greenlaw Drive
Greenlaw Av
Mansionhouse Rd
Wallneuk Road
Carthland La
Bn St
Surg
GLASGOW ROAD
A761
A726
Paisley Grammar Sch
Crossflat Crs
Wllmsbrgh Ter
Lacy St
Clarence St
Clinic Dr
Williamsburgh Primary School
McKerrell St
Howard St
Dunn St
Reid Paisley Ice Rink
Cochran St
Bank St
Ladyburn St
Lang St
Violet St
Cyril Street
Cncl Bldg
Victoria Bldgs Bus Cen & Ind Est
St John Ogilvie Primary School
Hawkhead Road
Springfield Av
Seedhill Rd
Seedhill Road
Linside Av
Achntrl
Abbey Mill Business Cen
Cncl Bldg
Millstream Ct
Benn Av
Raeburn Av
Anchor Dr
Anchor Av
Anchor Crsh
Hawkhead Station
Wood St
Blackhall La
Blackhall Street
The Wickets
Ross St
Hunterhill Tutorial Centre
Hunterhill Road
BARRHEAD ROAD
Cathcart Crs
Dunearn Pl
Rannoch Pl
Blackford Rd
Clvrhs Pl
Cartha Crs
Whiteford Rd
Portland Rd
Ladykirk Crs
Auldbar Ter
Marnock Ter
Whinhill Rd
Td Crs
1 grid square represents 500 metres

56
80
Oldhall
A761 GLASGOW ROAD
GLASGOW ROAD
A761
Kinpurnie Road
Balfron Road
Dunchurch Road
Roffey Park Road
Barshaw Pl
Tylney Rd
Oldhall Road
Blairmore Av
Penilee Road
Penilee Terrace
Atholl Crescent
School Road
Lanfine Road
Gartmore Road
Alton Road
Newtyle Road
Rosshall Av
Golf Drive
Marchbank Gdns
Drummond Dr
Strathmore Avenue
Ralston Golf Club
Woodend Dr
Rotherwick Drive
Bathgo Avenue
PO
Golf Course
Scott's Road
Hawkhead Cemetery
Rosshall
The Mary Russell Special School
Cart Water
Lovat Place
50
51
50
51
665
664
663

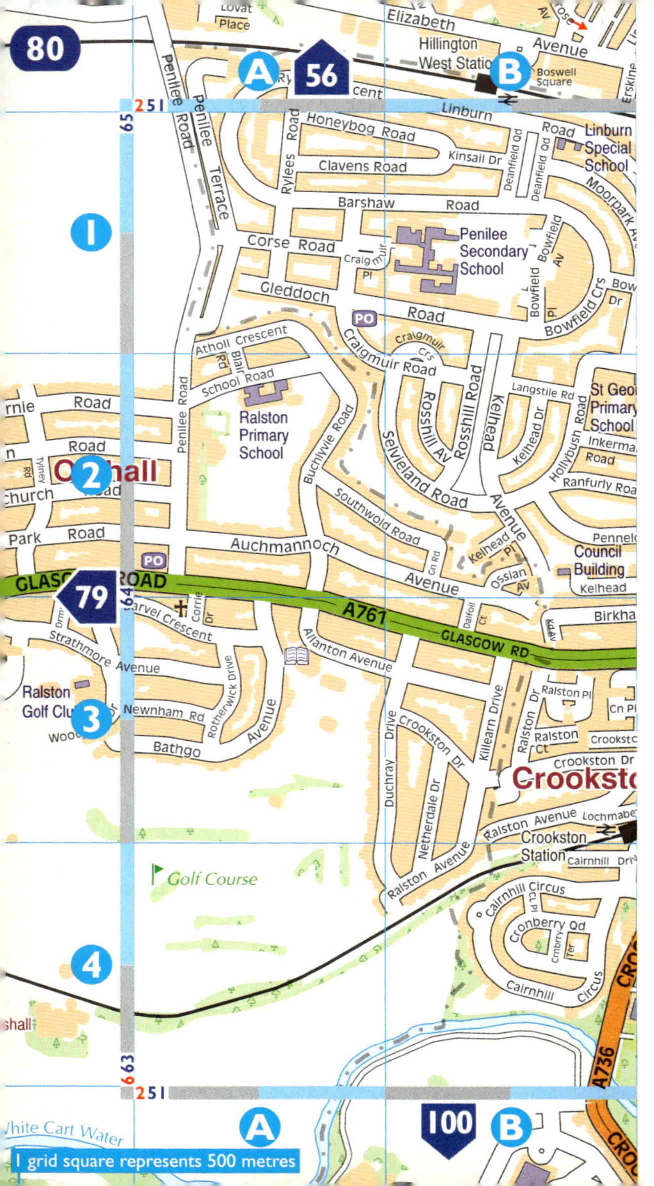
80
56
79
100
A
B
1
2
3
4
251
65
64
663
Lovat Place
Elizabeth Avenue
Hillington West Station
Boswell Square
Erskine
Penilee Road
Penilee Terrace
Linburn Road
Honeybog Road
Rylees Road
Clavens Road
Kinsail Dr
Deanfield Qd
Linburn Special School
Moorpark Av
Barshaw Road
Corse Road
Craigmuir Pl
Penilee Secondary School
Bowfield Av
Bowfield Pl
Bowfield Crs
Bowfield Dr
Gleddoch Road
PO
Craigmuir Crs
Craigmuir Road
Atholl Crescent
Blair Rd
School Road
Ralston Primary School
Langstile Rd
St George's Primary School
Rosshill Av
Rosshill Road
Kelhead Avenue
Kelhead Dr
Hollybush Road
Inkerman Road
Ranfurly Road
Buchlyvie Road
Selvieland Road
Southwold Road
Road
Tylney Rd
Cardonald
Church Road
Park Road
Auchmannoch Avenue
Gn Rd
Kelhead Pl
Ossian Av
Council Building
Kelhead
GLASGOW ROAD
A761
GLASGOW RD
Corrie Dr
Dalfoil Ct
Birkhall
Strathmore Avenue
Allanton Avenue
Ralston Golf Club
Newnham Rd
Rotherwick Drive
Avenue
Bathgo
Duchray Drive
Crookston Dr
Netherdale Dr
Killearn Drive
Ralston Dr
Ralston Pl
Ralston Ct
Crookston Dr
Crookston
Ralston Avenue
Crookston Station
Cairnhill Drive
Ralston Avenue
Golf Course
Cairnhill Circus
Cronberry Qd
Cairnhill Circus
A736
White Cart Water
1 grid square represents 500 metres

Crookston 81
Fifty Pitches Place
Junction 25
Hillington
Hillington Primary School
Hillington East Station
Cardonald
Cardonald Primary Sch
Sandwood Primary Sch
St George's School
Rosshall Academy
Bonnyholm Primary School
Ross Hall Hospital
Howford Special School
McGill Primary School
Mosspark Station
PAISLEY ROAD WEST A761
SANDWOOD RD A736
Carnegie Road
Chirnside Road
Gladsmuir Road
Bearford Drive
Dryburn Avenue
Wedderlea
Swinton Drive
Ladykirk Drive
Queensland
Kingsland
Redpath
Hatton Gardens
Crookston Avenue
Cardonald Drive
Berwick Drive
Moulin Circus
Arbroath Avenue
Dundee Dr
White Cart Water
Linthaugh Road
Dormanside Road
Bargaran Road
Barochan Road
58
82
101

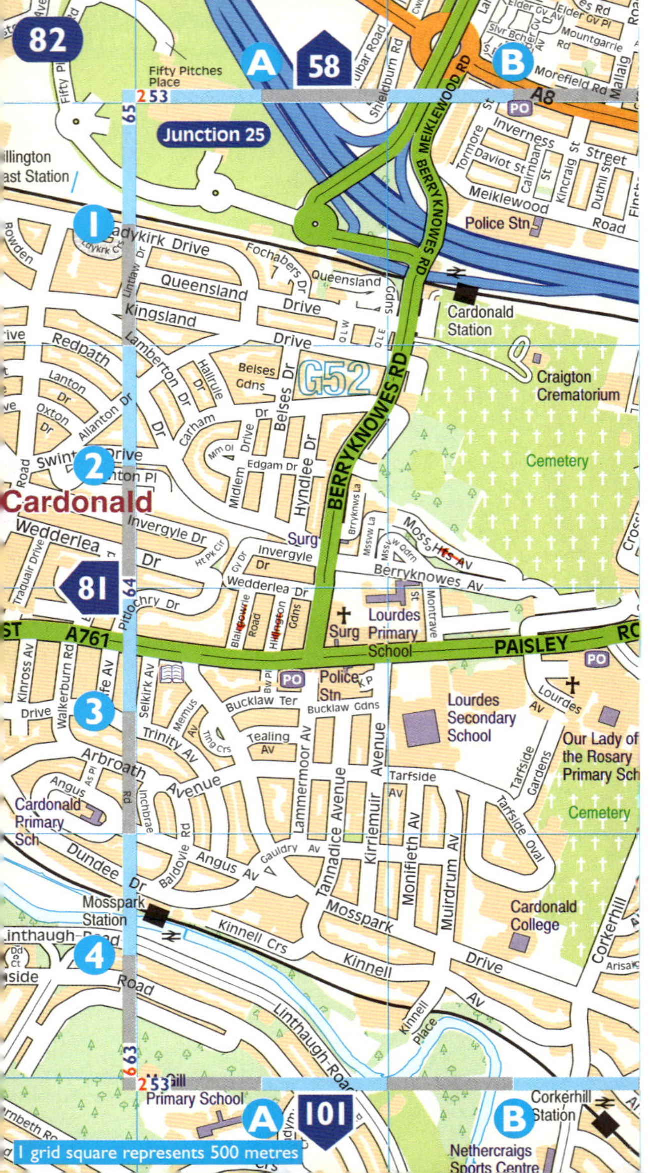
82
58
81
101
Junction 25
Cardonald
Fifty Pitches Place
Cardonald Station
Craigton Crematorium
Cemetery
Police Stn
Lourdes Primary School
Lourdes Secondary School
Our Lady of the Rosary Primary Sch
Cardonald Primary Sch
Cardonald College
Mosspark Station
Corkerhill Station
Nethercraigs Sports Centre
McGill Primary School
G52
A8
A761
PAISLEY RD
BERRYKNOWES RD
MEIKLEWOOD RD
Queensland Drive
Kingsland Drive
Ladykirk Drive
Wedderlea Dr
Invergyle Dr
Berryknowes Av
Mosspark Drive
Kinnell Crs
Linthaugh Road
Dundee Dr
Arbroath Avenue
Angus Av
Tarfside Av
Tarfside Oval
Tarfside Gardens
Lammermoor Av
Tannadice Avenue
Kirriemuir Avenue
Monifieth Av
Muirdrum Av
Corkerhill Rd
Morefield Rd
Inverness Street
Meiklewood Road
Daviot St
Lamberton Dr
Redpath Dr
Hyndlee Dr
Belses Dr
Edgam Dr
Bucklaw Ter
Bucklaw Gdns
Trinity Av
Selkirk Av
Walkerburn Rd
Kinross Av
Traquair Drive
Pitlochry Dr
1 grid square represents 500 metres

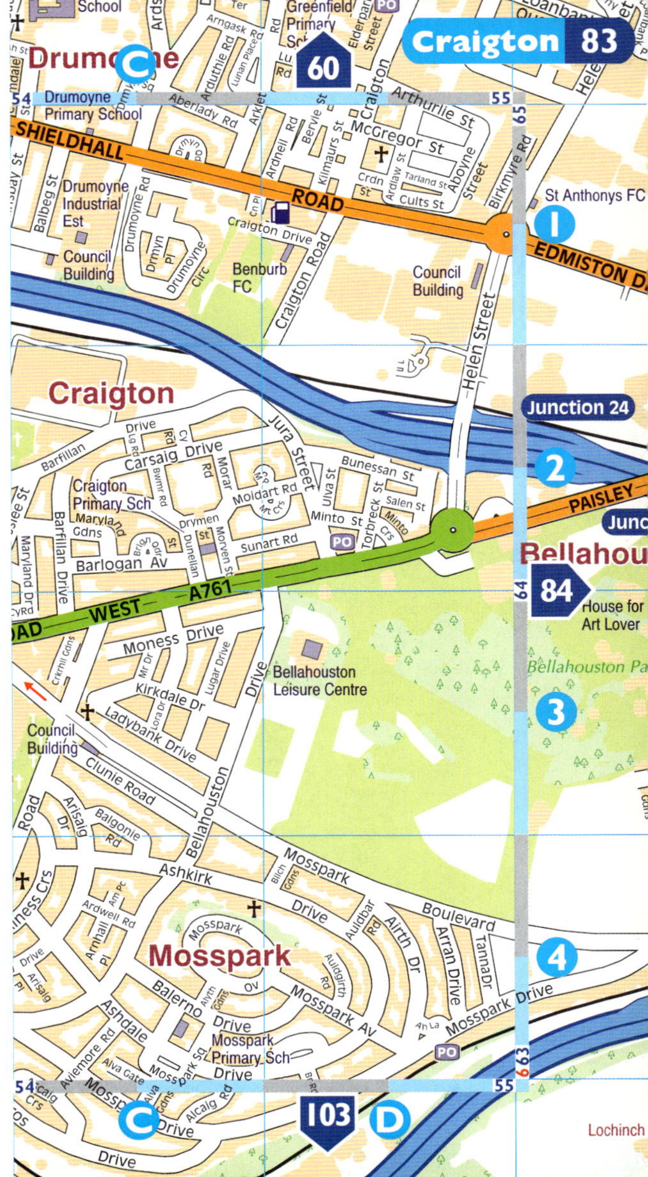
Drumoyne
Craigton
Mosspark
Bellahouston Park
60
84
103
Drumoyne Primary School
Drumoyne Industrial Est
Council Building
Benburb FC
St Anthonys FC
Craigton Primary Sch
Bellahouston Leisure Centre
House for Art Lover
Mosspark Primary Sch
Greenfield Primary School
Junction 24
SHIELDHALL ROAD
EDMISTON D
PAISLEY
WEST A761
Craigton Road
Helen Street
Arthurlie St
McGregor St
Aboyne Street
Birkmyre Rd
Carsaig Drive
Jura Street
Bunessan St
Moidart Rd
Minto St
Sunart Rd
Barlogan Av
Barfillan Drive
Moness Drive
Kirkdale Dr
Ladybank Drive
Clunie Road
Bellahouston Drive
Mosspark Boulevard
Mosspark Drive
Mosspark Av
Ashkirk
Balerno Drive
Ashdale
Aviemore Rd
Arran Drive
Tanna Dr
Airth Dr
Lochinch

84
60
83
103
A
B
1
2
3
4
Loanbank Quadrant
Helen Street
Dava St
Broomloan
Summertown
St Saviour's Primary School
Merryland St
Copeland Primary
Arthurlie St
Birkmyre Rd
Woodville Park Ind Est
Orton Pl
Brighton St
Brighton Pl
Copland Pl
Woodville Pk
Kintra St
Iona St
Clynder Street
St Anthonys FC
Woodville Park Industrial Est
Ibrox Stn
Rangers FC (Ibrox Stadium)
Ibrox Industrial
Mafeking St
Fairley St
Aboyne Street
Tarland St
Cults St
Ardlaw St
Council Building
EDMISTON DR
EDMISTON DRIVE A8
Ibrox
Ibrox Ter
Ibroxholm Oval
Copland Rd
Cairnlea Dr
BROOMLOAN RD
Ibrox Primary Sch
Surg
Junction 24
PO
PAISLEY ROAD WEST A761
B768
Clifford Gdns
Clifford Street
Beech Av
Junction 23
Bellahouston
Salen St
Urrdale Road
Farm Rd
Rowan Road
Rowan Gdns
Larch Rd
Maple Rd
House for an Art Lover
Bellahouston Park
DUMBRECK ROAD
Dalkeith Av
Dumbre
Melfort Av
Erskine Av
Nithsdale Rd
Avenue
Dargarvel Avenue
Torridon Av
Fleurs Road
Fleurs
Dumbreck Av
Dumbreck Ct
Third Gdns
Fourth Gdns
Scnd Gdns
First Gdns
Dmbrck
Boulevard
Airth Dr
Arran Drive
Mosspark Drive
M77
Junction 1
Hamilto
Springke
Haggs Castle Golf Club
Springkell Drive
Lochi
255
65
64
63

Prince's Dock
62
Glasgow Science Centre and IMAX Theatre
Bells Bridge
Council Building
Govan Road
Festival Business Cen
Strathclyde Business Cen
Lorne Street Primary School
Bellahouston Prim Sch
Cessnock Stn
PAISLEY ROAD WEST
A8
Midlock Medical Centre
IQRA Academy
Kinning Park Station
Strathclyde Business Cen
Maclellan Street
Junction 22
Bellahouston Academy
Durham Street
M8 Trading Estate
86
St Alberts Primary School
Maxwell Drive
Sherbrooke Drive
Nithsdale Road
Albert Drive
St Andrew's Dr
Craigholme School
Pollokshields
Surgery
Council Building
Dalziel Drive
Sherbrooke Av
Sutherland Avenue
Matilda Road
Aytoun Road
Newark
Glencairn
105
Maxwell Park Station
Fotheringay
Terregles

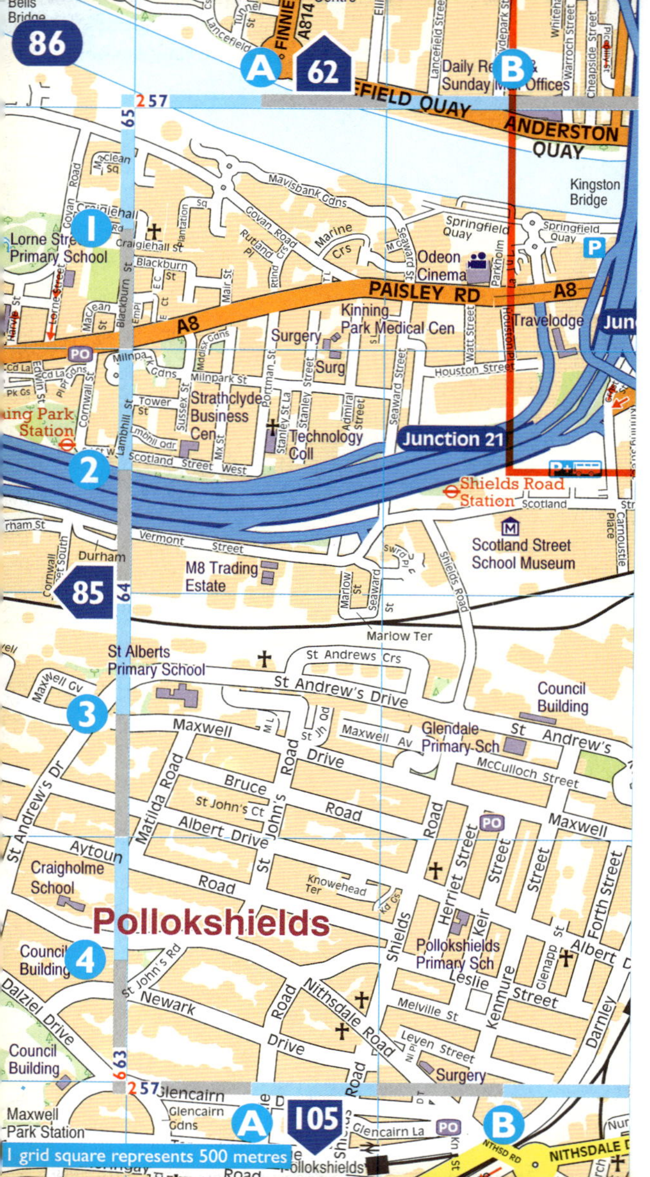
86
62
A
B
Daily Record & Sunday Mail Offices
LANCEFIELD QUAY
ANDERSTON QUAY
Kingston Bridge
Springfield Quay
Mavisbank Gdns
Govan Road
Marine Crs
Seaward St
Odeon Cinema
PAISLEY RD
A8
Kinning Park Medical Cen
Travelodge
Surgery
Surg
Houston Street
Lorne Street Primary School
Craigiehall St
Blackburn St
Milnpark St
Strathclyde Business Cen
Technology Coll
Junction 21
Kinning Park Station
Scotland Street West
Shields Road Station
Scotland Street School Museum
Vermont Street
Durham St
M8 Trading Estate
85
Marlow Ter
St Andrews Crs
St Alberts Primary School
St Andrew's Drive
Council Building
Maxwell Drive
Glendale Primary Sch
McCulloch Street
Bruce Road
St John's Ct
Albert Drive
Matilda Road
St John's Road
Aytoun Road
Craigholme School
Knowehead Ter
Pollokshields
Herriet Street
Keir Street
Pollokshields Primary Sch
Leslie Street
Kenmure Street
Glenapp St
Albert Dr
Forth Street
Darnley
Council Building
Dalziel Drive
Newark Drive
Nithsdale Road
Melville St
Leven Street
Surgery
Shields Road
Glencairn Dr
Glencairn Gdns
Glencairn La
Maxwell Park Station
105
NITHSDALE DR
1 grid square represents 500 metres
Pollokshields

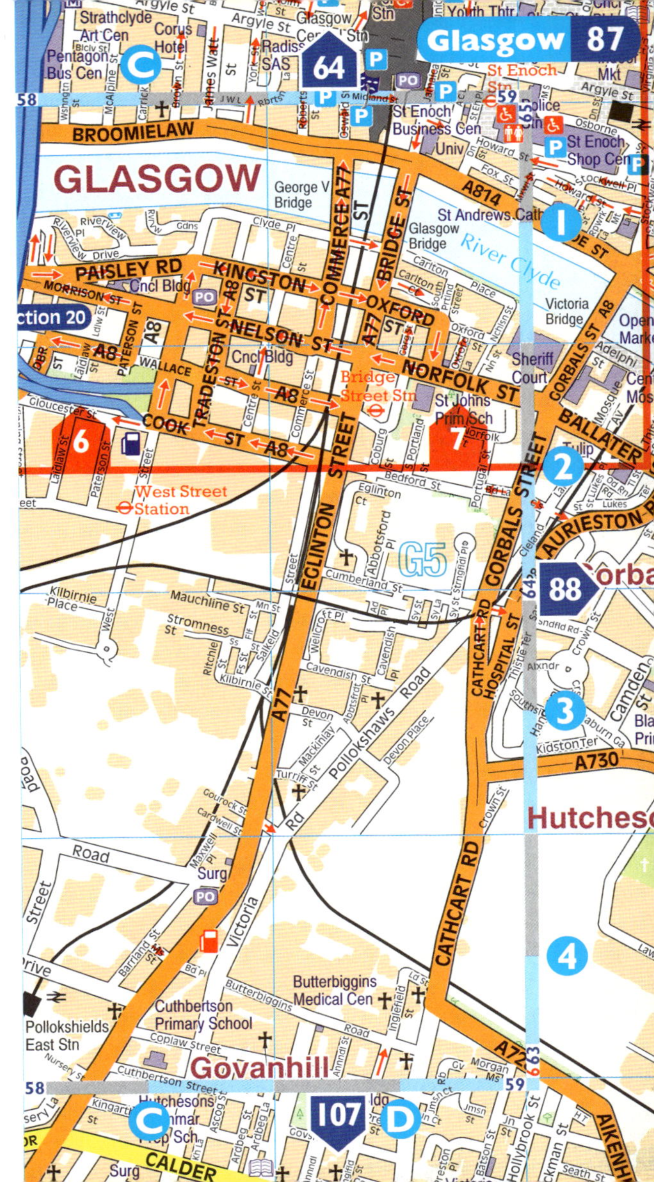
Strathclyde Art Cen
Corus Hotel
Pentagon Bus Cen
Argyle St
Glasgow Cen Stn
Radisson SAS
64
St Enoch
St Enoch Business Cen
Univ
St Enoch Shop Cen
Police
Howard St
Fox St
Osborne
Argyle St
Mkt
58
59
BROOMIELAW
GLASGOW
George V Bridge
Glasgow Bridge
St Andrews Cath
River Clyde
Victoria Bridge
Riverview Pl
Riverview Drive
Clyde Pl
PAISLEY RD
MORRISON ST
Cncl Bldg
KINGSTON ST
COMMERCE ST
BRIDGE ST
OXFORD ST
NELSON ST
WALLACE
Cncl Bldg
TRADESTON ST
PATERSON ST
NORFOLK ST
Bridge Street Stn
St Johns Prim Sch
Sheriff Court
CORBALS ST
BALLATER ST
Gloucester St
COOK ST
A8
A77
A814
6
7
2
3
4
88
C
D
West Street Station
Eglinton Ct
Bedford St
Abbotsford Pl
G5
Cumberland St
CORBALS ST
LAURIESTON
Kilbirnie Place
Mauchline St
Stromness St
ECLINTON STREET
Cavendish St
Devon St
Pollokshaws Road
Devon Place
CATHCART RD
HOSPITAL ST
Kidston Ter
A730
Hutcheso
Gourock St
Cardwell St
Victoria Rd
Road
Street
Surg
Barrland St
Butterbiggins Medical Cen
Butterbiggins Road
Cuthbertson Primary School
Coplaw Street
Pollokshields East Stn
Govanhill
Cuthbertson Street
Hutchesons Gmmar Sch
107
CALDER
Hollybrook St
Batson St
Morgan Ms
AIKENHEAD

88
64
87
107
A
B
1
2
3
4
G5
Youth Thtr
Shop Ctr
The Lighthouse
Cncl Bldg
Indoor Mkt
St Enoch Stn
St Enoch Business Cen
Univ
Police Stn
St Enoch Shop Cen
Argyle St Stn
Trongate
City Halls
Tolbooth Steeple
Tron Thtr
Glasgow Cross
Express by Holiday Inn
Gallowgate Mkt
GALLOWGATE
LONDON ROAD
Glasgow Bridge
River Clyde
CLYDE ST
Victoria Bridge
BRIDGEGATE
SALTMARKET
High Court & Court of Justiciary
Council Building
Glasgow Green
Open Air Market Stall
Albert Bridge
Central Mosque
Glasgow College of Nautical Studies
Gorbals Leisure Centre
Sheriff Court
NORFOLK ST
St Johns Prim Sch
GORBALS ST A8
CROWN ST
BALLATER ST
LAURIESTON RD
Florence Street Clinic
Council Building
Gorbals
Cem
Gorbals Health Cen
A74 BALLATER ST
St Francis Primary Sch
Blackfriars Primary School
A730
Hutchesontown
CALEDONIA ROAD
Cemetery
CATHCART RD
Oatlands
Richmond Park Sch
1 grid square represents 500 metres

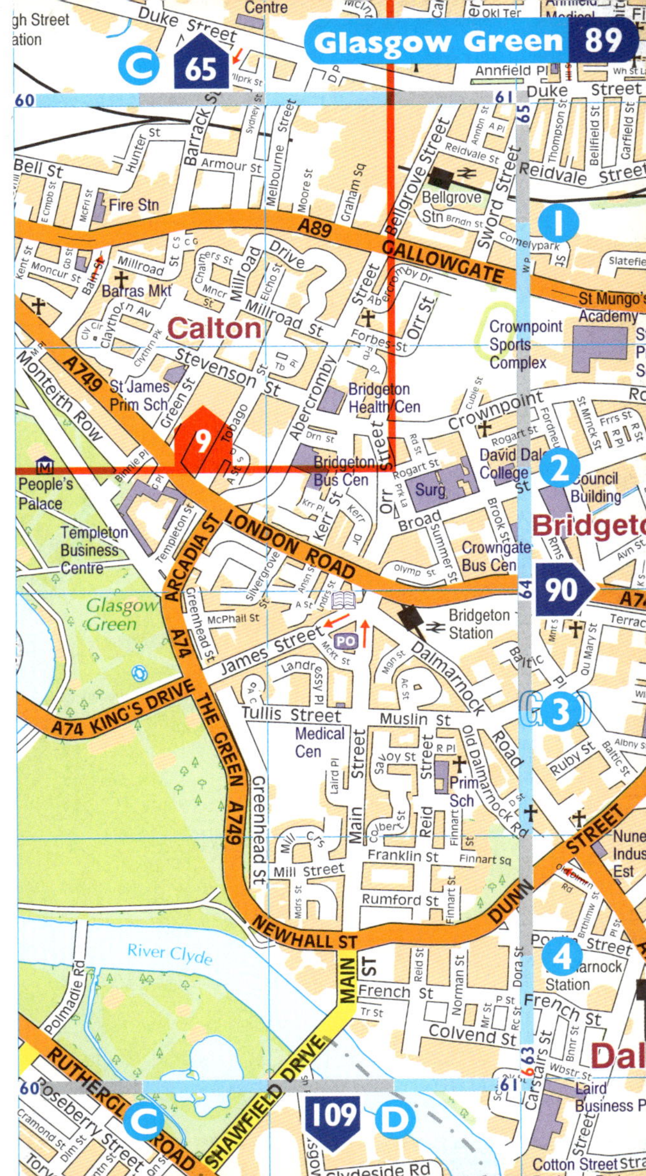
Calton
Bridgeton
Glasgow Green
River Clyde
A89 GALLOWGATE
A749 LONDON ROAD
ARCADIA ST
A74 KING'S DRIVE
THE GREEN A749
NEWHALL ST
MAIN ST
SHAWFIELD DRIVE
RUTHERGLEN ROAD
DUNN STREET
Duke Street
Reidvale Street
Bellgrove Street
Sword Street
Barrack St
Armour St
Bell St
Hunter St
Sydney St
Melbourne Street
Moore St
Graham Sq
Bellgrove Stn
Fire Stn
Barras Mkt
Millroad Drive
Millroad St
Abercromby Street
Forbes St
Orr St
Stevenson St
Monteith Row
St James Prim Sch
Green St
Tobago St
Bridgeton Health Cen
Bridgeton Bus Cen
Crownpoint Sports Complex
Crownpoint Rd
St Mungo's Academy
David Dale College
Council Building
Crowngate Bus Cen
People's Palace
Templeton Business Centre
Templeton St
McPhail St
James Street
Bridgeton Station
Dalmarnock Road
Tullis Street
Medical Cen
Muslin St
Main Street
Reid Street
Prim Sch
Franklin St
Finnart Sq
Mill Street
Rumford St
Greenhead St
French St
Colvend St
Norman St
Dora St
Polmadie Rd
Roseberry Street
Clydeside Rd
Cotton Street
Laird Business P
Carstairs St
Ruby St
Albny St
Baltic St
Nuneaton Indus Est
Dalmarnock Station
Slatefield
Comelypark
Broad St
Brook St
Olymp St
Summer St
Kerr St
Silvergrove St
Landressy Pl
Savoy St
Old Dalmarnock Rd
65
90
109
9

90
66
89
109
A
B
1
2
3
4
Medical Cen
Finlay Drive
St Denis Prim Sch
Paton St
Street Station
Aitken Street
Annfield Pl
Duke Street
Bellgrove Street
Reidvale St
Reidvale Street
Thompson St
Bellfield St
Garfield St
Bathgate St
Bluevale St
Glendale St
Glenpark Industrial Est
Glenpark Road
Bellgrove Stn
Comelypark St
Slatefield St
GALLOWGATE
MILLERSTON ST
G31
BIGGAR ST
Orr St
St Mungo's Academy
Crownpoint Sports Complex
St Annes Primary Sch
Crownpoint Road
Crownpoint Rd
Mountainblue St
Yate Street
Stamford St
Holywell St
Rogart St
Fordneuk St
David Dale College
Council Building
Surg
Broad St
Brook St
FIELDEN STREET
Law Street
Celtic FC
Dalserf St
Bridgeton
Crowngate
Frazer St
Cncl Bldg
Barrowfield Primary Sch
Barrowfield St
A74
LONDON ROAD
Bernard Terrace
Bridgeton Station
Dalmarnock Road
Qu Mary St
Bernard Street
Boden St
London Road Primary School
G40
Ruby St
Albany St
Baltic St
Dalmarnock Primary School
Muslin St
Old Dalmarnock Rd
Gailes St
Gretna Street
Bogside St
Road
Reid St
Finnart St
Finnart Sq
Nuneaton Industrial Est
Nuneaton St
Baltic Street
Mordaunt St
Kinnear Road
Irvine St
Patna St
Sorn St
Troon St
Lily Street
Springfield
DUNN STREET
Poplin Street
Baltic La
Dalmarnock Station
Council Building
Millerfield Road
Millerfield Pl
French St
Colvend St
A749
PO
Surg
Garvald St
Summerfield St
Dalmarnock
Laird Business
Allan Street
DALMARNOCK
Dunclutha Street
1 grid square represents 500 metres

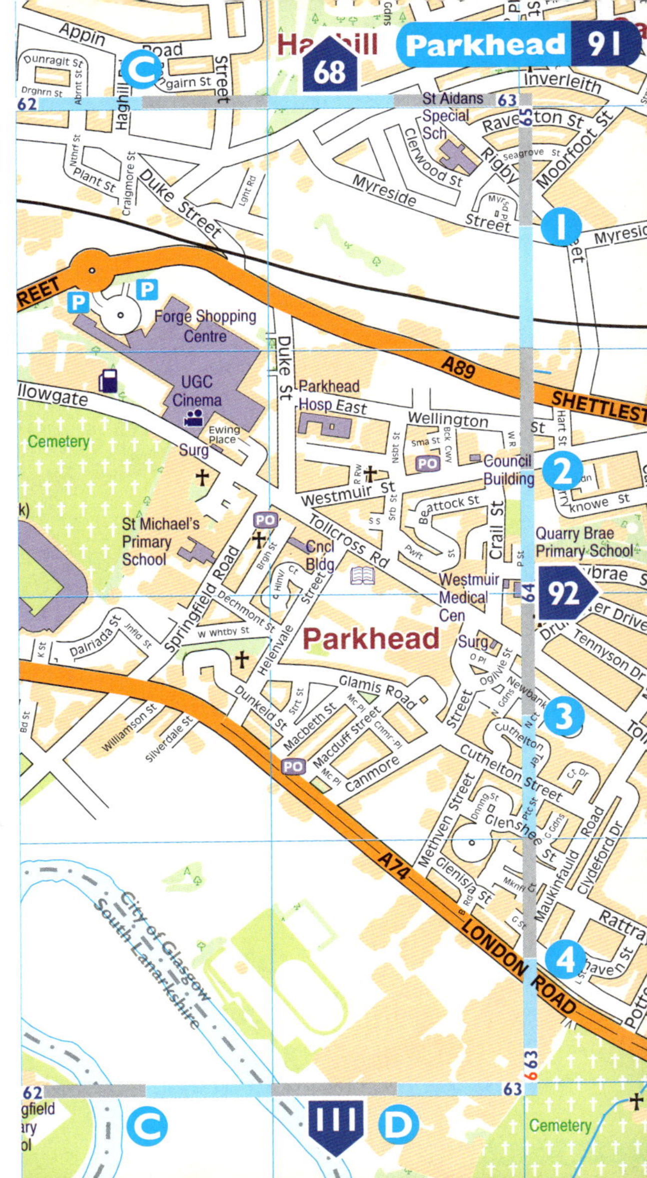
Appin
Road
Dunragit St
Drgnrn St
Haghill Rd
Street
Plant St
Craigmore St
Duke Street
Lght Rd
St Aidans Special Sch
Inverleith
Raveston St
Moorfoot St
Seagrove St
Rigby
Clerwood St
Myreside
Street
Myreside
Forge Shopping Centre
UGC Cinema
llowgate
A89
SHETTLESTON
Duke St
Parkhead Hosp East
Wellington
St
Hart St
Cemetery
Ewing Place
Surg
Council Building
Westmuir St
Beattock St
Crail St
knowe St
Quarry Brae Primary School
St Michael's Primary School
Tollcross Rd
Cncl Bldg
Westmuir Medical Cen
Springfield Road
Dechmont St
Dalriada St
Jnfld St
W Whtby St
Helenvale
Street
Parkhead
Surg
Ogilvie St
Newbank
Tennyson Dr
Glamis Road
Dunkeld St
Macbeth St
Macduff Street
Canmore
Williamson St
Silverdale St
Cuthelton Street
Cuthelton Ter
Methven Street
Glenshee St
Maukinfauld Road
Clydeford Dr
Glenisla St
A74
LONDON ROAD
Rattray
City of Glasgow
South Lanarkshire
Cemetery
Potter

68
92
111

92
Carntyne
68
91
111
A
B
1
2
3
4
Carntyne Road
Inverleith
St Aidans Special Sch
Clerwood St
Moorfoot St
Myreside Street
Banknock St
Camelon St
Bainsford St
Brckv St
Carntynehall Road
Merchiston
Whitburn Street
Ruchazie
Newington St
Cardowan
Westerburn St
Carntyne Stn
Sheddens Pl
Camburn St
A89
SHETTLESTON ROAD
Wellington St
Hart St
Fernan St
Denbeck Street
Darleith St
Council Building
Caroline St
Dalton St
St Mark St
Kilmany Dr
Cree Gardens
Elvan St
Edrom Street
Edrom Ct
Quarry Brae Primary School
Quarrybrae St
St Mark's Primary School
Denbrae St
Hillview St
Anstruther St
Ern St
Ardlui St
Beattock St
Crail St
Drumover Drive
Tennyson Dr
Muiryfauld Drive
Tollcross Park
Shettleston Day Hospital
Ogilvie St
Newbank Rd
Cuthelton Street
Cuthelton Ter
Tollcross Road
Wellshot Prim Sch
Wellshot Road
National Swimming Centre at Tollcross Leisure Centre
Trainard
Altyre
Methven Street
Glenshee St
Glenisla St
Maukinfauld Road
Clydeford Dr
Tollcross Park Gardens
Tollcross Road
Rattray St
Finhaven St
Potter St
Downfield Street
Quendale Dr
Dunira St
Easterhill Street
Cemetery
Braidfauld
Prosen St
London Rd
LONDON ROAD
Braidfauld Gdns
Cemetery

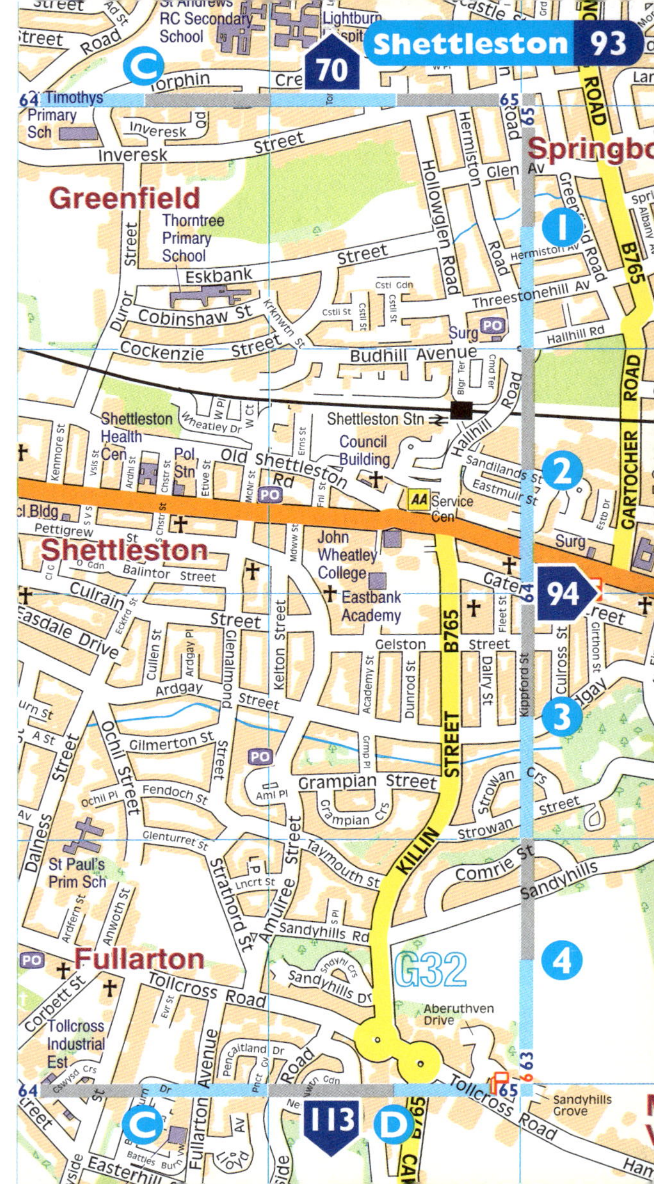
Greenfield
Shettleston
Fullarton
Springboig
St Andrews RC Secondary School
Lightburn Hospital
St Timothys Primary Sch
Thorntree Primary School
Shettleston Health Cen
Pol Stn
Shettleston Stn
Council Building
AA Service Cen
John Wheatley College
Eastbank Academy
St Paul's Prim Sch
Tollcross Industrial Est
Inveresk Street
Eskbank Street
Cobinshaw St
Cockenzie Street
Budhill Avenue
Old Shettleston Rd
Hallhill Road
Sandilands St
Eastmuir St
Hollowglen Road
Hermiston Road
Threestonehill Av
Hallhill Rd
Hermiston Av
Greenfield Road
Glen Av
Gartocher Road
B765
Pettigrew St
Balintor Street
Culrain Street
Easdale Drive
Ardgay Street
Glenalmond Street
Kelton Street
Gelston Street
Academy St
Dunrod St
Dairy St
Kipford St
Culross St
Fleet St
Gateside Street
Girthon St
Killin Street
Ochil Street
Gilmerton St
Fendoch St
Grampian Street
Grampian Crs
Strowan Street
Strowan Crs
Comrie St
Sandyhills Rd
Sandyhills Dr
Sandyhills Grove
Taymouth St
Glenturret St
Strathord St
Amulree Street
Dalness Street
Ardfern St
Anworth St
Tollcross Road
Corbett St
Fullarton Avenue
Aberuthven Drive
Duror Street
Kenmore St
Cullen St
Ardgay Pl
Ochil Pl
Aml Pl
Lncrt St
Gmrp Pl
Surg
PO
G32
70
94
113
C
D
1
2
3
4
64
65
663

94
70
93
113
A
B
1
2
3
4
265
65
64
63
Castle Street
Moredun
Barlanark Crescent
St Johns Approved School
Calvay Crs
Springboig
Hermiston
Glen Av
Hollowglen Road
Lrchgrv Av
Croftspar Avenue
Springboig Av
Albany Av
Albany Qd
Croftspar Dr
Croftspar Pl
Croftspar Grove
Eastmuir Special School
Kerrera Rd
Hermiston Av
Greenfield Road
B765
Mansionhouse Dr
Hallhill Road
Threestonehill Av
Hallhill Rd
Surg
PO
Glenduffhill Cemetery
GARTOCHER ROAD
Gartocher Ter
Mayberry Gardens
Gartocher Drive
Mayberry Crs
Carroglen Gdns
AA Service Cen
Eastbank Primary Sch
Crownhall Pl
Linacre Dr
Farmington Avenue
Old Manse Road
A89
BAILLIESTON ROAD
Fingask St
Ddsd Pl
Dds Gdn
Glen Ogle St
Sandyhills Rd
Manse Rd
Blackcroft Rd
Kippford St
Culross St
Girthon St
Ardgay
Dunrod St
KILLIN STREET
Balbeggie Street
Loch Achray St
Lochay St
Loch Laidon St
B Gdn
Strowan Crs
Strowan Street
Glen Luce Dr
Criffell
Wester Road
Comrie St
Sandyhills Road
New Luce Dr
Sandgate Av
Tiverton Av
Kirkinner
Bideford Crs
Torrington Crs
G32
Aberuthven Drive
Tollcross Road
Sandyhills Grove
Dornford Av
1 grid square represents 500 metres

Barrachnie 95
72
96
115
Crescent
Ogilvie Primary
Road
Stepford Road
St Judes Primary School
Garvel Rd
Bressay Rd
Blyth Rd
Barlanark Prim Sch
E Hallhill Rd
Springhill
Hallhill
Hallhill Road
Pendeen Rd
Sandaig Prim Sch
Council Building
Burnmouth Road
Carlieston Rd
Barlanark
Pndn Pl
Road
Sandaig Road
Pendeen Crescent
Pendeen Rd
Millbeg Pl
Pendeen
Glenduffhill Rd
Garrowhill Stn
Nurseries Rd
Barrachnie Gv
Bannercross
BARRACHNIE
Road
B7058
Springhill
Drive
Hillsborough Rd
Garrowhill Primary Sch
Council Building
Viewfield Dr
Viewfield Av
Gordon Av
Garrowhill
Stephen Crs
Hilary Dr
Douglas Dr
Maxwell
Coats Crs
Barrachnie
Blist Rd
PO
Weirwo
Glasgow
GLASGOW
ROAD
Aileen Dr
Juniper Ter
Br Pl
Birchwood Av
Ry Gdn
Dn Gdn
Carrick
Ln Gdn
Garforth Rd
Bedale Rd
Bowes Crs
Huntingtower
Bannerm High Sch
Cluny Gardens
Danby Rd
Coniston Crs
Gargrave
David Pl
Jagger Gdns
Mansionhouse Road
Mns Gv
All Gdn
Sherburn Gdns
Haig Drive
Avenue
St Francis of Assisi Prim Sch
Road
Beauly Rd
Tantallon Rd
Airlie Rd
Central Path
Drive
Kenmuir Av
Muirside Av
MOUNT VERNON AVENUE
Burntbroom Dr
Burntbroom Gdns
Greentree Dr
Oakhill Av
Orchard Street
Castle St
Albion St
Muirhead
B7058
Road
Brrwd Ct
HAMILTON
Daldowie Rd
Road

96
Junction 9
A
B
72
Stepford Road
Stpfd Pl
PO
Springhill Parkway
267
65
Springhill Dr S
Springhill Parkway
E Hallhill Rd
Hallhill Rd
Hallhill Rd
S F Pl
S F Wy
Springhill Farm Rd
S F Gv
Springcroft Dr
Springcroft Crescent
Springcroft Avenue
Springcroft Wynd
Sp Wynd
Sp Gv
Mc Pl
McKins Ov
Micklehouse Road
Micklehouse Wynd
McKins
Council Building
Pndn Pl
Road
Garrowhill Stn
Brrchn Crs
Brr Ct
Nurseries Rd
A8
EDINBURGH ROAD
Barrachnie Gv
Barrachnie Av
Bannercross Dr
B Pl
BARRACHNIE ROAD
B7058
Barony Dr
Bry Wd
Brn Wyn
Barony Gdns
B G
Bn Av
Bannercross Drive
T Av
Thrnb Gdns
Bakewell Rd
Bents Road
Ryecroft Dr
Dolan St
Greenshields Rd
St Bridgets Prim Sch
Camp Road
Hathersage Dr
Hathersage Av
Sugworth Av
H G
Garrowhill Primary Sch
Garrowhill
Springhill Drive
Hillsborough Rd
Hilary Dr
Douglas Dr
Council Building
Maxwell Drive
Beech Gdns
Beech Av
Whirlow Gdns
Whirlow Road
Thornbridge Rd
Coats Crs
Fl G
Ot G
Avenue
Buchanan Gv
Bchnn St
Stephen Crs
95
64
Wood Road
Maxwell Av
Glasgow Road
Mxwll St
Lngl St
S St
Cncl Bldgs
A89
GLASGOW ROAD
Rowandale Av
Rosedale Dr
Ladyhill Dr
W G
Willowdale Crs
Mr T
Baillieston Health Centre
Miller St
Nelson Street
Nelson Pl
Garforth Rd
Bedale Rd
Bowes Crs
3
Jagger Gdns
Huntingtower Road
Berriedale Av
Bannerman High School
Cluny Gardens
Road
Muirside Rd
George St
S Sctt St
Baillieston
Muirside St
Cld Pl
Loancroft Pl
David Pl
Haig Drive
C Crs
Wood
Ok Cr
Fr Pl
Ash Road
Drumpellier Road
Drm Pl
Drumpellier Av
St Francis of Assisi Prim Sch
Avenue
C Gdn
Beauly Rd
Bl C
Kl Gdn
Tantallon Rd
Old
Calderwood Dr
Provand Hall Crs
Cld Dr
Muirhead Road
Crw St
Caledonia Prim Sch
Orch St
Wm Gdn
Airlie Rd
Clc
Calderwood Av
Caledonia Road
Baillieston Station
4
Room Dr
Tdr St
Street
Castle St
Albion St
63
Road
Boghall
267
Br Rd
A
115
B
Baillieston
1 grid square represents 500 metres
Broomhouse

Baillieston 97
74
98
117
Swinton
Crosshill
Ellismuir Farm
Easterhouse Station
Swinton Primary Sch
Baillieston FC
COATBRIDGE ROAD
GLASGOW AND EDINBURGH ROAD
MAIN STREET
M8
North Calder Water
Rogerfield Road
Easterhouse Rd
Brodie Gdns
Rhindmuir Drive
Long Rw
Rhindmuir Road
Rhindmuir Av
Mainhill Pl
Mainhill Av
Swinton Crescent
Swinton Road
Swinton Av
Crossview Pl
Faulds
Fauldspark Crs
Glenburn Av
Rhindsdale Crs
Mainhill Dr
Dalreoch Av
Martin Crs
Dyke St
Gillies Lane
Ravenswood Rd
Bredisholm Rd
Bredisholm Ter
Bredisholm Dr
Ellismuir Road
Thornyburn Dr
Church St
Elmslie Ct
Station Road
Station Pk
Bracadale Rd
Brc Dr
B Gdn
B Ct
Mrh Gdn
Calderbank Vw
Loancroft Av
Swnt Rd
PO
C
D
68
69
65
64
663
1
2
3
4
Neth

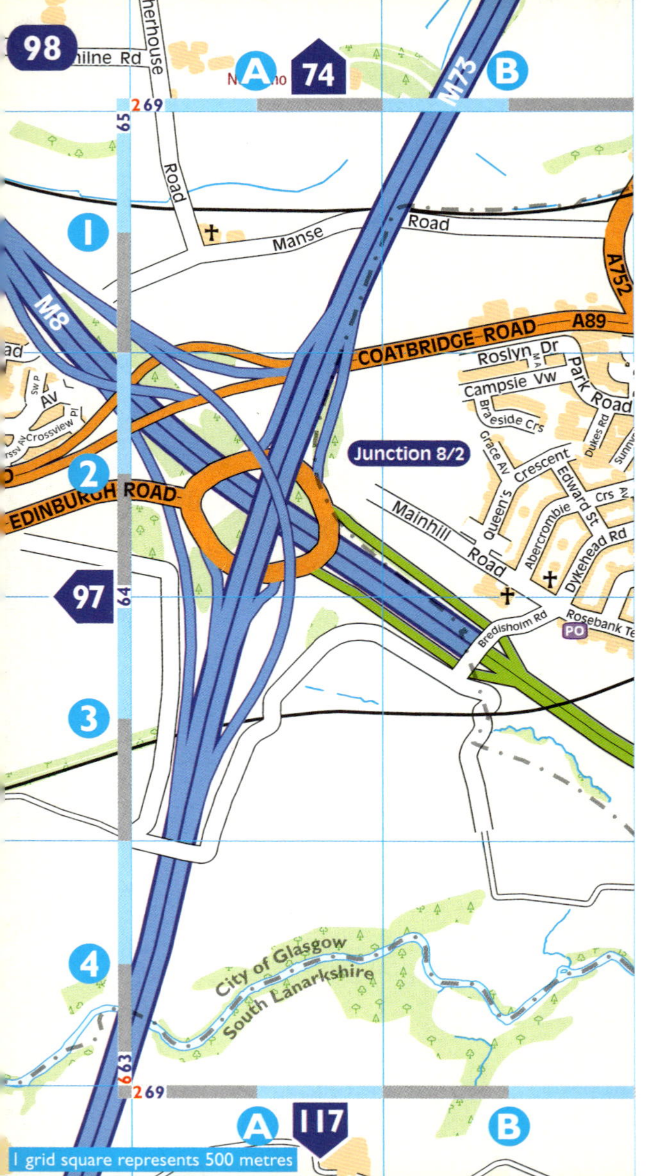

1 grid square represents 500 metres

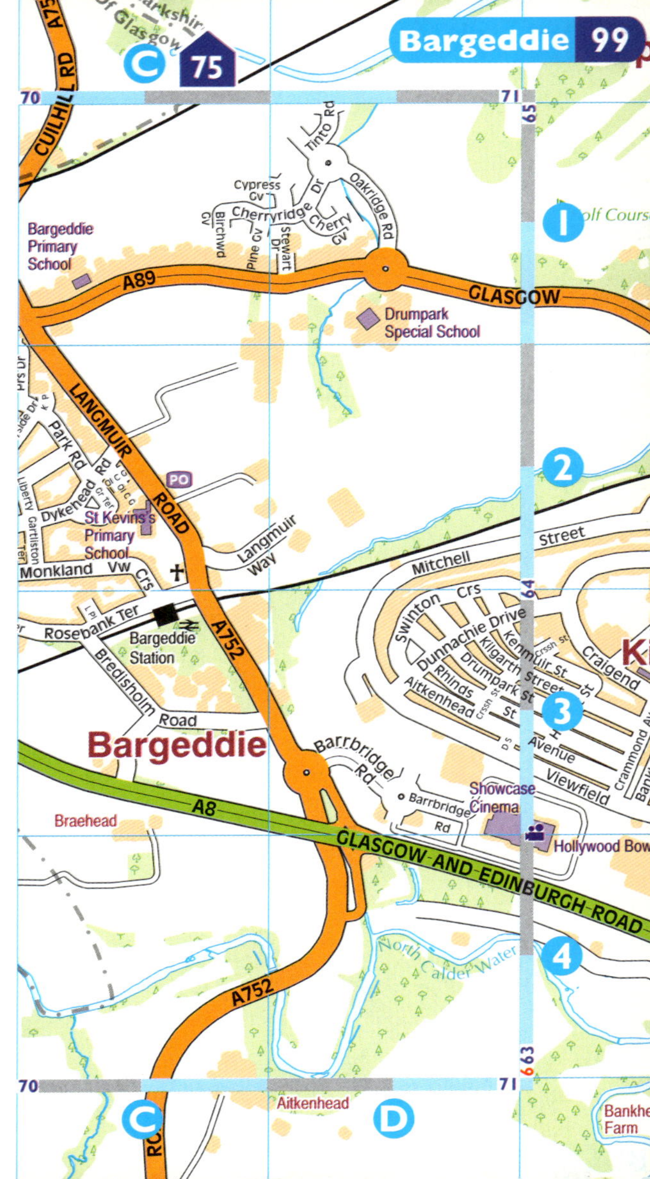

C
75
70
71
A75
CUILHILL RD
Cypress Gv
Cherryridge
Birchwd Gv
Pine Gv
Stewart Dr
Tinto Rd
Cherry Gv
Oakridge Rd
Bargeddie Primary School
A89
GLASGOW
Drumpark Special School
LANGMUIR ROAD
Park Rd
Dykehead Rd
PO
St Kevin's Primary School
Langmuir Way
Monkland Vw
Crs
Mitchell
Street
Rosebank Ter
Bargeddie Station
A752
Bredisholm Road
Swinton Crs
Dunnachie Drive
Kilgarth Street
Kenmuir St
Drumpark St
Rhinds St
Aitkenhead Avenue
Craigend
Viewfield
Crammond Av
Bargeddie
Barrbridge Rd
Barrbridge Rd
Showcase Cinema
Hollywood Bow
A8
GLASGOW-AND-EDINBURGH-ROAD
Braehead
North Calder Water
A752
Aitkenhead
Bankhe Farm
D
1
2
3
4
65
64
663
olf Cours

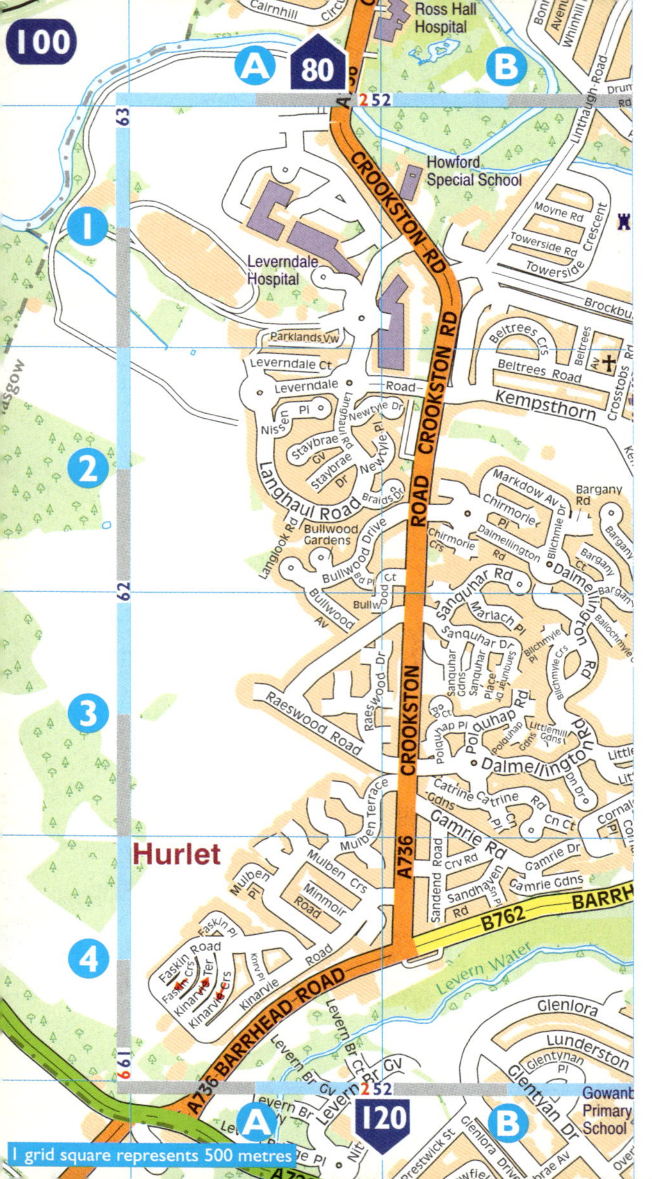

1 grid square represents 500 metres

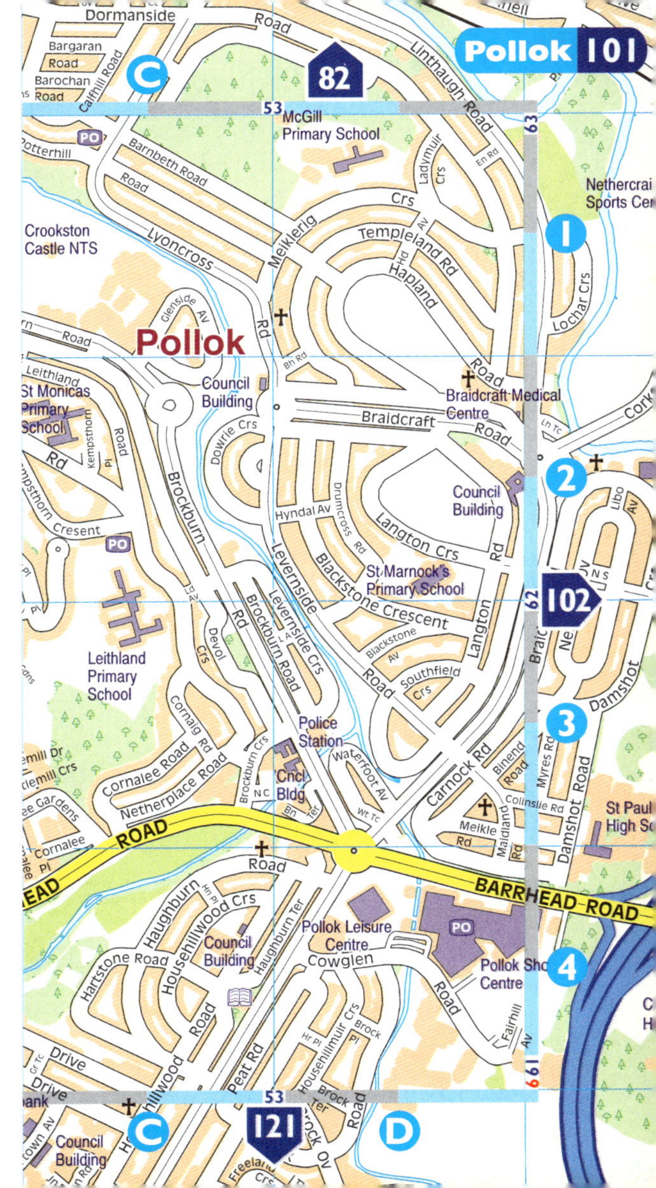

Pollok
Crookston Castle NTS
McGill Primary School
St Monicas Primary School
Leithland Primary School
Council Building
Braidcraft Medical Centre
St Marnock's Primary School
Police Station
Cncl Bldg
Pollok Leisure Centre
Pollok Shopping Centre
Nethercraig Sports Centre
St Paul's High School
Dormanside
Bargaran Road
Barochan Road
Calfhill Road
Potterhill
Barnbeth Road
Lyoncross Road
Meikleriq Crs
Templeland Rd
Hapland Road
Linthaugh Road
Braidcraft Road
Brockburn Road
Leverndale
Blackstone Crescent
Langton Crs
Carnock Rd
Damshot Road
BARRHEAD ROAD
Cowglen Road
Househillwood Crs
Hartstone Road
Haughburn Ter
Peat Rd
Cornalee Road
Netherplace Road
Lochar Crs
82
102
121
53
62
63
61

102
82
A
B
Corkerhill Station
Nethercraigs Sports Centre
Corkerhill
Braidcraft Medical Centre
St Edmunds Primary School
101
M77
St Paul's High School
Junction 2
BARRHEAD ROAD
B762
Cowglen Hospital
White Cart
122
1 grid square represents 500 metres

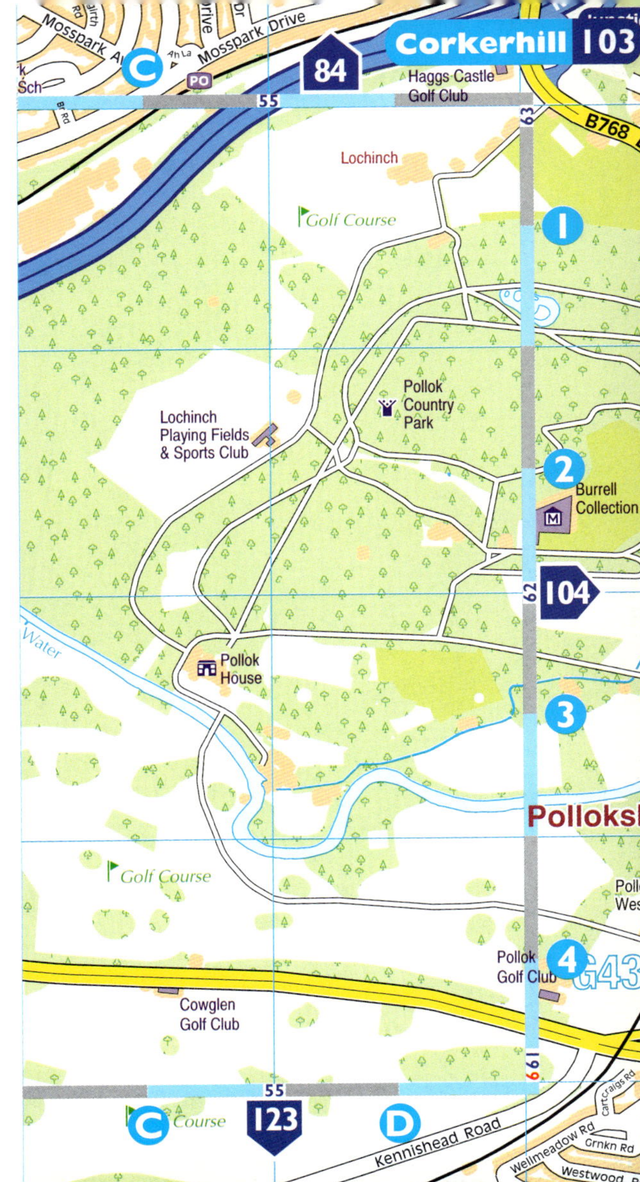

Corkerhill
103
84
Mosspark Drive
Haggs Castle
Golf Club
B768
Lochinch
Golf Course
Pollok
Country
Park
Lochinch
Playing Fields
& Sports Club
Burrell
Collection
104
Water
Pollok
House
Pollok
Golf Club
G43
Golf Course
Cowglen
Golf Club
Course
123
Kennishead Road
Wellmeadow Rd
Westwood

104
Junction 1
A
84
B
Haggs Castle Golf Club
B768 DUMBRECK ROAD
Springkell Drive
Terregles Avenue
Terregles Crs
Terregles Dr
Haggswood Av
Haggs Lane
Burrell Ct
St Andrew's
Albert Drive
Avenue
B768
HAGGS RD B769
Whins Rd
Road
Morton Gdns
Herries
Pollok Country Park
1
2
3
4
Burrell Collection
103
Ravenshall Road
Mannering Rd
Ellangowan Rd
Wellgreen Health Cen
Rssndl Rd
Surg
Cncl Bldg
Christian St
Pleasance
Kirk Lane Cem
Council Buildin
Sir John Maxwell Primary Sch
Bengal St
Pollokshaws
Pollokshaws West Station
POLLOKSHAWS ROAD
B769
Shawholm Crs
Riverbank Street
Pollok Golf Club
G43
Shawbridge St
Shawbridge Industrial Est
Police Station
Cogan St
Auldhouse
Harriet Pl
124
Westwood
Mamore St
grid square represents 500 metres

Dalziel Drive
Council Building
G41
Maxwell Park Station
Glencairn Drive
Glencairn Gdns
Terregles Avenue
Pollokshields West Stn
Glencairn La
Fotheringay Road
Fotheringay Lane
Kirkcaldy Road
Clydesdale CC
Hutchesons' Grammar Sch
Darnley Road
Strathbungo
Crossmyloof
Titwood Road
B763
Meldrum Gardens
Killiegrew Rd
Titwood Road
Crossmyloof Station
Crossmyloof Gdns
Minard Road
Waverley Gdns
Waverley St
Pollokshaws
Norham Street
Durward Avenue
Dinmont Road
Surgery
Shawlands Academy
Shawlands Primary School
Moss-Side Road
A77
Peveril Av
Woodstock Av
Kenilworth Av
Pollokshaws Road
Shawlands Stn
Shawlands
Eastwood Av
Skirving St
Afton St
Edgemont St
Deanston Dr
Tantallon Rd
Bellwood Street
Camphill Av
Camphill Avenue
Victoria Infirmary
Langside Primary Sch
St Convals Primary Sch
Coustonholm Rd
Pollokshaws East Station
Langside
Holmbank Av
Cartha St
Woodford St
Tantallon Road
Camphill Av
Mansionhouse Gdns
Millbrae
Cathkin Rd
Riverside Road
Corrour Road
Newlandsfield Rd
Kilmarnock Road
Langside Station
Millbrae Cr's
Cromarty Avenue
Earlspark Avenue
Battlefield Primary Sch
Newlands Rd
Monreith Rd
Ellisland Rd
Alloway Rd
Surgery
86
106
125
57
62
63
1
2
3
4
C
D

106
86
A
B
Pollokshields East Stn
Cuthbertson Primary School
Govan
Surgery
Strathbungo
Pollokshields West Stn
DARNLEY ROAD
NITHSDALE DR
CALDER
Hutchesons' Grammar Prep Sch
St Bride's Primary Sch
Queens Park Stn
Synagogue
Annette St Primary S
Mosque
The Ewington Hotel
Queen's Park
POLLOKSHAWS RD
A77
105
LANGSIDE AVENUE B768
Victoria Infirmary
A&E
Mount Florida Medical Centre
Langside College
Mount Florida Stn
Battlefield
Battlefield Primary Sch
Madhok Medical Cen
BATTLEFIELD RD
White Cart Water
Langside Station
126
1 grid square represents 500 metres
1
2
3
4
258

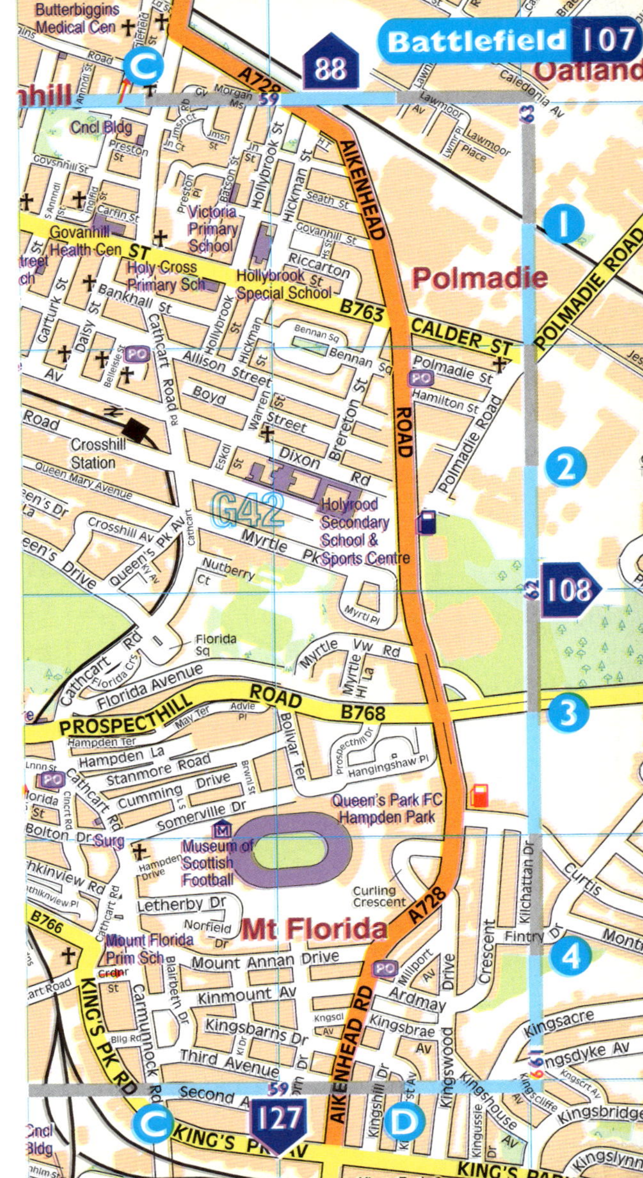

Butterbiggins Medical Cen
88
Oatland
Cncl Bldg
Govanhill Health Cen
Victoria Primary School
Holy Cross Primary Sch
Hollybrook Special School
Polmadie
AIKENHEAD ROAD
CALDER ST
B763
POLMADIE ROAD
Allison Street
Crosshill Station
Queen Mary Avenue
Holyrood Secondary School & Sports Centre
G42
Myrtle Pk
Queen's Drive
108
Florida Avenue
PROSPECTHILL ROAD
B768
Queen's Park FC Hampden Park
Museum of Scottish Football
Mt Florida
Mount Florida Prim Sch
Curling Crescent
A728
B766
KING'S PK RD
Mount Annan Drive
Kinmount Av
Kingsbarns Dr
Third Avenue
Second Av
127
KING'S PARK AV
Kingsacre
Kingsbridge
Kingslynn

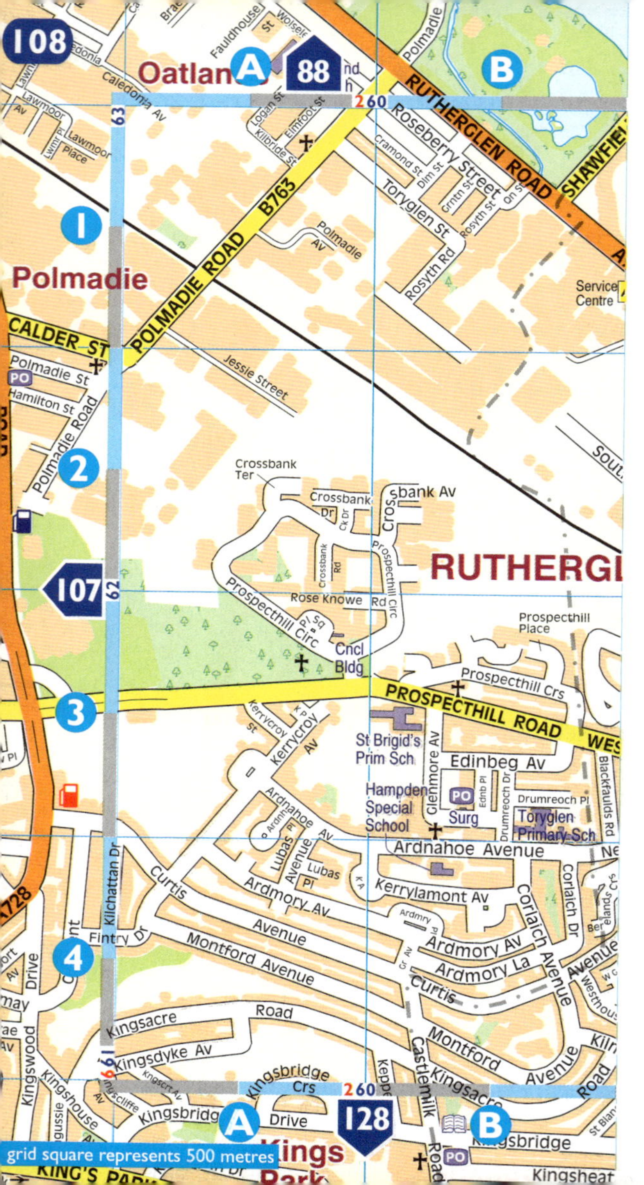

108
Oatlan
A
88
B
Polmadie
RUTHERGLEN ROAD
SHAWFIELD
POLMADIE ROAD
B763
CALDER ST
Roseberry Street
Toryglen St
Rosyth Rd
Jessie Street
Polmadie Av
Service Centre
Crossbank Ter
Crossbank Dr
Prospecthill Circ
Rose Knowe Rd
RUTHERGL
Prospecthill Place
Prospecthill Crs
PROSPECTHILL ROAD
Cncl Bldg
107
Kerrycroy Av
St Brigid's Prim Sch
Hampden Special School
Edinbeg Av
Drumreoch Pl
Toryglen Primary Sch
Blackfaulds Rd
Ardnahoe Avenue
Kerrylamont Av
Ardmory Av
Ardmory La
Curtis Avenue
Montford Avenue
Corlaich Avenue
Corlaich Dr
Kilchattan Dr
Fintry Dr
Kingsacre Road
Kingsdyke Av
Kingsbridge Crs
Kingsbridge Drive
Castlemilk Road
Kingswood Drive
Kingshouse
128
A
B
Kings Park
Kingsheat
grid square represents 500 metres

Dalmarnock
Laird Business Park
Davidson Street
Cotton Street Business Park
Strathclyde Street
Dalmarnock Trading Estate
Rutherglen Station
Burnhill Sports Centre
Burgh Prim Sch
Spectrum Bus Cen
Swimming Pool
St Columbkilles Prim Sch
Stonelaw High Sch
Rutherglen Health Cen
Bankhead Primary Sch
Bankhead
Glasgow Road
Glasgow Road
Quay Road
Seath Road
Ashton Rd
Queen St
King St
Victoria Street
Burnhill Street
Mill St
Greenhill Road
Farie St
Cathcart Rd
Clincarthill Rd
Parkhill Drive
Johnstone Drive
Overtoun Drive
Watson Av
Milrig Road
Bankhead Rd
Ewing St
Clydeside Rd
Camp Road
Millcroft Rd
Shore St
Cotton St
Swanston St
Downiebrae Road
Alleysbank Rd
Lloyd St
Dalmarnock
Farmeloan
Stonelaw
Pinkerton Av
Toryglen Road
Western Avenue
Colvend St
French St
Summerfield St
Landemer Dr
Strathclyde Dr
Cityford Dr
A730
A749
B768
G73

90
110
129

110
90
109
130
Dalmarnock Road
Cambuslang Road
Farmeloan Rd
Stonelaw Road
Main Street B768
Downiebrae Road
Springfield Primary School
Dalmarnock Industrial Estate
Duchess Ind Est
Dalmarnock Trading Estate
Farm Castle Ind Est
Rutherglen Station
Farmeloan Ind Est
Council Building
Rutherglen High School
Spectrum Bus Cen
Swimming Pool
St Columbkilles Prim Sch
Stonelaw High Sch
Rutherglen Health Cen
Calderwood Primary Sch
G73
1 grid square represents 500 metres

92
112
131
Cemetery
Clyde
Clyde Industrial Estate
Ballochmill Rd
John Hillhouse Industrial Estate
Eastfield
Cambuslang Road
Bogleshole Road
County Avenue
Trinity High School
Burn Ter
Richmond Drive
Eskdale
Annan Dr
Buckingham Dr
Berwick
Coldstream
Colville Dr
Bothwell Street
London Rd
Braidfauld
Potter
South Lanarksh
Peebles Dr

112 Braidfauld
A
92
B
264
63
62
61
1
2
3
4
111
132
Tollcross Road
Corbett St
Tollcross Industrial Est
Prosen St
London Rd
Braidfauld
Braidfauld Gdns
Dalbeth Rd
London Road
Causewayside Street
Easterhill St
St Vincents School Tollcross
Fullarton Avenue
Battles Burn
Fullarton La
Archerfield Dr
Westhorn Dr
Junction 1
Fullarton Rd
Drumhead Road
Drumhead Place
Cambuslang Road
Clydesmill Rd
Clydesmill
Cambuslang Road
Clydesmill Grove
Clydesmill Drive
City of Glasgow
South Lanarkshire
BRIDGE STREET
A763
Kincaid Gdns
Morriston Pk Dr
Aitor Prima School
1 grid square represents 500 metres

Mount Vernon
Carmyle
Junction 2
M74
A74
LONDON RD
B765 CARMYLE AVENUE
Tollcross Road
Hamilton Road
Sandyhills Grove
Aberuthven Drive
Willow La
Kenmuirhill Road
Carmyle Station
Inzievar Terrace
Montrose Avenue
St Joachims RC Primary School
Carmyle Prim Sch
Liddell St
Estate Road
Park Road
Noldrum Av
Duffus Ter
Duffus Pl
Drumshaw Dr
Mansionhouse Av
Ardargie Dr
Carmyle Av
Balmoral Dr
Gardenside Av
Gardenside Crs
Carmyle Medical Cen
PO
River Road
River Clyde
Kenmuir Road
Cambuslang Golf Club
Westburn Road
Westburn Farm Road
Luffness Gdns
Newbattle Rd
Newton Grange Av
94
114
133
65
63
62
661
1
2
3
4
C
D

Mount Vernon
Bideford Crs
Torrington Cr
Muirside Av
Mount Vernon
Primary Sch
94
B7058
Dornford
Meryon
Road
Woodend
Brrwd Ct
Wdnd Ct
Hamilton Road
Surg
Kenmuirhill Road
LONDON ROAD
A74
Kenmuir Road
St Bridgets
RC Primary
School
Kenmuir
Kenmuir Road
113
Duffus Ter
Duffus Pl
Drumshaw Dr
Park Road
River Clyde
City of Glasgow
South Lanarkshire
Light Burn
Avenue
134
Newton
Mitchell
Westburn Road
Westburn
A
B
1
2
3
4
63
62
61
266
1 grid square represents 500 metres

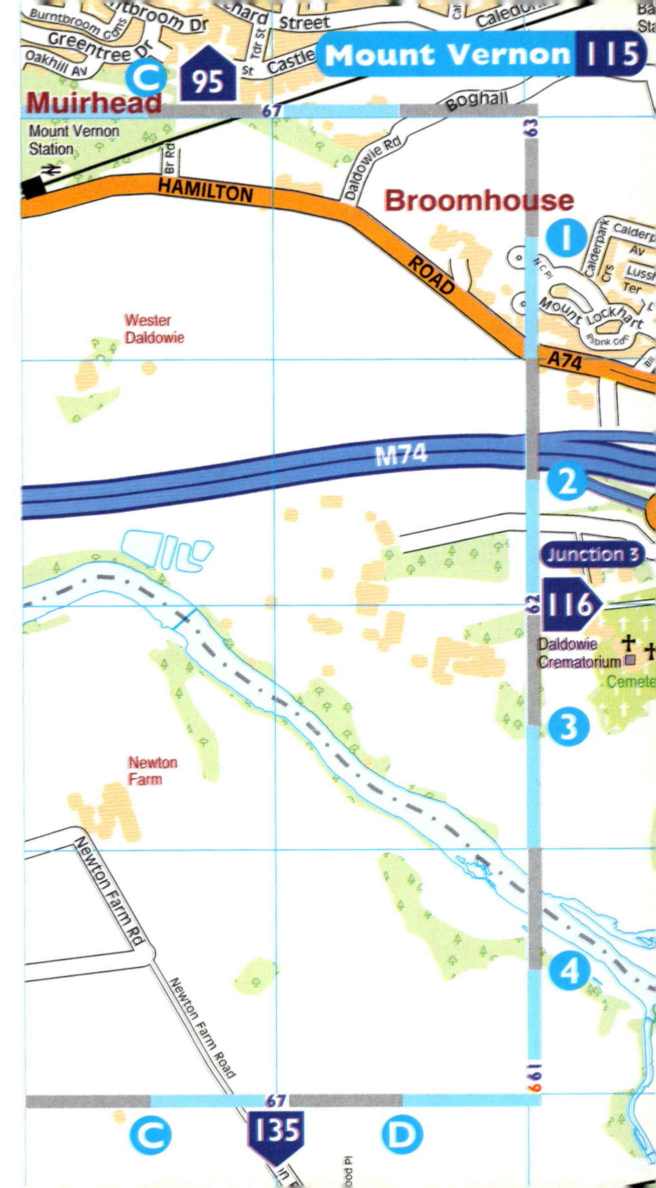

Mount Vernon 115
95
C
Muirhead
Burntbroom Gdns
Greentree Dr
Oakhill Av
Street
Castle
St
Boghall
Mount Vernon
Station
Br Rd
HAMILTON
Daldowie Rd
Broomhouse
ROAD
A74
Wester
Daldowie
M74
Junction 3
116
Daldowie
Crematorium
Newton
Farm
Newton Farm Rd
Newton Farm Road
1
2
3
4
67
63
62
61
C
135
D

116
Boghall Road
Station
A
96
B
268
63
Broomhouse
1
ROAD
Baillieston Road
Calderpark Av
Calderpark Crs
Lusshill Ter
Mount Lockhart
L t Pl
N C Pl
Rsbnk Gdn
Bll. Rd
Glasgow Zoopark
A74
Travel Inn
HAMILTON ROAD
Roundknowe Road
74
2
Junction 3
115
62
Daldowie Crematorium
Cemetery
Maryville
Junction 4/1
River Clyde
Greyfriars Road
3
FARM
4
61
TYRE
I grid square represents 500 metres

98
Calder Water
South Lanark
Woodhead Farm
Newlands Farm
Golf Course
M73
Birkenshaw Industrial Estate
Rannoch Road
Calderbraes Golf Club
Maryville Vw
Eighth St
Second Av
Sixth St
Old Edinburgh Road
Birkenshaw
Aitkenhead Primary School
B7001
The Cuillins
Watling St
Old Edinburgh Road
Fourth St
Second St
Hillview Crs
Milton Gdns
Calderbraes Avenue
Talbot Ter
First Avenue
Third St
Synth Av
First St
Dnvgn Pl
Boggknowe
Glenacre Crs
Mossgiel Gdns
Kirkhill Rd
Dalveen Dr
Glencroft Avenue
Hillfoot Gdns
Ardenlea
Ardgowan Dr
M74
Glasgow Road
Lucy Brae
Old Glasgow Road
Road
New Edinburgh Road
Kelvin Rd
B7071 Glasgow Road
Clydeneuk Dr
Powburn Crs
Kylepark
Brooklands Av
Alpine Gv
Kylepark Crescent
Clydfrd Dr
Priory Dr
Drive
Hume Drive
Sheepburn Road
Rosefield Gdns
Holmwood Av
Holmwood Gdns
Old Mill
Belleisle Av
Kylepark Av
Grammar School
Uddingston
C
D
1
2
3
4
69
61
62
63

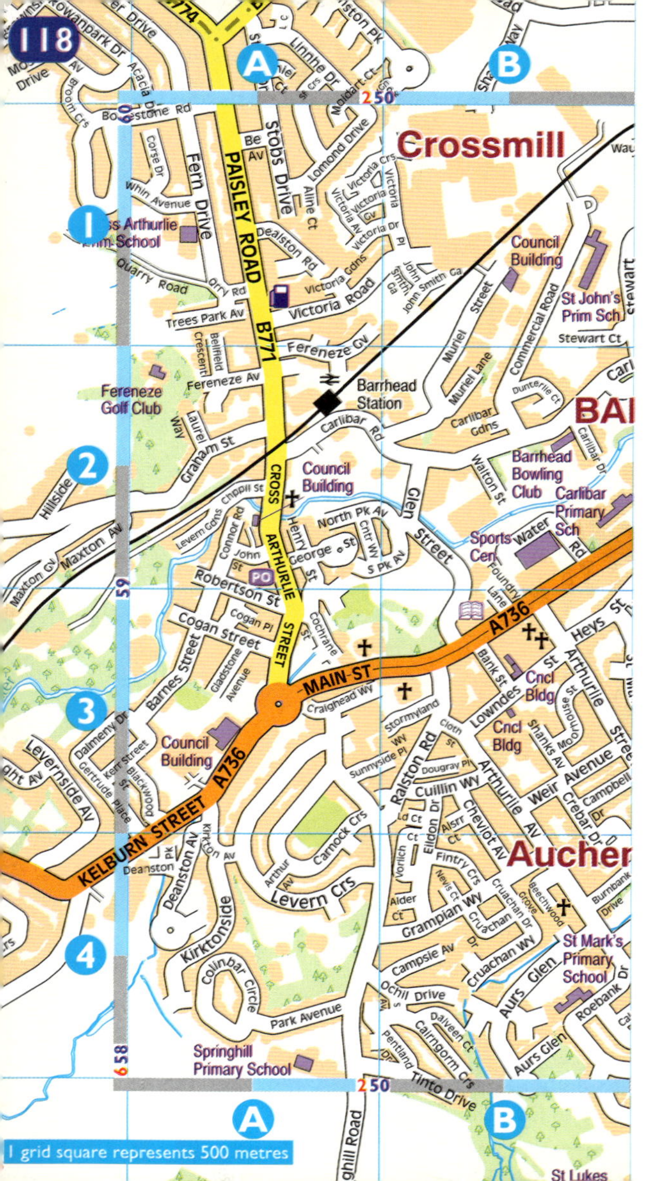

118
A
B
1
2
3
4
250
60
59
658
Crossmill
BA
Aucher
Rowanpark Dr
Acacia Dr
Broom Crs
Boydstone Rd
Corse Dr
Whin Avenue
Fern Drive
PAISLEY ROAD
B771
Stobs Drive
Linnhe Dr
Moidart Ct
Lomond Drive
Alline Ct
Victoria Crs
Victoria Gv
Victoria Av
Victoria Dr
Victoria Gdns
Victoria Road
Dealston Rd
John Smith Ga
Quarry Road
Qrry Rd
Trees Park Av
Bellfield Crescent
Fereneze Gv
Fereneze Av
Fereneze Golf Club
Barrhead Station
Muriel Street
Muriel Lane
Commercial Road
Council Building
St John's Prim Sch
Stewart Ct
Stewart
Dunterlie Ct
Carlibar Gdns
Carlibar Rd
Carlibar Dr
Laurel Way
Graham St
Hillside
Maxton Av
Maxton Gv
Chappll St
Levern Gdns
Connor Rd
John St
CROSS ARTHURLIE STREET
Henry St
North Pk Av
Cntr Wy
S Pk Av
George St
Glen Street
Walton St
Barrhead Bowling Club
Carlibar Primary Sch
Sports Cen
Water Rd
Foundry Lane
PO
Robertson St
Cogan Street
Cogan Pl
Barnes Street
Gladstone Avenue
Cochrane St
MAIN ST
A736
Craighead Wy
Stormyland Wy
Sunnyside Pl
Heys St
Bank St
Lowndes St
Arthurlie St
Cncl Bldg
Moorhouse St
Shanks Av
Weir Avenue
Campbell Dr
Crebar Dr
Cloth St
Dougray Pl
Ralston Rd
Cuillin Wy
Arthurlie Av
Cheviot Av
Eildon Dr
Alsrr Ct
Fintry Crs
Nevis Ct
Cruachan Dr
Cruachan Wy
Beechwood Grove
Burnbank Drive
Grampian Wy
Campsie Av
Ochil Drive
Aurs Glen
Aurs Glen Dr
Roebank Dr
St Mark's Primary School
Dalmeny Dr
Gertrude Place
Kerr Street
Blackwood St
Leverndale Av
Council Building
KELBURN STREET
Kirkton Av
Deanston Av
Deanston
Kirktonside
Colinbar Circle
Park Avenue
Carnock Crs
Arthur Av
Levern Crs
Vorlich Ct
Alder Ct
Dalveen Ct
Cairngorm Crs
Pentland Dr
Tinto Drive
Springhill Primary School
St Lukes
1 grid square represents 500 metres

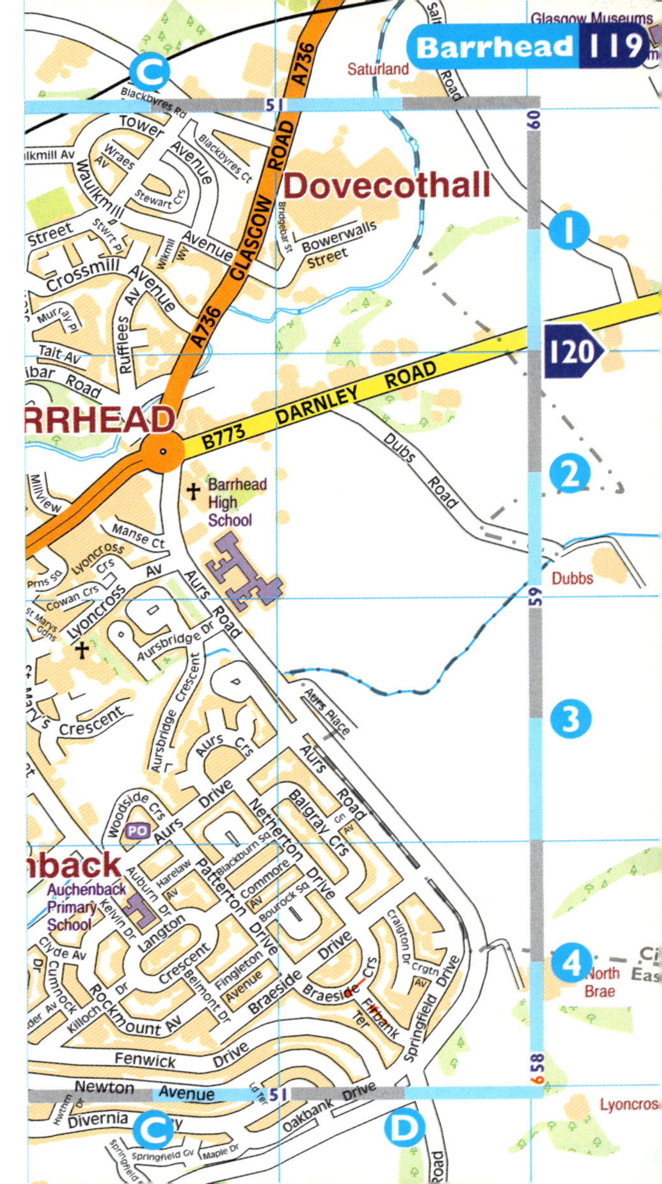
Glasgow Museums
Saturland
Dovecothall
Bowerwalls Street
Bridgebar St
Blackbyres Rd
Blackbyres Ct
Tower Avenue
Waulkmill Av
Wraes Av
Stewart Crs
Waulkmill Street
Stwrt Pl
Wlkmill Wy
Avenue
Crossmill Avenue
Murray Pl
Ruffles Av
Tait Av
Road
GLASGOW ROAD
A736
BARRHEAD
B773
DARNLEY ROAD
Dubs Road
Dubbs
120
Barrhead High School
Millview
Manse Ct
Lyoncross Crs
Lyoncross Av
Prns Sq
Cowan Crs
St Marys Gdns
Aurs Road
Aursbridge Dr
Aursbridge Crescent
St Mary's Crescent
Aurs Place
Aurs Crs
Aurs Drive
Aurs Road
Woodside Crs
PO
Balgray Crs
Gn Av
Netherton Drive
Blackburn Sq
Patterton Drive
Commore Av
Harelaw Av
Auburn Dr
Auchenback Primary School
Kelvin Dr
Langton Crescent
Bourock Sq
Craigton Dr
Crgtn Av
Springfield Drive
Braeside Drive
Braeside Crs
Fifbank Ter
Fingleton Avenue
Belmont Dr
Clyde Av
Cumnock Dr
Killoch Dr
Rockmount Av
Fenwick Drive
Newton Avenue
Oakbank Drive
Divernia Wy
Springfield Gv
Maple Dr
Springfield
Road
North Brae
Lyoncross
60
59
58
51
1
2
3
4
C
D

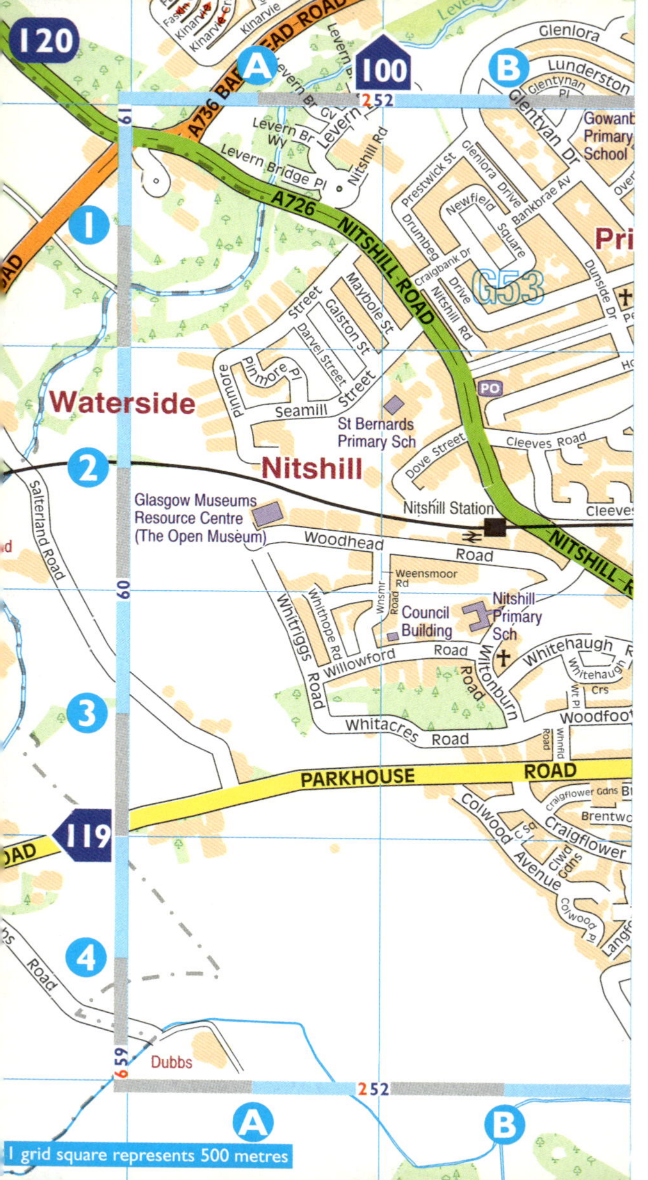

120
100
119
A
B
1
2
3
4
252
61
60
659
Glenlora
Lunderston
Glentynan Pl
Glentyan Dr
Gowanbank Primary School
Levern Br Cv
Levern Br Wy
Levern Bridge Pl
Nitshill Rd
A736 BARRHEAD ROAD
A726
NITSHILL ROAD
Prestwick St
Glenlora Drive
Newfield Square
Bankbrae Av
Drumbeg Drive
Craigbank Dr
Dunside Dr
G53
Street
Maybole St
Galston St
Darvel Street
Pinmore Pl
Pinmore
Seamill Street
Waterside
St Bernards Primary Sch
PO
Dove Street
Cleeves Road
Nitshill
Glasgow Museums Resource Centre (The Open Museum)
Nitshill Station
Woodhead Road
Salterland Road
Weensmoor Rd
Whitriggs Road
Whithope Rd
Council Building
Nitshill Primary Sch
Willowford Road
Wiltonburn Road
Whitehaugh Crs
Woodfoot Road
Whitacres Road
PARKHOUSE ROAD
Craigflower Gdns
Brentwood
Colwood Avenue
Craigflower
Colwood Pl
Dubbs
Road
1 grid square represents 500 metres

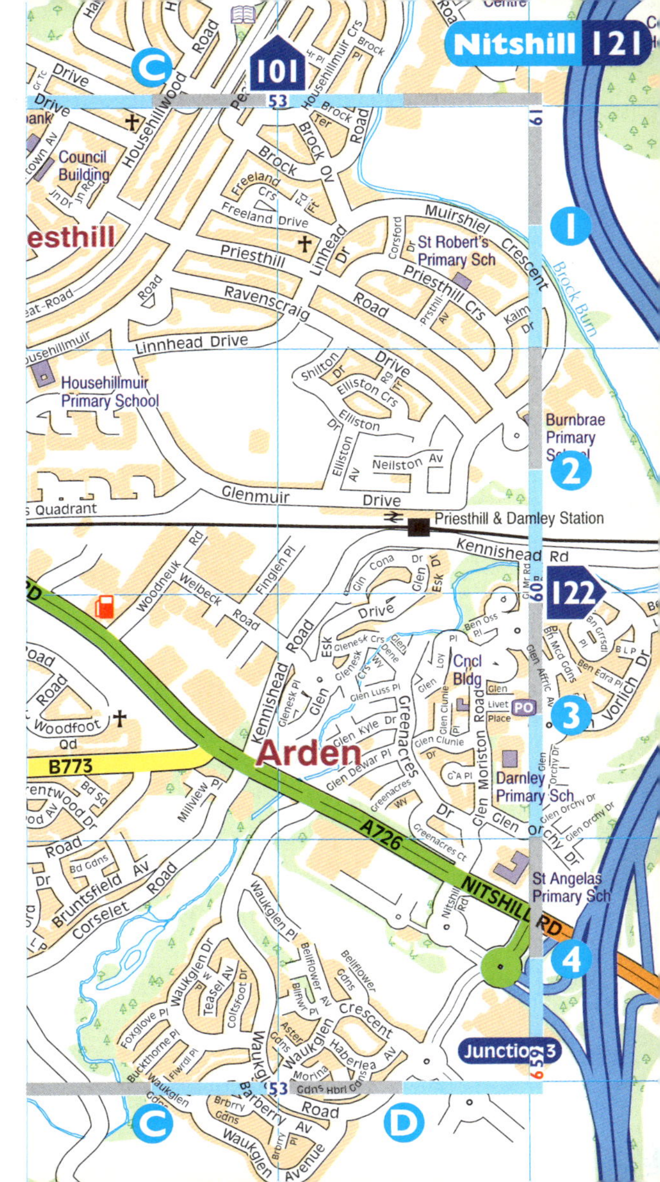

Nitshill 121
101
122
Priesthill
Arden
Council Building
Househillmuir Primary School
St Robert's Primary Sch
Burnbrae Primary School
Priesthill & Darnley Station
Darnley Primary Sch
St Angelas Primary Sch
Cncl Bldg
Househillwood Road
Househillmuir Crs
Brock Road
Brock Ter
Brock Ov
Brock Pl
Freeland Crs
Freeland Drive
Priesthill Road
Priesthill Crs
Ravenscraig Drive
Linnhead Dr
Linnhead Drive
Muirshiel Crescent
Corsford Dr
Kaim Dr
Shilton Dr
Elliston Crs
Elliston Dr
Elliston Av
Neilston Av
Glenmuir Drive
Kennishead Rd
Kennishead Road
Woodneuk Rd
Welbeck Road
Finglen Pl
Esk Road
Esk Dr
Gln Cona Drive
Ben Oss Pl
Glen Affric Av
Glenesk Crs
Glen Luss Pl
Glen Kyle Dr
Glen Dewar Pl
Greenacres
Greenacres Wy
Greenacres Ct
Glen Clunie
Glen Clunie Dr
Glen Moriston Road
Glen Livet Place
Glen Orchy Dr
Vorlich Dr
Ben Edra Pl
Millview Pl
Woodfoot Qd
B773
A726
NITSHILL RD
Nitshill Rd
Bruntsfield Av
Corselet Road
Waukglen Pl
Waukglen Dr
Waukglen Crs
Teasel Av
Coltsfoot Dr
Foxglove Pl
Buckthorne Pl
Bellflower Pl
Bellflower Gdns
Bellflower Av
Crescent
Haberlea Av
Morina Gdns
Barberry Av
Road
Waukglen Avenue
Brock Burn
Junction 3
Quadrant
53
60
59
61
C
D
1
2
3
4

122
Cowglen Hospital
A
102
B
254
61
Muirshiel Crescent
1
St Robert's Primary Sch
Priesthill Crs
Kaim Dr
Brock Burn
Boydstone Road
Kennishead
Burnbrae Primary School
2
Priesthill & Darnley Station
Kennishead Rd
121
60
Ben Vorlich Dr
Ben Uird Pl
Cncl Bldg
3
PO
M77
Hopeman Dr
Carnwadric Road
Hopeman St
Crebar Street
Kilmuir Crescent
Kilmuir Dr
Arden Prim Sch
St Louise Prim Sch
Darnley Primary Sch
Glen Moriston
Glen Orchy Dr
Greenacres Ct
Kilbeg Ter
Kyleakin Road
Surg
Kilvaxter Dr
Kilmuir Road
Thornlieb
St Angelas Primary Sch
NITSHILL RD
4
Kyleakin Ter
Kylerhea Rd
Spiersbridge Business Park
Spiersbridge Lane
Evanton Dr
Spiersbridge Ter
Nitshill Road
Junction 3
59
Thornliebank Ind Est
Thornliebank Ind Estate
A
B
Arden
1 grid square represents 500 metres

Cowglen Golf Club
103
55
Golf Course
Kennishead Road
Wellmeadow Rd
Grnkn Rd
Cartcraigs Rd
Westwood Road
Auld
1
Stoneside Drive
Scarba
Garvock Dr
Stoneside Sq
Fieldhead Dr
Bonnyrigg Dr
Banchory Av
Fyvie Av
2
B769
THORNLIEBANK
Kennishead Av
Kennishead Station
Foinaven Wy
Foinaven Gdns
Foinaven Dr
Brent Rd
Brent Gdns
Brent Dr
Forties Crs
Viking Wy
Boydstone Pl
Cemetery
Hutchesons St Aloysians RFC
Barrmill Rd
Burnfield Rd
124
60
Thornliebank Station
St Vincent's Primary Sch
Boydstone Road
Cruachan St
Carnwadric Primary Sch
Bangorshill Street
Carnwadric
Clova St
Thornliebank Primary School
3
Cemetery
Lochiel Road
Ardconnel St
Thornliebank Hlth Cen
Summerlea Rd
MAIN STREET
Main Street
Crosslees Drive
Orchard Av
Groveburn Av
Robslee Drive
Treeburn Av
Addison Pl
Spiers Gv
Spiersbridge Avenue
Hillside Ct
Library Lane
Crosslees Park
Braefield Dr
Sherwood Dr
Southlea Av
Rockmount Avenue
Heathwood Dr
Park
4
SPIERSBRIDGE ROAD
Woodlands Gate
Woodlands Crs
Woodside Av
Westfield Road
Woodfarm High Sch
Crum Av
Robslee Road
Moorfoot Av
59
55
Our Lady of the Missions Prim Sch
Robslee Primary School
C
136
D
Woodlands
Rouken Glen Rd
Newfield Place

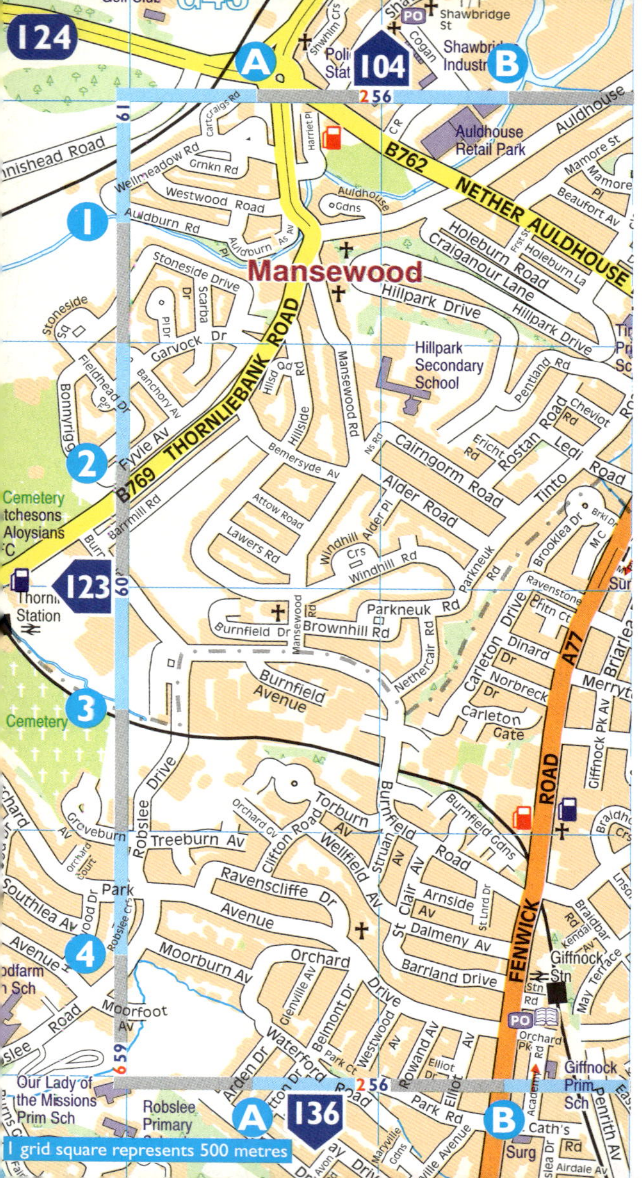

124
104
123
136
A
B
1
2
3
4
256
61
60
659
Shawbridge St
Shawbridge Industrial
Police Stat
Cogan St
Cartcraigs Rd
Harriet Pl
CR
Auldhouse Retail Park
B762 NETHER AULDHOUSE
Auldhouse
Mamore St
Mamore Pl
Beaufort Av
Nitshead Road
Wellmeadow Rd
Grnkn Rd
Westwood Road
Auldburn Rd
Auldburn Pl
Auldhouse Gdns
As Av
Mansewood
Holeburn Road
Holeburn La
Frst St
Craiganour Lane
Hillpark Drive
Stoneside Drive
Stoneside Sq
Scarba Dr
Pl Dr
Garvock Dr
Fieldhead Dr
Bonnyrigg
Banchory Av
B769 THORNLIEBANK ROAD
Hillsd Qd
Rd
Hillside
Mansewood Rd
Hillpark Secondary School
Pentland Rd
Cheviot Rd
Legi
Road
Ericht Rd
Rostan Road
Tinto
Fyvie Av
Bemersyde Av
Ns Rd
Cairngorm Road
Alder Road
Alder Pl
Cemetery
Aloysians
Barrmill Rd
Attow Road
Lawers Rd
Windhill Crs
Windhill Rd
Parkneuk Rd
Brooklea Dr
Brkl Dr
MC
Thornliebank Station
Burnfield Dr
Mansewood Rd
Brownhill Rd
Parkneuk Rd
Nethercairn Rd
Ravenstone
Crltn Ct
Carleton Drive
Dinard Dr
Norbreck Dr
Carleton Gate
A77
Briarlea
Merryton
Burnfield Avenue
Giffnock Pk Av
Cemetery
Robslee Drive
Torburn Av
Burnfield Road
Burnfield Gdns
FENWICK ROAD
Greveburn Av
Orchard Court
Orchard Gv
Clifton Road
Treeburn Av
Robslee Rd
Wellfield Av
Struan Av
St Clair Av
Arnside Av
St Lnrd Dr
Braidholm Crs
Park
Southlea Av
Robslee Crs
Ravenscliffe Dr
Avenue
Dalmeny Av
Kendal Rd
Kendal Av
Braidbar Rd
May Terrace
Giffnock Stn
Stn Rd
Moorburn Av
Orchard Drive
Barrland Drive
Avenue
Moorfoot Av
Road
Glenville Av
Belmont Dr
Westwood Av
Rowand Av
Elliot Dr
Elliot Av
Orchard Pk Rd
Giffnock Prim Sch
Our Lady of the Missions Prim Sch
Robslee Primary
Arden Dr
Waterford Road
Park Ct
Park Rd
Academy
Penrith Av
Cath's Surg
Rd
Airdale Av
Maryville Gdns
Avon
1 grid square represents 500 metres

105
126
137
57
60
59
Newlands
Merrylee
Netherlee
Giffnock
Langside Station
Muirend Stn
KILMARNOCK
MERRYLEE
CLARKSTON ROAD
Newlands Road
Monreith Road
Carlaverock Road
Calderwood Road
Beverley Road
Ellisland Rd
Alloway Rd
Kirkoswald Rd
Mossgiel Road
Lochlea Road
St Bride's Rd
Lubnaig
Airlour Rd
Langside Drive
Mochrum Rd
Quadrant Rd
Dairsie House School
Calderwood Lodge Jewish Primary School
Our Lady of the Annunciation Primary School
Surgery
Surg
Woodburn Rd
Mulberry Rd
Broom Rd
Briar Road
Briar Gdns
Tavistock Dr
Letham Dr
Burnhead Rd
Lanton Rd
Langside Dr
Laggan Road
Fernleigh Road
Merryburn Avenue
Merryvale Avenue
Merrycroft Av
Merrycrest Avenue
Ashlea Dr
Woodlea Dr
Rowanlea Drive
Birchlea Dr
Hazellea Dr
Thornlea Dr
Merrylee Park Av
Braidholm Road
Parkgrove Av
Braidbar Farm Rd
Brisbane Ct
Melbourne Ct
Braidbar Primary School
Heathside Rd
Whitton Drive
Graffham Avenue
Kyle Drive
Braidpark Drive
Kilmaurs Dr
Cunningham Dr
Forres Avenue
Huntly Av
Braidbar Farm Rd
Muirhill Ct
Braermar Ct
Muirend Road
Hazelden Pk
Hillcrest Av
Harelaw Ave
Kingsford Av
Whittlemuir Av
Cairndow Ct
Bogton Av
Deanwood Av
Deanwood Rd
Windlaw Gdns
Ormonde Avenue
Ormonde Dr
Ormonde Ct
Parklands Crs
Gordon Dr
Gordon Road
Gordon Av
Williamwood Drive
Williamwood Pk W
Coylton Rd
Glasserton
Cherrybank Rd
Friarton Rd
Ardle Rd
Ossian Rd
Aylmer Rd
Tannahill Rd
Earlspark Avenue
Cromarty Avenue
Kintore
Newlands
Muirskeith
Riverside Rd

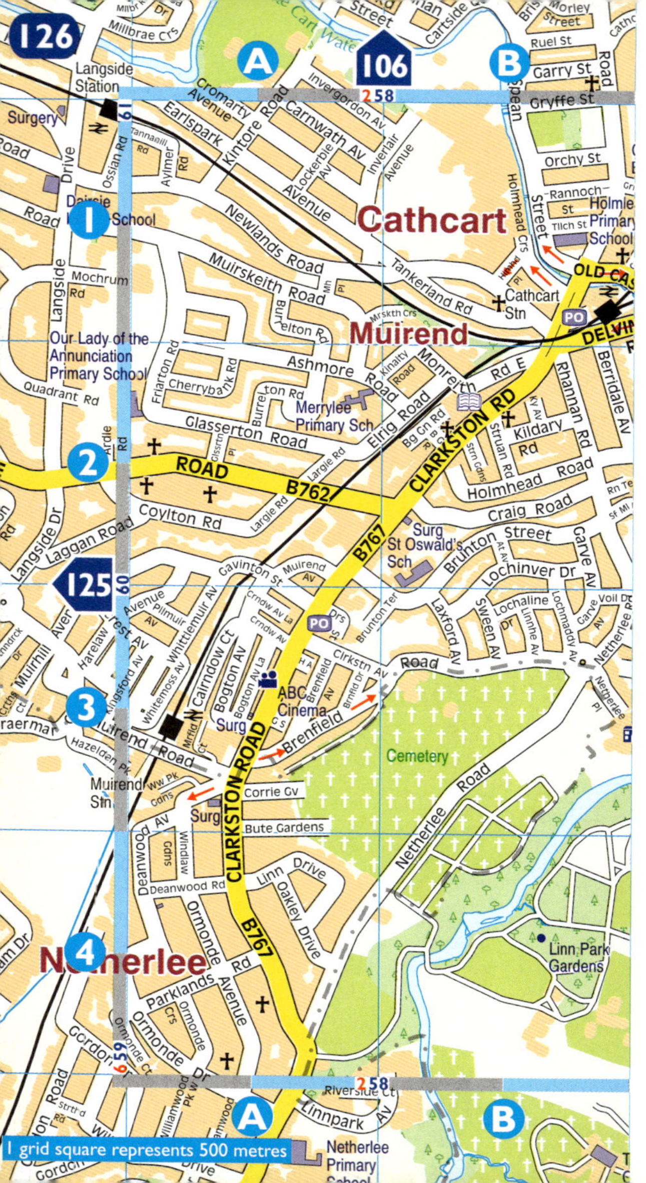

126
106
125
258
61
60
659
A
B
1
2
3
4
Langside Station
Cathcart
Muirend
Netherlee
Cathcart Stn
Muirend Stn
Surgery
Dairsie School
Our Lady of the Annunciation Primary School
Merrylee Primary Sch
St Oswald's Sch
Holmlea Primary School
Netherlee Primary School
ABC Cinema
Cemetery
Linn Park Gardens
Surg
PO
Clarkston Road
Clarkston Rd
B767
B762
Road
Old Castle Rd
Delvin Rd
Newlands Road
Muirskeith Road
Tankerland Rd
Ashmore Road
Glasserton Road
Coylton Rd
Laggan Road
Langside Dr
Langside Drive
Mochrum Rd
Quadrant Rd
Ardle Rd
Ossian Rd
Aylmer Rd
Kintore Road
Earlspark Avenue
Cromarty Avenue
Carnwath Av
Invergordon Av
Inverlair Avenue
Lockerbie Av
Avenue
Friarton Rd
Cherrybank Rd
Burrelton Rd
Burnelton Rd
Monreith Rd E
Kinalty Road
Elrig Road
Largie Rd
Gavinton St
Muirend Av
Whittlemuir Av
Cairndow Ct
Bogton Av
Bogton Av La
Clarkston Av
Brenfield Av
Brenfield Rd
Brunton Ter
Brunton Street
Craig Road
Holmhead Road
Struan Rd
Kildary Rd
Rhannan Rd
Berridale Av
Lochinver Dr
Laxford Av
Sween Av
Lochaline Dr
Linnhe Av
Lochmaddy Av
Garve Av
Voil Dr
Netherlee Rd
Netherlee Pl
Netherlee Road
Corrie Gv
Bute Gardens
Deanwood Av
Deanwood Rd
Windlaw Gdns
Linn Drive
Oakley Drive
Ormonde Avenue
Ormonde Crs
Ormonde Dr
Ormonde Ct
Parklands Rd
Riverside Ct
Linnpark Av
Muirend Road
Hazelden Pk
Kingsford Av
Whitemoss Av
Harelaw Av
Pilmuir Av
Muirhill Ct
Holmhead Crs
Holmhead Pl
Spean Street
Ruel St
Garry St
Gryffe St
Orchy St
Rannoch St
Tilch St
Morley Street
Millbrae Crs
Cartside St
I grid square represents 500 metres

107
128
C
D
1
2
3
4
59
60
G44
King's Pk Rd
King's Pk Av
King's Park Avenue
Kings Park Station
Aikenhead Rd
Menock Road
Mansebrae
B762
B766
Carmunnock Rd
Kinmount Av
Third Avenue
Second Av
Kingsbridge
Kingsdyke Av
Kingslynn Dr
Kingshouse Av
Kingshurst Av
Kingshill Dr
Kinghorn Dr
Broadwood Dr
Firwood Dr
Woodgreen Av
Woodholm Av
Overwood Dr
Southwood Drive
St Fillans Primary School
St Mirins Primary School
Kings Park Secondary School
Kilmailing Rd
Kirkwell Rd
Crompton Av
Elmore Avenue
Madison Av
Fairfax Av
Rmny Av
Courthill Avenue
Castle Greenock Av
Woodlinn Avenue
Carna Drive
Fetlar Dr
Tanera Av
Taynish Dr
Seil Drive
Shetland Drive
Orcades Drive
Farne Drive
Rockall Drive
Magnus Crs
Rodil Av
Simshill Road
Simshill Primary Sch
Old Castle Rd
Millholm Road
Holmwood House NTS
Linn Park Golf Club
Golf Course
Drakemire Drive
Drakemire Av
Raithburn Rd
Raithburn Avenue
Surg
PO
Thorncroft Road
Crofton
Croftfoot
Arnprior
Arnprior Qd
Glenacre Ter
Glenacre St
Westcastle Gdns
Castleton Prim Sch
Dougrie Gdns
Downcraig
Brigidale
Linnpark Industrial Est
The Linn Crematorium
Carmunnock Road

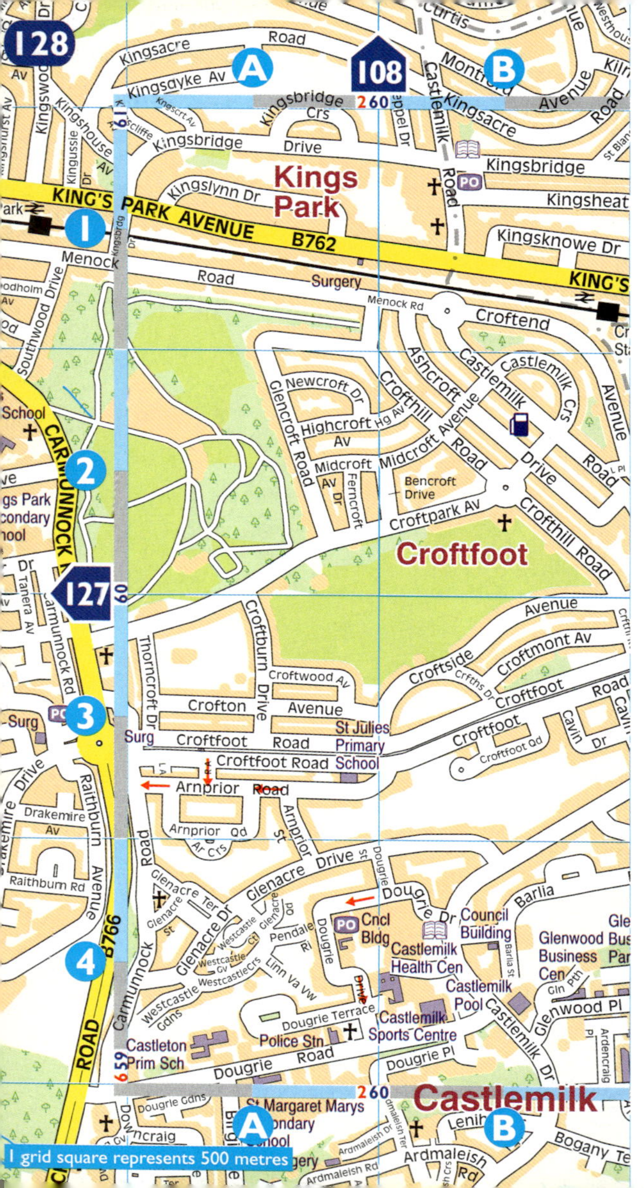

128
108
127
Kings Park
Croftfoot
Castlemilk
KING'S PARK AVENUE
B762
CARMUNNOCK ROAD
B766
Kingsacre Road
Kingsayke Av
Kingsbridge Crs
Kingsbridge Drive
Kingslynn Dr
Kingsbridge
Kingsheat
Kingsknowe Dr
Montford Avenue
Castlemilk Road
Menock Road
Surgery
Croftend
Castlemilk Drive
Castlemilk Crs
Ashcroft
Crofthill Road
Newcroft Dr
Glencroft Road
Highcroft Av
Midcroft Av
Midcroft Avenue
Bencroft Drive
Ferncroft Dr
Croftpark Av
Crofthill Road
Croftburn Drive
Croftwood Av
Crofton Avenue
Thorncroft Dr
Croftside Avenue
Croftmont Av
Croftfoot Road
Croftfoot Qd
Cavin Dr
St Julies Primary School
Arnprior Road
Arnprior Qd
Arnprior St
Glenacre Drive
Glenacre Ter
Glenacre Dr
Westcastle Crs
Westcastle Gdns
Pendale Ri
Linn Va Vw
Dougrie Dr
Dougrie Terrace
Dougrie Road
Dougrie Pl
Barlia Dr
Council Building
Cncl Bldg
Castlemilk Health Cen
Castlemilk Pool
Castlemilk Sports Centre
Castlemilk Dr
Glenwood Business Cen
Glenwood Pl
Castleton Prim Sch
Police Stn
Carmunnock Road
Raithburn Avenue
Raithburn Rd
Drakemire Av
Drakemire Drive
Southwood Drive
Menock Road
School
Carmunnock Rd
Tanera Av
St Margaret Marys Secondary School
Dougrie Gdns
Ardmaleish Rd
Bogany Ter
1 grid square represents 500 metres

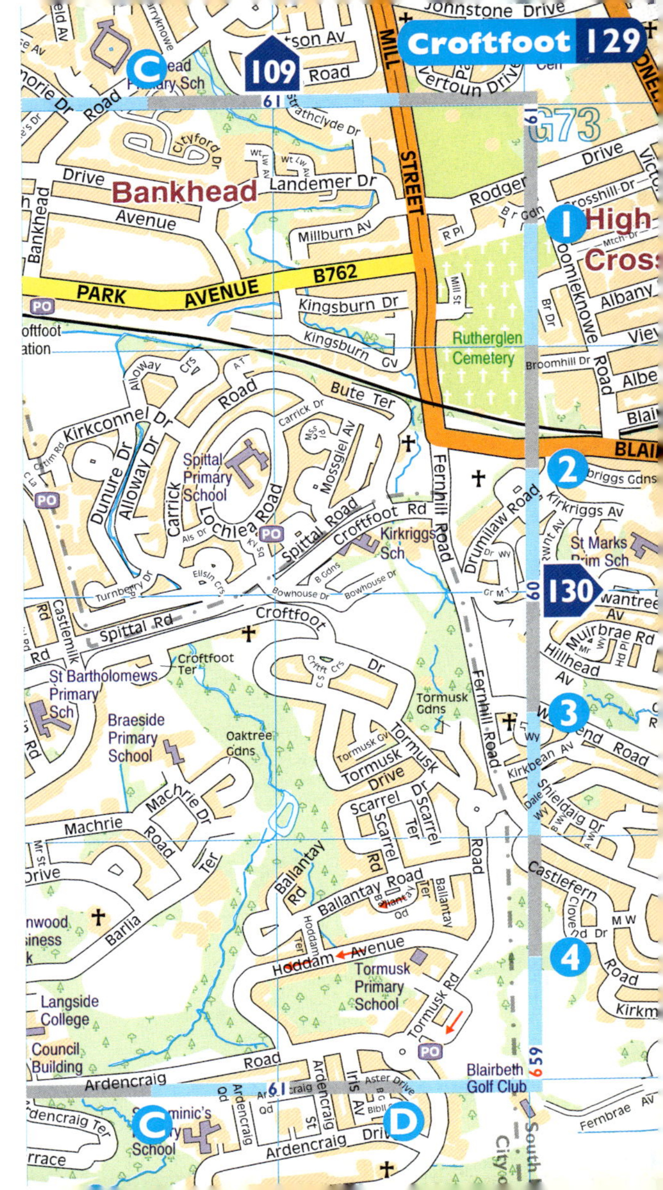
Johnstone Drive
109
Road
Mill Street
Vertoun Drive
G73
Strathclyde Dr
Cityford Dr
Drive
Bankhead
Avenue
Landemer Dr
Millburn Av
Rodger Drive
Crosshill Dr
High Cross
Albany
Park Avenue
B762
PO
Kingsburn Dr
Kingsburn Gv
Mill St
Rutherglen Cemetery
Broomhill Dr
Croftfoot Station
Alloway Crs
Road
Bute Ter
Carrick Dr
Kirkconnel Dr
Dunure Dr
Alloway Dr
Spittal Primary School
Carrick
Lochlea Road
Mossgiel Av
Spittal Road
Croftfoot Rd
Kirkriggs Sch
Fernhill Road
Drumilaw Road
Kirkriggs Av
St Marks Prim Sch
2
130
Turnberry Dr
Ellisln Crs
Bowhouse Dr
Muirbrae Rd
Hillhead Av
Castlemilk Rd
Spittal Rd
Croftfoot Dr
Croftfoot Ter
St Bartholomews Primary Sch
Braeside Primary School
Oaktree Gdns
Tormusk Gdns
Tormusk Drive
Tormusk Gv
Fernhill Road
3
Kirkbean Av
Shieldaig Dr
Machrie Dr
Machrie Road
Scarrel Dr
Scarrel Rd
Scarrel Ter
Ballantay Rd
Ballantay Road
Ballantay Ter
Castlefern Road
Cloverbank Dr
Barlia
Hoddam Avenue
Tormusk Primary School
Tormusk Rd
4
Langside College
Council Building
Ardencraig Road
Aster Drive
Iris Av
Blairbeth Golf Club
Ardencraig Ter
St Dominic's Primary School
Ardencraig Qd
Ardencraig Drive
Fernbrae Av
South City Way

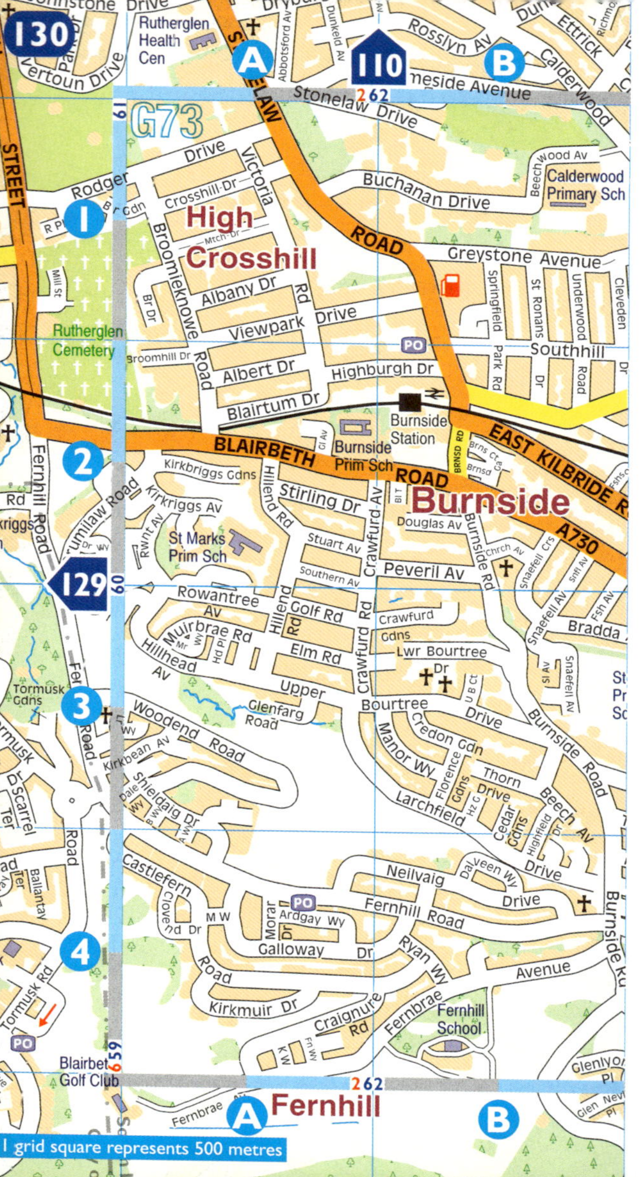

130
110
129
A
B
1
2
3
4
G73
262
61
60
659
Rutherglen Health Cen
Stonelaw Drive
Rosslyn Av
Calderwood
Ettrick
Buchanan Drive
Calderwood Primary Sch
Beechwood Av
High Crosshill
Rodger Drive
Crosshill Dr
Victoria Rd
Broomieknowe Road
Albany Dr
Viewpark Drive
Albert Dr
Broomhill Dr
Highburgh Dr
Blairtum Dr
Greystone Avenue
Springfield Park Rd
St Ronans Dr
Underwood Road
Cleveden Dr
Southhill
PO
Rutherglen Cemetery
Mill St
STREET
ROAD
Burnside Station
Burnside Prim Sch
BLAIRBETH ROAD
EAST KILBRIDE ROAD
A730
Burnside
Kirkbriggs Gdns
Kirkriggs Av
St Marks Prim Sch
Hillend Rd
Stirling Dr
Stuart Av
Southern Av
Crawfurd Av
Douglas Av
Peveril Av
Burnside Rd
Fernhill Road
Rowantree Av
Muirbrae Rd
Hillhead Av
Golf Rd
Elm Rd
Crawfurd Gdns
Lwr Bourtree Dr
Upper Bourtree Drive
Glenfarg Road
Woodend Road
Tormusk Gdns
Kirkbean Av
Shieldaig Dr
Bradda
Snaefell Av
Snaefell Crs
Credon Gdn
Manor Wy
Florence Gdns
Thorn Drive
Larchfield
Cedar Gdns
Beech Av
Highfield Dr
Burnside Road
Castlefern Road
Neilvaig Drive
Dalveen Wy
Fernhill Road
Ardgay Wy
Morar Dr
Galloway Dr
Ryan Wy
Avenue
Kirkmuir Dr
Craignure Rd
Fernbrae Av
Fernhill School
Blairbeth Golf Club
Tormusk Rd
Scarrel Dr
Ballantay
Glenlyon Pl
Fernbrae
Fernhill
1 grid square represents 500 metres

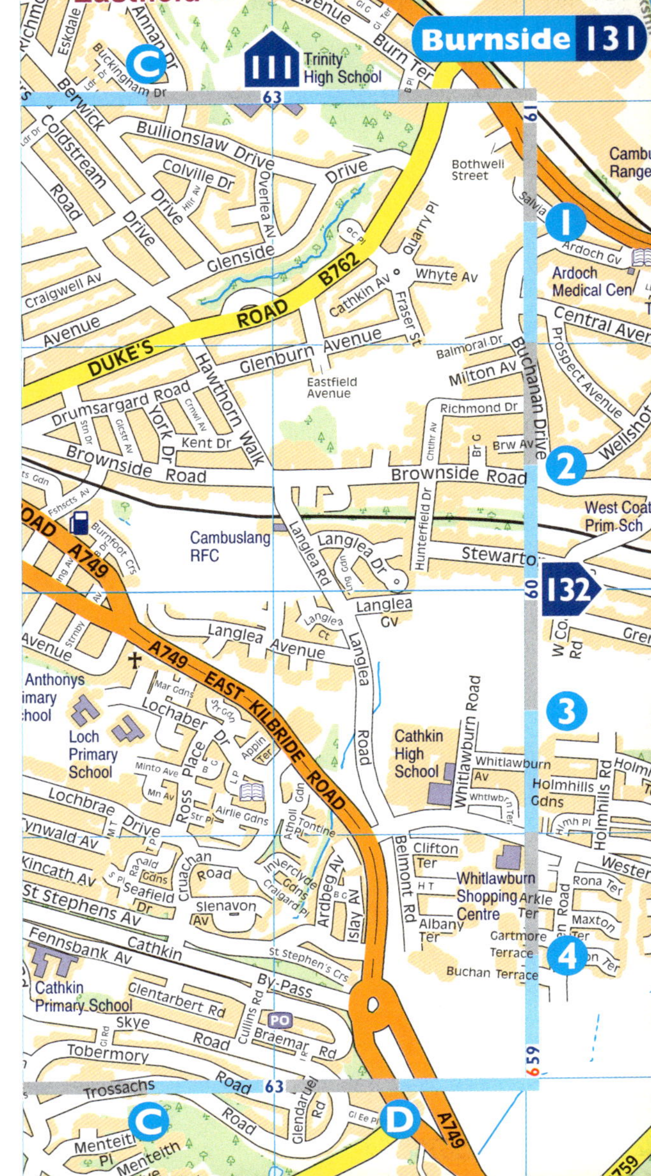
Trinity High School
Buckingham Dr
Annan Dr
Eskdale
Berwick
Coldstream
Road
Burn Ter
Bullionslaw Drive
Colville Dr
Drive
Overlea Av
Glenside
Craigwell Av
Avenue
DUKE'S ROAD
B762
Cathkin Av
Fraser St
Quarry Pl
Whyte Av
Bothwell Street
Salvia
Cambuslang Range
Ardoch Gv
Ardoch Medical Cen
Central Aven
Prospect Avenue
Balmoral Dr
Milton Av
Buchanan Drive
Glenburn Avenue
Eastfield Avenue
Richmond Dr
Drumsargard Road
Hawthorn Walk
York Dr
Kent Dr
Brw Av
Wellshot
Brownside Road
West Coats Prim Sch
Cambuslang RFC
Burnfoot Crs
Langlea Rd
Langlea Dr
Hunterfield Dr
Stewarton
132
A749
Langlea Gv
Langlea Ct
Langlea Avenue
Langlea Road
Avenue
A749 EAST KILBRIDE ROAD
Mar Gdns
Lochaber Dr
Appin Ter
Anthonys Primary School
Loch Primary School
Cathkin High School
Whitlawburn Road
Whitlawburn Av
Holmhills Gdns
Holmhills Rd
Minto Ave
Ross Place
Airlie Gdns
Atholl Gdn
Tontine Pl
Lochbrae Drive
Tynwald Av
Kincath Av
St Stephens Av
Cruachan Road
Seafield Dr
Slenavon Av
Inverclyde Gdns
Craigard Pl
Ardbeg Av
Islay Av
Belmont Rd
Clifton Ter
Whitlawburn Shopping Centre
Albany Ter
Arkle Ter
Rona Ter
Maxton Ter
Cartmore Terrace
Buchan Terrace
Fennsbank Av
Cathkin By-Pass
St Stephen's Crs
Cathkin Primary School
Glentarbert Rd
Cullins Rd
Braemar Rd
Skye Road
Tobermory Road
Trossachs Road
Glendarue Rd
Menteith Pl
Menteith
63
60
61
659

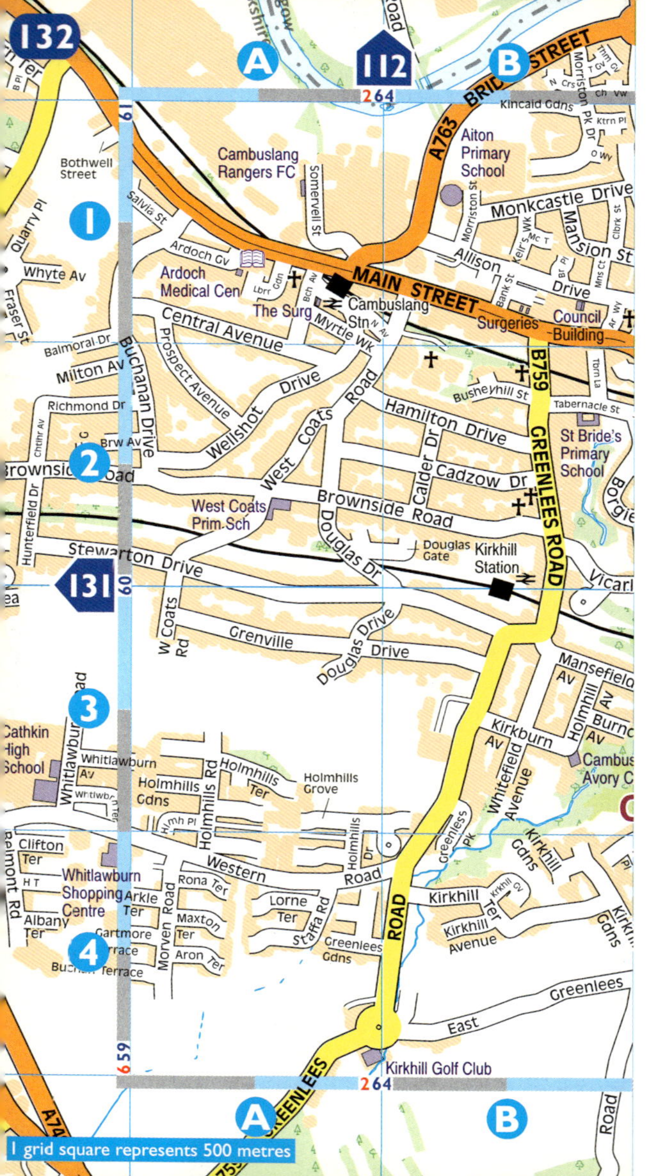
132
112
131
A
B
1
2
3
4
264
61
60
659
MAIN STREET
BRIDGE STREET
A763
B759
GREENLEES ROAD
Cambuslang Rangers FC
Aiton Primary School
Somervell St
Morriston St
Monkcastle Drive
Mansion St
Allison Drive
Kincaid Gdns
Bothwell Street
Salvia St
Quarry Pl
Whyte Av
Fraser St
Ardoch Gv
Ardoch Medical Cen
The Surg
Cambuslang Stn
Myrtle Wk
Bank St
Surgeries
Council Building
Central Avenue
Prospect Avenue
Balmoral Dr
Milton Av
Richmond Dr
Buchanan Drive
Wellshot Drive
West Coats Road
Hamilton Drive
Busheyhill St
Tabernacle St
St Bride's Primary School
Calder Dr
Cadzow Dr
Brownside Road
West Coats Prim Sch
Douglas Dr
Douglas Gate
Kirkhill Station
Hunterfield Dr
Stewarton Drive
W Coats Rd
Grenville Drive
Douglas Drive
Mansefield Av
Holmhill Av
Burnside Av
Kirkburn Av
Whitefield Avenue
Cathkin High School
Whitlawburn Av
Holmhills Gdns
Holmhills Rd
Holmhills Ter
Holmhills Grove
Holmhills Dr
Greenlees Pk
Kirkhill Gdns
Clifton Ter
Whitlawburn Shopping Centre
Arkle Ter
Western Road
Rona Ter
Lorne Ter
Staffa Rd
Kirkhill Ter
Kirkhill Avenue
Albany Ter
Gartmore Terrace
Maxton Ter
Aron Ter
Morven Road
Greenlees Gdns
East Greenlees Road
Kirkhill Golf Club
Belmont Rd
Road
1 grid square represents 500 metres

113
65
Cambuslang Golf Club
Clydeford Road
Golf Course
Westburn Road
Mill Road
Birch Dr
Elm Dr
Rwn Pl
Fir Pl
Birch Dr
Queen's Av
Kings Cres
Elm Drive
Westburn Cemetery
Old Mill Rd
Hmltn Rd
Surgery
Vicars Wk
Crescent
Croft Road
Cadoc St
Meek Pl
Kirkton Rd
Cambuslang College
Cairns Av
Robert Templeton Dr
A724
HAMILTON ROAD
Hwshl Av
Howieshill Rd
Macarthur Wynd
Macdougal Dr
M Wy
Macfarlane Crs
Cambuslang
134
Braeside Pl
Huntly Dr
Cairns
Kinloch Av
Woodland Pl
Janebank Av
Hamilton Crs
Langcroft Dr
Rosebank Drive
Cairnswell Avenue
Lilybank Avenue
Ivybank Avenue
St Cadoc's Primary Sch
Cairns Primary Sch
Wellside Dr
Mill Road
Wlfr
Overton St
Craigallian Avenue
Castle
CAMBUSLANG
Flemington
Tanzieknowe Road
E Greenlees Crs
E Greenlees Av
Auld Kirk Rd
Gilbertfield
East Greenlees Drive
Road
659
65
C
D
1
2
3
4

A
114
B
266
Westburn
Westburn Road
Mill Road
Newton
Lockhart Avenue
Mitchell Av
Henderson Av
McIver St
Dunlop St
Westburn Rd
Northbank Avenue
PO
Westburn Cemetery
Westburn
Old Mill Rd
Mill Road
Annick St
Wiston St
Montgomery St
Medwin St
Graham Av
Gateside Avenue
Acacia Way
Station Rd
Newton Station
Alder Gate
Ash Wynd
Hall
Village
Glencairn Gardens
Macfarlane Crs
M Wy
Macarthur Wynd
133
Cambuslang Recreation Centre
Overton Road
Mill Road
Overton St
Clyde Place
Graham Av
Hallside Primary Sch
Newton St Rd
Cedar Ct
Beech
Cherrytree Dr
Hallside Rd
New Rd
Overton Rd
School La
Elm Wy
Elder Ct
Fir
Hawthorn Gdns
Hamilton
Crs
Drive
St Cadoc's Primary Sch
Avenue
Wellside Dr
Surg
PO
Dn Pk Dr
Craigallian Avenue
A724
Castle Chimmins Av
Lightburn
Helenslea
Claude Av
Council Building
Flemington Industrial Est
Hutchinson Pl
Laburnum Av
Larch Cl
Deans Av
Dechmont
Castle Chimmins Road
Quarry Av
Road
Campsie View
Auld Kirk Rd
Gilbertfield Road
Letterickhills Crs
Gilbertfield Road
1
2
3
4
A
B
G72
266
I grid square represents 500 metres

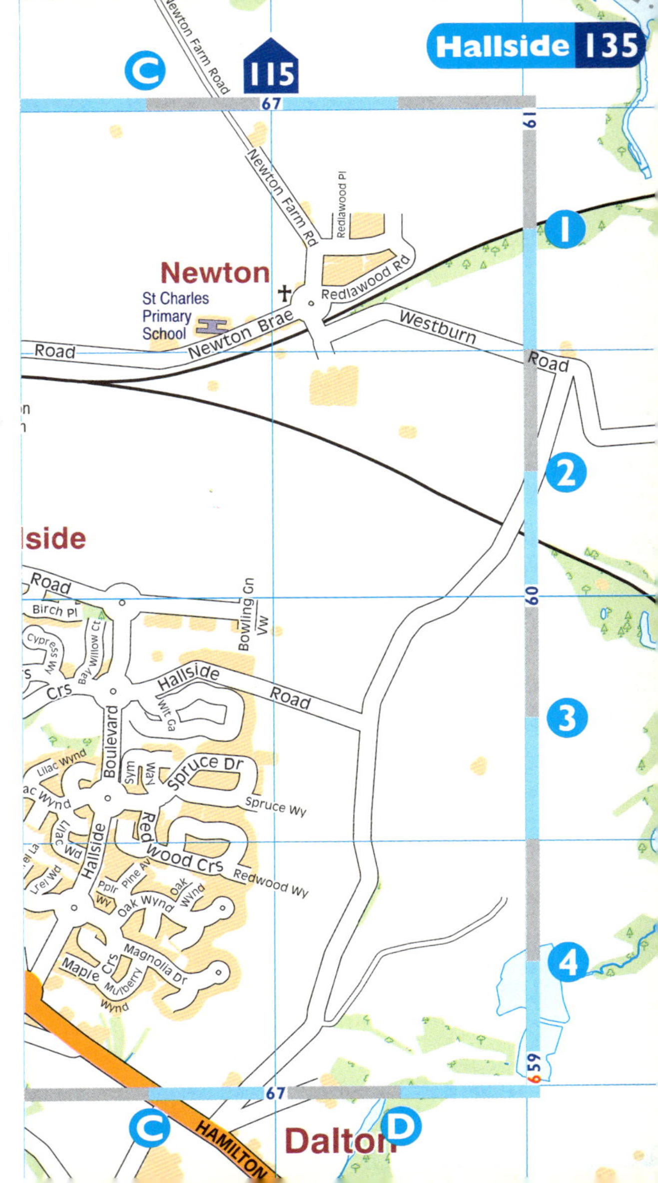
C
115
67
61
Newton Farm Road
Newton Farm Rd
Redlawood Pl
Redlawood Rd
Newton
St Charles
Primary
School
Newton Brae
Road
Westburn
Road
1
2
lside
Road
Birch Pl
Bay Willow Ct
Bowling Gn
Vw
60
3
Hallside
Road
Crs
Wit Ga
Boulevard
Lilac Wynd
Spruce Dr
Spruce Wy
Red
wood Crs
Redwood Wy
Hallside
Pine Av
Oak Wynd
Oak Wynd
Magnolia Dr
Maple Crs
Mulberry Wynd
4
659
67
C
D
HAMILTON
Dalton

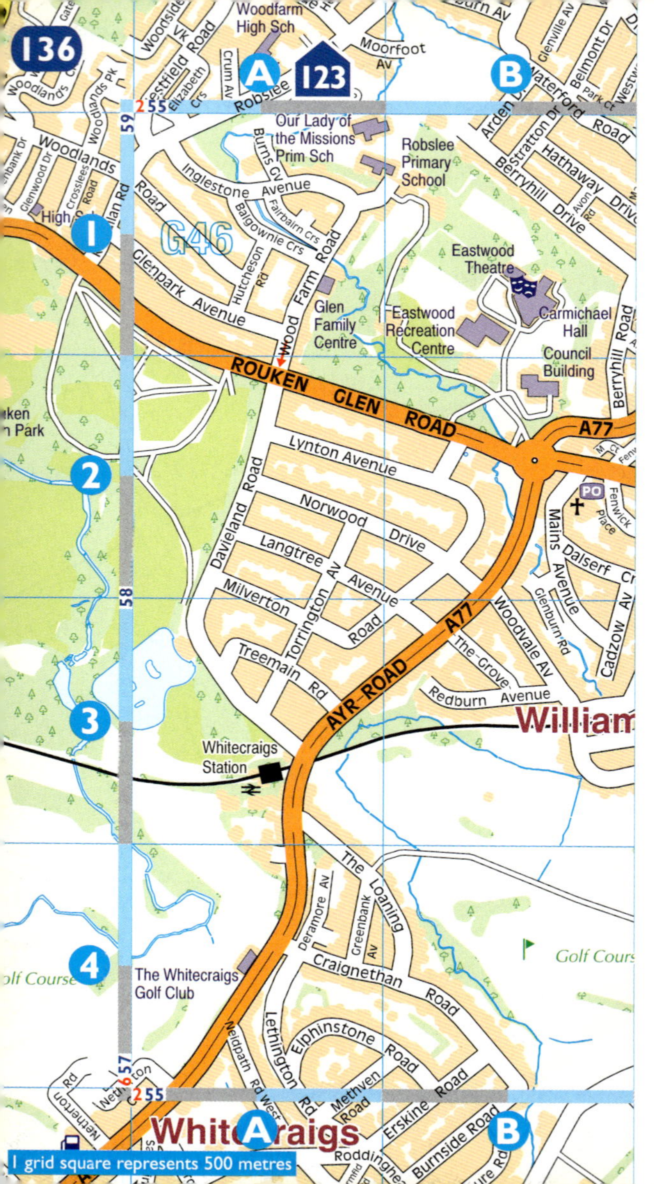
123
A
B
Woodfarm High Sch
Moorfoot Av
Robslee
Crum Av
Elizabeth Crs
Woodlands Pk
Woodlands Cr
Woodlands Road
Glenwood Dr
Crosslees Road
High Sch
Our Lady of the Missions Prim Sch
Burns Gv
Robslee Primary School
Inglestone Avenue
Fairbairn Crs
Balgownie Crs
Hutcheson Rd
Wood Farm Road
G46
Glenpark Avenue
Glen Family Centre
Eastwood Recreation Centre
Eastwood Theatre
Carmichael Hall
Council Building
Arden Dr
Waterford Road
Stratton Dr
Hathaway Drive
Berryhill Drive
Avon Rd
Belmont Dr
Glenville Av
Park Ct
Berryhill Road
ROUKEN GLEN ROAD
A77
Lynton Avenue
Davieland Road
Norwood Drive
Langtree Av
Avenue
Milverton Road
Torrington Av
Treemain Rd
AYR ROAD
The Grove
Woodvale Av
Redburn Avenue
Mains Avenue
Dalserf Cr
Glenburn Rd
Cadzow Av
Fenwick Place
PO
William
Whitecraigs Station
The Loaning
Deramore Av
Greenbank Av
Craignethan Road
The Whitecraigs Golf Club
Golf Course
Golf Cours
Neidpath Rd West
Lethington Rd
Elphinstone Road
Methven Road
Erskine Road
Burnside Road
Netherton Rd
Whitecraigs
1
2
3
4
59
58
57
256
255
1 grid square represents 500 metres

124
Giffnock
Clarkston
Williamwood
Eastwoodmains Road
Williamwood Station
Williamwood Medical Cen
Williamwood High Sch
Isobel Mair School
Cathcart Castle Golf Club
Council Building
Synagogue
Hotel
Surg
Giffnock Prim Sch
Church Road
Mearns Road
Beechlands Drive
Sunnybank
Queensberry Avenue
Dumgoyne Place
Golf Road
Stewart Drive
Lomondside Avenue
Campsie Gardens
Fereneze Avenue
Cathkin Gardens
Kilpatrick Drive
Vardar Avenue
Seres Road
Quarrybrae Av
Burnside Gdns
Greenwood
Gloucester Av
Highfield Dr
Knollpark Drive
Sunbury Avenue
Lothian Drive
Sunnyside
Cleuch Gdns
Morven Dr
Lembert Dr
Moraine Dr
Rockburn Dr
Struma
Dorian Drive
Atholl Drive
Balmeg Av
Dornoch Av
Denholm Dr
Greenhill Av
Ailsa Drive
Carrick Crs
Etive Dr
Sutherland Drive
Ruthven Av
Lawrence Av
Bromley Dr
Bromley La
Douglas Gdns
Percy Drive
Douglas Av
Seyton Av
Montgomery Drive
Otterburn Drive
Florence Drive
Claremont Avenue
St Ann's Dr
Arthurlie Drive
Eglinton Dr
Maryville Avenue
Park Rd
Elliot Dr
Rowand Av
Penrith Av
Eastwood Av
Huntly Av
Forres Avenue
Forres Gate
Keith Av
Bulloch Rd
Melford Avenue
Brora Dr
Clyth Drive
Deveron Av
Evan Crescent
Evan Drive
Drumby Crs
Hillview Drive
Mayfield Av
Mansfield Road
Mansfield Crs
Daleview
Flenders Rd
Golf C

Annlesland 39 C1
Arden 121 C3
Auchenback 118 B4
Auchinairn 32 B4
Baillieston 96 B3
Balornock 47 C1
Bankhead 129 C1
Bargeddie 99 C3
Barlanark 95 C1
Barmulloch 48 A2
Barrachnie 95 C2
Barrhead 118 B2
Battlefield 106 A3
Bearsden 15 C2
Bellahouston 84 A2
Birkenshaw 117 D2
Bishopbriggs 32 B1
Blackhall 78 A4
Blythswood 35 D2
Braidfauld 92 A4
Bridgeton 90 A2
Broomhill 40 A4
Broomhouse 115 D1
Burnside 130 B2
Cadder 19 D2
Calton 9 E4
Cambuslang 132 B3
Cardonald 81 D2
Carmyle 113 C3
Carntyne 68 B4
Carnwadric 123 C3
Castlehead 76 B4
Cathcart 126 A1
Clarkston 137 D4
Clydebank 20 A2
Colston 31 C3
Corkerhill 102 B1
Cowlairs 46 A4
Craigend 50 B4
Craigton 83 C2
Cranhill 69 D3
Criagendmuir 51 D3
Croftfoot 128 B2
Crookston 80 B3
Crosshill 97 D2
Crossmill 118 B1
Crossmyloof 105 C1
Dalmarnock 90 A4
Dean Park 56 A1
Dennistoun 66 B4
Dovecothall 119 D1
Dowanhill 41 D4
Drumchapel 13 C4
Drumry 21 C1
Dumbreck 84 B3
Easterhouse 72 B3
Eastfield 111 C4
Flemington 133 D4
Fullarton 93 C4
Gallowhill 54 B4
Garrowhill 96 A2
Garthamlock 71 C1
Germiston 67 C1
Giffnock 137 D1
Glasgow 8 A1
Gorbals 88 A2
Govan 61 C3
Govanhill 87 C4
Greenfield 93 C1
Haghill 68 A4
Hallside 134 B2
High Crosshill 130 A1
Hillington 81 C1
Hogganfield 69 C1
Hurlet 100 A4
Hutchesontown 88 A3
Ibrox 84 B1
Jordanhill 39 C2
Kelvindale 41 D1
Kelvinside 40 B2
Kennishead 122 B2
Kessington 17 C3
Kings Park 128 A1
Knightswood 24 A4
Kylepark 117 C4
Lambhill 29 D4
Langside 105 D4
Lochwood 74 A2
Mansewood 124 A1
Maryhill 26 B4
Merrylee 125 C3
Millerston 49 D3
Milngavie 11 D2
Milton 30 A4
Mosspark 83 C4
Mount Florida 107 C4
Mount Vernon 113 D1
Muirend 126 A1
Muirhead 95 D4
Netherlee 125 D4
Newlands 125 C1
Newton 135 C1
Nitshill 120 A2
Oatlands 88 B4
Old Balornock 47 C2
Oldhall 79 D2
Paisley 77 D3
Parkhead 91 D3
Partick 60 B1
Petershill 47 C4
Pollok 101 C1
Pollokshaws 104 A3
Pollokshields 85 D4
Polmadie 107 D1
Port Dundas 3 F1
Porterfield 54 B1
Possil Park 44 B2
Priesthill 120 B1
Provanmill 48 B4
Queenslie 71 C3
Renfrew 35 D4
Riddrie 68 A2
Robroyston 48 B1
Royston 5 D2
Ruchazie 70 A2
Ruchill 43 D2
Rutherglen 108 B2
Scotstoun 38 A2
Shawlands 105 C3
Shettleston 93 C2
Shieldhall 58 B3
Shortroods 52 B3
Sighthill 5 D1
Springboig 94 A1
Springburn 46 A3
Stepps 50 B2
Strathbungo 105 D1
Summerston 28 B2
Swinton 97 C1
Temple 25 C4
Thornliebank 122 B4
Townhead 4 B4
Victory Gardens 55 D2
Westburn 134 B1
West Drumoyne 59 D4
Whitecrook 21 D3
Whiteinch 59 D1
Williamwood 136 B3
Yoker 22 A4
Yorkhill 61 D3

USING THE STREET INDEX

Street names are listed alphabetically. Each street name is followed by its postal town or area locality, the Postcode District, the page number, and the reference to the square in which the name is found.

Standard index entries are shown as follows:

Abbey Cl *PSLY* PA1 ....**77** C2

Street names and selected addresses not shown on the map due to scale restrictions are shown in the index with an asterisk:

Beechgrove St *DMNK/BRGTN* G40 * **110** A1

GENERAL ABBREVIATIONS

ACC	ACCESS
ALY	ALLEY
AP	APPROACH
AR	ARCADE
ASS	ASSOCIATION
AV	AVENUE
BCH	BEACH
BLDS	BUILDINGS
BND	BEND
BNK	BANK
BR	BRIDGE
BRK	BROOK
BTM	BOTTOM
BUS	BUSINESS
BVD	BOULEVARD
BY	BYPASS
CATH	CATHEDRAL
CEM	CEMETERY
CEN	CENTRE
CFT	CROFT
CH	CHURCH
CHA	CHASE
CHYD	CHURCHYARD
CIR	CIRCLE
CIRC	CIRCUS
CL	CLOSE
CLFS	CLIFFS
CMP	CAMP
CNR	CORNER
CO	COUNTY
COLL	COLLEGE
COM	COMMON
COMM	COMMISSION
CON	CONVENT
COT	COTTAGE
COTS	COTTAGES
CP	CAPE
CPS	COPSE
CR	CREEK
CREM	CREMATORIUM
CRS	CRESCENT
CSWY	CAUSEWAY
CT	COURT
CTRL	CENTRAL
CTS	COURTS
CTYD	COURTYARD
CUTT	CUTTINGS
CV	COVE
CYN	CANYON
DEPT	DEPARTMENT
DL	DALE
DM	DAM
DR	DRIVE
DRO	DROVE
DRY	DRIVEWAY
DWGS	DWELLINGS
E	EAST
EMB	EMBANKMENT
EMBY	EMBASSY
ESP	ESPLANADE
EST	ESTATE
EX	EXCHANGE
EXPY	EXPRESSWAY
EXT	EXTENSION
F/O	FLYOVER
FC	FOOTBALL CLUB
FK	FORK
FLD	FIELD
FLDS	FIELDS
FLS	FALLS
FLS	FLATS
FM	FARM
FT	FORT
FWY	FREEWAY
FY	FERRY
GA	GATE
GAL	GALLERY
GDN	GARDEN
GDNS	GARDENS
GLD	GLADE
GLN	GLEN
GN	GREEN
GND	GROUND
GRA	GRANGE
GRG	GARAGE
GT	GREAT
GTWY	GATEWAY
GV	GROVE
HGR	HIGHER
HL	HILL
HLS	HILLS
HO	HOUSE
HOL	HOLLOW
HOSP	HOSPITAL
HRB	HARBOUR
HTH	HEATH
HTS	HEIGHTS
HVN	HAVEN
HWY	HIGHWAY
IMP	IMPERIAL
IN	INLET
IND EST	INDUSTRIAL ESTATE
INF	INFIRMARY
INFO	INFORMATION
INT	INTERCHANGE
IS	ISLAND
JCT	JUNCTION
JTY	JETTY
KG	KING
KNL	KNOLL
L	LAKE
LA	LANE
LDG	LODGE
LGT	LIGHT
LK	LOCK
LKS	LAKES
LNDG	LANDING
LTL	LITTLE
LWR	LOWER
MAG	MAGISTRATE
MAN	MANSIONS
MD	MEAD
MDW	MEADOWS
MEM	MEMORIAL
MKT	MARKET
MKTS	MARKETS
ML	MALL
ML	MILL
MNR	MANOR
MS	MEWS
MSN	MISSION
MT	MOUNT
MTN	MOUNTAIN
MTS	MOUNTAINS
MUS	MUSEUM
MWY	MOTORWAY
N	NORTH
NE	NORTH EAST
NW	NORTH WEST
O/P	OVERPASS
OFF	OFFICE
ORCH	ORCHARD
OV	OVAL
PAL	PALACE
PAS	PASSAGE
PAV	PAVILION
PDE	PARADE
PH	PUBLIC HOUSE
PK	PARK
PKWY	PARKWAY
PL	PLACE
PLN	PLAIN
PLNS	PLAINS
PLZ	PLAZA
POL	POLICE STATION
PR	PRINCE
PREC	PRECINCT
PREP	PREPARATORY
PRIM	PRIMARY
PROM	PROMENADE
PRS	PRINCESS
PRT	PORT
PT	POINT
PTH	PATH
PZ	PIAZZA
QD	QUADRANT
QU	QUEEN
QY	QUAY
R	RIVER
RBT	ROUNDABOUT
RD	ROAD
RDG	RIDGE
REP	REPUBLIC
RES	RESERVOIR

RFC .... RUGBY FOOTBALL CLUB
RI .... RISE
RP .... RAMP
RW .... ROW
S .... SOUTH
SCH .... SCHOOL
SE .... SOUTH EAST
SER .... SERVICE AREA
SH .... SHORE
SHOP .... SHOPPING
SKWY .... SKYWAY
SMT .... SUMMIT
SOC .... SOCIETY
SP .... SPUR
SPR .... SPRING
SQ .... SQUARE
ST .... STREET
STN .... STATION
STR .... STREAM
STRD .... STRAND
SW .... SOUTH WEST
TDG .... TRADING
TER .... TERRACE
THWY .... THROUGHWAY
TNL .... TUNNEL
TOLL .... TOLLWAY
TPK .... TURNPIKE
TR .... TRACK
TRL .... TRAIL
TWR .... TOWER
U/P .... UNDERPASS
UNI .... UNIVERSITY
UPR .... UPPER
V .... VALE
VA .... VALLEY
VIAD .... VIADUCT
VIL .... VILLA
VIS .... VISTA
VLG .... VILLAGE
VLS .... VILLAS
VW .... VIEW
W .... WEST
WD .... WOOD
WHF .... WHARF
WK .... WALK
WKS .... WALKS
WLS .... WELLS
WY .... WAY
YD .... YARD
YHA .... YOUTH HOSTEL

POSTCODE TOWNS AND AREA ABBREVIATIONS

BAIL/MDB/MHD ......Baillieston/Moodiesburn/Muirhead
BLTYR/CAMB ....Blantyre/Cambuslang
BRHD/NEIL ....Barrhead/Neilston
BSDN ....Bearsden
BSHPBGS ....Bishopbriggs
CAR/SHTL ....Carmyle/Shettleston
CARD/HILL/MSPK ....Cardonald/Hillington/Mosspark
CGLE ....Central Glasgow east
CGLW ....Central Glasgow west
CLYDBK ....Clydebank
COWCAD ....Cowcaddens
CRMNK/CLK/EAG ......Carmunnock/Clarkston/Eaglesham
CSMK ....Castlemilk
CTBR ....Coatbridge
DEN/PKHD ....Dennistoun/Parkhead
DMNK/BRGTN ....Dalmarnock/Bridgeton
DRUM ....Drumchapel
ESTRH ....Easterhouse
GBLS ....Gorbals
GIF/THBK ....Giffnock/Thornliebank
GOV/IBX ....Govan/Ibrox
GVH/MTFL ....Govanhill/Mount Florida
KNTSWD ....Knightswood
KVD/HLHD ....Kelvindale/Hillhead
KVGV ....Kelvingrove
LNPK/KPK ....Linn Park/King's Park
MLNGV ....Milngavie
MRYH/FIRH ....Maryhill/Firhill
NMRNS ....Newton Mearns
PLK/PH/NH ....Pollock/Priesthill/Nitshill
PLKSD/SHW ....Pollockshields/Shawlands
PLKSW/MSWD ....Pollockshaws/Mansewood
PPK/MIL ....Possil Park/Milton
PSLY ....Paisley
PSLYN/LNWD ....Paisley north/Linwood
PSLYS ....Paisley south
PTCK ....Partick
RNFRW ....Renfrew
RUTH ....Rutherglen
SCOT ....Scotstoun
SMSTN ....Summerston
SPRGB/BLRNK ....Springburn/Balornock
STPS/GTHM/RID ....Stepps/Garthamlock/Riddrie
UD/BTH/TAN ....Uddingston/Bothwell/Tannochside

Index - streets

Abb - Aco

A

Abbey Cl *PSLY* PA1 ....**77** C2
Abbeycraig Rd *ESTRH* G34 ....**74** B3
Abbey Dr *SCOT* G14 ....**39** D3
Abbeygreen St *ESTRH* G34 ....**74** B2
Abbeyhill St *CAR/SHTL* G32 ....**68** B4
Abbotsford *BSHPBGS* G64 ....**33** C1
Abbotsford Av *RUTH* G73 ....**110** A4
Abbotsford Pl *GBLS* G5 ....**87** D3
Abbotsford Rd *BSDN* G61 ....**14** A1
CLYDBK G81 ....**20** B2
Abbotshall Av *DRUM* G15 ....**12** A4
Abbotsinch Rd *PSLYN/LNWD* PA3 ....**53** D2
Abbot St *PLKSD/SHW* G41 ....**105** D2
PSLYN/LNWD PA3 ....**77** D1
Abbott Crs *CLYDBK* G81 ....**21** D3
Aberconway St *CLYDBK* G81 ....**21** C3
Abercorn Av *CARD/HILL/MSPK* G52 ....**56** B4
Abercorn Pl *SMSTN* G23 ....**28** A2
Abercorn St *PSLYN/LNWD* PA3 ....**77** D2
Abercrombie Crs *BAIL/MDB/MHD* G69 ....**98** B2
Abercromby Dr *DMNK/BRGTN* G40 ....**9** F4
Abercromby St *DMNK/BRGTN* G40 ....**9** F5
Aberdalgie Gdns *ESTRH* G34 ....**73** C3
Aberdalgie Rd *ESTRH* G34 ....**73** C3
Aberdour St *DEN/PKHD* G31 ....**67** D4
Aberfeldy St *DEN/PKHD* G31 ....**67** D4
Aberfoyle St *DEN/PKHD* G31 ....**67** D4
Aberlady Rd *GOV/IBX* G51 ....**59** D4
Abernethy St *DEN/PKHD* G31 ....**67** D4
Aberuthven Dr *CAR/SHTL* G32 ....**93** D4
Aboukir St *GOV/IBX* G51 ....**59** D3
Aboyne St *GOV/IBX* G51 ....**83** D1
Acacia Wy *BLTYR/CAMB* G72 ....**134** B2
Academy Pk *PLKSD/SHW* G41 ....**85** C3
Academy Rd *GIF/THBK* G46 ....**137** C1
Academy St *CAR/SHTL* G32 ....**93** D3
Achamore Crs *DRUM* G15 ....**12** A3
Achamore Dr *DRUM* G15 ....**12** A3
Achamore Rd *DRUM* G15 ....**12** A3
Acherhill Gdns *KNTSWD* G13 ....**23** C3
Acorn St *DMNK/BRGTN* G40 ....**89** D3

Acre Dr *MRYH/FIRH* G20 26 B2
Acredyke Crs *SPRGB/BLRNK* G21 32 B4
Acredyke Pl *SPRGB/BLRNK* G21 47 D1
Acredyke Rd *RUTH* G73 109 C3
SPRGB/BLRNK G21 32 B4
Acre Rd *MRYH/FIRH* G20 26 B2
Adams Court La *CGLE* G1 7 E3
Adamswell St *SPRGB/BLRNK* G21 45 D4
Addiewell St *CAR/SHTL* G32 69 D4
Addison Gv *GIF/THBK* G46 122 B3
Addison Pl *GIF/THBK* G46 122 B3
Addison Rd *GIF/THBK* G46 122 B3
KVD/HLHD G12 42 A3
Adelphi St *GBLS* G5 88 B3
Admiral St *PLKSD/SHW* G41 86 A2
Advie Pl *GVH/MTFL* G42 107 C3
Afton Crs *BSDN* G61 16 B4
Afton Dr *RNFRW* PA4 56 B1
Afton St *PLKSD/SHW* G41 105 D3
Agnew La *GVH/MTFL* G42 106 B2
Aikenhead Rd *GVH/MTFL* G42 107 D1
LNPK/KPK G44 127 D1
Ailean Dr *CAR/SHTL* G32 95 C3
Ailean Gdns *CAR/SHTL* G32 95 C3
Ailort Av *LNPK/KPK* G44 126 B2
Ailsa Dr *GIF/THBK* G46 137 C3
GVH/MTFL G42 106 A4
RUTH G73 129 C2
Ailsa Rd *BSHPBGS* G64 32 B1
RNFRW PA4 55 D1
Ainslie Av *CARD/HILL/MSPK* G52 57 D3
Ainslie Rd *CARD/HILL/MSPK* G52 57 D4
Airdale Av *GIF/THBK* G46 137 C1
Airgold Dr *DRUM* G15 12 B3
Airlie Gdns *RUTH* G73 131 C3
Airlie La *KVD/HLHD* G12 41 C4
Airlie Rd *BAIL/MDB/MHD* G69 96 A4
Airlie St *KVD/HLHD* G12 41 C4
Airlour Rd *PLKSW/MSWD* G43 125 D2
Airth Dr *CARD/HILL/MSPK* G52 83 D4
Airth La *CARD/HILL/MSPK* G52 83 D4
Airthrey Av *SCOT* G14 39 D3
Airthrey La *SCOT* G14 39 D3
Aitkenhead Av *CTBR* ML5 99 D3
Aitken St *DEN/PKHD* G31 90 B1
Alasdair Ct *BRHD/NEIL* G78 118 B3
Albany Av *CAR/SHTL* G32 94 A1
Albany Dr *RUTH* G73 130 A1
Albany Qd *CAR/SHTL* G32 94 A1
Albany St *DMNK/BRGTN* G40 90 A3
Albany Ter *BLTYR/CAMB* G72 131 D4
Albert Av *GVH/MTFL* G42 106 B2
Albert Br *GBLS* G5 8 A5
Albert Dr *BSDN* G61 16 B4
PLKSD/SHW G41 86 A3
RUTH G73 130 A2
Albert Rd *GVH/MTFL* G42 106 B2
RNFRW PA4 35 D4
Albion Ga *CGLE* G1 8 B2
Albion St *BAIL/MDB/MHD* G69 95 D4
CGLE G1 8 B2
PSLYN/LNWD PA3 76 B1
Alcaig Rd *CARD/HILL/MSPK* G52 102 B1
Alder Ct *BRHD/NEIL* G78 118 B4
Alder Ga *BLTYR/CAMB* G72 134 B2
Alderman Pl *KNTSWD* G13 38 B1
Alderman Rd *KNTSWD* G13 22 B4
Alder Pl *PLKSW/MSWD* G43 124 A2
Alder Rd *PLKSW/MSWD* G43 124 B2
Alderside Gdns *UD/BTH/TAN* G71 117 D4
Alexander Crs *GBLS* G5 88 A3
Alexander St *CLYDBK* G81 20 B2
Alexandra Av *STPS/GTHM/RID* G33 51 C1
Alexandra Ct *DEN/PKHD* G31 67 C3
Alexandra Dr *RNFRW* PA4 36 A4
Alexandra Pde *DEN/PKHD* G31 5 F4
Alexandra Park St *DEN/PKHD* G31 67 C3
Alford St *SPRGB/BLRNK* G21 45 C4
Alfred La *KVD/HLHD* G12 42 B4
Algie St *PLKSD/SHW* G41 106 A3
Aline Ct *BRHD/NEIL* G78 118 A1
Allan Av *RNFRW* PA4 56 B2
Allander Gdns *BSHPBGS* G64 18 B3
Allander Rd *MLNGV* G62 10 B1
Allander St *PPK/MIL* G22 44 B3
Allan Glen Gdns *BSHPBGS* G64 19 D3
Allan Pl *DMNK/BRGTN* G40 90 B4
Allan St *DMNK/BRGTN* G40 110 A1
Allanton Av *PSLY* PA1 80 A3
Allanton Dr *CARD/HILL/MSPK* G52 81 D2
Allender Rd *BSDN* G61 14 B4
Allen Wy *RNFRW* PA4 56 A2
Allerdyce Dr *DRUM* G15 22 B2
Allerton Gdns *CAR/SHTL* G32 95 D3
Alleysbank Rd *RUTH* G73 109 D2
Allison Dr *BLTYR/CAMB* G72 132 B1
Allison St *GVH/MTFL* G42 106 B1
Allnach Pl *ESTRH* G34 74 B3
Alloway Crs *RUTH* G73 129 C2
Alloway Dr *RUTH* G73 129 C2
Alloway Rd *PLKSW/MSWD* G43 125 C1
Almond Av *RNFRW* PA4 56 B1
Almond Rd *BSDN* G61 24 A1
STPS/GTHM/RID G33 50 B2
Almond St *STPS/GTHM/RID* G33 68 A2
Alness Crs *CARD/HILL/MSPK* G52 82 B4
Alsatian Av *CLYDBK* G81 21 D1
Alton Rd *PSLY* PA1 79 C3
Altyre St *CAR/SHTL* G32 92 B4
Alva Gdns *CARD/HILL/MSPK* G52 102 B1
Alva Ga *CARD/HILL/MSPK* G52 83 C4
Alyth Gdns *CARD/HILL/MSPK* G52 83 C4
Amisfield St *MRYH/FIRH* G20 42 B2
Amulree Pl *CAR/SHTL* G32 93 C3
Amulree St *CAR/SHTL* G32 93 C4
Ancaster Dr *KNTSWD* G13 40 A1
Ancaster La *KNTSWD* G13 40 A1
Anchor Av *PSLY* PA1 78 A3
Anchor Crs *PSLY* PA1 78 A4
Anchor Dr *PSLY* PA1 78 A3
Anchor La *CGLE* G1 7 F1
Anchor Wynd *PSLY* PA1 78 A4
Ancroft St *MRYH/FIRH* G20 43 D4
Anderson Dr *RNFRW* PA4 36 A3
Anderson St *PTCK* G11 61 C1
Anderston Quay *KVGV* G3 6 A3
Andrew Av *RNFRW* PA4 36 B4
Andrew Dr *CLYDBK* G81 21 C3
Andrew Sillars Av *BLTYR/CAMB* G72 133 D2
Andrews St *PSLYN/LNWD* PA3 76 B1
Angle Ga *SCOT* G14 39 C3
Angus Av *BSHPBGS* G64 33 D2
CARD/HILL/MSPK G52 82 A4
Angus Ov *CARD/HILL/MSPK* G52 81 D3
Angus Pl *CARD/HILL/MSPK* G52 81 D3
Angus St *CLYDBK* G81 22 A3
SPRGB/BLRNK G21 45 D3
Anish Pl *DRUM* G15 12 A3
Annandale St *GVH/MTFL* G42 87 D4
Annan Dr *BSDN* G61 14 A4
RUTH G73 111 C4
Annan St *GVH/MTFL* G42 106 B3
Annbank Pl *DEN/PKHD* G31 89 D1
Annbank St *DEN/PKHD* G31 89 D1
Anne Av *RNFRW* PA4 36 A3
Annes Ct *DMNK/BRGTN* G40 89 C3
Annette St *GVH/MTFL* G42 106 B1
Annfield Pl *DEN/PKHD* G31 66 A4
Annick Dr *BSDN* G61 14 A4
Annick St *BLTYR/CAMB* G72 134 A2
Anniesdale Av *STPS/GTHM/RID* G33 51 C1
Anniesland Crs *SCOT* G14 37 D2
Anniesland Rd *KNTSWD* G13 39 C1
SCOT G14 37 D2
Anson St *DMNK/BRGTN* G40 89 D3
Anstruther St *CAR/SHTL* G32 92 B3
Anthony St *CGLW* G2 6 B1
Antonine Rd *BSDN* G61 13 D1
Anwoth St *CAR/SHTL* G32 93 C4
Appin Crs *DEN/PKHD* G31 67 C4
Appin Rd *DEN/PKHD* G31 67 D4
Appin Ter *RUTH* G73 131 C3
Appleby St *PPK/MIL* G22 44 A4
Applecross St *MRYH/FIRH* G20 44 A4
Apsley La *PTCK* G11 60 B1
Apsley St *PTCK* G11 60 B1
Aranthrue Crs *RNFRW* PA4 35 D3
Aranthrue Dr *RNFRW* PA4 35 D3
Aray St *MRYH/FIRH* G20 42 A1
Arbroath Av *CARD/HILL/MSPK* G52 81 D3
Arcadia St *DMNK/BRGTN* G40 89 C3
Arcan Crs *DRUM* G15 23 D1
Archerfield Av *CAR/SHTL* G32 112 B1
Archerfield Crs *CAR/SHTL* G32 112 B1
Archerfield Dr *CAR/SHTL* G32 112 B1
Archerfield Gv *CAR/SHTL* G32 112 B1
Archerhill Av *KNTSWD* G13 23 C3
Archerhill Crs *KNTSWD* G13 23 D3
Archerhill Rd *KNTSWD* G13 23 D3
Archerhill Sq *KNTSWD* G13 22 B3

Archerhill Ter *KNTSWD* G13 ....23 C3
Ardargie Dr *CAR/SHTL* G32 ....113 D3
Ardargie Gv *CAR/SHTL* G32 ....113 D3
Ardargie Pl *CAR/SHTL* G32 ....113 D3
Ardbeg Av *BSHPBGS* G64 ....33 C2
RUTH G73 ....131 D4
Ardbeg La *GVH/MTFL* G42 ....106 B1
Ardbeg St *GVH/MTFL* G42 ....106 B1
Ardconnel St *GIF/THBK* G46 ....123 C3
Ardencraig Pl *CSMK* G45 ....128 B4
Ardencraig St *CSMK* G45 ....129 D4
Arden Dr *GIF/THBK* G46 ....136 B1
Ardenlea St *DMNK/BRGTN* G40 ....90 B4
Ardery St *PTCK* G11 ....60 B1
Ardessie St *SMSTN* G23 ....27 D2
Ardfern St *CAR/SHTL* G32 ....93 C4
Ardgay Pl *CAR/SHTL* G32 ....93 C3
Ardgay St *CAR/SHTL* G32 ....93 C3
Ardgay Wy *RUTH* G73 ....130 A4
Ardgowan Av *PSLYS* PA2 ....77 D4
Ardholm St *CAR/SHTL* G32 ....93 C2
Ardhu Pl *DRUM* G15 ....12 B3
Ardlaw St *GOV/IBX* G51 ....83 D1
Ardle Rd *PLKSW/MSWD* G43 ....125 D2
Ardlui St *CAR/SHTL* G32 ....92 B3
Ardmay Crs *LNPK/KPK* G44 ....107 D4
Ardmillan St *STPS/GTHM/RID* G33 ....69 C3
Ardmory Av *GVH/MTFL* G42 ....108 B4
Ardmory La *RUTH* G73 ....108 B4
Ardmory Pl *GVH/MTFL* G42 ....108 B4
Ardnahoe Av *GVH/MTFL* G42 ....108 B4
Ardnahoe Pl *GVH/MTFL* G42 ....108 A3
Ardneil Rd *GOV/IBX* G51 ....83 D1
Ardnish St *GOV/IBX* G51 ....59 C4
Ardoch Gv *BLTYR/CAMB* G72 ....132 A1
Ardoch Rd *BSDN* G61 ....16 B2
Ardoch St *PPK/MIL* G22 ....44 B3
Ardo Gdns *GOV/IBX* G51 ....84 A2
Ard Rd *RNFRW* PA4 ....35 C3
Ardshiel Rd *GOV/IBX* G51 ....59 D4
Ardsloy Pl *SCOT* G14 ....37 D3
Ard St *CAR/SHTL* G32 ....93 C3
Ardtoe Crs *STPS/GTHM/RID* G33 ....51 D2
Ardtoe Pl *STPS/GTHM/RID* G33 ....51 D2
Arduthie Rd *GOV/IBX* G51 ....59 D4
Ardwell Rd *CARD/HILL/MSPK* G52 ....83 C4
Argyle St *CGLW* G2 ....6 B2
KVGV G3 ....62 A2
KVGV G3 ....62 B4
PSLY PA1 ....76 B3
Argyll Ar *CGLE* G1 ....7 E2
Argyll Av *PSLYN/LNWD* PA3 ....53 D2
RNFRW PA4 ....35 C3
Argyll Rd *CLYDBK* G81 ....20 B3
Arisaig Dr *BSDN* G61 ....16 B4
CARD/HILL/MSPK G52 ....82 B4
Arisaig Pl *CARD/HILL/MSPK* G52 ....83 C4
Ark La *DEN/PKHD* G31 ....9 F1
Arkleston Crs *PSLYN/LNWD* PA3 ....55 C4
Arkleston Rd *PSLY* PA1 ....78 B1
PSLYN/LNWD PA3 ....55 D4
Arkle Ter *BLTYR/CAMB* G72 ....131 D4
Arklet Rd *GOV/IBX* G51 ....83 C1
Arlington St *KVGV* G3 ....2 A2
Armadale Pl *DEN/PKHD* G31 ....66 B3
Armadale St *DEN/PKHD* G31 ....66 B3
Armour St *COWCAD* G4 ....9 E3
Arngask Rd *GOV/IBX* G51 ....59 D4
Arnhall Pl *CARD/HILL/MSPK* G52 ....83 C4
Arnhem St *BLTYR/CAMB* G72 ....134 A2
Arnholm Pl *CARD/HILL/MSPK* G52 ....83 C4
Arnisdale Pl *ESTRH* G34 ....72 B3
Arnisdale Rd *ESTRH* G34 ....72 B3
Arnisdale Wy *RUTH* G73 ....130 A4
Arniston St *CAR/SHTL* G32 ....69 C4
Arniston Wy *PSLYN/LNWD* PA3 ....54 B4
Arnold Av *BSHPBGS* G64 ....32 A2
Arnol Pl *STPS/GTHM/RID* G33 ....72 A4
Arnott Wy *BLTYR/CAMB* G72 ....132 B1
Arnprior Crs *CSMK* G45 ....128 A4
Arnprior Qd *CSMK* G45 ....128 A3
Arnprior Rd *CSMK* G45 ....128 A3
Arnprior St *CSMK* G45 ....128 A3
Arnside Av *GIF/THBK* G46 ....124 B4
Arnwood Dr *KVD/HLHD* G12 ....40 B2
Aron Ter *BLTYR/CAMB* G72 ....132 A4
Aros Dr *CARD/HILL/MSPK* G52 ....102 A1
Arran Av *PSLYN/LNWD* PA3 ....53 D2
Arran Dr *CARD/HILL/MSPK* G52 ....83 D4
GIF/THBK G46 ....136 B1
Arran Pl *CLYDBK* G81 ....21 C1
Arran Rd *RNFRW* PA4 ....56 A1
Arran Ter *RUTH* G73 ....129 C2
Arrochar Ct *SMSTN* G23 ....27 D3
Arrochar Dr *SMSTN* G23 ....27 D2
Arrochar St *MRYH/FIRH* G20 ....27 D3
Arrol St *CARD/HILL/MSPK* G52 ....56 B4
Arrowsmith Av *KNTSWD* G13 ....24 B3
Arthur Av *BRHD/NEIL* G78 ....118 A4
Arthurlie Av *BRHD/NEIL* G78 ....118 B3
Arthurlie Dr *GIF/THBK* G46 ....137 C2
Arthurlie St *BRHD/NEIL* G78 ....118 B3
GOV/IBX G51 ....60 A4
Arthur St *KVGV* G3 ....62 A2
PSLY PA1 ....76 A2
Arundel Dr *BSHPBGS* G64 ....19 D3
GVH/MTFL G42 ....106 B4
Ascaig Crs *CARD/HILL/MSPK* G52 ....102 B1
Ascog Rd *BSDN* G61 ....25 D1
Ascog St *GVH/MTFL* G42 ....106 B1
Ascot Av *KVD/HLHD* G12 ....40 A1
Ashburton La *KVD/HLHD* G12 ....41 C1
Ashburton Rd *KVD/HLHD* G12 ....40 B1
Ashby Crs *KNTSWD* G13 ....25 C2
Ashcroft Dr *LNPK/KPK* G44 ....128 B1
Ashdale Dr *CARD/HILL/MSPK* G52 ....83 C4
Ashdene St *PPK/MIL* G22 ....29 D4
Ashfield *BSHPBGS* G64 ....19 C4
Ashfield Rd *MLNGV* G62 ....10 B2
Ashfield St *PPK/MIL* G22 ....44 B3
Ashgill Pl *PPK/MIL* G22 ....44 B1
Ashgill Rd *PPK/MIL* G22 ....44 A1
Ash Gv *BSHPBGS* G64 ....32 B3
Ashgrove St *DMNK/BRGTN* G40 ....109 D1
Ashkirk Dr *CARD/HILL/MSPK* G52 ....83 C4
Ashlea Dr *GIF/THBK* G46 ....125 C3
Ashley La *KVGV* G3 ....2 A2
Ashley St *COWCAD* G4 ....2 A2
Ashmore Rd *PLKSW/MSWD* G43 ....126 A2
Ash Rd *BAIL/MDB/MHD* G69 ....96 A4
Ashton La *KVD/HLHD* G12 ....62 A1
Ashton Rd *KVD/HLHD* G12 ....62 A1
RUTH G73 ....109 D2
Ashtree Rd *PLKSW/MSWD* G43 ....104 B4
Ashvale Crs *SPRGB/BLRNK* G21 ....45 D3
Ash Wynd *BLTYR/CAMB* G72 ....134 B3
Aspen Dr *SPRGB/BLRNK* G21 ....46 B4
Aspen Pl *BLTYR/CAMB* G72 ....134 B2
Aster Gdns *PLK/PH/NH* G53 ....121 C4
Athelstane Rd *KNTSWD* G13 ....24 A4
Athole Gdns *KVD/HLHD* G12 ....41 D4
Athole La *KVD/HLHD* G12 ....41 D4
Atholl Av *CARD/HILL/MSPK* G52 ....56 B4
Atholl Crs *PSLY* PA1 ....80 A2
Atholl Dr *GIF/THBK* G46 ....137 C3
Atholl Gdns *BSHPBGS* G64 ....18 B4
RUTH G73 ....131 D4
Atlas Pl *SPRGB/BLRNK* G21 ....46 A4
Atlas Rd *SPRGB/BLRNK* G21 ....45 D3
Atlas St *CLYDBK* G81 ....20 B3
Attlee Av *CLYDBK* G81 ....21 D2
Attow Rd *PLKSW/MSWD* G43 ....124 A2
Auburn Dr *BRHD/NEIL* G78 ....119 C4
Auchenbothie Crs
STPS/GTHM/RID G33 ....48 B1
Auchenbothie Pl *STPS/GTHM/RID* G33 ....48 B2
Auchencrow St *ESTRH* G34 ....74 A3
Auchencruive *MLNGV* G62 ....11 D3
Auchenhowie Rd *MLNGV* G62 ....11 D3
Auchentorlie Qd *PSLY* PA1 ....78 B3
Auchentorlie St *PTCK* G11 ....60 A1
Auchentoshan Ter *SPRGB/BLRNK* G21 ....65 D1
Auchinairn Rd *BSHPBGS* G64 ....33 D4
Auchingill Pl *ESTRH* G34 ....74 A2
Auchingill Rd *ESTRH* G34 ....73 D2
Auchinlea Rd *ESTRH* G34 ....72 A2
Auchinleck Av *STPS/GTHM/RID* G33 ....48 B1
Auchinleck Crs *STPS/GTHM/RID* G33 ....48 B1
Auchinleck Dr *STPS/GTHM/RID* G33 ....48 B1
Auchinleck Gdns *STPS/GTHM/RID* G33 ....48 B1
Auchinloch St *SPRGB/BLRNK* G21 ....46 A4
Auchmannoch Av *PSLY* PA1 ....80 A2
Auckland St *PPK/MIL* G22 ....44 A3
Auldbar Rd *CARD/HILL/MSPK* G52 ....83 D4
Auldburn Pl *PLKSW/MSWD* G43 ....124 A1
Auldburn Rd *PLKSW/MSWD* G43 ....123 D1
Auldearn Rd *SPRGB/BLRNK* G21 ....33 C4
Auldgirth Rd *CARD/HILL/MSPK* G52 ....83 D4
Auldhouse Av *PLKSW/MSWD* G43 ....124 A1
Auldhouse Gdns *PLKSW/MSWD* G43 ....124 A1

Auldhouse Rd *PLKSW/MSWD* G43 124 B1
Auldhouse Ter *PLKSW/MSWD* G43 125 C1
Auld Kirk Rd *BLTYR/CAMB* G72 133 D4
Aultbea St *PPK/MIL* G22 29 D3
Aultmore Rd *STPS/GTHM/RID* G33 72 A4
Aursbridge Crs *BRHD/NEIL* G78 119 C3
Aursbridge Dr *BRHD/NEIL* G78 119 C3
Aurs Crs *BRHD/NEIL* G78 119 C3
Aurs Dr *BRHD/NEIL* G78 119 C4
Aurs Gln *BRHD/NEIL* G78 118 B4
Aurs Pl *BRHD/NEIL* G78 119 D3
Aurs Rd *BRHD/NEIL* G78 119 D3
Austen La *KNTSWD* G13 39 D2
Austen Rd *KNTSWD* G13 39 D2
Avenel Rd *KNTSWD* G13 25 C2
Avenue End Rd *STPS/GTHM/RID* G33 50 A3
Avenuepark St *MRYH/FIRH* G20 42 B3
Avenue St *DMNK/BRGTN* G40 90 A2
RUTH G73 110 A2
Aviemore Gdns *BSDN* G61 16 A2
Aviemore Rd *CARD/HILL/MSPK* G52 102 B1
Avoch St *ESTRH* G34 73 C2
Avon Av *BSDN* G61 16 B3
Avonbank Rd *RUTH* G73 109 C4
Avondale Dr *PSLY* PA1 78 B1
Avondale St *STPS/GTHM/RID* G33 69 D2
Avon Rd *BSHPBGS* G64 32 A3
GIF/THBK G46 136 B1
Avonspark St *SPRGB/BLRNK* G21 46 B4
Aylmer Rd *PLKSW/MSWD* G43 126 A1
Ayr St *SPRGB/BLRNK* G21 46 A4
Aytoun Rd *PLKSD/SHW* G41 85 D4

B

Back Cswy *DEN/PKHD* G31 91 D2
Backmuir Rd *DRUM* G15 13 D2
Back Sneddon St *PSLY* PA1 77 C2
Bagnell St *SPRGB/BLRNK* G21 46 A2
Baillieston Rd *CAR/SHTL* G32 94 B3
UD/BTH/TAN G71 116 A2
Bainsford St *CAR/SHTL* G32 92 B1
Bain St *DMNK/BRGTN* G40 9 D4
Baird Av *CARD/HILL/MSPK* G52 56 B3
Baird Brae *MRYH/FIRH* G20 44 A4
Baird Dr *BSDN* G61 14 B2
Baird St *COWCAD* G4 4 B3
Baker St *PLKSD/SHW* G41 105 D2
Bakewell Rd *BAIL/MDB/MHD* G69 96 A2
Balaclava St *CGLW* G2 6 B2
Balado Rd *STPS/GTHM/RID* G33 71 D4
Balbeggie St *CAR/SHTL* G32 94 A3
Balbeg St *GOV/IBX* G51 83 C1
Balblair Rd *CARD/HILL/MSPK* G52 83 D4
Balcarres Av *KVD/HLHD* G12 41 D2
Balcomie St *STPS/GTHM/RID* G33 69 D2
Balcurvie Rd *ESTRH* G34 72 B1
Baldinnie Rd *ESTRH* G34 73 C3
Baldovan Crs *STPS/GTHM/RID* G33 72 A3
Baldovie Rd *CARD/HILL/MSPK* G52 82 A4
Baldragon Rd *ESTRH* G34 73 C2
Baldric Rd *KNTSWD* G13 38 B1
Baldwin Av *KNTSWD* G13 24 B2
Balerno Dr *CARD/HILL/MSPK* G52 83 C4
Balfleurs St *MLNGV* G62 11 C1
Balfluig St *ESTRH* G34 72 A2
Balfour St *MRYH/FIRH* G20 42 A1
Balfron Rd *GOV/IBX* G51 59 D4
PSLY PA1 79 D2
Balgair Dr *PSLY* PA1 78 B2
Balgair St *PPK/MIL* G22 44 A2
Balgair Ter *CAR/SHTL* G32 93 D2
Balglass St *PPK/MIL* G22 44 A3
Balgonie Rd *CARD/HILL/MSPK* G52 83 C3
Balgownie Crs *GIF/THBK* G46 136 A1
Balgraybank St *SPRGB/BLRNK* G21 46 B3
Balgray Crs *BRHD/NEIL* G78 119 D3
Balgrayhill Rd *SPRGB/BLRNK* G21 46 A1
Balintore St *CAR/SHTL* G32 93 C2
Baliol La *KVGV* G3 2 A3
Baliol St *KVGV* G3 2 A2
Ballaig Av *BSDN* G61 14 B2
Ballaig Crs *STPS/GTHM/RID* G33 50 B2
Ballantay Qd *CSMK* G45 129 D4
Ballantay Rd *CSMK* G45 129 D4
Ballantay Ter *CSMK* G45 129 D4
Ballantine Av *CARD/HILL/MSPK* G52 57 D4
Ballater Dr *BSDN* G61 25 D1
Ballater Pl *GBLS* G5 88 B3
Ballater St *GBLS* G5 7 F5
Ballindalloch Dr *DEN/PKHD* G31 66 B3
Ballindalloch La *DEN/PKHD* G31 66 B3
Balloch Gdns *CARD/HILL/MSPK* G52 83 D4
Ballochmill Rd *BLTYR/CAMB* G72 111 C3
Ballochmyle Crs *PLK/PH/NH* G53 100 B3
Ballochmyle Dr *PLK/PH/NH* G53 100 B2
Ballochmyle Gdns *PLK/PH/NH* G53 100 B3
Ballochmyle Pl *PLK/PH/NH* G53 100 B3
Ballogie Rd *LNPK/KPK* G44 107 C4
Balmartin Rd *SMSTN* G23 27 D2
Balmeg Av *GIF/THBK* G46 137 C3
Balmoral Dr *BLTYR/CAMB* G72 131 D2
BSDN G61 26 A1
CAR/SHTL G32 113 C3
Balmoral St *SCOT* G14 38 A4
Balmore Pl *PPK/MIL* G22 44 A1
Balmore Rd *SMSTN* G23 29 C4
Balmore Sq *MRYH/FIRH* G20 44 A2
Balmuildy Rd *BSHPBGS* G64 18 A2
Balornock Rd *SPRGB/BLRNK* G21 46 B2
Balruddery Pl *BSHPBGS* G64 33 D3
Balshagray Av *PTCK* G11 40 A4
Balshagray Crs *PTCK* G11 59 D1
Balshagray Dr *PTCK* G11 40 A4
Balshagray La *PTCK* G11 40 A4
Balshagray Pl *PTCK* G11 40 A4
Baltic Ct *DMNK/BRGTN* G40 90 A4
Baltic La *DMNK/BRGTN* G40 90 A4
Baltic Pl *DMNK/BRGTN* G40 89 D3
Baltic St *DMNK/BRGTN* G40 90 A4
Balure St *DEN/PKHD* G31 67 D4
Balvaird Crs *RUTH* G73 109 D4
Balvaird Dr *RUTH* G73 109 D4
Balveny St *STPS/GTHM/RID* G33 71 C1
Balvicar Dr *GVH/MTFL* G42 106 A2
Balvicar St *GVH/MTFL* G42 106 A1
Balvie Av *DRUM* G15 23 C2
GIF/THBK G46 137 D1
Balvie Crs *MLNGV* G62 10 A1
Balvie Rd *MLNGV* G62 10 A1
Banavie Rd *PTCK* G11 41 C4
Banchory Av *PLKSW/MSWD* G43 124 A2
Banchory Crs *BSDN* G61 26 A1
Banff St *STPS/GTHM/RID* G33 70 A1
Bangorshill St *GIF/THBK* G46 123 C3
Bankbrae Av *PLK/PH/NH* G53 120 B1
Bankend St *STPS/GTHM/RID* G33 69 D2
Bankfoot Dr *CARD/HILL/MSPK* G52 81 D3
Bankfoot Rd *CARD/HILL/MSPK* G52 81 D3
Bankglen Rd *DRUM* G15 13 D3
Bankhall St *GVH/MTFL* G42 107 C1
Bankhead Av *KNTSWD* G13 37 D1
Bankhead Dr *RUTH* G73 109 D4
Bankhead Rd *RUTH* G73 109 C4
Banknock St *CAR/SHTL* G32 92 A1
Bank Rd *CAR/SHTL* G32 113 D3
Bank St *BLTYR/CAMB* G72 132 B1
BRHD/NEIL G78 118 B3
KVD/HLHD G12 62 B1
PSLY PA1 77 D3
Bannercross Av *BAIL/MDB/MHD* G69 96 A2
Bannercross Dr *BAIL/MDB/MHD* G69 96 A1
Bannercross Gdns
BAIL/MDB/MHD G69 96 A2
Banner Dr *KNTSWD* G13 24 A2
Bannerman Pl *CLYDBK* G81 20 B1
Banner Rd *BSDN* G61 24 B1
Bantaskin St *MRYH/FIRH* G20 27 C4
Banton Pl *STPS/GTHM/RID* G33 72 B4
Barbreck Rd *GVH/MTFL* G42 106 A1
Barclay St *SPRGB/BLRNK* G21 46 A2
Bard Av *KNTSWD* G13 23 D3
Bardowie St *PPK/MIL* G22 44 B3
Bardrill Dr *BSHPBGS* G64 31 C2
Barfillan Dr *CARD/HILL/MSPK* G52 83 C2
Bargany Ct *PLK/PH/NH* G53 100 B2
Bargany Pl *PLK/PH/NH* G53 100 B3
Bargany Rd *PLK/PH/NH* G53 100 B2
Bargaran Rd *PLK/PH/NH* G53 81 D4
Bargarron Dr *PSLYN/LNWD* PA3 54 B4
Bargeddie St *STPS/GTHM/RID* G33 68 A1
Barholm Sq *STPS/GTHM/RID* G33 71 C2
Barlanark Av *CAR/SHTL* G32 70 B4
Barlanark Crs *CAR/SHTL* G32 71 C4
Barlanark Pl *STPS/GTHM/RID* G33 71 D4

Barlanark Rd *STPS/GTHM/RID* G33 .... **71** C4
Barlanark Wy *CAR/SHTL* G32 .... **71** C4
Barlia Dr *CSMK* G45 .... **128** B4
Barlia St *CSMK* G45 .... **128** B4
Barlia Ter *CSMK* G45 .... **129** C4
Barloch Av *MLNGV* G62 .... **10** B1
Barloch Rd *MLNGV* G62 .... **11** C1
Barloch St *PPK/MIL* G22 .... **44** B3
Barlogan Av *CARD/HILL/MSPK* G52 .... **83** C2
Barlogan Qd *CARD/HILL/MSPK* G52 .... **83** C2
Barmulloch Rd *SPRGB/BLRNK* G21 .... **46** B3
Barnbeth Rd *PLK/PH/NH* G53 .... **101** C1
Barnes Rd *MRYH/FIRH* G20 .... **43** D1
Barness Pl *STPS/GTHM/RID* G33 .... **69** D3
Barnes St *BRHD/NEIL* G78 .... **118** A3
Barnflat St *RUTH* G73 .... **110** A2
Barnhill Dr *SPRGB/BLRNK* G21 .... **46** B4
Barnkirk Av *DRUM* G15 .... **13** C4
Barns St *CLYDBK* G81 .... **21** C3
Barnton St *CAR/SHTL* G32 .... **68** B4
Barnwell Ter *GOV/IBX* G51 .... **59** D4
Barochan Rd *PLK/PH/NH* G53 .... **81** D4
Baronald Dr *KVD/HLHD* G12 .... **41** C1
Baronald Ga *KVD/HLHD* G12 .... **41** C1
Baronald St *RUTH* G73 .... **110** A2
Barone Dr *CRMNK/CLK/EAG* G76 .... **137** C3
Baron Rd *PSLYN/LNWD* PA3 .... **78** A1
Baron St *RNFRW* PA4 .... **55** D1
Barony Dr *BAIL/MDB/MHD* G69 .... **96** B1
Barony Gdns *BAIL/MDB/MHD* G69 .... **96** B2
Barony Wynd *BAIL/MDB/MHD* G69 .... **96** B2
Barra Av *RNFRW* PA4 .... **55** D2
Barrachnie Av *BAIL/MDB/MHD* G69 .... **96** A2
Barrachnie Ct *BAIL/MDB/MHD* G69 .... **95** D2
Barrachnie Crs *BAIL/MDB/MHD* G69 .... **95** D2
Barrachnie Gv *BAIL/MDB/MHD* G69 .... **96** A1
Barrachnie Pl *BAIL/MDB/MHD* G69 .... **96** A1
Barrachnie Rd *BAIL/MDB/MHD* G69 .... **96** A2
Barrack St *COWCAD* G4 .... **9** E3
Barra St *MRYH/FIRH* G20 .... **27** C3
Barrbridge Rd *BAIL/MDB/MHD* G69 .... **99** D3
Barrhead Rd *PLK/PH/NH* G53 .... **100** B4
PLK/PH/NH G53 .... **101** D4
PSLYS PA2 .... **77** D4
Barrie Rd *CARD/HILL/MSPK* G52 .... **57** D4
Barrington Dr *COWCAD* G4 .... **63** C1
Barrisdale Rd *MRYH/FIRH* G20 .... **27** D4
Barrisdale Wy *RUTH* G73 .... **130** A3
Barrland Dr *GIF/THBK* G46 .... **124** B4
Barrland St *PLKSD/SHW* G41 .... **87** C4
Barrmill Rd *PLKSW/MSWD* G43 .... **123** D2
Barrowfield St *DMNK/BRGTN* G40 .... **90** B3
Barr Pl *PSLY* PA1 .... **76** B3
Barr St *MRYH/FIRH* G20 .... **43** D4
Barrwood St *STPS/GTHM/RID* G33 .... **68** B1
Barshaw Dr *PSLY* PA1 .... **78** A1
Barshaw Pl *PSLY* PA1 .... **79** D2
Barshaw Rd *CARD/HILL/MSPK* G52 .... **80** A1
Bartholomew St *DMNK/BRGTN* G40 .... **90** A4
Bartiebeith Rd *STPS/GTHM/RID* G33 .... **71** C4
Bassett Av *KNTSWD* G13 .... **23** D3
Bassett Crs *KNTSWD* G13 .... **23** D3
Bathgate St *DEN/PKHD* G31 .... **90** A1
Bathgo Av *PSLY* PA1 .... **80** A3
Bath La *CGLW* G2 .... **2** B4
Bath St *CGLW* G2 .... **2** B4
Batson St *GVH/MTFL* G42 .... **107** C1
Battlefield Av *GVH/MTFL* G42 .... **106** B4
Battlefield Gdns *GVH/MTFL* G42 .... **106** B4
Battlefield Rd *GVH/MTFL* G42 .... **106** B3
Battles Burn Dr *CAR/SHTL* G32 .... **112** B1
Battles Burn Ga *CAR/SHTL* G32 .... **112** B1
Battles Burn Vw *CAR/SHTL* G32 .... **112** B1
Bavelaw St *STPS/GTHM/RID* G33 .... **71** C1
Bayfield Av *DRUM* G15 .... **13** C4
Bayfield Ter *DRUM* G15 .... **13** C4
Bay Willow Ct *BLTYR/CAMB* G72 .... **135** C3
Beaconsfield Rd *KVD/HLHD* G12 .... **41** C2
Bearford Dr *CARD/HILL/MSPK* G52 .... **81** D2
Bearsden Rd *BSDN* G61 .... **25** D3
KNTSWD G13 .... **40** A1
Beaton Rd *PLKSD/SHW* G41 .... **105** D1
Beattock St *DEN/PKHD* G31 .... **91** D2
Beaufort Av *PLKSW/MSWD* G43 .... **124** B1
Beaufort Gdns *BSHPBGS* G64 .... **31** C2
Beauly Pl *MRYH/FIRH* G20 .... **42** A2
Beauly Rd *BAIL/MDB/MHD* G69 .... **96** A4
Beaumont Ga *KVD/HLHD* G12 .... **61** D1
Beckfield Crs *STPS/GTHM/RID* G33 .... **33** D4
Beckfield Dr *STPS/GTHM/RID* G33 .... **33** D4
Beckfield Ga *SPRGB/BLRNK* G21 .... **33** D4
Beckfield Gv *STPS/GTHM/RID* G33 .... **33** D4
Beckfield Wk *STPS/GTHM/RID* G33 .... **33** D4
Bedale Rd *BAIL/MDB/MHD* G69 .... **95** D3
Bedford Av *CLYDBK* G81 .... **21** D1
Bedford La *GBLS* G5 .... **87** D2
Bedford St *GBLS* G5 .... **87** D2
Beech Av *BAIL/MDB/MHD* G69 .... **96** A2
BLTYR/CAMB G72 .... **132** A1
BSDN G61 .... **10** B4
GOV/IBX G51 .... **84** B2
RUTH G73 .... **130** B3
Beech Crs *BLTYR/CAMB* G72 .... **134** B3
Beech Gdns *BAIL/MDB/MHD* G69 .... **96** A2
Beechgrove St *DMNK/BRGTN* G40 * **110** A1
Beech Pl *BSHPBGS* G64 .... **32** B3
Beech Rd *BSHPBGS* G64 .... **32** B3
Beechwood Av *RUTH* G73 .... **130** B1
Beechwood Ct *BSDN* G61 .... **15** D4
Beechwood Dr *PTCK* G11 .... **40** A3
RNFRW PA4 .... **55** C2
Beechwood Gv *BRHD/NEIL* G78 .... **118** B4
Beechwood La *BSDN* G61 .... **15** D4
Beechwood Pl *PTCK* G11 .... **40** A3
Beil Dr *KNTSWD* G13 .... **22** B4
Beith St *PTCK* G11 .... **60** B2
Belgrave La *KVD/HLHD* G12 .... **42** B4
Belhaven Ter *KVD/HLHD* G12 .... **41** D3
Belhaven Terrace La *KVD/HLHD* G12 .... **41** D3
Belhaven Ter West *KVD/HLHD* G12 .... **41** D3
Belhaven Ter West La *KVD/HLHD* G12 .... **41** D3
Bellahouston Dr *CARD/HILL/MSPK* G52 .... **83** C4
Belleisle St *GVH/MTFL* G42 .... **107** C2
Bellfield Crs *BRHD/NEIL* G78 .... **118** A1
Bellfield St *DEN/PKHD* G31 .... **90** A1
Bellflower Av *PLK/PH/NH* G53 .... **121** D4
Bellflower Gdns *PLK/PH/NH* G53 .... **121** D4
Bellflower Pl *PLK/PH/NH* G53 .... **121** D4
Bellgrove St *DMNK/BRGTN* G40 .... **89** D1
Bellrock Ct *STPS/GTHM/RID* G33 .... **70** A3
Bellrock Crs *STPS/GTHM/RID* G33 .... **69** D3
Bellrock St *STPS/GTHM/RID* G33 .... **69** D3
Bells Br *GOV/IBX* G51 .... **62** A4
Bellscroft Av *RUTH* G73 .... **109** C4
Bellshaugh Ct *KVD/HLHD* G12 .... **41** D2
Bellshaugh Gdns *KVD/HLHD* G12 .... **41** D2
Bellshaugh La *KVD/HLHD* G12 .... **41** D2
Bellshaugh Pl *KVD/HLHD* G12 .... **41** D2
Bellshaugh Rd *KVD/HLHD* G12 .... **41** D2
Bell St *CGLE* G1 .... **8** C3
CLYDBK G81 .... **21** D4
COWCAD G4 .... **9** D3
RNFRW PA4 .... **36** A3
Bell View Ct *RNFRW* PA4 .... **36** A3
Bellwood St *PLKSD/SHW* G41 .... **105** D4
Belmont Crs *KVD/HLHD* G12 .... **42** B4
Belmont Dr *BRHD/NEIL* G78 .... **119** C4
GIF/THBK G46 .... **124** A4
RUTH G73 .... **110** A4
Belmont La *KVD/HLHD* G12 .... **42** B4
Belmont Rd *BLTYR/CAMB* G72 .... **131** D4
PSLYN/LNWD PA3 .... **78** A1
Belmont St *CLYDBK* G81 .... **20** B2
KVD/HLHD G12 .... **42** B4
MRYH/FIRH G20 .... **43** C4
Belses Dr *CARD/HILL/MSPK* G52 .... **82** A2
Belses Gdns *CARD/HILL/MSPK* G52 .... **82** A2
Belsyde Av *DRUM* G15 .... **23** C1
Beltane St *KVGV* G3 .... **2** A4
Beltrees Av *PLK/PH/NH* G53 .... **100** B2
Beltrees Crs *PLK/PH/NH* G53 .... **100** B1
Beltrees Rd *PLK/PH/NH* G53 .... **100** B2
Belvidere Crs *BSHPBGS* G64 .... **32** B1
Bemersyde *BSHPBGS* G64 .... **33** C1
Bemersyde Av *PLKSW/MSWD* G43 .... **124** A2
Benalder St *PTCK* G11 .... **61** D2
Bencroft Dr *LNPK/KPK* G44 .... **128** B2
Ben Donich Pl *PLK/PH/NH* G53 .... **122** A2
Ben Edra Pl *PLK/PH/NH* G53 .... **122** A3
Bengairn St *DEN/PKHD* G31 .... **67** D4
Bengal Pl *PLKSW/MSWD* G43 .... **104** B4
Bengal St *PLKSW/MSWD* G43 .... **104** B4
Ben Garrisdale Pl *PLK/PH/NH* G53 .... **122** A3
Benhar Pl *STPS/GTHM/RID* G33 .... **69** C4
Benholm St *CAR/SHTL* G32 .... **92** B4
Ben Laga Pl *PLK/PH/NH* G53 .... **122** A3
Ben Lui Pl *PLK/PH/NH* G53 .... **122** A3
Ben Macdui Gdns *PLK/PH/NH* G53 .... **122** A3
Bennan Sq *GVH/MTFL* G42 .... **107** D2
Benn Av *PSLY* PA1 .... **77** D3

Ben Oss Pl *PLK/PH/NH* G53 ....**121** D3
Benthall St *GBLS* G5....................**88** B3
Bentinck St *KVGV* G3 ....**62** B2
Bents Rd *BAIL/MDB/MHD* G69....................**96** B2
Ben Uird Pl *PLK/PH/NH* G53....................**122** A3
Benview St *MRYH/FIRH* G20 ....**43** C3
Ben Vorlich Dr *PLK/PH/NH* G53....................**122** A3
Berelands Crs *RUTH* G73....................**108** B4
Berelands Pl *RUTH* G73....................**109** C4
Beresford Av *SCOT* G14....................**39** D3
Berkeley St *KVGV* G3 ....**62** B3
Berkeley Terrace La *KVGV* G3....................**63** C3
Bernard St *DMNK/BRGTN* G40....................**90** A3
Bernard Ter *DMNK/BRGTN* G40 ....**90** A3
Berneray St *PPK/MIL* G22....................**30** A4
Berridale Av *LNPK/KPK* G44 ....**126** B2
Berriedale Av *BAIL/MDB/MHD* G69....................**96** A3
Berryburn Rd *SPRGB/BLRNK* G21 ....**47** D3
Berryhill Dr *GIF/THBK* G46 ....**136** B1
Berryhill Rd *GIF/THBK* G46 ....**136** B2
Berryknowes Av *CARD/HILL/MSPK* G52..**82** A2
Berryknowes La *CARD/HILL/MSPK* G52 ..**82** A2
Berryknowes Rd *CARD/HILL/MSPK* G52..**82** A2
Bertram St *PLKSD/SHW* G41....................**105** D2
Bervie St *GOV/IBX* G51 ....**83** D1
Berwick Dr *CARD/HILL/MSPK* G52 ....**81** D3
RUTH G73 ....**111** C4
Beverley Rd *PLKSW/MSWD* G43 ....**125** C1
Bevin Av *CLYDBK* G81 ....**21** D2
Bideford Crs *CAR/SHTL* G32 ....**94** B4
Biggar St *DEN/PKHD* G31 ....**90** B1
Bigton St *STPS/GTHM/RID* G33 ....**70** A1
Bilsland Ct *MRYH/FIRH* G20 ....**44** A2
Bilsland Dr *MRYH/FIRH* G20 ....**43** C2
Binend Rd *PLK/PH/NH* G53 ....**101** D3
Binnie Pl *DMNK/BRGTN* G40....................**89** C2
Binns Rd *STPS/GTHM/RID* G33....................**70** B1
Birch Dr *BLTYR/CAMB* G72 ....**133** D1
Birchend Dr *SPRGB/BLRNK* G21....................**67** C1
Birchend Pl *SPRGB/BLRNK* G21 ....**66** B1
Birchfield Dr *SCOT* G14 ....**38** A3
Birch Knowe *BSHPBGS* G64 ....**32** B3
Birchlea Dr *GIF/THBK* G46....................**125** C3
Birch Pl *BLTYR/CAMB* G72....................**135** C3
Birch St *GBLS* G5....................**88** B4
Birch Vw *BSDN* G61 ....**16** A2
Birchwood Av *CAR/SHTL* G32....................**95** C3
Birchwood Gv *CTBR* ML5 ....**99** C1
Birchwood Pl *CAR/SHTL* G32 ....**95** C3
Birdston Rd *SPRGB/BLRNK* G21 ....**47** D1
Birkenshaw St *DEN/PKHD* G31 ....**67** C4
Birkhall Av *CARD/HILL/MSPK* G52 ....**80** B3
Birkhall Dr *BSDN* G61....................**25** D1
Birkhill Av *BSHPBGS* G64....................**32** B1
Birkhill Gdns *BSHPBGS* G64 ....**32** B1
Birkmyre Rd *GOV/IBX* G51 ....**83** D1
Birkwood St *DMNK/BRGTN* G40 ....**110** A1
Birmingham Rd *RNFRW* PA4 ....**55** C2
Birnam Av *BSHPBGS* G64 ....**32** B1
Birnam Crs *BSDN* G61 ....**16** B2
Birnam Rd *DEN/PKHD* G31....................**91** D4
Birness Dr *PLKSW/MSWD* G43 ....**105** C4
Birnie Ct *SPRGB/BLRNK* G21....................**47** D4
Birnie Rd *SPRGB/BLRNK* G21 ....**47** D3
Birnock Av *RNFRW* PA4 ....**56** B2
Birsay Rd *PPK/MIL* G22....................**29** D4
Bishop Gdns *BSHPBGS* G64....................**31** C1
Bishop La *CGLW* G2 ....**6** B1
Bishopmill Pl *SPRGB/BLRNK* G21....................**47** D3
Bishopsgate Rd *SPRGB/BLRNK* G21 ....**31** C4
Blackburn Sq *BRHD/NEIL* G78 ....**119** C4
Blackburn St *GOV/IBX* G51 ....**85** D1
Blackbyres Ct *BRHD/NEIL* G78....................**119** C1
Blackcraig Av *DRUM* G15 ....**13** C4
Blackcroft Gdns *CAR/SHTL* G32....................**94** B3
Blackcroft Rd *CAR/SHTL* G32 ....**94** B3
Blackfaulds Rd *RUTH* G73....................**108** B3
Blackford Rd *PSLYS* PA2 ....**78** A4
Blackfriars St *CGLE* G1 ....**8** B2
Blackhall La *PSLY* PA1 ....**77** D4
Blackhall St *PSLY* PA1 ....**77** D4
Blackhill Pl *STPS/GTHM/RID* G33....................**68** A1
Blackhill Rd *SMSTN* G23 ....**28** B1
Blackie St *KVGV* G3....................**62** A3
Blacklaw La *PSLYN/LNWD* PA3....................**77** C2
Blackstone Av *PLK/PH/NH* G53 ....**101** D3
Blackstone Crs *PLK/PH/NH* G53 ....**101** D2
Black St *COWCAD* G4 ....**4** C3
Blackthorn St *PPK/MIL* G22 ....**45** D2
Blackwood St *KNTSWD* G13 ....**25** C4
Bladda La *PSLY* PA1 ....**77** D3
Bladnoch Dr *DRUM* G15 ....**24** A1
Blairatholl Av *PTCK* G11 ....**40** B4
Blairatholl Gdns *PTCK* G11 ....**40** B4
Blairbeth Dr *LNPK/KPK* G44 ....**107** C4
Blairbeth Rd *RUTH* G73....................**130** A2
Blairbeth Ter *RUTH* G73....................**130** B2
Blairbuie Dr *MRYH/FIRH* G20 ....**27** C4
Blair Crs *BAIL/MDB/MHD* G69 ....**96** A4
Blairdardie Rd *DRUM* G15 ....**23** D2
Blairgowrie Rd *CARD/HILL/MSPK* G52 ....**82** A3
Blairhall Av *PLKSD/SHW* G41 ....**106** A3
Blairlogie St *STPS/GTHM/RID* G33....................**70** A2
Blairmore Av *PSLY* PA1 ....**79** C2
Blair Rd *PSLY* PA1....................**80** A1
Blair St *CAR/SHTL* G32 ....**92** B2
Blairtum Dr *RUTH* G73....................**130** A2
Blairtummock Rd *STPS/GTHM/RID* G33..**70** B3
Blaneview *STPS/GTHM/RID* G33 ....**51** C3
Blantyre St *KVGV* G3 ....**62** A2
Blaven Ct *BAIL/MDB/MHD* G69 ....**97** C3
Blawarthill St *SCOT* G14 ....**37** C2
Bleasdale Ct *CLYDBK* G81 ....**20** B1
Blenheim Av *STPS/GTHM/RID* G33 ....**51** C1
Blenheim Ct *PSLY* PA1....................**76** B2
Blochairn Rd *SPRGB/BLRNK* G21 ....**66** B2
Bluevale St *DEN/PKHD* G31 ....**90** A1
Blythe Pl *STPS/GTHM/RID* G33....................**71** D4
Blyth Rd *STPS/GTHM/RID* G33....................**95** C1
Blythswood Av *RNFRW* PA4....................**36** A3
Blythswood Dr *PSLYN/LNWD* PA3....................**76** B1
Blythswood Rd *RNFRW* PA4....................**36** A2
Blythswood Sq *CGLW* G2 ....**2** C5
Blythswood St *CGLW* G2....................**3** D4
Boclair Av *BSDN* G61 ....**15** D3
Boclair Crs *BSDN* G61 ....**16** A3
BSHPBGS G64 ....**32** A2
Boclair Rd *BSDN* G61 ....**16** A2
BSHPBGS G64 ....**32** A1
Boclair St *KNTSWD* G13 ....**25** C3
Boden St *DMNK/BRGTN* G40 ....**90** A3
Bogbain Rd *ESTRH* G34....................**72** B3
Boggknowe *UD/BTH/TAN* G71....................**117** C3
Boghall Rd *UD/BTH/TAN* G71....................**96** A4
Boghall St *STPS/GTHM/RID* G33 ....**70** A2
Boghead Rd *SPRGB/BLRNK* G21 ....**46** B2
Bogleshole Rd *BLTYR/CAMB* G72....................**111** D4
Bogmoor Pl *GOV/IBX* G51....................**58** B2
Bogmoor Rd *GOV/IBX* G51 ....**58** B3
Bogside Rd *STPS/GTHM/RID* G33 ....**49** D2
Bogside St *DMNK/BRGTN* G40 ....**90** B3
Bogton Av *LNPK/KPK* G44....................**126** A3
Bogton Avenue La *LNPK/KPK* G44 ....**126** A3
Boleyn Rd *PLKSD/SHW* G41 ....**105** D1
Bolivar Ter *GVH/MTFL* G42 ....**107** D3
Bolton Dr *GVH/MTFL* G42 ....**106** B3
Bon Accord Sq *CLYDBK* G81 ....**20** B3
Bonawe St *MRYH/FIRH* G20 ....**43** C4
Boness St *DMNK/BRGTN* G40....................**90** B3
Bonhill St *PPK/MIL* G22....................**44** A4
Bonnar St *DMNK/BRGTN* G40....................**90** A4
Bonnaughton Rd *BSDN* G61 ....**13** D1
Bonnyholm Av *PLK/PH/NH* G53 ....**81** C4
Bonnyrigg Dr *PLKSW/MSWD* G43 ....**123** D2
Bonyton Av *KNTSWD* G13 ....**37** C1
Boon Dr *DRUM* G15 ....**23** D1
Borden La *KNTSWD* G13 ....**39** D2
Borden Rd *KNTSWD* G13 ....**39** D2
Boreland Dr *KNTSWD* G13....................**23** D4
Boreland Pl *KNTSWD* G13 ....**38** A1
Borgie Crs *BLTYR/CAMB* G72 ....**132** B2
Borland Rd *BSDN* G61 ....**16** A4
Borron St *COWCAD* G4....................**44** B4
Borthwick St *STPS/GTHM/RID* G33....................**70** A2
Boswell Ct *PLKSD/SHW* G41....................**106** A4
Boswell Sq *CARD/HILL/MSPK* G52 ....**57** C4
Botanic Crs *MRYH/FIRH* G20 ....**42** A3
Bothlin Dr *STPS/GTHM/RID* G33 ....**51** C1
Bothwell La *CGLW* G2 ....**6** C1
KVD/HLHD G12 ....**62** B1
Bothwell St *BLTYR/CAMB* G72 ....**131** D1
CGLW G2 ....**6** C1
Bourock Sq *BRHD/NEIL* G78....................**119** C4
Bouverie St *RUTH* G73....................**109** C3
SCOT G14 ....**36** B1
Bowden Dr *CARD/HILL/MSPK* G52....................**81** D1
Bower St *KVD/HLHD* G12 ....**42** B4
Bowerwalls St *BRHD/NEIL* G78 ....**119** D1
Bowes Crs *BAIL/MDB/MHD* G69 ....**95** D3
Bowfield Av *CARD/HILL/MSPK* G52....................**80** B1

Bowfield Crs CARD/HILL/MSPK G52 80 B1
Bowfield Dr CARD/HILL/MSPK G52 80 B1
Bowfield Pl CARD/HILL/MSPK G52 80 B1
Bowhouse Dr CSMK G45 129 D3
Bowhouse Gdns CSMK G45 129 D2
Bowling Green La SCOT G14 39 C4
Bowling Green Rd CAR/SHTL G32 94 B3
LNPK/KPK G44 126 B2
SCOT G14 39 C4
Bowling Green Vw BLTYR/CAMB G72 135 C3
Bowman St GVH/MTFL G42 106 B1
Bowmont Ter KVD/HLHD G12 41 D4
Bowmore Gdns RUTH G73 131 D4
UD/BTH/TAN G71 117 D3
Bowmore Rd CARD/HILL/MSPK G52 83 C2
Bowmount Gdns KVD/HLHD G12 41 D4
Boydstone Pl GIF/THBK G46 123 C2
Boydstone Rd GIF/THBK G46 123 C3
PLKSW/MSWD G43 122 B1
Boyd St GVH/MTFL G42 107 C2
Boyle St CLYDBK G81 21 D3
Boyndie St ESTRH G34 73 C3
Brabloch Crs PSLYN/LNWD PA3 77 D1
Bracadale Dr BAIL/MDB/MHD G69 97 D3
Bracadale Gdns BAIL/MDB/MHD G69 97 D3
Bracadale Gv BAIL/MDB/MHD G69 97 C3
Bracadale Rd BAIL/MDB/MHD G69 97 C3
Brackenbrae Av BSHPBGS G64 31 C1
Brackenbrae Rd BSHPBGS G64 31 D2
Bracken St PPK/MIL G22 44 A1
Brackla Av KNTSWD G13 22 A3
Bradan Av KNTSWD G13 22 A4
Bradda Av RUTH G73 130 B3
Bradfield Av KVD/HLHD G12 41 D2
Braefield Dr GIF/THBK G46 123 D4
Braefoot Av MLNGV G62 10 B3
Braehead Av MLNGV G62 10 A2
Braehead St GBLS G5 88 B4
Braemar Ct GIF/THBK G46 125 D3
Braemar Crs BSDN G61 25 D1
Braemar Rd RUTH G73 131 C4
Braemar St GVH/MTFL G42 106 A4
Braemore Gdns PPK/MIL G22 45 C3
Braes Av CLYDBK G81 21 D3
Braeside Av MLNGV G62 10 B3
RUTH G73 110 B4
Braeside Crs BAIL/MDB/MHD G69 98 B2
BRHD/NEIL G78 119 D4
Braeside Dr BRHD/NEIL G78 119 C4
Braeside Pl BLTYR/CAMB G72 133 C3
Braeside St MRYH/FIRH G20 43 C4
Braidbar Farm Rd GIF/THBK G46 125 C4
Braidbar Rd GIF/THBK G46 124 B4
Braidcraft Rd PLK/PH/NH G53 101 D2
Braidcraft Ter PLK/PH/NH G53 102 A2
Braidfauld Gdns CAR/SHTL G32 92 B4
Braidfauld Pl CAR/SHTL G32 112 A1
Braidfauld St CAR/SHTL G32 112 A1
Braidholm Crs GIF/THBK G46 124 B3
Braidholm Rd GIF/THBK G46 125 C3
Braidpark Dr GIF/THBK G46 125 C4
Braids Dr PLK/PH/NH G53 100 A2
Braid Sq COWCAD G4 2 C1
Braid St COWCAD G4 2 C1
Branchock Av BLTYR/CAMB G72 134 A3
Brandon Gdns BLTYR/CAMB G72 131 D2
Brandon St DEN/PKHD G31 89 D1
Brand Pl GOV/IBX G51 85 C1
Brand St GOV/IBX G51 85 D1
Branklyn Cl KNTSWD G13 39 C1
Branklyn Crs KNTSWD G13 39 C1
Branklyn Gv KNTSWD G13 39 C1
Branklyn Pl KNTSWD G13 39 C1
Brassey St MRYH/FIRH G20 42 B1
Breadalbane Gdns RUTH G73 131 C3
Breadalbane St KVGV G3 63 C3
Breadie Dr MLNGV G62 10 A3
Brechin Rd BSHPBGS G64 33 C2
Brechin St KVGV G3 62 B3
Bredisholm Dr BAIL/MDB/MHD G69 97 C3
Bredisholm Rd BAIL/MDB/MHD G69 97 C3
BAIL/MDB/MHD G69 98 B3
BAIL/MDB/MHD G69 99 C3
Bredisholm Ter BAIL/MDB/MHD G69 97 C3
Brenfield Av LNPK/KPK G44 126 A3
Brenfield Dr LNPK/KPK G44 126 A3
Brenfield Rd LNPK/KPK G44 126 A3
Brent Dr GIF/THBK G46 123 C2
Brent Gdns GIF/THBK G46 123 C2
Brent Rd GIF/THBK G46 123 D2
Brent Wy GIF/THBK G46 123 C2
Brentwood Av PLK/PH/NH G53 120 B3
Brentwood Dr PLK/PH/NH G53 120 B3
Brentwood Sq PLK/PH/NH G53 121 C3
Brereton St GVH/MTFL G42 107 D2
Bressay Rd STPS/GTHM/RID G33 95 C1
Brewster Av PSLYN/LNWD PA3 54 B4
Briarcroft Dr SPRGB/BLRNK G21 48 A1
STPS/GTHM/RID G33 33 D4
Briarcroft Pl STPS/GTHM/RID G33 48 B1
Briarcroft Rd SPRGB/BLRNK G21 48 A1
STPS/GTHM/RID G33 33 D4
Briar Gdns PLKSW/MSWD G43 125 C2
Briar Gv PLKSW/MSWD G43 125 C2
Briarlea Dr GIF/THBK G46 124 B3
Briar Neuk BSHPBGS G64 32 B3
Briar Rd PLKSW/MSWD G43 125 C2
Briarwell La MLNGV G62 11 C2
Briarwell Rd MLNGV G62 11 C2
Briarwood Ct CAR/SHTL G32 114 B1
Brick La PSLY PA1 77 D2
Bridgebar St BRHD/NEIL G78 119 D1
Bridgegait MLNGV G62 11 D3
Bridgegate CGLE G1 8 A4
Bridge-Gate CGLE G1 8 A4
Bridge St BLTYR/CAMB G72 132 B1
GBLS G5 7 E4
PSLY PA1 77 D3
Brigham Pl SMSTN G23 28 A3
Brighton Pl GOV/IBX G51 84 B1
Brighton St GOV/IBX G51 84 B1
Brisbane Ct GIF/THBK G46 125 C4
Brisbane St LNPK/KPK G44 106 B4
Broadford St COWCAD G4 64 B1
Broadholm St PPK/MIL G22 44 B1
Broadleys Av BSHPBGS G64 31 D1
Broadlie Dr KNTSWD G13 37 D1
Broadloan RNFRW PA4 55 D1
Broad St DMNK/BRGTN G40 89 D2
Broadwood Dr LNPK/KPK G44 127 C1
Brockburn Crs PLK/PH/NH G53 101 C3
Brockburn Rd PLK/PH/NH G53 100 B1
Brockburn Ter PLK/PH/NH G53 101 D3
Brock Ov PLK/PH/NH G53 121 D1
Brock Pl PLK/PH/NH G53 101 D4
Brock Rd PLK/PH/NH G53 121 C1
Brock Ter PLK/PH/NH G53 121 D1
Brockville St CAR/SHTL G32 92 B1
Brodick St SPRGB/BLRNK G21 66 B2
Brodie Gdns BAIL/MDB/MHD G69 97 C1
Brodie Rd SPRGB/BLRNK G21 33 C4
Brookfield Av STPS/GTHM/RID G33 33 D4
Brookfield Avenue Ga
STPS/GTHM/RID G33 33 D4
Brookfield Cnr STPS/GTHM/RID G33 33 D4
Brookfield Dr STPS/GTHM/RID G33 33 D4
Brookfield Gdns STPS/GTHM/RID G33 33 D4
Brookfield Rd STPS/GTHM/RID G33 33 D4
Brooklands Av UD/BTH/TAN G71 117 D4
Brooklea Dr GIF/THBK G46 124 B2
Brookside St DMNK/BRGTN G40 90 A2
Brook St DMNK/BRGTN G40 89 D2
Broomfield Av BLTYR/CAMB G72 111 C4
Broomfield La SPRGB/BLRNK G21 46 A2
Broomfield Pl SPRGB/BLRNK G21 46 A2
Broomfield Rd SPRGB/BLRNK G21 46 A2
Broomhill Av CAR/SHTL G32 113 C3
PTCK G11 60 A1
Broomhill Dr PTCK G11 40 A4
RUTH G73 130 A2
Broomhill Gdns PTCK G11 40 A4
Broomhill La PTCK G11 40 A4
Broomhill Pl PTCK G11 60 A1
Broomhill Ter PTCK G11 60 A1
Broomieknowe Dr RUTH G73 130 A1
Broomieknowe Gdns RUTH G73 129 D1
Broomieknowe Rd RUTH G73 130 A1
Broomielaw KVGV G3 6 B3
Broomknowes Rd SPRGB/BLRNK G21 46 B3
Broomlands St PSLY PA1 76 A3
Broomley Dr GIF/THBK G46 137 C2
Broomley La GIF/THBK G46 137 C2
Broomloan Rd GOV/IBX G51 61 C4
Broompark Circ DEN/PKHD G31 66 A3
Broompark Dr DEN/PKHD G31 9 F1
Broompark La DEN/PKHD G31 66 A4
Broompark St DEN/PKHD G31 66 A4
Broom Rd PLKSW/MSWD G43 125 C2
Broomton Rd SPRGB/BLRNK G21 33 C4
Brora Dr BSDN G61 16 B3

GIF/THBK G46 ....137 D1
RNFRW PA4 ....36 B4
Brora Gdns *BSHPBGS* G64 ....32 B2
Brora Rd *BSHPBGS* G64 ....32 B2
Brora St *STPS/GTHM/RID* G33 ....68 A2
Broughton Dr *SMSTN* G23 ....28 A3
Broughton Gdns *SMSTN* G23 ....28 A2
Broughton Rd *SMSTN* G23 ....28 A3
Brown Av *CLYDBK* G81 ....21 D3
Brownhill Rd *GIF/THBK* G46 ....124 A3
Brownlie St *GVH/MTFL* G42 ....107 C3
Brown Pl *BLTYR/CAMB* G72 ....132 B1
Brownsdale Rd *RUTH* G73 ....109 C4
Brownside Av *BLTYR/CAMB* G72 ....131 D2
Brownside Dr *KNTSWD* G13 ....37 C1
Brownside Rd *RUTH* G73 ....131 C2
Brown's La *PSLY* PA1 ....77 C3
Brown St *CGLW* G2 ....6 C2
PSLY PA1 ....76 A2
RNFRW PA4 ....55 C1
Bruce Av *PSLYN/LNWD* PA3 ....54 B4
Brucefield Pl *ESTRH* G34 ....74 A3
Bruce Rd *PLKSD/SHW* G41 ....86 A3
PSLYN/LNWD PA3 ....78 A1
RNFRW PA4 ....54 B2
Bruce St *CLYDBK* G81 ....20 B2
Brunstane Rd *ESTRH* G34 ....72 B2
Brunswick La *CGLE* G1 ....8 A2
Brunswick St *CGLE* G1 ....8 A2
Brunton St *LNPK/KPK* G44 ....126 B2
Brunton Ter *LNPK/KPK* G44 ....126 A3
Bruntsfield Av *PLK/PH/NH* G53 ....121 C4
Bruntsfield Gdns *PLK/PH/NH* G53 ....121 C4
Buccleuch Av *CARD/HILL/MSPK* G52 ....56 B3
CRMNK/CLK/EAG G76 ....137 D4
Buccleuch La *COWCAD* G4 ....2 C3
Buccleuch St *KVGV* G3 ....2 B3
Buchanan Crs *BSHPBGS* G64 ....33 C3
Buchanan Dr *BLTYR/CAMB* G72 ....131 D1
BSDN G61 ....16 A3
BSHPBGS G64 ....33 C3
RUTH G73 ....130 A1
Buchanan Gv *BAIL/MDB/MHD* G69 ....96 B2
Buchanan St *BAIL/MDB/MHD* G69 ....96 B3
CGLE G1 ....3 F5
MLNGV G62 ....11 C1
Buchan Ter *BLTYR/CAMB* G72 ....131 D4
Buchlyvie Gdns *BSHPBGS* G64 ....31 D3
Buchlyvie Rd *PSLY* PA1 ....80 A2
Buchlyvie St *ESTRH* G34 ....73 C4
Buckingham Dr *CAR/SHTL* G32 ....113 C3
RUTH G73 ....111 C4
Buckingham St *KVD/HLHD* G12 ....42 A4
Buckingham Ter *KVD/HLHD* G12 ....42 A4
Bucklaw Gdns *CARD/HILL/MSPK* G52 ....82 A3
Bucklaw Pl *CARD/HILL/MSPK* G52 ....82 A3
Bucklaw Ter *CARD/HILL/MSPK* G52 ....82 A3
Buckley St *PPK/MIL* G22 ....45 C1
Bucksburn Rd *SPRGB/BLRNK* G21 ....47 D3
Buddon St *DMNK/BRGTN* G40 ....91 C3
Budhill Av *CAR/SHTL* G32 ....93 D2
Bulldale Ct *SCOT* G14 ....36 B2
Bulldale St *SCOT* G14 ....36 B1
Bullionslaw Dr *RUTH* G73 ....131 C1
Bulloch Rd *GIF/THBK* G46 ....137 D1
Bullwood Av *PLK/PH/NH* G53 ....100 A2
Bullwood Ct *PLK/PH/NH* G53 ....100 A3
Bullwood Dr *PLK/PH/NH* G53 ....100 A2
Bullwood Gdns *PLK/PH/NH* G53 ....100 A2
Bullwood Pl *PLK/PH/NH* G53 ....100 A2
Bunessan St *CARD/HILL/MSPK* G52 ....83 D2
Bunhouse Rd *KVGV* G3 ....61 D2
Burghead Dr *GOV/IBX* G51 ....59 D3
Burghead Pl *GOV/IBX* G51 ....59 D3
Burgher St *DEN/PKHD* G31 ....91 C2
Burgh Hall La *PTCK* G11 ....61 C1
Burgh Hall St *PTCK* G11 ....61 C1
Burgh La *KVD/HLHD* G12 ....42 A4
Burleigh St *GOV/IBX* G51 ....60 B3
Burlington Av *KVD/HLHD* G12 ....41 C1
Burmola St *PPK/MIL* G22 ....44 A3
Burnacre Gdns *UD/BTH/TAN* G71 ....117 D4
Burnawn Gdns *STPS/GTHM/RID* G33 ....33 D4
Burnawn Gv *STPS/GTHM/RID* G33 ....33 D4
Burnawn Pl *STPS/GTHM/RID* G33 ....33 D4
Burnbank Dr *BRHD/NEIL* G78 ....118 B4
Burnbank Gdns *MRYH/FIRH* G20 ....63 C1
Burnbank Pl *MRYH/FIRH* G20 ....63 C1
Burnbank Ter *COWCAD* G4 ....2 A1
Burnbrae Av *BSDN* G61 ....10 B4
Burnbrae Dr *RUTH* G73 ....131 C2
Burnbrae St *SPRGB/BLRNK* G21 ....46 B3
Burncleuch Av *BLTYR/CAMB* G72 ....132 B3
Burndyke Ct *GOV/IBX* G51 ....61 C4
Burndyke Sq *GOV/IBX* G51 ....61 D4
Burnett Rd *STPS/GTHM/RID* G33 ....71 D4
Burnfield Av *GIF/THBK* G46 ....124 A3
Burnfield Dr *GIF/THBK* G46 ....124 A3
Burnfield Gdns *GIF/THBK* G46 ....124 B3
Burnfield Rd *GIF/THBK* G46 ....123 D2
Burnfoot Crs *RUTH* G73 ....131 C2
Burnfoot Dr *CARD/HILL/MSPK* G52 ....81 D2
Burnham Rd *SCOT* G14 ....37 D3
Burnhead Rd *PLKSW/MSWD* G43 ....125 D2
Burnhill Qd *RUTH* G73 ....109 C3
Burnhill St *RUTH* G73 ....109 C3
Burnhouse St *MRYH/FIRH* G20 ....41 D1
Burnmouth Pl *BSDN* G61 ....16 A2
Burnmouth Rd *STPS/GTHM/RID* G33 ....95 D1
Burnpark Av *UD/BTH/TAN* G71 ....117 C4
Burn Pl *BLTYR/CAMB* G72 ....111 D4
Burns Gv *GIF/THBK* G46 ....136 A1
Burnside Av *BRHD/NEIL* G78 ....118 A1
Burnside Ct *RUTH* G73 ....130 B2
Burnside Gdns *CRMNK/CLK/EAG* G76 ....137 D4
Burnside Ga *RUTH* G73 ....130 B2
Burnside Rd *RUTH* G73 ....130 B2
Burns St *COWCAD* G4 ....64 A1
Burntbroom Dr *BAIL/MDB/MHD* G69 ....95 D4
Burntbroom Gdns *CAR/SHTL* G32 ....95 D4
Burntbroom Rd *UD/BTH/TAN* G71 ....115 C1
Burntbroom St *STPS/GTHM/RID* G33 ....71 C4
Burn Ter *BLTYR/CAMB* G72 ....111 D4
Burra Gdns *BSHPBGS* G64 ....33 D1
Burrell Ct *PLKSD/SHW* G41 ....104 B1
Burrell's La *COWCAD* G4 ....9 D1
Burrelton Rd *PLKSW/MSWD* G43 ....126 A2
Busheyhill St *BLTYR/CAMB* G72 ....132 B2
Bute Av *RNFRW* PA4 ....56 A2
Bute Crs *BSDN* G61 ....25 D1
Bute Gdns *KVD/HLHD* G12 ....62 A1
LNPK/KPK G44 ....126 A4
Bute La *KVD/HLHD* G12 ....62 A1
Bute Rd *PSLYN/LNWD* PA3 ....53 C2
Bute Ter *RUTH* G73 ....129 D2
Butterbiggins Rd *GVH/MTFL* G42 ....87 C4
Butterfield Pl *PLKSD/SHW* G41 ....87 C4
Byrebush Rd *PLK/PH/NH* G53 ....101 D2
Byres Av *PSLYN/LNWD* PA3 ....78 A1
Byres Crs *PSLYN/LNWD* PA3 ....78 A1
Byres Rd *KVD/HLHD* G12 ....62 A1
Byron St *PTCK* G11 ....60 A1
Byshot St *PPK/MIL* G22 ....45 C3

C

Cadder Ct *BSHPBGS* G64 ....19 D2
Cadder Pl *MRYH/FIRH* G20 ....28 A4
Cadder Rd *BSHPBGS* G64 ....19 D2
MRYH/FIRH G20 ....28 A4
Cadder Wy *BSHPBGS* G64 ....19 D2
Cadoc St *BLTYR/CAMB* G72 ....133 C2
Cadogan St *CGLW* G2 ....6 C1
Cadzow Av *GIF/THBK* G46 ....136 B3
Cadzow Dr *BLTYR/CAMB* G72 ....132 B2
Cadzow St *CGLW* G2 ....6 B2
Caird Dr *PTCK* G11 ....61 C1
Cairn Av *RNFRW* PA4 ....56 B2
Cairnban St *GOV/IBX* G51 ....82 B1
Cairnbrook Rd *ESTRH* G34 ....73 D3
Cairndow Av *LNPK/KPK* G44 ....126 A3
Cairndow Avenue La *LNPK/KPK* G44 ....126 A3
Cairndow Ct *LNPK/KPK* G44 ....126 A3
Cairngorm Crs *BRHD/NEIL* G78 ....118 B4
BSDN G61 ....13 D1
Cairngorm Rd *PLKSW/MSWD* G43 ....124 B2
Cairnhill Circ *CARD/HILL/MSPK* G52 ....80 B4
Cairnhill Dr *CARD/HILL/MSPK* G52 ....80 B4
Cairnhill Pl *CARD/HILL/MSPK* G52 ....80 B4
Cairnhill Rd *BSDN* G61 ....25 D2
Cairnlea Dr *GOV/IBX* G51 ....84 B1
Cairns Av *BLTYR/CAMB* G72 ....133 C2
Cairns Dr *MLNGV* G62 ....10 B1
Cairnsmore Rd *DRUM* G15 ....22 B1
Cairns Rd *BLTYR/CAMB* G72 ....133 C3

Cairn St *SPRGB/BLRNK* G21 **46** A1
Cairnswell Av *BLTYR/CAMB* G72 **133** D3
Cairnswell Pl *BLTYR/CAMB* G72 **133** D3
Cairntoul Dr *KNTSWD* G13 **37** D1
Cairntoul Pl *SCOT* G14 **37** D2
Caithness St *MRYH/FIRH* G20 **43** C3
Calcots Pl *ESTRH* G34 **73** D2
Caldarvan St *PPK/MIL* G22 **44** A4
Calder Av *BRHD/NEIL* G78 **118** B4
Calderbank Vw *BAIL/MDB/MHD* G69 **96** B4
Calderbraes Av *UD/BTH/TAN* G71 **117** D3
Caldercuilt Rd *MRYH/FIRH* G20 **27** C3
Calder Dr *BLTYR/CAMB* G72 **132** B2
Calder Ga *BSHPBGS* G64 **18** B3
Calderpark Av *UD/BTH/TAN* G71 **116** A1
Calder Pl *BAIL/MDB/MHD* G69 **96** B3
Calder St *GVH/MTFL* G42 **106** B1
Calderwood Av *BAIL/MDB/MHD* G69 **96** A4
Calderwood Dr *BAIL/MDB/MHD* G69 **96** A4
Calderwood Gdns *BAIL/MDB/MHD* G69 **96** A4
Calderwood Rd *PLKSW/MSWD* G43 **125** C1
RUTH G73 **110** B4
Caldwell Av *KNTSWD* G13 **37** D1
Caledonia Av *GBLS* G5 **88** A4
RUTH G73 **110** A3
Caledonia Ct *PSLYN/LNWD* PA3 **76** B1
Caledonia Dr *BAIL/MDB/MHD* G69 **96** B4
Caledonian Crs *KVD/HLHD* G12 **62** B1
Caledonia Rd *GBLS* G5 **88** A4
UD/BTH/TAN G71 **96** A4
Caledonia St *GBLS* G5 **88** B4
PSLYN/LNWD PA3 **76** B2
Caledonia Wy *PSLYN/LNWD* PA3 **53** C2
Caledonia Wy East *PSLYN/LNWD* PA3 **53** D2
Caledonia Wy West *PSLYN/LNWD* PA3 **53** C2
Caledon La *KVD/HLHD* G12 **61** D1
Caledon St *KVD/HLHD* G12 **41** D4
Calfhill Rd *PLK/PH/NH* G53 **81** D4
Calgary St *COWCAD* G4 **4** A3
Callander St *MRYH/FIRH* G20 **43** D4
Callieburn Rd *BSHPBGS* G64 **32** A3
Cally Av *DRUM* G15 **13** C4
Calside Av *PSLYS* PA2 **76** B4
Calvay Crs *STPS/GTHM/RID* G33 **71** C4
Calvay Rd *STPS/GTHM/RID* G33 **71** D4
Cambridge Av *CLYDBK* G81 **21** C1
Cambridge Rd *RNFRW* PA4 **55** D1
Cambridge St *CGLW* G2 **3** D4
Camburn St *CAR/SHTL* G32 **92** B2
Cambusdoon Rd *STPS/GTHM/RID* G33 **70** B1
Cambuskenneth Gdns *CAR/SHTL* G32 **94** B2
Cambuslang Rd *BLTYR/CAMB* G72 **111** D3
CAR/SHTL G32 **112** A3
RUTH G73 **110** B2
Cambus Pl *STPS/GTHM/RID* G33 **70** B1
Camden St *GBLS* G5 **88** A3
Camelon St *CAR/SHTL* G32 **92** B1
Cameron Ct *CLYDBK* G81 **21** C3
Cameron Dr *BSDN* G61 **16** A4
Cameron St *CARD/HILL/MSPK* G52 **56** B4
Camlachie St *DEN/PKHD* G31 **90** B2
Campbell Av *MLNGV* G62 **10** B2
Campbell Dr *BRHD/NEIL* G78 **118** B3
BSDN G61 **14** B2
Campbell St *MRYH/FIRH* G20 **27** D4
RNFRW PA4 **36** A3
Camphill *PSLYS* PA2 **76** B4
Camphill Av *PLKSD/SHW* G41 **105** D4
Camp Rd *BAIL/MDB/MHD* G69 **96** B2
RUTH G73 **109** C1
Camps Crs *RNFRW* PA4 **56** B1
Campsie Av *BRHD/NEIL* G78 **118** B4
Campsie Dr *MLNGV* G62 **11** C1
PSLYN/LNWD PA3 **53** D2
PSLYN/LNWD PA3 **54** B3
Campsie Gdns *CRMNK/CLK/EAG* G76 **137** C3
Campsie St *SPRGB/BLRNK* G21 **46** A2
Campsie Vw *BAIL/MDB/MHD* G69 **98** B2
BLTYR/CAMB G72 **134** B4
STPS/GTHM/RID G33 **51** C3
Campston Pl *STPS/GTHM/RID* G33 **70** A2
Camsbusmore Pl *STPS/GTHM/RID* G33 **70** B1
Camstradden Dr East *BSDN* G61 **14** A3
Camstradden Dr West *BSDN* G61 **14** A3
Camus Pl *DRUM* G15 **12** B3
Canal St *COWCAD* G4 **4** A2
PSLY PA1 **76** B3
RNFRW PA4 **36** A3
Canal Ter *PSLY* PA1 **76** B3
Cander Rigg *BSHPBGS* G64 **19** C3
Candleriggs *CGLE* G1 **8** B3
Canmore Pl *DEN/PKHD* G31 **91** D3
Canmore St *DEN/PKHD* G31 **91** D3
Canniesburn Rd *BSDN* G61 **24** A1
Canonbie St *ESTRH* G34 **74** A2
Canting Wy *GOV/IBX* G51 **61** D4
Capelrig St *GIF/THBK* G46 **122** B3
Caprington St *STPS/GTHM/RID* G33 **69** D2
Cara Dr *GOV/IBX* G51 **59** D3
Carberry Rd *PLKSD/SHW* G41 **105** C1
Carbeth Rd *MLNGV* G62 **10** A2
Carbeth St *PPK/MIL* G22 **44** A3
Carbisdale St *PPK/MIL* G22 **45** D2
Carbost St *SMSTN* G23 **27** D2
Carbrook St *PSLY* PA1 **76** A3
SPRGB/BLRNK G21 **66** B2
Cardarrach St *SPRGB/BLRNK* G21 **46** B3
Cardonald Dr *CARD/HILL/MSPK* G52 **81** C3
Cardonald Gdns *CARD/HILL/MSPK* G52 **81** C3
Cardonald Place Rd
CARD/HILL/MSPK G52 **81** D3
Cardowan Dr *STPS/GTHM/RID* G33 **51** C2
Cardowan Rd *CAR/SHTL* G32 **92** B1
STPS/GTHM/RID G33 **51** D1
Cardow Rd *SPRGB/BLRNK* G21 **47** D3
Cardrona St *STPS/GTHM/RID* G33 **50** A4
Cardross St *DEN/PKHD* G31 **66** A4
Cardwell St *PLKSD/SHW* G41 **87** C3
Cardyke St *SPRGB/BLRNK* G21 **46** B3
Careston Pl *BSHPBGS* G64 **33** D2
Carfin St *GVH/MTFL* G42 **107** C1
Carfrae St *KVGV* G3 **61** D3
Cargill Sq *BSHPBGS* G64 **33** C3
Carham Dr *CARD/HILL/MSPK* G52 **82** A2
Carillon Rd *GOV/IBX* G51 **85** C2
Carisbrooke Crs *BSHPBGS* G64 **19** D3
Carlaverock Rd *PLKSW/MSWD* G43 **125** C1
Carleith Qd *GOV/IBX* G51 **59** C4
Carleston St *SPRGB/BLRNK* G21 **46** A3
Carleton Ct *GIF/THBK* G46 **124** B3
Carleton Dr *GIF/THBK* G46 **124** B3
Carleton Ga *GIF/THBK* G46 **124** B3
Carlibar Av *KNTSWD* G13 **37** C1
Carlibar Dr *BRHD/NEIL* G78 **118** B2
Carlibar Gdns *BRHD/NEIL* G78 **118** B2
Carlibar Rd *BRHD/NEIL* G78 **118** B2
Carlile Pl *PSLYN/LNWD* PA3 **77** C1
Carlisle St *PPK/MIL* G22 **45** C3
Carlton Ct *GBLS* G5 **7** D4
Carlton Pl *GBLS* G5 **7** E4
Carlyle Av *CARD/HILL/MSPK* G52 **57** D3
Carmaben Rd *STPS/GTHM/RID* G33 **71** C3
Carment Dr *PLKSD/SHW* G41 **105** C3
Carmichael Pl *GVH/MTFL* G42 **106** A4
Carmichael St *GOV/IBX* G51 **84** B1
Carmunnock Rd *LNPK/KPK* G44 **107** C4
Carmyle Av *CAR/SHTL* G32 **113** C1
Carna Dr *LNPK/KPK* G44 **127** D2
Carnarvon St *KVGV* G3 **2** A2
Carnegie Rd *CARD/HILL/MSPK* G52 **57** D4
Carnoch St *SMSTN* G23 **27** D2
Carnock Crs *BRHD/NEIL* G78 **118** A4
Carnock Rd *PLK/PH/NH* G53 **101** D3
Carnoustie Crs *BSHPBGS* G64 **33** C2
Carnoustie Pl *GBLS* G5 **86** B2
Carntynehall Rd *CAR/SHTL* G32 **92** B1
Carntyne Pl *CAR/SHTL* G32 **68** A4
Carntyne Rd *CAR/SHTL* G32 **68** A4
Carnwadric Rd *GIF/THBK* G46 **122** B3
Carnwath Av *PLKSW/MSWD* G43 **126** A1
Caroline St *DEN/PKHD* G31 **92** A2
Carolside Dr *DRUM* G15 **13** D4
Carrbridge Dr *MRYH/FIRH* G20 **42** A1
Carrickarden Rd *BSDN* G61 **15** D4
Carrick Crs *GIF/THBK* G46 **137** C2
Carrick Dr *CAR/SHTL* G32 **95** C3
RUTH G73 **129** D2
Carrick Gv *CAR/SHTL* G32 **95** C3
Carrick Rd *BSHPBGS* G64 **33** C2
RUTH G73 **129** C2
Carrick St *KVGV* G3 **6** C3
Carrington St *COWCAD* G4 **2** A1
Carroglen Gdns *CAR/SHTL* G32 **94** B2
Carroglen Gv *CAR/SHTL* G32 **94** B2
Carron Crs *BSDN* G61 **14** A4
BSHPBGS G64 **32** B2
SPRGB/BLRNK G21 **45** D2
Carron Pl *PPK/MIL* G22 **45** D2
Carron St *PPK/MIL* G22 **45** D2
Carrour Gdns *BSHPBGS* G64 **31** D1

Carsaig Dr *CARD/HILL/MSPK* G52 **83** C2
Carseview Dr *BSDN* G61 **16** A1
Carstairs St *DMNK/BRGTN* G40 **109** D1
Carswell Gdns *PLKSD/SHW* G41 **105** D1
Cartcraigs Rd *PLKSW/MSWD* G43 **124** A1
Cartha Crs *PSLYS* PA2 **78** A4
Cartha St *PLKSD/SHW* G41 **105** C4
Cart La *PSLYN/LNWD* PA3 **77** C1
Cartside Qd *PLKSW/MSWD* G43 **106** B4
Cartside St *GVH/MTFL* G42 **106** A4
Cart St *CLYDBK* G81 **20** B3
Cartvale La *PSLYN/LNWD* PA3 **77** C1
Cartvale Rd *GVH/MTFL* G42 **106** A4
Cassley Av *RNFRW* PA4 **57** C1
Castlebank Ct *KNTSWD* G13 **39** D1
Castlebank Crs *PTCK* G11 **60** B2
Castlebank Gdns *KNTSWD* G13 **39** D1
Castlebank St *PTCK* G11 **60** A2
Castlebank Vls *KNTSWD* G13 **39** D1
Castlebay Dr *PPK/MIL* G22 **30** A2
Castlebay Pl *PPK/MIL* G22 **30** A3
Castlebay St *PPK/MIL* G22 **30** A3
Castlebrae Gdns *LNPK/KPK* G44 **127** C1
Castle Chimmins Av *BLTYR/CAMB* G72 **134** A3
Castle Chimmins Rd *BLTYR/CAMB* G72 **134** A4
Castlefern Rd *RUTH* G73 **129** D4
Castle Gait *PSLY* PA1 **77** C4
Castlehill Crs *RNFRW* PA4 **36** A3
Castlehill Rd *BSDN* G61 **13** D1
Castlelaw Gdns *CAR/SHTL* G32 **93** D1
Castlelaw St *CAR/SHTL* G32 **93** D1
Castlemilk Crs *LNPK/KPK* G44 **128** B2
Castlemilk Dr *CSMK* G45 **128** B4
Castlemilk Rd *LNPK/KPK* G44 **108** B4
RUTH G73 **129** C3
Castle St *BAIL/MDB/MHD* G69 **95** D4
COWCAD G4 **5** D5
PSLY PA1 **76** A3
PTCK G11 **61** D2
RUTH G73 **110** A3
SPRGB/BLRNK G21 **5** E3
Castleton Av *SPRGB/BLRNK* G21 **31** C4
Cathay St *PPK/MIL* G22 **30** A3
Cathcart Crs *PSLYS* PA2 **78** A4
Cathcart Pl *RUTH* G73 **109** C4
Cathcart Rd *GBLS* G5 **87** D3
LNPK/KPK G44 **106** B4
RUTH G73 **109** C4
Cathedral Sq *COWCAD* G4 **9** D1
Cathedral St *COWCAD* G4 **4** A5
Cathkin Av *BLTYR/CAMB* G72 **131** D1
RUTH G73 **110** B4
Cathkin By-Pass *RUTH* G73 **131** C4
Cathkin Dr *CRMNK/CLK/EAG* G76 **137** C3
Cathkin Pl *BLTYR/CAMB* G72 **131** D1
Cathkin Rd *GVH/MTFL* G42 **106** A4
UD/BTH/TAN G71 **117** D2
Cathkinview Pl *GVH/MTFL* G42 **106** B4
Cathkinview Rd *GVH/MTFL* G42 **106** B4
Catrine Ct *PLK/PH/NH* G53 **100** B3
Catrine Gdns *PLK/PH/NH* G53 **100** B3
Catrine Pl *PLK/PH/NH* G53 **100** B3
Catrine Rd *PLK/PH/NH* G53 **100** B3
Causewayside Crs *CAR/SHTL* G32 **112** B1
Causewayside St *CAR/SHTL* G32 **112** B1
Causeyside St *PSLY* PA1 **77** C3
Cavendish Pl *GBLS* G5 **87** D3
Cavendish St *GBLS* G5 **87** D3
Cavin Dr *CSMK* G45 **128** B3
Cavin Rd *CSMK* G45 **128** B3
Cayton Gdns *BAIL/MDB/MHD* G69 **95** D3
Cecil St *KVD/HLHD* G12 **42** A4
Cedar Ct *BLTYR/CAMB* G72 **134** B3
MRYH/FIRH G20 **63** D1
Cedar Gdns *RUTH* G73 **130** B4
Cedar Rd *BSHPBGS* G64 **32** B3
Cedar St *MRYH/FIRH* G20 **63** D1
Cedric Pl *KNTSWD* G13 **24** B4
Cedric Rd *KNTSWD* G13 **24** B4
Celtic St *MRYH/FIRH* G20 **27** C4
Cemetery Rd *CARD/HILL/MSPK* G52 **82** B3
Centenary Ct *CLYDBK* G81 **20** B2
Central Av *BLTYR/CAMB* G72 **132** A1
CAR/SHTL G32 **94** B4
CLYDBK G81 **20** A1
PTCK G11 **60** A1
Central Gv *CAR/SHTL* G32 **94** B3
Central Pth *CAR/SHTL* G32 **95** C4
Central Rd *PSLY* PA1 **77** C2
Central Wy *PSLY* PA1 **77** C2
Centre St *GBLS* G5 **6** C5
Centre Wy *BRHD/NEIL* G78 **118** A2
Ceres Gdns *BSHPBGS* G64 **33** D2
Cessnock Rd *STPS/GTHM/RID* G33 **49** D2
Cessnock St *GOV/IBX* G51 **85** C2
Chalmers Ga *DMNK/BRGTN* G40 **9** E4
Chalmers St *CLYDBK* G81 **20** B2
DMNK/BRGTN G40 **9** E4
Chamberlain La *KNTSWD* G13 **39** D2
Chamberlain Rd *KNTSWD* G13 **39** D2
Chancellor St *PTCK* G11 **61** C1
Chapel Ct *RUTH* G73 **109** C3
Chapel St *MRYH/FIRH* G20 **42** B2
RUTH G73 **109** C3
Chapelton Av *BSDN* G61 **15** D3
Chapelton Gdns *BSDN* G61 **15** D3
Chapelton St *PPK/MIL* G22 **44** B1
Chaplet Av *KNTSWD* G13 **24** A3
Chapman St *GVH/MTFL* G42 **106** B1
Chappell St *BRHD/NEIL* G78 **118** A2
Charing Cross La *KVGV* G3 **2** A4
Charles Av *RNFRW* PA4 **36** A3
Charles St *SPRGB/BLRNK* G21 **5** F2
Charlotte St *CGLE* G1 **8** C4
Chatelherault Av *BLTYR/CAMB* G72 **131** D2
Chatton St *SMSTN* G23 **27** D2
Cheapside St *KVGV* G3 **6** A2
Chelmsford Dr *KVD/HLHD* G12 **41** C2
Cherrybank Rd *PLKSW/MSWD* G43 **126** A2
Cherry Gv *CTBR* ML5 **99** D1
Cherry Pl *BSHPBGS* G64 **32** B3
Cherryridge Dr *CTBR* ML5 **99** C1
Cherrytree Dr *BLTYR/CAMB* G72 **134** B3
Chesterfield Av *KVD/HLHD* G12 **40** B2
Chesters Pl *RUTH* G73 **109** C4
Chesters Rd *BSDN* G61 **14** A3
Chester St *CAR/SHTL* G32 **93** C2
Chestnut St *PPK/MIL* G22 **45** C2
Chestnut Wy *BLTYR/CAMB* G72 **134** B3
Cheviot Av *BRHD/NEIL* G78 **118** B3
Cheviot Rd *PLKSW/MSWD* G43 **124** B2
Chirmorie Crs *PLK/PH/NH* G53 **100** B2
Chirmorie Pl *PLK/PH/NH* G53 **100** B2
Chirnside Pl *CARD/HILL/MSPK* G52 **81** C1
Chirnside Rd *CARD/HILL/MSPK* G52 **81** C1
Chisolm St *CGLE* G1 **8** B3
Christian St *PLKSW/MSWD* G43 **104** B3
Christie La *PSLY* PA1 **77** C2
Christie St *PSLY* PA1 **77** D2
Christopher St *SPRGB/BLRNK* G21 **66** B2
Church Av *RUTH* G73 **130** B2
STPS/GTHM/RID G33 **51** C1
Church Hl *PSLY* PA1 **77** C2
Churchill Dr *PTCK* G11 **40** B4
Church Rd *GIF/THBK* G46 **137** C1
Church St *BAIL/MDB/MHD* G69 **97** C3
PTCK G11 **61** D2
Church Vw *BLTYR/CAMB* G72 **112** B4
Circus Dr *DEN/PKHD* G31 **66** A4
Circus Place La *DEN/PKHD* G31 **66** A4
Citizen La *CGLE* G1 **7** F1
Cityford Dr *RUTH* G73 **129** C1
Civic St *COWCAD* G4 **3** D2
Clachan Dr *GOV/IBX* G51 **59** D3
Claddens Qd *PPK/MIL* G22 **44** B1
Claddens St *PPK/MIL* G22 **44** A1
Clairinch Gdns *RNFRW* PA4 **55** D2
Clairmont Gdns *KVGV* G3 **63** C2
Clair Rd *BSHPBGS* G64 **33** D2
Claremont Dr *MLNGV* G62 **10** B1
Claremont Gdns *MLNGV* G62 **10** B2
Claremont Pas *KVGV* G3 **63** C2
Claremont Pl *KVGV* G3 **63** C2
Claremont St *KVGV* G3 **62** B3
Claremont Ter *KVGV* G3 **63** C2
Claremount Av *GIF/THBK* G46 **137** C1
Claremount Terrace La *KVGV* G3 **62** B2
Clarence Dr *PSLY* PA1 **78** A2
PTCK G11 **40** B4
Clarence Gdns *PTCK* G11 **40** B4
Clarence La *KVD/HLHD* G12 **41** C4
Clarence St *CLYDBK* G81 **21** C1
PSLY PA1 **78** A2
Clarendon Pl *COWCAD* G4 **2** B1
Clarendon St *MRYH/FIRH* G20 **2** B1
Clare St *SPRGB/BLRNK* G21 **66** B2
Clarion Crs *KNTSWD* G13 **23** C3
Clarion Rd *KNTSWD* G13 **23** C4
Clarkston Av *LNPK/KPK* G44 **126** A3
Clarkston Rd *LNPK/KPK* G44 **126** B2

Clark St *PSLYN/LNWD* PA3 ....76 A1
RNFRW PA4 ....35 C4
Clathic Av *BSDN* G61 ....16 A4
Claude Av *BLTYR/CAMB* G72 ....134 B4
Claud Rd *PSLYN/LNWD* PA3 ....78 A1
Clavens Rd *CARD/HILL/MSPK* G52 ....80 A1
Claverhouse Pl *PSLYS* PA2 ....78 A4
Claverhouse Rd *CARD/HILL/MSPK* G52 ....57 C4
Clavering St East *PSLY* PA1 ....76 A2
Clavering St West *PSLY* PA1 ....76 A3
Clayhouse Rd *STPS/GTHM/RID* G33 ....51 D3
Claypotts Pl *STPS/GTHM/RID* G33 ....69 D2
Claypotts Rd *STPS/GTHM/RID* G33 ....69 D2
Clayslaps Rd *KVGV* G3 ....62 A2
Claythorn Av *DMNK/BRGTN* G40 ....9 D5
Claythorn Circ *DMNK/BRGTN* G40 ....9 D5
Claythorn Pk *DMNK/BRGTN* G40 ....9 D5
Claythorn Ter *DMNK/BRGTN* G40 ....9 E4
Clayton Ter *DEN/PKHD* G31 ....66 A4
Cleddens Ct *BSHPBGS* G64 ....32 A2
Cleeves Qd *PLK/PH/NH* G53 ....120 B2
Cleeves Rd *PLK/PH/NH* G53 ....120 B2
Cleghorn St *PPK/MIL* G22 ....44 A4
Cleland La *GBLS* G5 ....88 A2
Cleland St *GBLS* G5 ....88 A2
Clelland Av *BSHPBGS* G64 ....32 A3
Clerwood St *CAR/SHTL* G32 ....91 D1
Cleuch Gdns *CRMNK/CLK/EAG* G76 ....137 D3
Cleveden Crs *KVD/HLHD* G12 ....41 C2
Cleveden Crescent La *KVD/HLHD* G12 ....41 C2
Cleveden Dr *KVD/HLHD* G12 ....41 C2
RUTH G73 ....130 B1
Cleveden Drive La *KVD/HLHD* G12 ....41 D3
Cleveden Gdns *KVD/HLHD* G12 ....41 D2
Cleveden La *KVD/HLHD* G12 ....41 C1
Cleveden Pl *KVD/HLHD* G12 ....41 C1
Cleveden Rd *KVD/HLHD* G12 ....41 C1
Cleveland La *CGLW* G2 ....2 A4
Cleveland St *KVGV* G3 ....2 A4
Clifford Gdns *GOV/IBX* G51 ....84 B2
Clifford La *GOV/IBX* G51 ....85 D2
Clifford St *GOV/IBX* G51 ....84 B2
Cliff Rd *KVGV* G3 ....63 C2
Clifton Pl *KVGV* G3 ....62 B3
Clifton Rd *GIF/THBK* G46 ....124 A4
Clifton St *KVGV* G3 ....62 B2
Clifton Ter *BLTYR/CAMB* G72 ....131 D4
Clincarthill Rd *RUTH* G73 ....109 D4
Clincart Rd *GVH/MTFL* G42 ....107 C3
Cloan Av *DRUM* G15 ....23 D1
Cloan Crs *BSHPBGS* G64 ....19 D3
Cloberhill Rd *KNTSWD* G13 ....24 A2
Clober Rd *MLNGV* G62 ....10 B1
Clochbar Gdns *MLNGV* G62 ....10 A1
Cloch St *STPS/GTHM/RID* G33 ....69 D3
Clonbeith St *STPS/GTHM/RID* G33 ....71 D1
Closeburn St *PPK/MIL* G22 ....44 B2
Cloth St *BRHD/NEIL* G78 ....118 B3
Clouston La *MRYH/FIRH* G20 ....42 B3
Clouston St *MRYH/FIRH* G20 ....42 A3
Clova St *GIF/THBK* G46 ....123 C3
Cloverbank St *SPRGB/BLRNK* G21 ....66 B2
Clovergate *BSHPBGS* G64 ....31 C2
Clunie Rd *CARD/HILL/MSPK* G52 ....83 C3
Cluny Av *BSDN* G61 ....26 A1
Cluny Dr *BSDN* G61 ....26 A1
PSLYN/LNWD PA3 ....78 A1
Cluny Gdns *BAIL/MDB/MHD* G69 ....96 A3
SCOT G14 ....39 D3
Clutha St *GOV/IBX* G51 ....85 D1
Clyde Av *BRHD/NEIL* G78 ....119 C4
Clydebrae St *GOV/IBX* G51 ....61 C3
Clydeford Dr *CAR/SHTL* G32 ....92 A4
UD/BTH/TAN G71 ....117 C4
Clydeford Rd *BLTYR/CAMB* G72 ....133 C1
CAR/SHTL G32 ....112 B4
Clydeholm Rd *SCOT* G14 ....59 C1
Clydeholm Ter *CLYDBK* G81 ....21 D4
Clydeneuk Dr *UD/BTH/TAN* G71 ....117 C4
Clyde Pl *BLTYR/CAMB* G72 ....134 A3
GBLS G5 ....6 C3
Clyde Rd *PSLYN/LNWD* PA3 ....55 C4
Clydesdale Av *PSLYN/LNWD* PA3 ....54 B2
Clydeside Rd *RUTH* G73 ....109 C1
Clydesmill Dr *CAR/SHTL* G32 ....112 B4
Clydesmill Gv *CAR/SHTL* G32 ....112 B4
Clydesmill Pl *CAR/SHTL* G32 ....112 B3
Clydesmill Rd *CAR/SHTL* G32 ....112 B3
Clyde St *CGLE* G1 ....7 E3
CLYDBK G81 ....21 C4
RNFRW PA4 ....36 A2
Clydeview Ter *CAR/SHTL* G32 ....113 D3
Clynder St *GOV/IBX* G51 ....84 B1
Clyth Dr *GIF/THBK* G46 ....137 D1
Coalhill St *DEN/PKHD* G31 ....90 B2
Coatbridge Rd *BAIL/MDB/MHD* G69 ....97 C2
CTBR ML5 ....99 C1
Coats Crs *BAIL/MDB/MHD* G69 ....96 A2
Cobington Pl *STPS/GTHM/RID* G33 ....70 A2
Cobinshaw St *CAR/SHTL* G32 ....93 C1
Coburg St *GBLS* G5 ....7 E5
Cochno St *CLYDBK* G81 ....21 C3
Cochrane St *BRHD/NEIL* G78 ....118 A3
CGLE G1 ....8 A1
Cochran St *PSLY* PA1 ....77 D3
Cockels Loan *RNFRW* PA4 ....55 D3
Cockenzie St *CAR/SHTL* G32 ....93 C2
Cockmuir St *SPRGB/BLRNK* G21 ....46 B3
Cogan Pl *BRHD/NEIL* G78 ....118 A3
Cogan Rd *PLKSW/MSWD* G43 ....124 B1
Cogan St *BRHD/NEIL* G78 ....118 A3
PLKSW/MSWD G43 ....104 B4
Colbert St *DMNK/BRGTN* G40 ....89 D4
Colchester Dr *KVD/HLHD* G12 ....40 B1
Coldingham Av *SCOT* G14 ....36 B1
Coldstream Dr *RUTH* G73 ....131 C1
Coldstream Pl *COWCAD* G4 ....44 B4
Coldstream Rd *CLYDBK* G81 ....20 B2
Colebrooke Pl *KVD/HLHD* G12 ....42 B4
Colebrooke St *BLTYR/CAMB* G72 ....132 B1
KVD/HLHD G12 ....42 B4
Colebrooke Ter *KVD/HLHD* G12 ....42 B4
Colfin St *ESTRH* G34 ....73 D2
Colgrain Av *MRYH/FIRH* G20 ....43 D1
Colgrain St *MRYH/FIRH* G20 ....43 D2
Colgrain Ter *MRYH/FIRH* G20 ....43 D1
Colgrave Crs *CAR/SHTL* G32 ....92 B4
Colinbar Cir *BRHD/NEIL* G78 ....118 A4
Colinslie Rd *PLK/PH/NH* G53 ....101 D3
Colinton Pl *CAR/SHTL* G32 ....70 A4
Colintraive Av *STPS/GTHM/RID* G33 ....48 B4
Colintraive Crs *STPS/GTHM/RID* G33 ....48 B4
Colla Gdns *BSHPBGS* G64 ....33 D1
Coll Av *RNFRW* PA4 ....56 A2
College La *CGLE* G1 ....8 C2
College St *CGLE* G1 ....8 B2
Collessie Dr *STPS/GTHM/RID* G33 ....70 B1
Collina St *MRYH/FIRH* G20 ....41 D1
Collins St *COWCAD* G4 ....9 D1
Coll Pl *SPRGB/BLRNK* G21 ....67 C1
Coll St *SPRGB/BLRNK* G21 ....67 C1
Collylinn Rd *BSDN* G61 ....15 C3
Colmonell Av *KNTSWD* G13 ....22 B4
Colonsay Av *RNFRW* PA4 ....55 D2
Colonsay Rd *CARD/HILL/MSPK* G52 ....83 C2
Colquhoun Av *CARD/HILL/MSPK* G52 ....57 D4
Colquhoun Dr *BSDN* G61 ....14 B2
Colston Av *SPRGB/BLRNK* G21 ....31 D4
Colston Dr *BSHPBGS* G64 ....31 D4
Colston Gdns *BSHPBGS* G64 ....31 C4
Colston Pth *SPRGB/BLRNK* G21 ....31 C4
Colston Pl *SPRGB/BLRNK* G21 ....31 C4
Colston Rd *PPK/MIL* G22 ....31 C4
Coltmuir Crs *BSHPBGS* G64 ....31 C3
Coltmuir Dr *PPK/MIL* G22 ....31 C3
Coltmuir Gdns *PPK/MIL* G22 ....31 C3
Coltmuir St *PPK/MIL* G22 ....44 A1
Coltness La *STPS/GTHM/RID* G33 ....70 B4
Coltness St *STPS/GTHM/RID* G33 ....70 B3
Coltpark Av *BSHPBGS* G64 ....31 C3
Coltpark La *BSHPBGS* G64 ....31 C3
Coltsfoot Dr *PLK/PH/NH* G53 ....121 C4
Columba St *GOV/IBX* G51 ....61 C4
Colvend Dr *RUTH* G73 ....130 A4
Colvend St *DMNK/BRGTN* G40 ....89 D4
Colville Dr *RUTH* G73 ....131 C1
Colwood Av *PLK/PH/NH* G53 ....120 B3
Colwood Gdns *PLK/PH/NH* G53 ....120 B4
Colwood Pl *PLK/PH/NH* G53 ....120 B4
Colwood Sq *PLK/PH/NH* G53 ....120 B4
Comedie Rd *STPS/GTHM/RID* G33 ....51 D3
Comelypark St *DEN/PKHD* G31 ....89 D1
Commerce St *GBLS* G5 ....7 D5
Commercial Rd *BRHD/NEIL* G78 ....118 B2
GBLS G5 ....88 B2
Commonhead Rd *ESTRH* G34 ....74 A3
Commore Av *BRHD/NEIL* G78 ....119 C4
Commore Dr *KNTSWD* G13 ....23 C4
Comrie Rd *STPS/GTHM/RID* G33 ....50 B2
Comrie St *CAR/SHTL* G32 ....93 D4

Cona St *GIF/THBK* G46 **122** B3
Congress Rd *KVGV* G3 **62** A4
Congress Wy *KVGV* G3 **62** B4
Conisborough Rd *ESTRH* G34 **72** A1
Conistone Crs *BAIL/MDB/MHD* G69 **95** D3
Connal St *DMNK/BRGTN* G40 **90** B4
Connell Crs *MLNGV* G62 **11** D2
Conniston St *CAR/SHTL* G32 **68** B4
Connor Rd *BRHD/NEIL* G78 **118** A2
Conon Av *BSDN* G61 **14** B4
Consett La *STPS/GTHM/RID* G33 **70** B3
Consett St *STPS/GTHM/RID* G33 **70** B3
Contin Pl *MRYH/FIRH* G20 **42** A2
Cook St *GBLS* G5 **6** C5
Cooperage Ct *KNTSWD* G13 **36** A1
Copland Pl *GOV/IBX* G51 **84** B1
Copland Qd *GOV/IBX* G51 **84** B1
Copland Rd *GOV/IBX* G51 **84** B2
Coplaw St *GVH/MTFL* G42 **87** C4
Corbett Ct *CAR/SHTL* G32 **92** B4
Corbett St *CAR/SHTL* G32 **93** C4
Cordiner St *LNPK/KPK* G44 **107** C4
Corkerhill Gdns *CARD/HILL/MSPK* G52 **83** C3
Corkerhill Pl *CARD/HILL/MSPK* G52 **102** A1
Corkerhill Rd *CARD/HILL/MSPK* G52 **82** B4
Corlaich Av *GVH/MTFL* G42 **108** B4
Corlaich Dr *RUTH* G73 **108** B4
Cornaig Rd *PLK/PH/NH* G53 **101** C3
Cornalee Gdns *PLK/PH/NH* G53 **100** B3
Cornalee Pl *PLK/PH/NH* G53 **100** B3
Cornalee Rd *PLK/PH/NH* G53 **101** C3
Cornhill St *SPRGB/BLRNK* G21 **46** B2
Corn St *COWCAD* G4 **3** D1
Cornwall Av *RUTH* G73 **131** C2
Cornwall St *GOV/IBX* G51 **85** D2
Cornwall St South *PLKSD/SHW* G41 **85** D3
Coronation Wy *BSDN* G61 **25** D1
Corpach Pl *ESTRH* G34 **74** A2
Corran St *STPS/GTHM/RID* G33 **69** C3
Corrie Dr *PSLY* PA1 **80** A3
Corrie Gv *LNPK/KPK* G44 **126** A3
Corrour Rd *PLKSW/MSWD* G43 **105** C4
Corsebar Wy *PSLYS* PA2 **76** A4
Corse Dr *BRHD/NEIL* G78 **118** A1
Corsehill Pl *ESTRH* G34 **73** D3
Corsehill St *ESTRH* G34 **73** D3
Corselet Rd *PLK/PH/NH* G53 **121** C4
Corse Rd *CARD/HILL/MSPK* G52 **80** A1
Corsewall Av *CAR/SHTL* G32 **95** C4
Corsford Dr *PLK/PH/NH* G53 **121** D1
Corsock St *DEN/PKHD* G31 **67** C4
Corston St *STPS/GTHM/RID* G33 **68** A3
Cortachy Pl *BSHPBGS* G64 **33** D2
Coruisk Dr *CRMNK/CLK/EAG* G76 **137** D3
Corunna St *KVGV* G3 **62** B3
Coshneuk Rd *STPS/GTHM/RID* G33 **50** A2
Cottar St *MRYH/FIRH* G20 **28** A4
Cotton St *DMNK/BRGTN* G40 **109** C1
PSLY PA1 **77** D3
Coulin Gdns *PPK/MIL* G22 **45** C3
County Av *BLTYR/CAMB* G72 **111** C4
County Pl *PSLY* PA1 **77** C2
County Sq *PSLY* PA1 **77** C2
Couper St *COWCAD* G4 **4** B3
Courthill *BSDN* G61 **14** B1
Courthill Av *LNPK/KPK* G44 **127** C2
Coustonholm Rd *PLKSW/MSWD* G43 **105** C4
Coventry Dr *DEN/PKHD* G31 **67** C3
Cowal Rd *MRYH/FIRH* G20 **27** C4
Cowal St *MRYH/FIRH* G20 **27** C4
Cowan Crs *BRHD/NEIL* G78 **119** C3
Cowan La *KVD/HLHD* G12 **62** B1
Cowan St *KVD/HLHD* G12 **62** B1
Cowcaddens Rd *COWCAD* G4 **3** D3
Cowcaddens St *CGLW* G2 **3** E4
Cowdenhill Circ *KNTSWD* G13 **24** B3
Cowdenhill Pl *KNTSWD* G13 **24** B3
Cowdenhill Rd *KNTSWD* G13 **24** A3
Cowden St *GOV/IBX* G51 **59** C4
Cowdray Crs *RNFRW* PA4 **36** A4
Cowglen Rd *PLK/PH/NH* G53 **101** D4
Cowlairs Rd *SPRGB/BLRNK* G21 **45** D3
Coxhill St *SPRGB/BLRNK* G21 **45** C4
Coxton Pl *STPS/GTHM/RID* G33 **71** C2
Coylton Rd *PLKSW/MSWD* G43 **126** A2
Craggan Dr *KNTSWD* G13 **37** C1
Craigallian Av *BLTYR/CAMB* G72 **134** A4
Craiganour La *PLKSW/MSWD* G43 **124** B1
Craigard Pl *RUTH* G73 **131** C4
Craigbank Dr *PLK/PH/NH* G53 **120** B1
Craigbarnet Crs *STPS/GTHM/RID* G33 **50** A3
Craigbo Av *SMSTN* G23 **27** D2
Craigbo Rd *SMSTN* G23 **27** D2
Craigbo St *SMSTN* G23 **27** D2
Craigdhu Av *MLNGV* G62 **10** A2
Craigdhu Rd *MLNGV* G62 **10** A2
Craigellan Rd *PLKSW/MSWD* G43 **125** C1
Craigenbay St *SPRGB/BLRNK* G21 **47** C3
Craigend Crs *MLNGV* G62 **10** A1
Craigendmuir Rd *STPS/GTHM/RID* G33 **51** D3
Craigendmuir St *STPS/GTHM/RID* G33 **68** A1
Craigend Pl *KNTSWD* G13 **39** D1
Craigend St *KNTSWD* G13 **39** D1
Craigflower Gdns *PLK/PH/NH* G53 **120** B3
Craigflower Rd *PLK/PH/NH* G53 **120** B3
Craighall Rd *COWCAD* G4 **3** E1
Craighead Av *STPS/GTHM/RID* G33 **48** A4
Craighead Wy *BRHD/NEIL* G78 **118** A3
Craighouse St *STPS/GTHM/RID* G33 **69** D2
Craigieburn Gdns *MRYH/FIRH* G20 **26** B3
Craigiehall Pl *GOV/IBX* G51 **85** D1
Craigiehall St *GOV/IBX* G51 **85** D1
Craigielea Pk *RNFRW* PA4 **35** D4
Craigielea Rd *RNFRW* PA4 **35** D4
Craigielea St *DEN/PKHD* G31 **66** B3
Craigie St *GVH/MTFL* G42 **106** B1
Craigievar St *STPS/GTHM/RID* G33 **71** D1
Craigleith St *CAR/SHTL* G32 **92** A1
Craiglockhart St *STPS/GTHM/RID* G33 **71** C2
Craigmaddie Terrace La *KVGV* G3 **62** B2
Craigmillar Av *MLNGV* G62 **11** C1
Craigmillar Rd *GVH/MTFL* G42 **106** B4
Craigmont Dr *MRYH/FIRH* G20 **42** B2
Craigmont St *MRYH/FIRH* G20 **42** B1
Craigmore St *DEN/PKHD* G31 **91** C1
Craigmuir Crs *CARD/HILL/MSPK* G52 **80** B1
Craigmuir Pl *CARD/HILL/MSPK* G52 **80** A1
Craigmuir Rd *CARD/HILL/MSPK* G52 **80** A1
Craigneil St *STPS/GTHM/RID* G33 **71** D1
Craignestock Pl *DMNK/BRGTN* G40 **89** C2
Craignestock St *DMNK/BRGTN* G40 **9** E5
Craignethan Rd *GIF/THBK* G46 **136** A4
Craignure Rd *RUTH* G73 **130** A4
Craigpark *DEN/PKHD* G31 **66** B4
Craigpark Dr *DEN/PKHD* G31 **66** B4
Craig Rd *LNPK/KPK* G44 **126** B2
Craigton Av *BRHD/NEIL* G78 **119** D4
MLNGV G62 **10** A1
Craigton Dr *BRHD/NEIL* G78 **119** D4
GOV/IBX G51 **83** C1
Craigton Pl *GOV/IBX* G51 **83** C1
Craigton Rd *GOV/IBX* G51 **83** D1
Craigvicar Gdns *CAR/SHTL* G32 **94** B2
Craigwell Av *RUTH* G73 **131** C1
Crail St *DEN/PKHD* G31 **91** D2
Cramond Av *RNFRW* PA4 **56** B1
Cramond St *GBLS* G5 **108** A1
Cramond Ter *CAR/SHTL* G32 **93** D2
Cranborne Rd *KVD/HLHD* G12 **40** B2
Cranbrooke Dr *MRYH/FIRH* G20 **27** D4
Cranston St *KVGV* G3 **63** C4
Cranworth La *KVD/HLHD* G12 **42** A4
Cranworth St *KVD/HLHD* G12 **42** A4
Crarae Av *BSDN* G61 **25** C1
Crathes Ct *LNPK/KPK* G44 **125** D3
Crathie Dr *PTCK* G11 **60** B1
Crawford Crs *UD/BTH/TAN* G71 **117** D4
Crawford Dr *DRUM* G15 **23** C2
Crawford St *PTCK* G11 **60** B1
Crawfurd Av *RUTH* G73 **130** A2
Crawfurd Gdns *RUTH* G73 **130** B3
Crawfurd Rd *RUTH* G73 **130** A3
Craw Rd *PSLYS* PA2 **76** A4
Crebar Dr *BRHD/NEIL* G78 **118** B3
Crebar St *GIF/THBK* G46 **122** B3
Credon Gdns *RUTH* G73 **130** B3
Cree Av *BSHPBGS* G64 **33** D2
Cree Gdns *CAR/SHTL* G32 **92** B2
Creran Dr *RNFRW* PA4 **35** C3
Crescent Rd *SCOT* G14 **38** A2
Cresswell La *KVD/HLHD* G12 **42** A4
Cresswell St *KVD/HLHD* G12 **42** A4
Cressy St *GOV/IBX* G51 **59** D3
Crest Av *KNTSWD* G13 **23** D3
Crichton St *SPRGB/BLRNK* G21 **45** D3
Criffell Gdns *CAR/SHTL* G32 **94** B4
Criffell Rd *CAR/SHTL* G32 **94** B3
Crimea St *CGLW* G2 **6** B2
Crinan Gdns *BSHPBGS* G64 **33** C2
Crinan St *DEN/PKHD* G31 **67** C3

Cripps Av *CLYDBK* G81 **21** D2
Croftbank St *SPRGB/BLRNK* G21 **46** A3
Croftburn Dr *LNPK/KPK* G44 **128** A3
Croftcroighn Rd *STPS/GTHM/RID* G33 **70** A2
Croftend Av *LNPK/KPK* G44 **128** B1
Croftend La *RUTH* G73 **129** C2
Croftfoot Crs *CSMK* G45 **129** D3
Croftfoot Dr *CSMK* G45 **129** C3
Croftfoot Qd *CSMK* G45 **128** B3
Croftfoot Rd *CSMK* G45 **128** B3
Croftfoot St *CSMK* G45 **129** D3
Croftfoot Ter *CSMK* G45 **129** C3
Crofthill Rd *LNPK/KPK* G44 **128** B3
Crofthouse Dr *LNPK/KPK* G44 **128** B3
Croftmont Av *LNPK/KPK* G44 **128** B3
Crofton Av *LNPK/KPK* G44 **128** A3
Croftpark Av *LNPK/KPK* G44 **128** B2
Croft Rd *BLTYR/CAMB* G72 **133** C2
Croftside Av *LNPK/KPK* G44 **128** B3
Croftspar Av *CAR/SHTL* G32 **94** B1
Croftspar Ct *STPS/GTHM/RID* G33 **94** B1
Croftspar Dr *CAR/SHTL* G32 **94** A1
Croftspar Ga *STPS/GTHM/RID* G33 **94** B1
Croftspar Gv *CAR/SHTL* G32 **94** A1
Croftspar Pl *CAR/SHTL* G32 **94** A1
Croft Wy *RNFRW* PA4 **56** A2
Croftwood Av *LNPK/KPK* G44 **128** A3
Cromarty Av *BSHPBGS* G64 **33** D1
PLKSW/MSWD G43 **106** A4
Cromarty Crs *BSDN* G61 **10** A4
Crombie Gdns *BAIL/MDB/MHD* G69 **95** D4
Cromdale St *GOV/IBX* G51 **83** C1
Cromer St *MRYH/FIRH* G20 **43** C2
Crompton Av *LNPK/KPK* G44 **127** C2
Cromwell La *COWCAD* G4 **2** B1
Cromwell St *COWCAD* G4 **2** B1
Cronberry Qd *CARD/HILL/MSPK* G52 **80** B4
Cronberry Ter *CARD/HILL/MSPK* G52 **80** B4
Crookston Av *CARD/HILL/MSPK* G52 **81** C3
Crookston Ct *CARD/HILL/MSPK* G52 **81** C3
Crookston Dr *CARD/HILL/MSPK* G52 **80** B3
Crookston Gv *CARD/HILL/MSPK* G52 **81** C3
Crookston Pl *CARD/HILL/MSPK* G52 **80** B3
Crookston Qd *CARD/HILL/MSPK* G52 **80** B3
Crookston Rd *CARD/HILL/MSPK* G52 **80** B4
PLK/PH/NH G53 **100** A1
Crookston Ter *CARD/HILL/MSPK* G52 **81** C3
Crosbie La *MRYH/FIRH* G20 **27** C3
Crosbie St *MRYH/FIRH* G20 **27** C3
Cross Arthurlie St *BRHD/NEIL* G78 **118** A2
Crossbank Av *GVH/MTFL* G42 **108** B2
Crossbank Dr *GVH/MTFL* G42 **108** A2
Crossbank Rd *GVH/MTFL* G42 **108** A2
Crossbank Ter *GVH/MTFL* G42 **108** A2
Crossburn Av *MLNGV* G62 **10** A2
Crossflat Crs *PSLY* PA1 **78** A2
Crossford Dr *SMSTN* G23 **28** A2
Crosshill Av *GVH/MTFL* G42 **107** C2
Crosshill Dr *RUTH* G73 **130** A1
Crosshill St *CTBR* ML5 **99** D3
Crosslees Dr *GIF/THBK* G46 **123** C4
Crosslees Pk *GIF/THBK* G46 **123** C4
Crosslee St *CARD/HILL/MSPK* G52 **82** B2
Crossloan Rd *GOV/IBX* G51 **60** A4
Crossloan Ter *GOV/IBX* G51 **60** A4
Crossmill Av *BRHD/NEIL* G78 **119** C1
Crossmyloof Gdns *PLKSD/SHW* G41 **105** C2
Crosspoint Dr *SMSTN* G23 **28** A2
Cross St *CAR/SHTL* G32 **113** D2
Crosstobs Rd *PLK/PH/NH* G53 **100** B2
Crossveggate *MLNGV* G62 **11** C2
Crossview Av *BAIL/MDB/MHD* G69 **97** D2
Crossview Pl *BAIL/MDB/MHD* G69 **97** D2
Crovie Rd *PLK/PH/NH* G53 **100** B4
Crowhill Rd *BSHPBGS* G64 **31** D3
Crowhill St *PPK/MIL* G22 **44** B1
Crow La *KNTSWD* G13 **40** A2
Crowlin Crs *STPS/GTHM/RID* G33 **70** A3
Crown Circ *KVD/HLHD* G12 **41** D4
Crown Gdns *KVD/HLHD* G12 **41** D4
Crownhall Pl *CAR/SHTL* G32 **94** A2
Crownhall Rd *CAR/SHTL* G32 **94** A2
Crownpoint Rd *DMNK/BRGTN* G40 **9** F5
Crown Rd North *KVD/HLHD* G12 **41** C4
Crown Rd South *KVD/HLHD* G12 **41** D4
Crown St *BAIL/MDB/MHD* G69 **95** D4
GBLS G5 **8** A5
Crown Ter *KVD/HLHD* G12 **41** C4
Crow Rd *KNTSWD* G13 **25** D4
Croy Pl *SPRGB/BLRNK* G21 **47** D2
Croy Rd *SPRGB/BLRNK* G21 **47** D2
Cruachan Av *RNFRW* PA4 **55** D2
Cruachan Dr *BRHD/NEIL* G78 **118** B4
Cruachan Rd *RUTH* G73 **131** C4
Cruachan St *GIF/THBK* G46 **123** C3
Cruachan Wy *BRHD/NEIL* G78 **118** B4
Cruden St *GOV/IBX* G51 **83** D1
Crum Av *GIF/THBK* G46 **123** D4
Crusader Av *KNTSWD* G13 **24** B2
Cubie St *DMNK/BRGTN* G40 **89** D2
Cuilhill Rd *BAIL/MDB/MHD* G69 **99** C1
CTBR ML5 **75** C3
The Cuillins *UD/BTH/TAN* G71 **117** D2
Cuillin Wy *BRHD/NEIL* G78 **118** B3
Culbin Dr *KNTSWD* G13 **22** B3
Cullen St *CAR/SHTL* G32 **93** C3
Cullins Rd *RUTH* G73 **131** C4
Culloden St *DEN/PKHD* G31 **67** C3
Culrain Gdns *CAR/SHTL* G32 **93** C2
Culrain St *CAR/SHTL* G32 **93** C2
Culross St *CAR/SHTL* G32 **94** A3
Cults St *GOV/IBX* G51 **83** D1
Culzean Crs *BAIL/MDB/MHD* G69 **96** A3
Culzean Dr *CAR/SHTL* G32 **94** B2
Cumberland Pl *GBLS* G5 **88** A3
Cumberland St *GBLS* G5 **87** D2
Cumbernauld Rd *DEN/PKHD* G31 **67** C4
STPS/GTHM/RID G33 **49** D3
STPS/GTHM/RID G33 **68** A2
Cumbrae Ct *CLYDBK* G81 **20** B1
Cumbrae Rd *RNFRW* PA4 **56** A2
Cumbrae St *STPS/GTHM/RID* G33 **69** D3
Cumlodden Dr *MRYH/FIRH* G20 **27** C4
Cumming Dr *GVH/MTFL* G42 **107** C3
Cumnock Dr *BRHD/NEIL* G78 **119** C4
Cumnock Rd *STPS/GTHM/RID* G33 **48** B1
Cunard St *CLYDBK* G81 **20** B3
Cunningham Dr *GIF/THBK* G46 **125** D4
Cunninghame Rd *RUTH* G73 **110** B3
Cunningham Rd *CARD/HILL/MSPK* G52 **57** C3
Curfew Rd *KNTSWD* G13 **24** B2
Curle St *SCOT* G14 **59** D1
Curling Crs *GVH/MTFL* G42 **107** D4
Currie Pl *MRYH/FIRH* G20 **42** B2
Currie St *MRYH/FIRH* G20 **42** B1
Curtis Av *LNPK/KPK* G44 **108** B4
Curzon St *MRYH/FIRH* G20 **42** B1
Cuthbertson St *PLKSD/SHW* G41 **87** C4
Cuthelton Dr *DEN/PKHD* G31 **92** A3
Cuthelton St *DEN/PKHD* G31 **91** D3
Cuthelton Ter *DEN/PKHD* G31 **91** D3
Cypress Gv *CTBR* ML5 **99** C1
Cypress St *PPK/MIL* G22 **45** C2
Cypress Wy *BLTYR/CAMB* G72 **135** C3
Cyril St *PSLY* PA1 **78** A3

D

Daer Av *RNFRW* PA4 **56** B2
Dairsie Gdns *BSHPBGS* G64 **33** D3
Dairsie St *LNPK/KPK* G44 **126** A3
Daisy St *GVH/MTFL* G42 **107** C2
Dalbeth Rd *CAR/SHTL* G32 **112** A1
Dalcharn Pl *ESTRH* G34 **72** B3
Dalcross St *PTCK* G11 **61** D1
Daldowie Av *CAR/SHTL* G32 **94** B4
Daldowie Rd *UD/BTH/TAN* G71 **115** D1
Dale St *DMNK/BRGTN* G40 **89** D3
Daleview Av *KVD/HLHD* G12 **41** C1
Dale Wy *RUTH* G73 **129** D3
Dalfoil Ct *PSLY* PA1 **80** B3
Dalgarroch Av *KNTSWD* G13 **22** A3
Dalhousie Gdns *BSHPBGS* G64 **31** D1
Dalhousie La *KVGV* G3 **2** C3
Dalhousie St *COWCAD* G4 **3** D3
KVGV G3 **2** C4
Dalilea Dr *ESTRH* G34 **74** A2
Dalilea Pl *ESTRH* G34 **74** A2
Dalintober St *GBLS* G5 **6** B4
Dalkeith Av *BSHPBGS* G64 **19** D4
PLKSD/SHW G41 **84** B3
Dalkeith Rd *BSHPBGS* G64 **19** D3
Dalmahoy St *CAR/SHTL* G32 **68** B4
Dalmally St *MRYH/FIRH* G20 **43** C4
Dalmarnock Rd *DMNK/BRGTN* G40 **89** D3

Dalmary Dr *PSLY* PA1 78 B1
Dalmellington Dr *PLK/PH/NH* G53 100 B3
Dalmellington Rd *PLK/PH/NH* G53 100 B3
Dalmeny Av *GIF/THBK* G46 124 B4
Dalmeny St *GBLS* G5 108 B1
Dalnair St *KVGV* G3 61 D2
Dalness St *CAR/SHTL* G32 93 C4
Dalreoch Av *BAIL/MDB/MHD* G69 97 C2
Dalriada St *DMNK/BRGTN* G40 91 C3
Dalry St *CAR/SHTL* G32 93 D3
Dalserf Crs *GIF/THBK* G46 136 B2
Dalserf St *DMNK/BRGTN* G40 90 B2
Dalsetter Av *DRUM* G15 22 B1
Dalsetter Pl *DRUM* G15 23 C1
Dalsholm Rd *MRYH/FIRH* G20 26 B4
Dalswinton Pth *ESTRH* G34 73 D3
Dalswinton St *ESTRH* G34 73 D3
Dalton Av *CLYDBK* G81 22 A2
Dalton St *DEN/PKHD* G31 92 A2
Dalveen Ct *BRHD/NEIL* G78 118 B4
Dalveen Dr *UD/BTH/TAN* G71 117 D3
Dalveen St *CAR/SHTL* G32 92 B2
Dalveen Wy *RUTH* G73 130 B4
Dalziel Dr *PLKSD/SHW* G41 85 C4
Dalziel Rd *CARD/HILL/MSPK* G52 57 C3
Damshot Crs *PLK/PH/NH* G53 102 A3
Damshot Rd *PLK/PH/NH* G53 102 A4
Danby Rd *BAIL/MDB/MHD* G69 95 D3
Danes Av *SCOT* G14 38 B3
Danes Crs *SCOT* G14 38 A2
Danes Dr *SCOT* G14 38 B3
Danes La North *SCOT* G14 38 B3
Danes La South *SCOT* G14 38 B3
Dargarvel Av *PLKSD/SHW* G41 84 B3
Darleith St *CAR/SHTL* G32 92 B2
Darnaway Av *STPS/GTHM/RID* G33 71 C1
Darnaway Dr *STPS/GTHM/RID* G33 71 C1
Darnaway St *STPS/GTHM/RID* G33 71 C1
Darnick St *SPRGB/BLRNK* G21 66 B1
Darnley Crs *BSHPBGS* G64 18 B4
Darnley Gdns *PLKSD/SHW* G41 105 D1
Darnley Pl *PLKSD/SHW* G41 105 D1
Darnley Rd *BRHD/NEIL* G78 119 C2
PLKSD/SHW G41 105 D1
Darnley St *PLKSD/SHW* G41 86 B4
Dartford St *PPK/MIL* G22 44 A4
Darvel Crs *PSLY* PA1 79 D3
Darvel St *PLK/PH/NH* G53 120 A1
Davaar Rd *RNFRW* PA4 56 A2
Davaar St *DMNK/BRGTN* G40 90 B3
Dava St *GOV/IBX* G51 60 B4
Daventry Dr *KVD/HLHD* G12 40 B2
David Pl *BAIL/MDB/MHD* G69 95 D3
Davidson Pl *CAR/SHTL* G32 94 A1
Davidson St *CLYDBK* G81 22 A3
DMNK/BRGTN G40 109 D1
David St *DMNK/BRGTN* G40 90 A2
Davieland Rd *GIF/THBK* G46 136 A2
Daviot St *GOV/IBX* G51 82 B1
Dawson Pl *COWCAD* G4 44 A4
Dawson Rd *COWCAD* G4 44 A4
Dealston Rd *BRHD/NEIL* G78 118 A1
Deanfield Qd *CARD/HILL/MSPK* G52 80 B1
Dean Park Dr *BLTYR/CAMB* G72 134 A3
Dean Park Rd *RNFRW* PA4 56 A1
Deans Av *BLTYR/CAMB* G72 134 A4
Deanside Rd *CARD/HILL/MSPK* G52 57 D3
Deanston Av *BRHD/NEIL* G78 118 A4
Deanston Dr *PLKSD/SHW* G41 105 D3
Dean St *CLYDBK* G81 21 C2
Deanwood Av *GIF/THBK* G46 126 A4
Deanwood Rd *GIF/THBK* G46 126 A4
Dechmont Av *BLTYR/CAMB* G72 134 A4
Dechmont Pl *BLTYR/CAMB* G72 134 A4
Dechmont Rd *UD/BTH/TAN* G71 117 D2
Dechmont St *DEN/PKHD* G31 91 C3
Dee Av *RNFRW* PA4 36 B4
Deepdene Rd *BSDN* G61 24 B1
Dee St *STPS/GTHM/RID* G33 68 A3
Delny Pl *STPS/GTHM/RID* G33 71 D4
Delvin Rd *LNPK/KPK* G44 126 B1
Denbeck St *CAR/SHTL* G32 92 B2
Denbrae St *CAR/SHTL* G32 92 B2
Denham St *PPK/MIL* G22 44 A4
Denholm Dr *GIF/THBK* G46 137 C3
Denmark St *PPK/MIL* G22 44 B3
Denmilne Rd *BAIL/MDB/MHD* G69 74 A4
Denmilne St *ESTRH* G34 73 D4
Deramore Av *GIF/THBK* G46 136 A4
Derby St *KVGV* G3 62 B3
Derby Terrace La *KVGV* G3 62 A2
Derwent St *PPK/MIL* G22 44 A3
Despard Av *CAR/SHTL* G32 94 B3
Despard Gdns *CAR/SHTL* G32 95 C3
Deveron Av *GIF/THBK* G46 137 D1
Deveron Rd *BSDN* G61 24 A1
Deveron St *STPS/GTHM/RID* G33 68 A2
Devol Crs *PLK/PH/NH* G53 101 C3
Devon Gdns *BSHPBGS* G64 18 B4
Devon Pl *GVH/MTFL* G42 87 D3
Devonshire Gardens La *KVD/HLHD* G12 41 C3
Devonshire Ter *KVD/HLHD* G12 41 C3
Devonshire Terrace La *KVD/HLHD* G12 41 C3
Devon St *GBLS* G5 87 D3
Dewar Ga *DRUM* G15 13 C4
Diana Av *KNTSWD* G13 23 D3
Dick St *MRYH/FIRH* G20 43 C4
Dilwara Av *SCOT* G14 59 D1
Dinard Dr *GIF/THBK* G46 124 B3
Dinart St *STPS/GTHM/RID* G33 68 A2
Dinduff St *ESTRH* G34 73 D2
Dinmont Rd *PLKSD/SHW* G41 105 C2
Dinwiddie St *SPRGB/BLRNK* G21 67 D1
Dipple Pl *DRUM* G15 23 D1
Dirleton Dr *PLKSD/SHW* G41 105 D3
Dirleton Ga *BSDN* G61 14 B4
Dixon Av *GVH/MTFL* G42 106 B1
Dixon Rd *GVH/MTFL* G42 107 D2
Dixon St *CGLE* G1 7 E3
PSLY PA1 77 D3
Dobbie's Loan *COWCAD* G4 3 F2
Dobbie's Loan Pl *COWCAD* G4 4 B4
Dochart Av *RNFRW* PA4 56 B2
Dochart St *STPS/GTHM/RID* G33 68 B1
Dock St *CLYDBK* G81 21 D4
Dodhill Pl *KNTSWD* G13 38 A1
Dodside Gdns *CAR/SHTL* G32 94 A3
Dodside Pl *CAR/SHTL* G32 94 A3
Dodside St *CAR/SHTL* G32 94 A3
Dolan St *BAIL/MDB/MHD* G69 96 B2
Dollar Ter *MRYH/FIRH* G20 27 C3
Dolphin Rd *PLKSD/SHW* G41 105 C1
Donaldson Dr *RNFRW* PA4 35 D4
Don Av *RNFRW* PA4 56 B1
Don St *STPS/GTHM/RID* G33 68 A3
Doon Crs *BSDN* G61 14 B4
Doonfoot Rd *PLKSW/MSWD* G43 124 B1
Dora St *DMNK/BRGTN* G40 90 A4
Dorchester Av *KVD/HLHD* G12 40 B1
Dorchester Ct *KVD/HLHD* G12 40 B1
Dorchester Pl *KVD/HLHD* G12 40 B2
Dorian Dr *CRMNK/CLK/EAG* G76 137 C3
Dorlin Rd *STPS/GTHM/RID* G33 51 D2
Dormanside Ct *PLK/PH/NH* G53 81 D4
Dormanside Ga *PLK/PH/NH* G53 81 D4
Dormanside Gv *PLK/PH/NH* G53 81 D4
Dormanside Rd *PLK/PH/NH* G53 81 D4
Dornal Av *KNTSWD* G13 22 B4
Dornford Av *CAR/SHTL* G32 114 A1
Dornford Rd *CAR/SHTL* G32 114 A1
Dornie Dr *CAR/SHTL* G32 113 C3
Dornoch Av *GIF/THBK* G46 137 C2
Dornoch Rd *BSDN* G61 24 B1
Dornoch St *DMNK/BRGTN* G40 9 F5
Dorset St *KVGV* G3 63 C3
Dosk Av *KNTSWD* G13 22 A3
Dosk Pl *KNTSWD* G13 22 B3
Dougalston Av *MLNGV* G62 11 C2
Dougalston Crs *MLNGV* G62 11 C2
Dougalston Gdns North *MLNGV* G62 11 C2
Dougalston Gdns South *MLNGV* G62 11 C2
Dougalston Rd *SMSTN* G23 28 A2
Douglas Av *CAR/SHTL* G32 113 C2
GIF/THBK G46 137 C2
RUTH G73 130 B2
Douglas Dr *BAIL/MDB/MHD* G69 95 D2
BLTYR/CAMB G72 132 A3
DRUM G15 22 B2
Douglas Gdns *BSDN* G61 15 D3
GIF/THBK G46 137 C2
Douglas Ga *BLTYR/CAMB* G72 132 B2
Douglas La *CGLW* G2 2 C5
Douglas Park Crs *BSDN* G61 16 A1
Douglas Pl *BSDN* G61 15 C2
Douglas Rd *RNFRW* PA4 54 B3
Douglas St *CGLW* G2 2 C4
MLNGV G62 10 B2
PSLY PA1 76 A2
Douglas Ter *PLKSD/SHW* G41 106 A1
Dougray Pl *BRHD/NEIL* G78 118 B3

Dougrie Dr *CSMK* G45 ....128 B4
Dougrie Pl *CSMK* G45 ....128 B4
Dougrie Rd *CSMK* G45 ....128 A4
Dougrie St *CSMK* G45 ....128 A4
Dougrie Ter *CSMK* G45 ....128 A4
Doune Crs *BSHPBGS* G64 ....19 D3
Doune Gdns *MRYH/FIRH* G20 ....42 B4
Doune Gardens La *MRYH/FIRH* G20 ....42 B4
Doune Qd *MRYH/FIRH* G20 ....42 B4
Dovecot *PLKSW/MSWD* G43 ....104 B3
Dover St *KVGV* G3 ....63 C3
Dove St *PLK/PH/NH* G53 ....120 B2
Dowanhill St *PTCK* G11 ....61 D1
Dowanside La *KVD/HLHD* G12 ....41 D4
Dowanside Rd *KVD/HLHD* G12 ....41 D4
Downfield St *CAR/SHTL* G32 ....92 A4
Downhill St *KVD/HLHD* G12 ....41 D4
Downiebrae Rd *RUTH* G73 ....110 A1
Downs St *SPRGB/BLRNK* G21 ....46 A3
Dowrie Crs *PLK/PH/NH* G53 ....101 C2
Drakemire Av *CSMK* G45 ....127 D3
Drake St *DMNK/BRGTN* G40 ....9 E5
Dreghorn St *DEN/PKHD* G31 ....67 D4
Drive Rd *GOV/IBX* G51 ....59 D3
Drochil St *ESTRH* G34 ....72 B2
Drumbeg Dr *PLK/PH/NH* G53 ....120 B1
Drumbottie Rd *SPRGB/BLRNK* G21 ....46 B2
Drumby Crs *CRMNK/CLK/EAG* G76 ....137 D2
Drumby Dr *CRMNK/CLK/EAG* G76 ....137 D3
Drumcarn Dr *MLNGV* G62 ....10 A2
Drumchapel Gdns *DRUM* G15 ....23 C1
Drumchapel Pl *DRUM* G15 ....23 D1
Drumchapel Rd *DRUM* G15 ....23 D1
Drumclog Gdns *STPS/GTHM/RID* G33 ....49 C1
Drumcross Rd *PLK/PH/NH* G53 ....101 D2
Drumhead Pl *CAR/SHTL* G32 ....112 A2
Drumhead Rd *CAR/SHTL* G32 ....112 A2
Drumilaw Rd *RUTH* G73 ....129 D2
Drumilaw Wy *RUTH* G73 ....129 D2
Drumlaken Av *MRYH/FIRH* G20 ....27 C2
Drumlaken Ct *MRYH/FIRH* G20 ....27 C2
Drumlaken St *MRYH/FIRH* G20 ....27 C2
Drumlanrig Av *ESTRH* G34 ....74 A3
Drumlanrig Pl *ESTRH* G34 ....74 A3
Drumlin Dr *MLNGV* G62 ....10 A3
Drumlochy Rd *STPS/GTHM/RID* G33 ....69 D2
Drummond Av *RUTH* G73 ....109 C3
Drummond Dr *PSLY* PA1 ....79 D3
Drummore Rd *DRUM* G15 ....14 A3
Drumover Dr *DEN/PKHD* G31 ....92 A3
Drumoyne Av *GOV/IBX* G51 ....59 D4
Drumoyne Circ *GOV/IBX* G51 ....83 C1
Drumoyne Dr *GOV/IBX* G51 ....59 D4
Drumoyne Pl *GOV/IBX* G51 ....83 C1
Drumoyne Qd *GOV/IBX* G51 ....83 C1
Drumoyne Rd *GOV/IBX* G51 ....59 D4
Drumoyne Sq *GOV/IBX* G51 ....83 C1
Drumpark St *CTBR* ML5 ....99 D3
GIF/THBK G46 ....123 C3
Drumpellier Av *BAIL/MDB/MHD* G69 ....96 B4
Drumpellier Pl *BAIL/MDB/MHD* G69 ....96 B3
Drumpellier Rd *BAIL/MDB/MHD* G69 ....96 A4
Drumpellier St *STPS/GTHM/RID* G33 ....68 A1
Drumreoch Dr *GVH/MTFL* G42 ....108 B4
Drumreoch Pl *GVH/MTFL* G42 ....108 B3
Drumry Rd East *DRUM* G15 ....22 B1
Drumsargard Rd *RUTH* G73 ....131 C2
Drums Av *PSLYN/LNWD* PA3 ....76 A1
Drums Crs *PSLYN/LNWD* PA3 ....76 A1
Drumshaw Dr *CAR/SHTL* G32 ....113 D3
Drums Rd *PLK/PH/NH* G53 ....81 C4
Drury St *CGLW* G2 ....7 E1
Dryad St *GIF/THBK* G46 ....122 B2
Dryburgh Av *RUTH* G73 ....110 A4
Dryburgh Gdns *MRYH/FIRH* G20 ....43 C4
Dryburgh Rd *BSDN* G61 ....14 A1
Dryburn Av *CARD/HILL/MSPK* G52 ....81 C2
Drygate *COWCAD* G4 ....9 E2
Drygrange Rd *STPS/GTHM/RID* G33 ....70 B1
Drymen Rd *BSDN* G61 ....15 D4
Drymen St *CARD/HILL/MSPK* G52 ....83 C2
Drynoch Pl *PPK/MIL* G22 ....29 D4
Drysdale St *SCOT* G14 ....37 C2
Duart St *MRYH/FIRH* G20 ....27 C3
Dubs Rd *BRHD/NEIL* G78 ....119 D2
Dubton St *ESTRH* G34 ....73 C2
Duchall Pl *SCOT* G14 ....38 A3
Duchess Palace *RUTH* G73 ....110 B3
Duchess Rd *RUTH* G73 ....110 B2
Duchray Dr *PSLY* PA1 ....80 B3
Duchray La *STPS/GTHM/RID* G33 ....68 A2
Duchray St *STPS/GTHM/RID* G33 ....68 A2
Dudhope St *STPS/GTHM/RID* G33 ....71 C1
Dudley Dr *KVD/HLHD* G12 ....40 B4
Dudley La *KVD/HLHD* G12 ....40 B4
Duffus Pl *CAR/SHTL* G32 ....113 D3
Duffus St *ESTRH* G34 ....72 A2
Duffus Ter *CAR/SHTL* G32 ....113 D3
Duich Gdns *SMSTN* G23 ....28 A1
Duisdale Rd *CAR/SHTL* G32 ....113 D3
Dukes Rd *BAIL/MDB/MHD* G69 ....98 B2
RUTH G73 ....131 C2
Duke St *COWCAD* G4 ....9 D2
DEN/PKHD G31 ....91 D1
Dulnain St *BLTYR/CAMB* G72 ....134 A2
Dulsie Rd *SPRGB/BLRNK* G21 ....47 D1
Dumbarton Rd *PTCK* G11 ....60 B1
PTCK G11 ....61 D1
SCOT G14 ....36 B1
Dumbreck Av *CARD/HILL/MSPK* G52 ....84 A4
Dumbreck Ct *PLKSD/SHW* G41 ....84 A4
Dumbreck Pl *PLKSD/SHW* G41 ....84 A4
Dumbreck Rd *PLKSD/SHW* G41 ....104 A1
Dumbreck Sq *PLKSD/SHW* G41 ....84 A3
Dumgoyne Av *MLNGV* G62 ....10 A2
Dumgoyne Pl *CRMNK/CLK/EAG* G76 ....137 C4
Dunalastair Dr *STPS/GTHM/RID* G33 ....50 A2
Dunan Pl *STPS/GTHM/RID* G33 ....71 D4
Dunard Rd *RUTH* G73 ....110 A4
Dunard St *MRYH/FIRH* G20 ....43 C4
Dunaskin St *PTCK* G11 ....61 D2
Dunbar Av *RUTH* G73 ....110 B4
Dunbeith Pl *MRYH/FIRH* G20 ....42 A2
Dunblane St *COWCAD* G4 ....3 E3
Duncan Av *SCOT* G14 ....38 B4
Duncan La North *SCOT* G14 ....38 B3
Duncan La South *SCOT* G14 ....38 B4
Duncansby Rd *STPS/GTHM/RID* G33 ....94 B1
Dunchattan Pl *DEN/PKHD* G31 ....9 F3
Dunchattan St *DEN/PKHD* G31 ....9 F1
Dunchurch Rd *PSLY* PA1 ....79 D2
Dunclutha St *DMNK/BRGTN* G40 ....110 A1
Duncombe St *MRYH/FIRH* G20 ....27 D4
Duncrub Dr *BSHPBGS* G64 ....31 C2
Duncruin St *MRYH/FIRH* G20 ....27 C4
Duncruin Ter *MRYH/FIRH* G20 ....27 D4
Duncryne Av *CAR/SHTL* G32 ....94 B3
Duncryne Gdns *CAR/SHTL* G32 ....95 C3
Duncryne Pl *BSHPBGS* G64 ....31 C3
Duncryne Rd *CAR/SHTL* G32 ....94 B3
Dundashill *COWCAD* G4 ....3 E1
Dundas St *CGLE* G1 ....3 F5
Dundasvale Ct *COWCAD* G4 ....3 D2
Dundee Dr *CARD/HILL/MSPK* G52 ....81 D4
Dundonald Rd *KVD/HLHD* G12 ....41 D3
PSLYN/LNWD PA3 ....54 B4
Dundrennan Rd *GVH/MTFL* G42 ....106 A4
Dunearn Pl *PSLYS* PA2 ....78 A4
Dunearn St *COWCAD* G4 ....2 A1
Dunellan St *CARD/HILL/MSPK* G52 ....83 C2
Dungeonhill Rd *ESTRH* G34 ....74 A3
Dunglass Av *SCOT* G14 ....38 B3
Dunglass La *SCOT* G14 ....38 B3
Dunglass La North *SCOT* G14 ....38 B3
Dunglass La South *SCOT* G14 ....38 B3
Dungoyne St *MRYH/FIRH* G20 ....27 C3
Dunira St *CAR/SHTL* G32 ....92 B4
Dunivaig St *STPS/GTHM/RID* G33 ....71 C3
Dunkeld Av *RUTH* G73 ....110 A4
Dunkeld Dr *BSDN* G61 ....16 B3
Dunkeld St *DEN/PKHD* G31 ....91 C3
Dunkenny Rd *DRUM* G15 ....12 B3
Dunlin *KVD/HLHD* G12 ....40 B1
Dunlop St *BLTYR/CAMB* G72 ....134 B1
CGLE G1 ....7 F4
RNFRW PA4 ....36 A3
Dunmore Dr *MLNGV* G62 ....11 D3
Dunmore St *CLYDBK* G81 ....21 C3
Dunnachie Dr *CTBR* ML5 ....99 D3
Dunnichen Gdns *BSHPBGS* G64 ....33 D2
Dunning St *DEN/PKHD* G31 ....91 D3
Dunnottar St *BSHPBGS* G64 ....33 D1
STPS/GTHM/RID G33 ....70 A1
Dunn St *DMNK/BRGTN* G40 ....89 D4
PSLY PA1 ....78 A2
Dunolly St *SPRGB/BLRNK* G21 ....66 B2
Dunphail Dr *ESTRH* G34 ....74 A3
Dunphail Rd *ESTRH* G34 ....74 A3
Dunragit St *DEN/PKHD* G31 ....67 D4
Dunrobin St *DEN/PKHD* G31 ....90 B1

Dunrod St *CAR/SHTL* G32 ....93 D3
Dunside Dr *PLK/PH/NH* G53 ....120 B1
Dunskaith Pl *ESTRH* G34 ....74 A4
Dunskaith St *ESTRH* G34 ....74 A3
Dunsmuir St *GOV/IBX* G51 ....61 C4
Dunsyre Pl *SMSTN* G23 ....28 A2
Dunsyre St *STPS/GTHM/RID* G33 ....68 B3
Duntarvie Av *ESTRH* G34 ....73 D3
Duntarvie Cl *ESTRH* G34 ....73 D3
Duntarvie Crs *ESTRH* G34 ....73 D3
Duntarvie Dr *ESTRH* G34 ....73 C3
Duntarvie Gdns *ESTRH* G34 ....73 D3
Duntarvie Pl *ESTRH* G34 ....73 C3
Duntarvie Qd *ESTRH* G34 ....73 D3
Duntarvie Rd *ESTRH* G34 ....73 C3
Dunterlie Av *KNTSWD* G13 ....37 D1
Dunterlie Ct *BRHD/NEIL* G78 ....118 B2
Duntocher Rd *BSDN* G61 ....14 B1
Duntreath Av *DRUM* G15 ....22 B2
Duntreath Dr *DRUM* G15 ....22 B2
Duntreath Gdns *DRUM* G15 ....22 B1
Duntreath Gv *DRUM* G15 ....22 B2
Duntroon St *DEN/PKHD* G31 ....67 C3
Dunure Dr *RUTH* G73 ....129 C2
Dunure St *MRYH/FIRH* G20 ....27 D4
Dunvegan Dr *BSHPBGS* G64 ....19 C3
Dunvegan Pl *UD/BTH/TAN* G71 ....117 C3
Dunvegan Qd *RNFRW* PA4 ....35 C3
Dunwan Av *KNTSWD* G13 ....22 B4
Dunwan Pl *KNTSWD* G13 ....22 B4
Durham St *PLKSD/SHW* G41 ....85 D2
Durness Av *BSDN* G61 ....16 B2
Duror St *CAR/SHTL* G32 ....93 C1
Durris Gdns *CAR/SHTL* G32 ....94 B4
Durward Av *PLKSD/SHW* G41 ....105 C2
Durward Ct *PLKSD/SHW* G41 ....105 C2
Duthil St *GOV/IBX* G51 ....82 B1
Dyce La *PTCK* G11 ....60 B1
Dyer's La *CGLE* G1 ....8 B4
Dykebar Av *KNTSWD* G13 ....37 D1
Dykehead La *STPS/GTHM/RID* G33 ....71 C4
Dykehead Rd *BAIL/MDB/MHD* G69 ....98 B2
Dykehead St *STPS/GTHM/RID* G33 ....71 C4
Dykemuir Pl *SPRGB/BLRNK* G21 ....47 C3
Dykemuir Qd *SPRGB/BLRNK* G21 ....46 B3
Dykemuir St *SPRGB/BLRNK* G21 ....46 B3
Dyke Rd *KNTSWD* G13 ....37 C1
Dyke St *BAIL/MDB/MHD* G69 ....97 C2
CTBR ML5 ....99 D3

E

Eagle Crs *BSDN* G61 ....13 D1
Eaglesham Ct *GOV/IBX* G51 ....86 A1
Eaglesham Pl *GOV/IBX* G51 ....86 A1
Eagle St *COWCAD* G4 ....64 B1
Earlbank Av *SCOT* G14 ....38 B3
Earlbank La North *SCOT* G14 ....38 B3
Earlbank La South *SCOT* G14 ....38 B4
Earl Haig Rd *CARD/HILL/MSPK* G52 ....57 C4
Earl La *SCOT* G14 ....38 B4
Earl Pl *SCOT* G14 ....38 B3
Earlspark Av *PLKSW/MSWD* G43 ....126 A1
Earl St *SCOT* G14 ....38 B4
Earlybraes Gdns *CAR/SHTL* G32 ....94 B1
Earn Av *BSDN* G61 ....16 B3
RNFRW PA4 ....56 B1
Earnock St *STPS/GTHM/RID* G33 ....48 A3
Earnside St *CAR/SHTL* G32 ....93 D2
Earn St *STPS/GTHM/RID* G33 ....68 B2
Easdale Dr *CAR/SHTL* G32 ....92 B3
East Av *RNFRW* PA4 ....36 A4
Eastbank Dr *CAR/SHTL* G32 ....94 A2
East Barns St *CLYDBK* G81 ....21 D3
East Bath La *CGLE* G1 ....3 F5
East Buchanan St *PSLY* PA1 ....77 D2
Eastburn Crs *SPRGB/BLRNK* G21 ....47 C1
Eastburn Rd *SPRGB/BLRNK* G21 ....47 C2
East Campbell St *COWCAD* G4 ....9 D3
Eastcote Av *SCOT* G14 ....39 D3
Eastcroft *RUTH* G73 ....110 A3
Eastcroft Ter *SPRGB/BLRNK* G21 ....46 B3
Easter Craigs *DEN/PKHD* G31 ....67 C3
Easterhill Pl *CAR/SHTL* G32 ....92 B4
Easterhill St *CAR/SHTL* G32 ....92 B4
Easterhouse Pl *ESTRH* G34 ....73 D3
Easterhouse Qd *ESTRH* G34 ....73 D3
Easterhouse Rd *BAIL/MDB/MHD* G69 ....96 B2
Easter Queenslie Rd
STPS/GTHM/RID G33 ....71 D3
Eastfield Av *BLTYR/CAMB* G72 ....131 D2
Eastfield Rd *SPRGB/BLRNK* G21 ....45 D3
East Greenlees Av *BLTYR/CAMB* G72 ....133 D4
East Greenlees Crs *BLTYR/CAMB* G72 ....133 C4
East Greenlees Dr *BLTYR/CAMB* G72 ....133 D4
East Greenlees Rd *BLTYR/CAMB* G72 ....132 B4
East Hallhill Rd *BAIL/MDB/MHD* G69 ....95 D1
Easthall Pl *STPS/GTHM/RID* G33 ....72 A4
East Kilbride Rd *RUTH* G73 ....130 B2
East La *PSLY* PA1 ....78 B2
Eastmuir St *CAR/SHTL* G32 ....93 D2
East Springfield Ter *BSHPBGS* G64 ....32 B3
Eastvale Pl *KVGV* G3 ....61 D3
East Wellington St *DEN/PKHD* G31 ....91 D2
Eastwood Av *GIF/THBK* G46 ....137 C1
PLKSD/SHW G41 ....105 C3
Eastwood Crs *GIF/THBK* G46 ....123 C3
Eastwoodmains Rd *GIF/THBK* G46 ....137 C2
Eastwood Vw *BLTYR/CAMB* G72 ....134 B1
Eccles St *PPK/MIL* G22 ....45 D2
Eckford St *CAR/SHTL* G32 ....93 C3
Eday St *PPK/MIL* G22 ....45 C1
Edderton Pl *STPS/GTHM/RID* G33 ....72 B4
Edderton Wy *STPS/GTHM/RID* G33 ....72 B4
Eddlewood Ct *STPS/GTHM/RID* G33 ....72 A4
Eddlewood Pth *STPS/GTHM/RID* G33 ....72 A4
Eddlewood Pl *STPS/GTHM/RID* G33 ....72 A4
Eddlewood Rd *STPS/GTHM/RID* G33 ....72 A4
Eden La *STPS/GTHM/RID* G33 ....68 A2
Eden Pl *RNFRW* PA4 ....56 B1
Eden St *STPS/GTHM/RID* G33 ....68 A2
Edenwood St *DEN/PKHD* G31 ....92 A2
Edgam Dr *CARD/HILL/MSPK* G52 ....82 A2
Edgefauld Av *SPRGB/BLRNK* G21 ....46 A4
Edgefauld Dr *SPRGB/BLRNK* G21 ....46 A3
Edgefauld Pl *SPRGB/BLRNK* G21 ....46 A2
Edgefauld Rd *SPRGB/BLRNK* G21 ....46 B4
Edgehill La *PTCK* G11 ....40 B3
Edgehill Rd *BSDN* G61 ....15 C1
PTCK G11 ....40 A3
Edgemont St *PLKSD/SHW* G41 ....105 D3
Edinbeg Av *GVH/MTFL* G42 ....108 B3
Edinbeg Pl *GVH/MTFL* G42 ....108 B3
Edinburgh Rd *CAR/SHTL* G32 ....69 D4
STPS/GTHM/RID G33 ....68 B4
Edington St *COWCAD* G4 ....3 D1
Edison St *CARD/HILL/MSPK* G52 ....56 B3
Edmiston Dr *GOV/IBX* G51 ....84 A1
Edrom Ct *CAR/SHTL* G32 ....92 B2
Edrom St *CAR/SHTL* G32 ....92 B3
Edward Av *RNFRW* PA4 ....36 A3
Edward St *BAIL/MDB/MHD* G69 ....98 B2
CLYDBK G81 ....21 D4
Edwin St *GOV/IBX* G51 ....85 D2
Edzell Ct *SCOT* G14 ....59 C1
Edzell Gdns *BSHPBGS* G64 ....33 C3
Edzell Pl *SCOT* G14 ....39 C4
Edzell St *SCOT* G14 ....59 C1
Egidia Av *GIF/THBK* G46 ....136 B1
Egilsay Crs *PPK/MIL* G22 ....30 A3
Egilsay Pl *PPK/MIL* G22 ....30 A3
Egilsay St *PPK/MIL* G22 ....30 A3
Egilsay Ter *PPK/MIL* G22 ....30 A3
Eglinton Ct *GBLS* G5 ....87 D2
Eglinton Dr *GIF/THBK* G46 ....137 C1
Eglinton St *GBLS* G5 ....87 D3
Eider *KVD/HLHD* G12 ....26 A4
Eighth St *UD/BTH/TAN* G71 ....117 D2
Eildon Dr *BRHD/NEIL* G78 ....118 B4
Eileen Gdns *BSHPBGS* G64 ....32 B1
Elcho St *DMNK/BRGTN* G40 ....9 F4
Elderbank *BSDN* G61 ....15 C4
Elder Crs *BLTYR/CAMB* G72 ....134 B3
Elder Grove Av *GOV/IBX* G51 ....59 C4
Elder Grove Pl *GOV/IBX* G51 ....59 C4
Elderpark Gdns *GOV/IBX* G51 ....60 A4
Elderpark Gv *GOV/IBX* G51 ....60 A4
Elderpark St *GOV/IBX* G51 ....60 A4
Elderslie St *KVGV* G3 ....63 C3
Elder St *GOV/IBX* G51 ....60 A4
Eldon Gdns *BSHPBGS* G64 ....31 C2
Eldon St *KVGV* G3 ....62 B1
Elgin Rd *BSDN* G61 ....10 A4
Elibank St *STPS/GTHM/RID* G33 ....69 D2
Elie St *PTCK* G11 ....61 D1

Elizabeth Crs *GIF/THBK* G46 ....123 D4
Elizabeth St *GOV/IBX* G51 ....85 C2
Ellangowan Rd *MLNGV* G62 ....10 B1
PLKSD/SHW G41 ....104 B3
Ellergreen Rd *BSDN* G61 ....15 C3
Ellesmere St *PPK/MIL* G22 ....43 D4
Elliot Av *GIF/THBK* G46 ....137 C1
Elliot Dr *GIF/THBK* G46 ....124 B4
Elliot Pl *KVGV* G3 ....62 B4
Elliot St *KVGV* G3 ....62 B4
Ellisland Crs *CSMK* G45 ....129 C2
Ellisland Rd *PLKSW/MSWD* G43 ....125 C1
Ellismuir Farm Rd *BAIL/MDB/MHD* G69 ..97 D3
Ellismuir Pl *BAIL/MDB/MHD* G69 ....97 C3
Ellismuir Rd *BAIL/MDB/MHD* G69 ....97 C3
Elliston Av *PLK/PH/NH* G53 ....121 D2
Elliston Crs *PLK/PH/NH* G53 ....121 D2
Elliston Dr *PLK/PH/NH* G53 ....121 D2
Ellon Gv *PSLYN/LNWD* PA3 ....54 A4
Ellon Wy *PSLYN/LNWD* PA3 ....54 B4
Elm Av *RNFRW* PA4 ....35 D3
Elm Bank *BSHPBGS* G64 ....32 B2
Elmbank Crs *CGLW* G2 ....2 B4
Elmbank St *CGLW* G2 ....2 B5
Elmbank Street La *KVGV* G3 ....2 B5
Elm Dr *BLTYR/CAMB* G72 ....133 D1
Elmfoot St *GBLS* G5 ....108 A1
Elm Gdns *BSDN* G61 ....15 C1
Elmore Av *LNPK/KPK* G44 ....127 D3
Elm Rd *RUTH* G73 ....130 A3
Elmslie Ct *BAIL/MDB/MHD* G69 ....97 C3
Elm St *SCOT* G14 ....39 C4
Elmvale Rw *SPRGB/BLRNK* G21 ....45 D3
Elmvale St *PPK/MIL* G22 ....45 D2
Elm Wk *BSDN* G61 ....15 C1
Elm Wy *BLTYR/CAMB* G72 ....134 B3
Elmwood Av *PTCK* G11 ....40 A3
Elmwood La *PTCK* G11 ....40 A3
Elphinstone Pl *GOV/IBX* G51 ....61 D4
Elphinstone Rd *GIF/THBK* G46 ....136 A4
Elphin St *SMSTN* G23 ....27 D2
Elrig Rd *LNPK/KPK* G44 ....126 A2
Elspeth Gdns *BSHPBGS* G64 ....33 C1
Eltham St *PPK/MIL* G22 ....44 A4
Elvan St *CAR/SHTL* G32 ....92 B2
Embo Dr *KNTSWD* G13 ....38 A1
Emerson Rd *BSHPBGS* G64 ....32 A3
Emerson Rd West *BSHPBGS* G64 ....32 A2
Emerson St *MRYH/FIRH* G20 ....43 D1
Endfield Av *KVD/HLHD* G12 ....41 C1
Endrick Bank *BSHPBGS* G64 ....19 C3
Endrick Dr *BSDN* G61 ....15 D3
PSLY PA1 ....78 B1
Endrick St *SPRGB/BLRNK* G21 ....45 C4
Ensay St *PPK/MIL* G22 ....30 B4
Enterkin St *CAR/SHTL* G32 ....92 B3
Eriboll Pl *PPK/MIL* G22 ....29 D4
Eriboll St *PPK/MIL* G22 ....29 D4
Ericht Rd *PLKSW/MSWD* G43 ....124 B2
Eriska Av *SCOT* G14 ....37 D2
Erradale St *PPK/MIL* G22 ....29 C4
Errogie St *ESTRH* G34 ....73 C3
Erskine Av *PLKSD/SHW* G41 ....84 B3
Erskine Sq *CARD/HILL/MSPK* G52 ....57 C4
Ervie St *ESTRH* G34 ....73 D4
Esk Av *RNFRW* PA4 ....56 B1
Eskbank St *CAR/SHTL* G32 ....93 C1
Eskdale Dr *RUTH* G73 ....111 C4
Eskdale Rd *BSDN* G61 ....24 B1
Eskdale St *GVH/MTFL* G42 ....107 C2
Esk St *SCOT* G14 ....37 C2
Esmond St *KVGV* G3 ....61 D2
Espedair St *PSLYS* PA2 ....77 C4
Essenside Av *DRUM* G15 ....24 A1
Essex Dr *SCOT* G14 ....39 D3
Essex La *SCOT* G14 ....39 D4
Esslemont Av *SCOT* G14 ....38 A3
Estate Qd *CAR/SHTL* G32 ....113 D3
Estate Rd *CAR/SHTL* G32 ....113 D3
Etive Av *BSDN* G61 ....16 B3
Etive Crs *BSHPBGS* G64 ....32 B2
Etive Dr *GIF/THBK* G46 ....137 D2
Etive St *CAR/SHTL* G32 ....93 C2
Eton La *KVD/HLHD* G12 ....62 B1
Ettrick Av *RNFRW* PA4 ....57 C1
Ettrick Crs *RUTH* G73 ....110 B4
Ettrick Pl *PLKSD/SHW* G41 ....105 C4
Evan Crs *GIF/THBK* G46 ....137 D1
Evan Dr *GIF/THBK* G46 ....137 D2
Evanton Dr *GIF/THBK* G46 ....122 B4
Evanton Pl *GIF/THBK* G46 ....122 B4
Everard Ct *SPRGB/BLRNK* G21 ....31 C4
Everard Dr *SPRGB/BLRNK* G21 ....45 D1
Everard Pl *SPRGB/BLRNK* G21 ....31 C4
Everard Qd *SPRGB/BLRNK* G21 ....31 C4
Eversley St *CAR/SHTL* G32 ....93 C4
Everton Rd *PLK/PH/NH* G53 ....101 D1
Ewing Pl *DEN/PKHD* G31 ....91 C2
Ewing St *RUTH* G73 ....109 D4
Ewing Wk *MLNGV* G62 ....11 D2
Exeter Dr *PTCK* G11 ....60 B1
Eynort St *PPK/MIL* G22 ....29 C4
Eyrepoint Ct *STPS/GTHM/RID* G33 ....69 D3

F

Fairbairn Crs *GIF/THBK* G46 ....136 A1
Fairburn St *CAR/SHTL* G32 ....92 B3
Fairfax Av *LNPK/KPK* G44 ....127 D2
Fairfield Dr *RNFRW* PA4 ....56 A2
Fairfield Gdns *GOV/IBX* G51 ....60 A3
Fairfield Pl *GOV/IBX* G51 ....60 A3
Fairfield St *GOV/IBX* G51 ....60 A3
Fairhaven Rd *SMSTN* G23 ....27 D3
Fairhill Av *PLK/PH/NH* G53 ....101 D4
Fairholm St *CAR/SHTL* G32 ....92 B3
Fairley St *GOV/IBX* G51 ....84 B1
Fairlie Park Dr *PTCK* G11 ....60 B1
Fairway *BSDN* G61 ....13 D2
Falcon Ter *MRYH/FIRH* G20 ....27 C3
Falcon Terrace La *MRYH/FIRH* G20 ....27 C3
Falfield St *GBLS* G5 ....87 C3
Falkland Crs *BSHPBGS* G64 ....33 D3
Falkland La *KVD/HLHD* G12 ....41 C4
Falkland St *KVD/HLHD* G12 ....41 C4
Falloch Rd *BSDN* G61 ....24 A1
GVH/MTFL G42 ....106 B4
Falside Rd *CAR/SHTL* G32 ....112 B1
Fara St *SMSTN* G23 ....28 B3
Farie St *RUTH* G73 ....109 C3
Farme Castle Ct *RUTH* G73 ....110 B2
Farmeloan Rd *RUTH* G73 ....110 A3
Farmington Av *CAR/SHTL* G32 ....94 B2
Farmington Gdns *CAR/SHTL* G32 ....94 B2
Farmington Gv *CAR/SHTL* G32 ....94 B2
Farm Rd *PLKSD/SHW* G41 ....84 B2
Farne Dr *LNPK/KPK* G44 ....127 C3
Farnell St *COWCAD* G4 ....64 A1
Faskally Av *BSHPBGS* G64 ....18 A4
Faskin Crs *PLK/PH/NH* G53 ....100 A4
Faskin Pl *PLK/PH/NH* G53 ....100 A4
Faskin Rd *PLK/PH/NH* G53 ....100 A4
Fasque Pl *DRUM* G15 ....12 A3
Fauldhouse St *GBLS* G5 ....88 B4
Faulds *BAIL/MDB/MHD* G69 ....97 C2
Faulds Gdns *BAIL/MDB/MHD* G69 ....97 C2
Fauldshead Rd *RNFRW* PA4 ....35 D4
Fauldspark Crs *BAIL/MDB/MHD* G69 ....97 C1
Fearnach Pl *MRYH/FIRH* G20 ....26 B4
Fearnmore Rd *MRYH/FIRH* G20 ....27 D4
Felton Pl *KNTSWD* G13 ....22 B4
Fendoch St *CAR/SHTL* G32 ....93 C3
Fenella St *CAR/SHTL* G32 ....93 D2
Fennsbank Av *RUTH* G73 ....131 C4
Fenwick Dr *BRHD/NEIL* G78 ....119 C4
Fenwick Pl *GIF/THBK* G46 ....136 B2
Fenwick Rd *GIF/THBK* G46 ....136 B2
Fereneze Av *BRHD/NEIL* G78 ....118 A2
CRMNK/CLK/EAG G76 ....137 C3
RNFRW PA4 ....54 B3
Fereneze Crs *KNTSWD* G13 ....22 B4
Fereneze Gv *BRHD/NEIL* G78 ....118 A2
Fergus Dr *MRYH/FIRH* G20 ....42 B3
Fergus La *MRYH/FIRH* G20 ....43 C3
Ferguson Av *MLNGV* G62 ....10 B2
RNFRW PA4 ....36 A4
Ferguson St *RNFRW* PA4 ....36 A4
Ferguston Rd *BSDN* G61 ....15 D3
Fernan St *CAR/SHTL* G32 ....92 B2
Fern Av *BSHPBGS* G64 ....32 B3
Fernbank Av *BLTYR/CAMB* G72 ....133 D3
Fernbank St *PPK/MIL* G22 ....45 D2
Fernbrae Av *RUTH* G73 ....130 B4
Fernbrae Wy *RUTH* G73 ....130 A4
Ferncroft Dr *LNPK/KPK* G44 ....128 A2

Ferndale Ct *SMSTN* G23 .... **27** D3
Ferndale Dr *MRYH/FIRH* G20 .... **27** C3
Ferndale Gdns *SMSTN* G23 .... **27** D3
Ferndale Pl *SMSTN* G23 .... **27** D3
Fern Dr *BRHD/NEIL* G78 .... **118** A1
Ferness Ov *SPRGB/BLRNK* G21 .... **33** C4
Ferness Pl *SPRGB/BLRNK* G21 .... **33** C4
Ferness Rd *SPRGB/BLRNK* G21 .... **47** D1
Ferngrove Av *KVD/HLHD* G12 .... **41** C1
Fernhill Rd *RUTH* G73 .... **129** D3
Fernie Gdns *MRYH/FIRH* G20 .... **28** A4
Fern La *KNTSWD* G13 .... **40** A2
Fernlea *BSDN* G61 .... **15** C4
Fernleigh Rd *PLKSW/MSWD* G43 .... **125** C2
Ferryden St *SCOT* G14 .... **59** D1
Ferry Rd *KVGV* G3 .... **61** D2
RNFRW PA4 .... **36** A3
Fersit St *PLKSW/MSWD* G43 .... **124** B1
Fetlar Dr *LNPK/KPK* G44 .... **127** D2
Fettercairn Av *DRUM* G15 .... **12** A3
Fettes St *STPS/GTHM/RID* G33 .... **69** C3
Fidra St *STPS/GTHM/RID* G33 .... **69** C3
Fielden Pl *DMNK/BRGTN* G40 .... **90** A2
Fielden St *DMNK/BRGTN* G40 .... **90** A2
Fieldhead Dr *PLKSW/MSWD* G43 .... **123** D2
Fieldhead Sq *PLKSW/MSWD* G43 .... **123** D2
Fife Av *CARD/HILL/MSPK* G52 .... **81** D3
Fife Wy *BSHPBGS* G64 .... **33** D3
Fifth Av *KVD/HLHD* G12 .... **40** A2
RNFRW PA4 .... **55** D1
STPS/GTHM/RID G33 .... **50** A2
Fifty Pitches Pl *GOV/IBX* G51 .... **58** B4
Fifty Pitches Rd *GOV/IBX* G51 .... **81** D1
Finch Dr *KNTSWD* G13 .... **22** B3
Findhorn Av *RNFRW* PA4 .... **36** B4
Findhorn St *STPS/GTHM/RID* G33 .... **68** A3
Findochty St *STPS/GTHM/RID* G33 .... **71** D2
Fingal La *MRYH/FIRH* G20 .... **27** C4
Fingal St *MRYH/FIRH* G20 .... **27** D4
Fingask St *CAR/SHTL* G32 .... **94** A3
Finglen Pl *PLK/PH/NH* G53 .... **121** C3
Fingleton Av *BRHD/NEIL* G78 .... **119** C4
Finhaven St *CAR/SHTL* G32 .... **92** A4
Finlarig St *ESTRH* G34 .... **73** D4
Finlas St *PPK/MIL* G22 .... **45** C3
Finlay Dr *DEN/PKHD* G31 .... **66** B4
Finlay Ri *MLNGV* G62 .... **11** D3
Finnart Sq *DMNK/BRGTN* G40 .... **89** D4
Finnart St *DMNK/BRGTN* G40 .... **89** D4
Finnieston Sq *KVGV* G3 .... **62** B3
Finnieston St *KVGV* G3 .... **62** B4
Finsbay St *GOV/IBX* G51 .... **82** B1
Fintry Crs *BRHD/NEIL* G78 .... **118** B4
BSHPBGS G64 .... **33** C2
Fintry Dr *LNPK/KPK* G44 .... **107** D4
Firbank Ter *BRHD/NEIL* G78 .... **119** D4
Fir Ct *BLTYR/CAMB* G72 .... **134** B3
Firdon Crs *DRUM* G15 .... **23** C2
Firhill Rd *MRYH/FIRH* G20 .... **43** D3
Firhill St *MRYH/FIRH* G20 .... **43** D3
Firpark Rd *BSHPBGS* G64 .... **32** B3
Firpark St *DEN/PKHD* G31 .... **5** F5
Firpark Ter *DEN/PKHD* G31 .... **9** F1
Fir Pl *BAIL/MDB/MHD* G69 .... **96** A4
BLTYR/CAMB G72 .... **133** D1
First Av *BSDN* G61 .... **16** A4
RNFRW PA4 .... **55** D1
STPS/GTHM/RID G33 .... **50** A2
UD/BTH/TAN G71 .... **117** D3
First Gdns *PLKSD/SHW* G41 .... **84** A3
Firwood Dr *LNPK/KPK* G44 .... **127** D1
Fishescoates Av *RUTH* G73 .... **130** B3
Fishescoates Gdns *RUTH* G73 .... **130** B2
Fitzalan Dr *PSLYN/LNWD* PA3 .... **78** A1
Fitzalan Rd *PSLYN/LNWD* PA3 .... **54** B2
Fitzroy La *KVGV* G3 .... **62** B3
Fleet Av *RNFRW* PA4 .... **56** B2
Fleet St *CAR/SHTL* G32 .... **93** D3
Fleming Av *CLYDBK* G81 .... **21** D3
Fleming St *DEN/PKHD* G31 .... **90** B1
PSLYN/LNWD PA3 .... **53** D4
Flemington St *SPRGB/BLRNK* G21 .... **46** A4
Fleurs Av *PLKSD/SHW* G41 .... **84** B4
Fleurs Rd *PLKSD/SHW* G41 .... **84** B3
Flora Gdns *BSHPBGS* G64 .... **33** C1
Florence Dr *GIF/THBK* G46 .... **137** C1
Florence Gdns *RUTH* G73 .... **130** B3
Florence St *GBLS* G5 .... **8** A5
Florida Av *GVH/MTFL* G42 .... **107** C3
Florida Crs *GVH/MTFL* G42 .... **107** C3
Florida Dr *GVH/MTFL* G42 .... **106** B3
Florida Gdns *BAIL/MDB/MHD* G69 .... **96** A2
Florida Sq *GVH/MTFL* G42 .... **107** C3
Florida St *GVH/MTFL* G42 .... **106** B3
Flowerdale Pl *PLK/PH/NH* G53 .... **121** C4
Fochabers Dr *CARD/HILL/MSPK* G52 .... **82** A1
Foinaven Dr *GIF/THBK* G46 .... **123** C2
Foinaven Gdns *GIF/THBK* G46 .... **123** C1
Foinaven Wy *GIF/THBK* G46 .... **123** D1
Forbes Dr *DMNK/BRGTN* G40 .... **9** F5
Forbes Pl *PSLY* PA1 .... **77** C3
Forbes St *DMNK/BRGTN* G40 .... **9** F4
Fordneuk St *DMNK/BRGTN* G40 .... **90** A2
Fordoun St *ESTRH* G34 .... **74** A3
Ford Rd *KVD/HLHD* G12 .... **42** A3
Fordyce St *PTCK* G11 .... **61** C1
Foresthall Crs *SPRGB/BLRNK* G21 .... **46** B4
Foresthall Dr *SPRGB/BLRNK* G21 .... **46** B4
Foresthall Gdns *SPRGB/BLRNK* G21 .... **46** B4
Fore St *SCOT* G14 .... **38** B4
Forfar Av *CARD/HILL/MSPK* G52 .... **81** D3
Forfar Crs *BSHPBGS* G64 .... **33** C3
Forgan Gdns *BSHPBGS* G64 .... **33** D3
Forge Pl *SPRGB/BLRNK* G21 .... **67** C1
Forge St *SPRGB/BLRNK* G21 .... **67** C1
Forglen St *ESTRH* G34 .... **73** C2
Formby Dr *SMSTN* G23 .... **27** D3
Forres Av *GIF/THBK* G46 .... **125** C4
Forres Ga *GIF/THBK* G46 .... **137** D1
Forres St *SMSTN* G23 .... **28** A2
Forrester Ct *BSHPBGS* G64 .... **31** D3
Forrestfield St *SPRGB/BLRNK* G21 .... **66** B2
Forrest St *DMNK/BRGTN* G40 .... **90** A2
Forteviot Av *BAIL/MDB/MHD* G69 .... **97** C2
Forteviot Pl *BAIL/MDB/MHD* G69 .... **97** C2
Forth Rd *BSDN* G61 .... **24** B1
Forth St *CLYDBK* G81 .... **21** C3
PLKSD/SHW G41 .... **86** B4
Forties Ct *GIF/THBK* G46 .... **123** C2
Forties Crs *GIF/THBK* G46 .... **123** C2
Forties Gdns *GIF/THBK* G46 .... **123** D2
Forties Wy *GIF/THBK* G46 .... **123** D2
Fortingall Av *KVD/HLHD* G12 .... **41** D1
Fortingall Pl *KVD/HLHD* G12 .... **41** D1
Fortrose St *PTCK* G11 .... **61** C1
Foswell Dr *DRUM* G15 .... **12** B2
Foswell Pl *DRUM* G15 .... **12** B2
Fotheringay La *PLKSD/SHW* G41 .... **105** C1
Fotheringay Rd *PLKSD/SHW* G41 .... **105** C1
Foulis La *KNTSWD* G13 .... **40** A1
Foulis St *KNTSWD* G13 .... **40** A1
Foundry La *BRHD/NEIL* G78 .... **118** B2
Fountainwell Av *SPRGB/BLRNK* G21 .... **65** C1
Fountainwell Dr *SPRGB/BLRNK* G21 .... **65** C1
Fountainwell Pl *SPRGB/BLRNK* G21 .... **65** C1
Fountainwell Rd *SPRGB/BLRNK* G21 .... **65** D1
Fountainwell Sq *SPRGB/BLRNK* G21 .... **65** D1
Fourth Av *RNFRW* PA4 .... **55** D1
STPS/GTHM/RID G33 .... **50** A2
Fourth Gdns *PLKSD/SHW* G41 .... **84** A3
Foxbar Dr *KNTSWD* G13 .... **38** A1
Foxglove Pl *PLK/PH/NH* G53 .... **121** C4
Foxhills Pl *SMSTN* G23 .... **28** A2
Foxley St *CAR/SHTL* G32 .... **113** D2
Fox St *CGLE* G1 .... **7** E3
Foyers Ter *SPRGB/BLRNK* G21 .... **46** B3
Francis St *GBLS* G5 .... **87** C3
Frankfield Rd *STPS/GTHM/RID* G33 .... **51** D2
Frankfield St *STPS/GTHM/RID* G33 .... **68** A1
Frankfort St *PLKSD/SHW* G41 .... **105** D2
Franklin St *DMNK/BRGTN* G40 .... **89** D4
Fraser Av *RUTH* G73 .... **110** B4
Fraser St *BLTYR/CAMB* G72 .... **131** D1
Frazer St *DMNK/BRGTN* G40 .... **90** B2
Freeland Ct *PLK/PH/NH* G53 .... **121** D1
Freeland Crs *PLK/PH/NH* G53 .... **121** C1
Freeland Dr *PLK/PH/NH* G53 .... **121** C1
French St *DMNK/BRGTN* G40 .... **89** D4
RNFRW PA4 .... **55** C1
Freuchie St *ESTRH* G34 .... **73** C4
Friar Av *BSHPBGS* G64 .... **19** D3
Friarscourt Av *KNTSWD* G13 .... **24** B3
Friars Pl *KNTSWD* G13 .... **24** B3
Friarton Rd *PLKSW/MSWD* G43 .... **126** A2
Fruin Rd *DRUM* G15 .... **22** B2
Fruin St *PPK/MIL* G22 .... **44** B3
Fulbar Av *RNFRW* PA4 .... **35** D3
Fulbar Ct *RNFRW* PA4 .... **35** D3
Fulbar La *RNFRW* PA4 .... **36** A3
Fulbar Rd *GOV/IBX* G51 .... **58** B4

Fulbar St *RNFRW* PA4 **36** A3
Fullarton Av *CAR/SHTL* G32 **112** B1
Fullarton La *CAR/SHTL* G32 **112** B1
Fullarton Rd *CAR/SHTL* G32 **112** B2
Fullerton St *PSLYN/LNWD* PA3 **53** C4
Fullerton Ter *PSLYN/LNWD* PA3 **53** D4
Fulton Rd *MLNGV* G62 **11** C2
Fulton St *KNTSWD* G13 **25** C4
Fulwood Av *KNTSWD* G13 **22** B4
Fulwood Pl *KNTSWD* G13 **22** B4
Fyvie Av *PLKSW/MSWD* G43 **123** D2

G

Gadie Av *RNFRW* PA4 **56** B1
Gadie St *STPS/GTHM/RID* G33 **68** A3
Gadloch St *PPK/MIL* G22 **44** B1
Gadsburn Ct *SPRGB/BLRNK* G21 **47** D1
Gadshill St *SPRGB/BLRNK* G21 **5** F2
Gailes St *DMNK/BRGTN* G40 **90** B3
Gairbraid Av *MRYH/FIRH* G20 **41** D1
Gairbraid Ct *MRYH/FIRH* G20 **41** D1
Gairbraid Pl *MRYH/FIRH* G20 **42** A1
Gairbraid Ter *BAIL/MDB/MHD* G69 **99** C2
Gala Av *RNFRW* PA4 **56** B1
Gala St *STPS/GTHM/RID* G33 **68** B1
Galbraith Dr *GOV/IBX* G51 **59** C3
MLNGV G62 **10** A3
Galdenoch St *STPS/GTHM/RID* G33 **70** A1
Gallan Av *SMSTN* G23 **28** A2
Galloway Dr *RUTH* G73 **130** A4
Galloway St *SPRGB/BLRNK* G21 **46** A1
Gallowflat St *RUTH* G73 **110** A3
Gallowgate *CGLE* G1 **8** C3
COWCAD G4 **9** D4
DEN/PKHD G31 **90** B2
Gallowhill Rd *PSLYN/LNWD* PA3 **77** D1
Galston St *PLK/PH/NH* G53 **120** A1
Gamrie Dr *PLK/PH/NH* G53 **100** B4
Gamrie Gdns *PLK/PH/NH* G53 **100** B4
Gamrie Rd *PLK/PH/NH* G53 **100** B3
Gannochy Dr *BSHPBGS* G64 **33** C2
Gantock Crs *STPS/GTHM/RID* G33 **70** A4
Gardenside Av *CAR/SHTL* G32 **113** C3
Gardenside Crs *CAR/SHTL* G32 **113** C3
Gardenside Pl *CAR/SHTL* G32 **113** C3
Gardner St *PTCK* G11 **61** C1
Gardyne St *ESTRH* G34 **72** B2
Garfield St *DEN/PKHD* G31 **90** A1
Garforth Rd *BAIL/MDB/MHD* G69 **95** D3
Gargrave Av *BAIL/MDB/MHD* G69 **95** D3
Garion Dr *KNTSWD* G13 **38** A2
Garlieston Rd *STPS/GTHM/RID* G33 **95** D1
Garmouth Ct *GOV/IBX* G51 **60** B3
Garmouth Gdns *GOV/IBX* G51 **60** A3
Garmouth St *GOV/IBX* G51 **60** A3
Garnethill St *KVGV* G3 **2** C3
Garnet St *KVGV* G3 **2** B3
Garnkirk La *STPS/GTHM/RID* G33 **51** D2
Garnock St *SPRGB/BLRNK* G21 **66** A1
Garrioch Crs *MRYH/FIRH* G20 **42** A2
Garrioch Dr *MRYH/FIRH* G20 **42** A2
Garrioch Ga *MRYH/FIRH* G20 **42** A2
Garriochmill Rd *MRYH/FIRH* G20 **42** A3
Garrioch Qd *MRYH/FIRH* G20 **42** A2
Garrioch Rd *MRYH/FIRH* G20 **42** A3
Garrowhill Dr *BAIL/MDB/MHD* G69 **95** D2
Garry Av *BSDN* G61 **26** A1
Garry St *LNPK/KPK* G44 **106** B4
Garscadden Rd *DRUM* G15 **22** B1
Garscadden Rd South *DRUM* G15 **22** B3
KNTSWD G13 **23** C3
Garscube Rd *COWCAD* G4 **3** D3
MRYH/FIRH G20 **43** D4
Gartartan Rd *PSLY* PA1 **80** B2
Gartconnell Dr *BSDN* G61 **15** C1
Gartconnell Gdns *BSDN* G61 **15** C1
Gartconnell Rd *BSDN* G61 **15** C1
Gartcosh Rd *BAIL/MDB/MHD* G69 **98** B1
CTBR ML5 **75** D3
Gartcraig Pl *STPS/GTHM/RID* G33 **69** C2
Gartcraig Rd *STPS/GTHM/RID* G33 **68** B3
Gartferry St *SPRGB/BLRNK* G21 **46** B3
Garthamlock Rd *STPS/GTHM/RID* G33 **71** D2
Garthland Dr *DEN/PKHD* G31 **66** B4
Garthland La *PSLY* PA1 **77** D2
Garth St *CGLE* G1 **8** A2
Gartliston Ter *BAIL/MDB/MHD* G69 **99** C2
Gartloch Rd *BAIL/MDB/MHD* G69 **72** A1
STPS/GTHM/RID G33 **69** C2
Gartly St *LNPK/KPK* G44 **126** A3
Gartmore Gdns *UD/BTH/TAN* G71 **117** D3
Gartmore Rd *PSLY* PA1 **79** C3
Gartmore Ter *BLTYR/CAMB* G72 **131** D4
Gartocher Dr *CAR/SHTL* G32 **94** A2
Gartocher Rd *CAR/SHTL* G32 **94** A2
Gartocher Ter *CAR/SHTL* G32 **94** A2
Gartons Rd *SPRGB/BLRNK* G21 **47** D2
Garturk St *GVH/MTFL* G42 **107** C1
Garvald St *DMNK/BRGTN* G40 **90** B4
Garve Av *LNPK/KPK* G44 **126** B3
Garvel Crs *STPS/GTHM/RID* G33 **95** C1
Garvel Rd *STPS/GTHM/RID* G33 **95** C1
Garvock Dr *PLKSW/MSWD* G43 **124** A2
Garwhitter Dr *MLNGV* G62 **11** C1
Gask Pl *KNTSWD* G13 **22** B3
Gatehouse St *CAR/SHTL* G32 **93** D2
Gateside Av *BLTYR/CAMB* G72 **134** A2
Gateside St *DEN/PKHD* G31 **90** B1
Gauldry Av *CARD/HILL/MSPK* G52 **82** A4
Gauze St *PSLY* PA1 **77** D2
Gavin's Mill Rd *MLNGV* G62 **10** B2
Gavinton St *LNPK/KPK* G44 **126** A2
Geary St *SMSTN* G23 **27** D2
Geddes Rd *SPRGB/BLRNK* G21 **33** C4
Gelston St *CAR/SHTL* G32 **93** D3
George Gray St *RUTH* G73 **110** B3
George La *PSLY* PA1 **77** C3
George Mann Ter *RUTH* G73 **129** D3
George Pl *PSLY* PA1 **77** C3
George Reith Av *KVD/HLHD* G12 **40** A2
George Sq *CGLE* G1 **7** F1
George St *BAIL/MDB/MHD* G69 **96** B3
BRHD/NEIL G78 **118** A2
CGLE G1 **8** B1
PSLY PA1 **76** B3
George V Br *KVGV* G3 **7** D3
Gibson Rd *RNFRW* PA4 **55** C3
Gibson St *DMNK/BRGTN* G40 **9** D4
KVD/HLHD G12 **62** B1
Giffnock Park Av *GIF/THBK* G46 **124** B3
Gifford Dr *CARD/HILL/MSPK* G52 **81** C2
Gilbertfield Pl *STPS/GTHM/RID* G33 **70** A1
Gilbertfield Rd *BLTYR/CAMB* G72 **134** A4
Gilbertfield St *STPS/GTHM/RID* G33 **70** A1
Gilbert St *KVGV* G3 **61** D3
Gilhill St *MRYH/FIRH* G20 **27** D4
Gillies La *BAIL/MDB/MHD* G69 **97** C3
Gilmerton St *CAR/SHTL* G32 **93** C3
Gilmour Crs *RUTH* G73 **109** C3
Gilmour St *PSLY* PA1 **77** C2
Girthon St *CAR/SHTL* G32 **94** A3
Girvan St *STPS/GTHM/RID* G33 **68** A2
Gladney Av *KNTSWD* G13 **22** A3
Gladsmuir Rd *CARD/HILL/MSPK* G52 **81** C1
Gladstone Av *BRHD/NEIL* G78 **118** A3
Gladstone St *COWCAD* G4 **2** B1
Glaive Rd *KNTSWD* G13 **24** B2
Glamis Rd *DEN/PKHD* G31 **91** D3
Glanderston Av *BRHD/NEIL* G78 **119** D3
Glanderston Ct *KNTSWD* G13 **23** C4
Glanderston Dr *KNTSWD* G13 **23** C4
Glasgow & Edinburgh Rd
BAIL/MDB/MHD G69 **97** C2
BAIL/MDB/MHD G69 **99** D4
Glasgow Br *CGLE* G1 **7** E3
Glasgow Rd *BAIL/MDB/MHD* G69 **95** D3
BRHD/NEIL G78 **119** C1
CTBR ML5 **99** D1
MLNGV G62 **11** C3
PSLY PA1 **77** D2
RNFRW PA4 **56** B1
RUTH G73 **109** C1
UD/BTH/TAN G71 **116** B2
Glasgow St *KVD/HLHD* G12 **42** B4
Glassel Rd *ESTRH* G34 **74** A2
Glasserton Pl *PLKSW/MSWD* G43 **126** A2
Glasserton Rd *PLKSW/MSWD* G43 **126** A2
Glassford St *CGLE* G1 **8** A2
Glebe Ct *COWCAD* G4 **4** C4
Glebe Pl *BLTYR/CAMB* G72 **133** C2
RUTH G73 **109** C3
Glebe St *COWCAD* G4 **4** C3
COWCAD G4 **5** D5
RNFRW PA4 **36** A4

Gleddoch Rd *CARD/HILL/MSPK* G52 ....**80** A1
Glenacre Crs *UD/BTH/TAN* G71 ....**117** D3
Glenacre Dr *CSMK* G45 ....**128** A4
Glenacre Qd *CSMK* G45 ....**128** A4
Glenacre St *CSMK* G45..............................**128** A4
Glenacre Ter *CSMK* G45.............................**128** A4
Glen Affric Av *PLK/PH/NH* G53 ....**121** D3
Glen Alby Pl *PLK/PH/NH* G53 ....**121** D3
Glenalmond St *CAR/SHTL* G32 ....**93** C3
Glenapp St *PLKSD/SHW* G41........................**86** B4
Glen Av *CAR/SHTL* G32...............................**93** D1
Glenavon Rd *MRYH/FIRH* G20 ....**27** D4
Glenbarr St *SPRGB/BLRNK* G21 ....**5** E2
Glenbervie Pl *SMSTN* G23 ....**27** D2
Glenbuck Av *STPS/GTHM/RID* G33 ....**49** C1
Glenbuck Dr *STPS/GTHM/RID* G33...............**49** C1
Glenburn Av *BAIL/MDB/MHD* G69................**97** C2
BLTYR/CAMB G72 ....**131** C2
Glenburn Gdns *BSHPBGS* G64 ....**31** D1
Glenburnie Pl *STPS/GTHM/RID* G33 ....**72** B4
Glenburn La *MRYH/FIRH* G20 ....**28** A4
Glenburn Rd *BSDN* G61 ....**14** B2
GIF/THBK G46 ....**136** B2
Glenburn St *MRYH/FIRH* G20 ....**28** A4
Glencairn Ct *RUTH* G73 ....**109** C3
Glencairn Dr *PLKSD/SHW* G41 ....**105** D1
RUTH G73 ....**109** C3
Glencairn Gdns *BLTYR/CAMB* G72 ....**134** A2
PLKSD/SHW G41 ....**105** D1
Glencairn La *PLKSD/SHW* G41 ....**105** D1
Glencairn Rd *PSLYN/LNWD* PA3 ....**54** B4
Glencloy St *MRYH/FIRH* G20........................**27** C4
Glen Clunie Dr *PLK/PH/NH* G53 ....**121** D3
Glen Clunie Pl *PLK/PH/NH* G53 ....**121** D3
Glencoe Pl *KNTSWD* G13 ....**25** C4
Glencoe Rd *RUTH* G73...................................**131** C4
Glencoe St *KNTSWD* G13 ....**25** D4
Glen Cona Dr *PLK/PH/NH* G53 ....**121** D2
Glencorse St *STPS/GTHM/RID* G33 ....**68** B4
Glen Crs *KNTSWD* G13 ....**22** A4
Glencroft Av *UD/BTH/TAN* G71 ....**117** D3
Glencroft Rd *LNPK/KPK* G44.......................**128** A2
Glendale Crs *BSHPBGS* G64.........................**33** C3
Glendale Dr *BSHPBGS* G64 ....**33** C3
Glendale Pl *BSHPBGS* G64...........................**33** C4
DEN/PKHD G31..**90** B1
Glendale St *DEN/PKHD* G31 ....**90** B1
Glendaruel Av *BSDN* G61 ....**16** B3
Glendarvel Gdns *PPK/MIL* G22......................**45** C3
Glendee Gdns *RNFRW* PA4 ....**56** A1
Glendee Rd *RNFRW* PA4 ....**56** A1
Glen Dene Wy *PLK/PH/NH* G53 ....**121** D3
Glendevon Sq *STPS/GTHM/RID* G33 ....**70** A1
Glen Dewar Pl *PLK/PH/NH* G53 ....**121** D3
Glendinning Rd *KNTSWD* G13.......................**25** C2
Glendore St *SCOT* G14 ....**59** D1
Glenduffhill Rd *BAIL/MDB/MHD* G69 ....**95** D2
Gleneagles Gdns *BSHPBGS* G64....................**18** B4
Gleneagles La North *SCOT* G14 ....**38** B3
Gleneagles La South *SCOT* G14 ....**38** B4
Glenelg Qd *ESTRH* G34..................................**74** A2
Glenesk Crs *PLK/PH/NH* G53 ....**121** D3
Glen Esk Dr *PLK/PH/NH* G53 ....**121** D3
Glenesk Pl *PLK/PH/NH* G53 ....**121** D3
Glenfarg Crs *BSDN* G61 ....**16** B3
Glenfarg Rd *RUTH* G73 ....**130** A3
Glenfarg St *MRYH/FIRH* G20 ....**2** B1
Glenfinnan Dr *BSDN* G61 ....**16** B4
MRYH/FIRH G20 ....**42** A1
Glenfinnan Pl *MRYH/FIRH* G20 ....**42** A1
Glenfinnan Rd *MRYH/FIRH* G20....................**42** A2
Glengarry Dr *CARD/HILL/MSPK* G52 ....**82** A2
Glengavel Crs *STPS/GTHM/RID* G33 ....**49** C1
Glengyre St *ESTRH* G34 ....**73** D3
Glenhead Crs *PPK/MIL* G22 ....**44** B1
Glenhead St *PPK/MIL* G22 ....**44** B1
Gleniffer Av *KNTSWD* G13 ....**37** D1
Gleniffer Rd *RNFRW* PA4...............................**55** C3
Glenisla St *DEN/PKHD* G31 ....**91** D4
Glenkirk Dr *DRUM* G15 ....**23** D1
Glen Kyle Dr *PLK/PH/NH* G53......................**121** D3
Glen La *PSLYN/LNWD* PA3 ....**77** C2
Glen Livet Pl *PLK/PH/NH* G53.....................**121** D3
Glenlora Dr *PLK/PH/NH* G53.......................**100** B4
Glenlora Ter *PLK/PH/NH* G53 ....**101** C4
Glen Loy Pl *PLK/PH/NH* G53.......................**121** D3
Glen Luce Dr *CAR/SHTL* G32 ....**94** B4
Glenlui Av *RUTH* G73 ....**130** A2
Glen Luss Pl *PLK/PH/NH* G53 ....**121** D3
Glenlyon Pl *RUTH* G73 ....**130** B4
Glenmavis St *COWCAD* G4................................**3** E3
Glenmore Av *GVH/MTFL* G42 ....**108** B3
Glen Moriston Rd *PLK/PH/NH* G53 ....**121** D3
Glenmuir Dr *PLK/PH/NH* G53 ....**121** C2
Glen Ogle St *CAR/SHTL* G32 ....**94** A3
Glen Orchy Dr *PLK/PH/NH* G53 ....**122** A4
Glenpark Gdns *BLTYR/CAMB* G72 ....**111** D4
Glenpark Rd *DEN/PKHD* G31 ....**90** B1
Glenpark Ter *BLTYR/CAMB* G72 ....**111** D4
Glenraith Rd *STPS/GTHM/RID* G33 ....**50** A4
Glen Rd *CAR/SHTL* G32 ....**70** A4
Glen Sax Dr *RNFRW* PA4 ....**56** B2
Glenshee Gdns *DEN/PKHD* G31 ....**92** A4
Glenshee St *DEN/PKHD* G31 ....**91** D3
Glenside Av *PLK/PH/NH* G53 ....**101** C1
Glenside Dr *BLTYR/CAMB* G72 ....**131** C1
Glenspean St *PLKSW/MSWD* G43................**125** C1
Glen St *BLTYR/CAMB* G72 ....**134** A3
BRHD/NEIL G78 ....**118** B2
PSLYN/LNWD PA3..**76** B2
Glentanar Pl *PPK/MIL* G22 ....**29** D4
Glentanar Rd *PPK/MIL* G22 ....**29** D4
Glentarbert Rd *RUTH* G73...........................**131** C4
Glentrool Gdns *PPK/MIL* G22 ....**45** C3
Glenturret St *CAR/SHTL* G32...........................**93** C3
Glentyan Dr *PLK/PH/NH* G53......................**100** B4
Glentynan Pl *PLK/PH/NH* G53 ....**100** B4
Glenville Av *GIF/THBK* G46 ....**124** A4
Glenwood Pth *CSMK* G45 ....**128** B4
Glenwood Pl *CSMK* G45 ....**128** B4
Gloucester Av *CRMNK/CLK/EAG* G76......**137** D4
RUTH G73 ....**131** C2
Gloucester St *GBLS* G5 ....**6** B5
Gockston Rd *PSLYN/LNWD* PA3 ....**53** C4
Gogar Pl *STPS/GTHM/RID* G33 ....**68** B3
Gogar St *STPS/GTHM/RID* G33 ....**68** B3
Goldberry Av *SCOT* G14.................................**38** A2
Golf Dr *DRUM* G15 ....**22** B2
PSLY PA1 ....**79** C3
Golfhill Dr *DEN/PKHD* G31 ....**66** B3
Golf Rd *CRMNK/CLK/EAG* G76....................**137** D3
RUTH G73 ....**130** A3
Golfview *BSDN* G61 ....**13** D2
Golspie St *GOV/IBX* G51....................................**60** B3
Goosedubbs *CGLE* G1 ....**8** A4
Gorbals St *GBLS* G5 ....**7** F5
Gordon Av *BAIL/MDB/MHD* G69 ....**95** D2
CARD/HILL/MSPK G52 ....**56** B4
Gordon Dr *GIF/THBK* G46 ....**125** D4
Gordon La *CGLE* G1 ....**7** E1
Gordon St *CGLE* G1 ....**7** E1
PSLY PA1 ....**77** C3
Gorebridge St *CAR/SHTL* G32 ....**68** B4
Gorget Av *KNTSWD* G13 ....**24** A2
Gorget Pl *KNTSWD* G13 ....**24** A2
Gorget Qd *DRUM* G15 ....**23** D2
Gorsewood *BSHPBGS* G64 ....**31** C2
Gorstan Pl *MRYH/FIRH* G20 ....**41** D2
Gorstan St *SMSTN* G23 ....**27** D3
Gosford La *SCOT* G14.......................................**37** D3
Goudie St *PSLYN/LNWD* PA3...........................**53** C4
Gough St *STPS/GTHM/RID* G33 ....**68** A3
Gourlay St *SPRGB/BLRNK* G21 ....**45** D3
Gourock St *PLKSD/SHW* G41 ....**87** C3
Govanhill St *GVH/MTFL* G42 ....**107** D1
Govan Rd *GOV/IBX* G51 ....**59** C2
GOV/IBX G51 ....**85** C1
Gowanlea Av *DRUM* G15...................................**23** C2
Gowanlea Dr *GIF/THBK* G46 ....**125** C3
Gower St *PLKSD/SHW* G41 ....**85** C2
Gower Ter *PLKSD/SHW* G41 ....**85** C2
Goyle Av *DRUM* G15 ....**14** A4
Grace Av *BAIL/MDB/MHD* G69 ....**98** B2
Grace St *KVGV* G3 ....**63** C4
Graffham Av *GIF/THBK* G46 ....**125** C4
Grafton Pl *CGLE* G1 ....**4** A5
Graham Av *BLTYR/CAMB* G72.......................**134** A3
Graham Sq *DMNK/BRGTN* G40...........................**9** F4
Graham St *BRHD/NEIL* G78..........................**118** A2
Graham Ter *BSHPBGS* G64 ....**32** B4
Grainger Rd *BSHPBGS* G64 ....**33** D2
Grampian Crs *CAR/SHTL* G32 ....**93** D3
Grampian Pl *CAR/SHTL* G32 ....**93** D3
Grampian St *CAR/SHTL* G32 ....**93** D3
Grampian Wy *BRHD/NEIL* G78.....................**118** B4
Granby La *KVD/HLHD* G12...............................**62** A1
Grandtuly Dr *KVD/HLHD* G12 ....**41** D1
Grange Av *MLNGV* G62 ....**11** C1
Grange Rd *BSDN* G61..**15** D2
GVH/MTFL G42 ....**106** B3

Gran St *CLYDBK* G81 ..... **22** A3
Grantlea Gv *CAR/SHTL* G32 ..... **94** B3
Grantlea Ter *CAR/SHTL* G32 ..... **94** B3
Grantley Gdns *PLKSD/SHW* G41 ..... **105** C3
Grantley St *PLKSD/SHW* G41 ..... **105** C3
Granton St *GBLS* G5 ..... **108** B1
Grant St *COWCAD* G4 ..... **2** A2
Granville St *KVGV* G3 ..... **2** A4
Gray Dr *BSDN* G61 ..... **15** D4
Gray St *KVGV* G3 ..... **62** B2
Great Dovehill *COWCAD* G4 ..... **8** C3
Great George La *KVD/HLHD* G12 ..... **62** A1
Great George St *KVD/HLHD* G12 ..... **42** A4
Great Kelvin La *KVD/HLHD* G12 ..... **62** B1
Great Western Rd *KNTSWD* G13 ..... **24** A3
Great Western Ter *KVD/HLHD* G12 ..... **41** D3
Great Western Terrace La
KVD/HLHD G12 ..... **41** D3
Greenacres Ct *PLK/PH/NH* G53 ..... **121** D3
Greenacres Dr *PLK/PH/NH* G53 ..... **121** D3
Greenacres Wy *PLK/PH/NH* G53 ..... **121** D3
Greenan Av *LNPK/KPK* G44 ..... **108** B4
Greenbank Av *GIF/THBK* G46 ..... **136** A4
Greendyke St *CGLE* G1 ..... **8** B4
Greenend Pl *CAR/SHTL* G32 ..... **70** B4
Greenfield Rd *CAR/SHTL* G32 ..... **94** A1
Greenfield St *GOV/IBX* G51 ..... **60** A3
Greengairs Av *GOV/IBX* G51 ..... **59** C4
Greenhead Rd *BSDN* G61 ..... **15** D3
Greenhead St *DMNK/BRGTN* G40 ..... **89** C3
Greenhill *BSHPBGS* G64 ..... **33** C3
Greenhill Av *GIF/THBK* G46 ..... **137** C2
Greenhill Ct *RUTH* G73 ..... **109** D3
Greenhill Rd *PSLYN/LNWD* PA3 ..... **76** A1
RUTH G73 ..... **109** D4
Greenhill St *RUTH* G73 ..... **109** D4
Greenholm Av *UD/BTH/TAN* G71 ..... **117** D4
Greenholme St *LNPK/KPK* G44 ..... **126** B1
Greenknowe Rd *PLKSW/MSWD* G43 ..... **124** A1
Greenlaw Av *PSLY* PA1 ..... **78** A2
Greenlaw Crs *PSLY* PA1 ..... **78** A1
Greenlaw Dr *PSLY* PA1 ..... **78** A2
Greenlaw Rd *SCOT* G14 ..... **36** A1
Greenlea St *KNTSWD* G13 ..... **39** D1
Greenlees Gdns *BLTYR/CAMB* G72 ..... **132** A4
Greenlees Pk *BLTYR/CAMB* G72 ..... **132** B4
Greenlees Rd *BLTYR/CAMB* G72 ..... **132** B2
Greenloan Av *GOV/IBX* G51 ..... **59** C4
Greenmount *PPK/MIL* G22 ..... **29** C4
Greenock Av *LNPK/KPK* G44 ..... **127** C2
Greenock Rd *PSLYN/LNWD* PA3 ..... **52** B3
Greenrig St *STPS/GTHM/RID* G33 ..... **48** A4
Greenshields Rd *BAIL/MDB/MHD* G69 ..... **96** B2
Greenside Crs *STPS/GTHM/RID* G33 ..... **48** B4
Greenside St *STPS/GTHM/RID* G33 ..... **48** B4
Green St *DMNK/BRGTN* G40 ..... **9** E5
The Green *DMNK/BRGTN* G40 ..... **89** C3
Greentree Dr *BAIL/MDB/MHD* G69 ..... **95** D4
Greenview St *PLKSW/MSWD* G43 ..... **104** B3
Greenwood Av *BLTYR/CAMB* G72 ..... **134** A1
Greenwood Dr *BSDN* G61 ..... **16** A3
Greenwood Qd *CLYDBK* G81 ..... **21** D2
Greenwood Rd *CRMNK/CLK/EAG* G76 ..... **137** D4
Grenville Dr *BLTYR/CAMB* G72 ..... **132** A3
Gretna St *DMNK/BRGTN* G40 ..... **90** B3
Greyfriars Rd *UD/BTH/TAN* G71 ..... **116** B3
Greyfriars St *CAR/SHTL* G32 ..... **69** C4
Greystone Av *RUTH* G73 ..... **130** B1
Greywood St *KNTSWD* G13 ..... **25** C4
Grierson La *STPS/GTHM/RID* G33 ..... **68** A3
Grierson St *STPS/GTHM/RID* G33 ..... **68** A3
Grogarry Rd *DRUM* G15 ..... **13** C3
Grosvenor Crescent La *KVD/HLHD* G12 ..... **42** A4
Grosvenor La *KVD/HLHD* G12 ..... **42** A4
Grosvenor Ter *KVD/HLHD* G12 ..... **42** A4
Groveburn Av *GIF/THBK* G46 ..... **123** D3
Grovepark Ct *MRYH/FIRH* G20 ..... **63** D1
Grove Park Gdns *MRYH/FIRH* G20 ..... **63** D1
Grovepark St *MRYH/FIRH* G20 ..... **63** D1
The Groves *BSHPBGS* G64 ..... **33** C4
The Grove *GIF/THBK* G46 ..... **136** B3
Grudie St *ESTRH* G34 ..... **72** B3
Gryffe Av *RNFRW* PA4 ..... **35** C2
Gryffe St *LNPK/KPK* G44 ..... **126** B1
Guildford St *STPS/GTHM/RID* G33 ..... **70** B2
Gullane St *PTCK* G11 ..... **61** C2
Guthrie St *MRYH/FIRH* G20 ..... **42** A1

H

Haberlea Av *PLK/PH/NH* G53 ..... **121** D4
Haggs La *PLKSD/SHW* G41 ..... **104** B1
Haggs Rd *PLKSD/SHW* G41 ..... **104** B2
Haggswood Av *PLKSD/SHW* G41 ..... **104** B1
Haghill Rd *DEN/PKHD* G31 ..... **91** C1
Haig Dr *BAIL/MDB/MHD* G69 ..... **95** D3
Haig St *SPRGB/BLRNK* G21 ..... **46** A3
Hailes Av *CAR/SHTL* G32 ..... **94** B2
Haining Rd *RNFRW* PA4 ..... **36** A4
The Haining *RNFRW* PA4 ..... **56** A1
Hairmyres St *GVH/MTFL* G42 ..... **107** D1
Hairst St *RNFRW* PA4 ..... **36** A3
Halbeath Av *DRUM* G15 ..... **12** B4
Halbert St *PLKSD/SHW* G41 ..... **105** D2
Haldane La *SCOT* G14 ..... **39** C4
Haldane St *SCOT* G14 ..... **39** C4
Halgreen Av *DRUM* G15 ..... **12** A4
Hallbrae St *STPS/GTHM/RID* G33 ..... **68** B1
Halley Dr *KNTSWD* G13 ..... **22** A4
Halley Pl *KNTSWD* G13 ..... **36** B1
Halley St *KNTSWD* G13 ..... **22** A4
Hallforest St *STPS/GTHM/RID* G33 ..... **70** A1
Hallhill Crs *STPS/GTHM/RID* G33 ..... **95** C1
Hallhill Rd *BAIL/MDB/MHD* G69 ..... **96** A1
CAR/SHTL G32 ..... **93** D2
STPS/GTHM/RID G33 ..... **95** C1
Halliburton Crs *ESTRH* G34 ..... **72** A4
Halliburton Ter *ESTRH* G34 ..... **72** B4
Hallidale Crs *RNFRW* PA4 ..... **57** C1
Hallrule Dr *CARD/HILL/MSPK* G52 ..... **82** A2
Hallside Av *BLTYR/CAMB* G72 ..... **134** B2
Hallside Bvd *BLTYR/CAMB* G72 ..... **135** C4
Hallside Crs *BLTYR/CAMB* G72 ..... **134** B2
Hallside Dr *BLTYR/CAMB* G72 ..... **134** B2
Hallside Pl *GBLS* G5 ..... **88** A3
Hallside Rd *BLTYR/CAMB* G72 ..... **134** B3
Hall St *CLYDBK* G81 ..... **20** B2
Hallydown Dr *KNTSWD* G13 ..... **38** B2
Halton Gdns *BAIL/MDB/MHD* G69 ..... **95** D3
Hamilton Av *PLKSD/SHW* G41 ..... **84** B4
Hamilton Crs *BLTYR/CAMB* G72 ..... **133** D3
RNFRW PA4 ..... **36** A2
Hamilton Dr *BLTYR/CAMB* G72 ..... **132** B2
GIF/THBK G46 ..... **137** D1
KVD/HLHD G12 ..... **42** B4
Hamiltonhill Crs *PPK/MIL* G22 ..... **44** A3
Hamiltonhill Rd *PPK/MIL* G22 ..... **44** A4
Hamilton Park Av *KVD/HLHD* G12 ..... **42** B4
Hamilton Rd *BLTYR/CAMB* G72 ..... **133** C2
BLTYR/CAMB G72 ..... **134** A3
CAR/SHTL G32 ..... **113** D1
RUTH G73 ..... **110** A4
UD/BTH/TAN G71 ..... **115** C1
Hamilton St *CLYDBK* G81 ..... **21** D4
GVH/MTFL G42 ..... **107** D2
PSLYN/LNWD PA3 ..... **77** D2
Hamilton Ter *CLYDBK* G81 ..... **21** D4
Hampden Dr *GVH/MTFL* G42 ..... **107** C4
Hampden La *GVH/MTFL* G42 ..... **107** C3
Hampden Ter *GVH/MTFL* G42 ..... **107** C3
Handel Pl *GBLS* G5 ..... **88** A3
Hangingshaw Pl *GVH/MTFL* G42 ..... **107** D3
Hanover Cl *GVH/MTFL* G42 ..... **106** B3
Hanover Ct *CGLE* G1 ..... **4** A5
Hanover St *CGLE* G1 ..... **7** F1
Hanson St *DEN/PKHD* G31 ..... **66** A3
Hapland Av *PLK/PH/NH* G53 ..... **101** D1
Hapland Rd *PLK/PH/NH* G53 ..... **101** D1
Harbour La *PSLY* PA1 ..... **77** C2
Harbour Rd *PSLYN/LNWD* PA3 ..... **53** D4
Harburn Pl *SCOT* G14 ..... **37** C1
SMSTN G23 ..... **28** A1
Harcourt Dr *DEN/PKHD* G31 ..... **67** C3
Hardgate Dr *GOV/IBX* G51 ..... **58** B3
Hardgate Gdns *GOV/IBX* G51 ..... **58** B4
Hardgate Pl *GOV/IBX* G51 ..... **58** B4
Hardgate Rd *GOV/IBX* G51 ..... **58** B3
Hardie Av *RUTH* G73 ..... **110** B3
Hardridge Av *CARD/HILL/MSPK* G52 ..... **102** B1
Hardridge Pl *CARD/HILL/MSPK* G52 ..... **102** B1
Hardridge Rd *CARD/HILL/MSPK* G52 ..... **102** A1
Harefield Dr *SCOT* G14 ..... **38** A2
Harelaw Av *BRHD/NEIL* G78 ..... **119** C4
LNPK/KPK G44 ..... **125** D3
Harhill St *GOV/IBX* G51 ..... **60** B4

Harland St *SCOT* G14 ....38 B4
Harley St *GOV/IBX* G51 ....85 C2
Harmetray St *PPK/MIL* G22 ....45 C1
Harmony Pl *GOV/IBX* G51 ....60 B4
Harmony Rw *GOV/IBX* G51 ....60 B4
Harmony Sq *GOV/IBX* G51 ....60 B4
Harmsworth St *PTCK* G11 ....59 D1
Harport St *GIF/THBK* G46 ....122 B3
Harriet Pl *PLKSW/MSWD* G43 ....124 A1
Harriet St *RUTH* G73 ....109 D3
Harrison Dr *GOV/IBX* G51 ....84 B1
Harris Rd *SMSTN* G23 ....27 D2
Harrow Ct *DRUM* G15 ....12 B4
Harrow Pl *DRUM* G15 ....12 B4
Hartlaw Crs *CARD/HILL/MSPK* G52 ....81 C1
Hartree Av *KNTSWD* G13 ....22 A3
Hartstone Rd *PLK/PH/NH* G53 ....101 C4
Hart St *DEN/PKHD* G31 ....92 A2
Harvey St *COWCAD* G4 ....64 B1
Harvie St *GOV/IBX* G51 ....85 D1
Harwood St *CAR/SHTL* G32 ....68 B4
Hastie St *KVGV* G3 ....62 A2
Hatfield Dr *KVD/HLHD* G12 ....40 A2
Hathaway Dr *GIF/THBK* G46 ....136 B1
Hathaway La *MRYH/FIRH* G20 ....42 B2
Hathaway St *MRYH/FIRH* G20 ....42 B2
Hathersage Av *BAIL/MDB/MHD* G69 ....96 B2
Hathersage Dr *BAIL/MDB/MHD* G69 ....96 B2
Hathersage Gdns *BAIL/MDB/MHD* G69 ....96 B2
Hatton Gdns *CARD/HILL/MSPK* G52 ....81 C3
Haughburn Pl *PLK/PH/NH* G53 ....101 C4
Haughburn Rd *PLK/PH/NH* G53 ....101 C4
Haughburn Ter *PLK/PH/NH* G53 ....101 C4
Haugh Rd *KVGV* G3 ....62 A3
Havelock La *PTCK* G11 ....61 D1
Havelock St *PTCK* G11 ....61 D1
Hawick St *KNTSWD* G13 ....22 A4
Hawkhead Rd *PSLY* PA1 ....78 B3
Hawthorn Av *BSDN* G61 ....10 B4
BSHPBGS G64 ....32 B3
Hawthornden Gdns *SMSTN* G23 ....28 A1
Hawthorn Gdns *BLTYR/CAMB* G72 ....134 B3
Hawthorn Qd *PPK/MIL* G22 ....44 B2
Hawthorn St *PPK/MIL* G22 ....44 B2
SPRGB/BLRNK G21 ....46 A2
Hawthorn Wk *BLTYR/CAMB* G72 ....131 C2
Hayburn Crs *PTCK* G11 ....40 B4
Hayburn Ga *PTCK* G11 ....61 C1
Hayburn La *KVD/HLHD* G12 ....40 B4
Hayburn St *PTCK* G11 ....61 C2
Hayfield St *GBLS* G5 ....88 B3
Haymarket St *CAR/SHTL* G32 ....69 C4
Hayston Crs *MRYH/FIRH* G20 ....44 A2
Hayston St *MRYH/FIRH* G20 ....44 A2
Haywood St *PPK/MIL* G22 ....44 A1
Hazel Av *BSDN* G61 ....10 B4
LNPK/KPK G44 ....126 A3
Hazel Dene *BSHPBGS* G64 ....32 B2
Hazelden Pk *LNPK/KPK* G44 ....125 D3
Hazellea Dr *GIF/THBK* G46 ....125 C3
Hazelwood Gdns *RUTH* G73 ....130 B3
Hazelwood Rd *PLKSD/SHW* G41 ....85 C3
Hazlitt Gdns *MRYH/FIRH* G20 ....43 D1
Hazlitt Pl *MRYH/FIRH* G20 ....43 D1
Hazlitt St *MRYH/FIRH* G20 ....44 A2
Heath Av *BSHPBGS* G64 ....32 B3
Heathcot Av *DRUM* G15 ....22 A1
Heathcot Pl *DRUM* G15 ....21 D1
Heatherbrae *BSHPBGS* G64 ....31 C2
Heatheryknowe Rd
BAIL/MDB/MHD G69 ....74 B3
Heathfield St *STPS/GTHM/RID* G33 ....70 B3
Heathside Rd *GIF/THBK* G46 ....125 C4
Heathwood Dr *GIF/THBK* G46 ....123 D4
Hecla Av *DRUM* G15 ....12 B4
Hecla Pl *DRUM* G15 ....12 B4
Hecla Sq *DRUM* G15 ....12 B4
Hector Rd *PLKSD/SHW* G41 ....105 C3
Helensburgh Dr *KNTSWD* G13 ....39 C1
Helenslea *BLTYR/CAMB* G72 ....134 A3
Helen St *GOV/IBX* G51 ....83 D2
Helenvale Ct *DEN/PKHD* G31 ....91 D2
Helenvale St *DEN/PKHD* G31 ....91 C3
Hemlock St *KNTSWD* G13 ....25 D4
Henderland Dr *BSDN* G61 ....25 C1
Henderland Rd *BSDN* G61 ....25 D2
Henderson Av *BLTYR/CAMB* G72 ....134 A1
Henderson St *KNTSWD* G13 ....22 A3
MRYH/FIRH G20 ....43 C4
PSLY PA1 ....76 B2
Henrietta St *SCOT* G14 ....38 B4
Henry St *BRHD/NEIL* G78 ....118 A2
Hepburn Rd *CARD/HILL/MSPK* G52 ....57 D4
Herald Av *KNTSWD* G13 ....24 B2
Herbert St *MRYH/FIRH* G20 ....43 C4
Heriot Crs *BSHPBGS* G64 ....19 C4
Herma St *SMSTN* G23 ....28 A3
Hermiston Av *CAR/SHTL* G32 ....93 D1
Hermiston Rd *CAR/SHTL* G32 ....93 D1
Hermitage Av *KNTSWD* G13 ....24 A4
Herries Rd *PLKSD/SHW* G41 ....104 B2
Herriet St *PLKSD/SHW* G41 ....86 B4
Herschell St *KNTSWD* G13 ....40 A1
Hertford Av *KVD/HLHD* G12 ....41 C1
Hexham Gdns *PLKSD/SHW* G41 ....105 C2
Heys St *BRHD/NEIL* G78 ....118 B3
Hickman St *GVH/MTFL* G42 ....107 D1
Hickman Ter *GVH/MTFL* G42 ....107 D1
Hickory St *PPK/MIL* G22 ....45 D2
Highburgh Dr *RUTH* G73 ....130 A2
Highburgh Rd *KVD/HLHD* G12 ....61 D1
High Calside *PSLYS* PA2 ....76 B4
High Craighall Rd *COWCAD* G4 ....3 E1
Highcroft Av *LNPK/KPK* G44 ....128 A2
Highfield Dr *CRMNK/CLK/EAG* G76 ....137 D4
KVD/HLHD G12 ....41 C1
RUTH G73 ....130 B4
Highfield Pl *KVD/HLHD* G12 ....41 C1
Highland La *GOV/IBX* G51 ....61 D4
High Rd *PSLYS* PA2 ....76 A4
High St *COWCAD* G4 ....8 C2
PSLY PA1 ....76 B3
RNFRW PA4 ....36 A4
RUTH G73 ....109 D3
Hilary Dr *BAIL/MDB/MHD* G69 ....95 D2
Hillary Av *RUTH* G73 ....131 C1
Hillcrest Av *CAR/SHTL* G32 ....113 C3
LNPK/KPK G44 ....125 D3
Hillcrest Rd *BSDN* G61 ....15 D3
CAR/SHTL G32 ....113 D3
Hillcrest St *MLNGV* G62 ....11 C1
Hillcroft Ter *BSHPBGS* G64 ....31 D3
Hillend Rd *PPK/MIL* G22 ....29 C4
RUTH G73 ....130 A3
Hillfoot Av *RUTH* G73 ....109 D4
Hillfoot Dr *BSDN* G61 ....15 D2
Hillfoot Gdns *UD/BTH/TAN* G71 ....117 D3
Hillfoot St *DEN/PKHD* G31 ....66 B4
Hillhead Av *RUTH* G73 ....130 A3
Hillhead Pl *RUTH* G73 ....130 A3
Hillhead Rd *SPRGB/BLRNK* G21 ....33 D4
Hillhead St *KVD/HLHD* G12 ....62 A1
MLNGV G62 ....10 B1
Hillhouse St *SPRGB/BLRNK* G21 ....46 B3
Hillington Gdns *CARD/HILL/MSPK* G52 ....82 A3
Hillington Park Circ
CARD/HILL/MSPK G52 ....82 A2
Hillington Qd *CARD/HILL/MSPK* G52 ....81 C2
Hillington Rd *CARD/HILL/MSPK* G52 ....57 C2
Hillington Rd South
CARD/HILL/MSPK G52 ....81 C1
Hillington Ter *CARD/HILL/MSPK* G52 ....81 C2
Hillkirk Pl *SPRGB/BLRNK* G21 ....46 A3
Hillkirk St *SPRGB/BLRNK* G21 ....46 A3
Hillneuk Av *BSDN* G61 ....15 D2
Hillneuk Dr *BSDN* G61 ....16 A2
Hillpark Dr *PLKSW/MSWD* G43 ....124 B1
Hillsborough Rd *BAIL/MDB/MHD* G69 ....95 D2
Hillside Av *BSDN* G61 ....15 D2
CRMNK/CLK/EAG G76 ....137 D4
Hillside Ct *GIF/THBK* G46 ....123 C4
Hillside Dr *BSDN* G61 ....16 A2
BSHPBGS G64 ....32 A1
Hillside Gardens La *KVD/HLHD* G12 ....41 C4
Hillside Qd *PLKSW/MSWD* G43 ....124 A2
Hillside Rd *PLKSW/MSWD* G43 ....124 A2
Hill St *KVGV* G3 ....2 C3
Hillswick Crs *PPK/MIL* G22 ....29 D3
Hillview Crs *UD/BTH/TAN* G71 ....117 D3
Hillview Dr *CRMNK/CLK/EAG* G76 ....137 D4
Hillview Gdns *BSHPBGS* G64 ....33 D4
Hillview St *CAR/SHTL* G32 ....92 B2
Hilton Gdns *KNTSWD* G13 ....25 D4
Hilton Pk *BSHPBGS* G64 ....18 B4
Hilton Rd *BSHPBGS* G64 ....18 B4
Hilton Ter *BLTYR/CAMB* G72 ....131 D4
BSHPBGS G64 ....18 B4
KNTSWD G13 ....25 C4
Hinshaw St *MRYH/FIRH* G20 ....43 D4
Hinshelwood Dr *GOV/IBX* G51 ....84 A2

Hinshelwood Pl *GOV/IBX* G51 **84** B2
Hobart St *PPK/MIL* G22 **44** A3
Hobden St *SPRGB/BLRNK* G21 **46** B4
Hoddam Av *CSMK* G45 **129** C4
Hoddam Ter *CSMK* G45 **129** D4
Hogarth Av *CAR/SHTL* G32 **68** A4
Hogarth Gdns *CAR/SHTL* G32 **68** A4
Hogganfield St *STPS/GTHM/RID* G33 **68** A1
Holeburn La *PLKSW/MSWD* G43 **124** B1
Holeburn Rd *PLKSW/MSWD* G43 **124** B1
Holehouse Dr *KNTSWD* G13 **37** D1
Holland St *CGLW* G2 **2** B5
Hollinwell Rd *SMSTN* G23 **27** D3
Hollowglen Rd *CAR/SHTL* G32 **93** D1
Hollybank Pl *BLTYR/CAMB* G72 **133** C3
Hollybank St *SPRGB/BLRNK* G21 **66** B2
Hollybrook St *GVH/MTFL* G42 **107** C2
Hollybush Rd *CARD/HILL/MSPK* G52 **80** B2
Holly Dr *SPRGB/BLRNK* G21 **46** B4
Hollymount *BSDN* G61 **25** D1
Holm Av *UD/BTH/TAN* G71 **117** D4
Holmbank Av *PLKSD/SHW* G41 **105** C4
Holmes Av *RNFRW* PA4 **55** D2
Holmfauldhead Dr *GOV/IBX* G51 **59** D3
Holmfauldhead Pl *GOV/IBX* G51 **59** D2
Holmfauld Rd *GOV/IBX* G51 **59** D2
Holmhead Crs *LNPK/KPK* G44 **126** B1
Holmhead Pl *LNPK/KPK* G44 **126** B1
Holmhead Rd *LNPK/KPK* G44 **126** B2
Holmhill Av *BLTYR/CAMB* G72 **132** B3
Holmhills Dr *BLTYR/CAMB* G72 **132** A4
Holmhills Gdns *BLTYR/CAMB* G72 **132** A3
Holmhills Gv *BLTYR/CAMB* G72 **132** A3
Holmhills Pl *BLTYR/CAMB* G72 **132** A4
Holmhills Rd *BLTYR/CAMB* G72 **132** A4
Holmhills Ter *BLTYR/CAMB* G72 **132** A3
Holmlea Rd *GVH/MTFL* G42 **106** B4
Holm St *CGLW* G2 **7** D2
Holyrood Crs *MRYH/FIRH* G20 **63** C1
Holyrood Qd *MRYH/FIRH* G20 **63** C1
Holywell St *DEN/PKHD* G31 **90** B2
Honeybog Rd *CARD/HILL/MSPK* G52 **80** A1
Hood St *CLYDBK* G81 **21** C1
Hopefield Av *KVD/HLHD* G12 **41** D2
Hopehill Gdns *MRYH/FIRH* G20 **43** D4
Hopehill Rd *MRYH/FIRH* G20 **43** D4
Hopeman Av *GIF/THBK* G46 **122** B3
Hopeman Dr *GIF/THBK* G46 **122** B3
Hopeman Rd *GIF/THBK* G46 **122** B3
Hopeman St *GIF/THBK* G46 **122** B3
Hope St *CGLW* G2 **7** E1
Hopetoun Pl *SMSTN* G23 **28** A1
Hopetoun Ter *SPRGB/BLRNK* G21 **46** B4
Horne St *PPK/MIL* G22 **45** D2
Hornshill St *SPRGB/BLRNK* G21 **46** B3
Horsburgh St *STPS/GTHM/RID* G33 **71** C1
Horse Shoe Rd *BSDN* G61 **15** C3
Horslethill Rd *KVD/HLHD* G12 **41** D3
Hospital St *GBLS* G5 **87** D3
Hotspur St *MRYH/FIRH* G20 **42** B3
Houldsworth La *KVGV* G3 **62** B3
Househillmuir Crs *PLK/PH/NH* G53 **121** D1
Househillmuir Pl *PLK/PH/NH* G53 **101** D4
Househillmuir Rd *PLK/PH/NH* G53 **120** B2
Househillwood Crs *PLK/PH/NH* G53 **101** C4
Househillwood Rd *PLK/PH/NH* G53 **121** C1
Housel Av *KNTSWD* G13 **38** A1
Houston Pl *GBLS* G5 **86** B1
Houston St *PLKSD/SHW* G41 **86** B2
RNFRW PA4 **36** A3
Howard St *CGLE* G1 **7** F3
PSLY PA1 **78** A2
Howat St *GOV/IBX* G51 **60** B3
Howford Rd *CARD/HILL/MSPK* G52 **81** D3
Howgate Av *DRUM* G15 **12** B4
Howieshill Av *BLTYR/CAMB* G72 **133** C2
Howieshill Rd *BLTYR/CAMB* G72 **133** C3
Howth Dr *KNTSWD* G13 **25** D3
Howth Ter *KNTSWD* G13 **25** D3
Hoylake Pl *SMSTN* G23 **28** A2
Hughenden Dr *KVD/HLHD* G12 **41** C3
Hughenden Gdns *KVD/HLHD* G12 **40** B3
Hughenden La *KVD/HLHD* G12 **41** C3
Hughenden Rd *KVD/HLHD* G12 **41** C3
Hugh Murray Gv *BLTYR/CAMB* G72 **133** D2
Hugo St *MRYH/FIRH* G20 **43** C2
Hume Dr *UD/BTH/TAN* G71 **117** D4
Hume St *CLYDBK* G81 **20** B2
Hunterfield Dr *BLTYR/CAMB* G72 **131** D2
Hunterhill Av *PSLYS* PA2 **77** D4
Hunterhill Rd *PSLYS* PA2 **77** D4
Hunter Rd *RUTH* G73 **110** B2
Hunters Hill Ct *SPRGB/BLRNK* G21 **46** A1
Huntershill Rd *BSHPBGS* G64 **31** D3
Huntershill St *SPRGB/BLRNK* G21 **45** D1
Huntershill Wy *BSHPBGS* G64 **31** D4
Hunter St *COWCAD* G4 **9** E2
PSLY PA1 **77** C2
Huntingdon Rd *SPRGB/BLRNK* G21 **5** D1
Huntingdon Sq *SPRGB/BLRNK* G21 **65** D1
Huntingtower Rd *BAIL/MDB/MHD* G69 **95** D3
Huntley Gdns *KVD/HLHD* G12 **42** A4
Huntly Av *GIF/THBK* G46 **125** C4
Huntly Ct *BSHPBGS* G64 **32** A3
Huntly Dr *BLTYR/CAMB* G72 **133** C3
Huntly Rd *CARD/HILL/MSPK* G52 **57** C3
KVD/HLHD G12 **41** D4
Hurlford Av *KNTSWD* G13 **22** B4
Hurly Hawkin *BSHPBGS* G64 **33** D3
Hutcheson Rd *GIF/THBK* G46 **136** A1
Hutcheson St *CGLE* G1 **8** A3
Hutchinson Pl *BLTYR/CAMB* G72 **134** B4
Hutchison Dr *BSDN* G61 **26** A1
Hutton *KVD/HLHD* G12 **40** B1
Hutton Dr *GOV/IBX* G51 **59** D3
Huxley Pl *MRYH/FIRH* G20 **43** C1
Huxley St *MRYH/FIRH* G20 **43** C1
Hydepark St *KVGV* G3 **63** C4
Hyndal Av *PLK/PH/NH* G53 **101** D2
Hyndland Av *PTCK* G11 **61** C1
Hyndland Rd *KVD/HLHD* G12 **41** D4
Hyndland St *PTCK* G11 **61** D1
Hyndlee Dr *CARD/HILL/MSPK* G52 **82** A2

I

Iain Dr *BSDN* G61 **14** A1
Iain Rd *BSDN* G61 **14** A1
Ian Smith Ct *CLYDBK* G81 **21** D3
Ibroxholm Ov *GOV/IBX* G51 **84** B1
Ibroxholm Pl *GOV/IBX* G51 **84** B2
Ibrox St *GOV/IBX* G51 **85** C1
Ibrox Ter *GOV/IBX* G51 **84** B1
Iddesleigh Av *MLNGV* G62 **10** B1
Ilay Av *BSDN* G61 **26** A3
Ilay Ct *BSDN* G61 **26** A3
Ilay Rd *BSDN* G61 **26** A3
Inchbrae Rd *CARD/HILL/MSPK* G52 **82** A3
Inchfad Crs *DRUM* G15 **12** A4
Inchfad Dr *DRUM* G15 **12** A4
Inchfad Pl *DRUM* G15 **12** A4
Inchholm La *PTCK* G11 **59** D1
Inchinnan Rd *PSLYN/LNWD* PA3 **53** D4
RNFRW PA4 **34** B3
Inchkeith Pl *CAR/SHTL* G32 **70** A4
Inchlaggan Pl *DRUM* G15 **12** A3
Inchlee St *SCOT* G14 **59** D1
Inchoch St *STPS/GTHM/RID* G33 **71** D1
Inchrory Pl *DRUM* G15 **12** A3
Incle St *PSLY* PA1 **77** D2
India St *CGLW* G2 **2** B4
Inga St *MRYH/FIRH* G20 **28** A4
Ingerbreck Av *RUTH* G73 **131** C2
Ingleby Dr *DEN/PKHD* G31 **66** B4
Inglefield St *GVH/MTFL* G42 **87** D4
Ingleneuk Av *STPS/GTHM/RID* G33 **50** A2
Inglestone Av *GIF/THBK* G46 **136** A1
Inglis St *DEN/PKHD* G31 **90** A1
Ingram St *CGLE* G1 **8** B2
Inishail Rd *STPS/GTHM/RID* G33 **70** B2
Inkerman Rd *CARD/HILL/MSPK* G52 **80** B2
Innellan Gdns *MRYH/FIRH* G20 **26** B4
Innellan Pl *MRYH/FIRH* G20 **26** B4
Innerwick Dr *CARD/HILL/MSPK* G52 **81** D2
Inveraray Dr *BSHPBGS* G64 **19** D3
Invercanny Dr *DRUM* G15 **13** C3
Invercanny Pl *DRUM* G15 **13** C3
Inverclyde Gdns *RUTH* G73 **131** C4
Inveresk Qd *CAR/SHTL* G32 **93** C1
Inveresk St *CAR/SHTL* G32 **93** C1
Inverewe Pl *GIF/THBK* G46 **122** A4
Inverglas Av *RNFRW* PA4 **57** C2
Invergordon Av *PLKSW/MSWD* G43 **106** A4
Invergyle Dr *CARD/HILL/MSPK* G52 **81** D2
Inverlair Av *PLKSW/MSWD* G43 **126** A1

Inverleith St *CAR/SHTL* G32 ....68 B4
Inverlochy St *STPS/GTHM/RID* G33....71 C2
Inverness St *GOV/IBX* G51 ....82 B1
Inveroran Dr *BSDN* G61 ....16 B3
Inver Rd *STPS/GTHM/RID* G33 ....71 D4
Invershiel Rd *SMSTN* G23 ....27 D2
Invershin Dr *MRYH/FIRH* G20....42 A2
Inverurie St *SPRGB/BLRNK* G21 ....45 C4
Inzievar Ter *CAR/SHTL* G32 ....113 C2
Iona Rd *RNFRW* PA4....55 D2
RUTH G73 ....131 D4
Iona St *GOV/IBX* G51 ....61 C4
Iona Wy *STPS/GTHM/RID* G33 ....51 D3
Iris Av *CSMK* G45 ....129 D4
Irongray St *DEN/PKHD* G31 ....67 D4
Irvine St *DMNK/BRGTN* G40 ....90 B4
Islay Av *RUTH* G73 ....131 D4
Ivanhoe Rd *KNTSWD* G13 ....24 B3
Ivybank Av *BLTYR/CAMB* G72 ....133 D3

J

Jagger Gdns *BAIL/MDB/MHD* G69....95 D3
Jamaica St *CGLE* G1 ....7 E3
James Dunlop Gdns *BSHPBGS* G64 ....32 B4
James Gray St *PLKSD/SHW* G41....105 D2
James Morrison St *CGLE* G1 ....8 B4
James Nisbet St *SPRGB/BLRNK* G21 ....5 F4
James St *DMNK/BRGTN* G40....89 C3
James Watt St *CGLW* G2 ....6 C2
Jamieson Ct *GVH/MTFL* G42....107 C1
Jamieson St *GVH/MTFL* G42....107 C1
Janebank Av *BLTYR/CAMB* G72 ....133 D3
Janefield St *DEN/PKHD* G31....90 B2
DMNK/BRGTN G40 ....91 C3
Jane Rae Gdns *CLYDBK* G81 ....21 D3
Jardine St *MRYH/FIRH* G20....43 C4
Jean Maclean Pl *BSHPBGS* G64 ....19 D3
Jedburgh Av *RUTH* G73....110 A4
Jedburgh Gdns *MRYH/FIRH* G20 ....43 C4
Jedworth Av *DRUM* G15....13 D4
Jedworth Rd *DRUM* G15....14 A4
Jerviston Rd *STPS/GTHM/RID* G33 ....70 B1
Jessie St *GVH/MTFL* G42 ....108 A2
Jocelyn Sq *CGLE* G1 ....8 A4
John Knox St *CLYDBK* G81 ....21 D4
COWCAD G4....9 E1
John Marshall Dr *PPK/MIL* G22 ....31 C3
Johnsburn Dr *PLK/PH/NH* G53 ....121 C1
Johnsburn Rd *PLK/PH/NH* G53 ....121 C1
Johnshaven St *PLKSW/MSWD* G43 ....104 B4
John Smith Ga *BRHD/NEIL* G78 ....118 B1
Johnson Dr *BLTYR/CAMB* G72 ....132 B2
Johnstone Av *CARD/HILL/MSPK* G52 ....58 A4
CLYDBK G81....21 D3
Johnstone Dr *RUTH* G73....109 D4
Johnston St *PSLY* PA1 ....77 C3
John St *BRHD/NEIL* G78 ....118 A2
CGLE G1 ....8 A2
Joppa St *STPS/GTHM/RID* G33....68 B3
Jordanhill Crs *KNTSWD* G13 ....39 C2
Jordanhill Dr *KNTSWD* G13....39 C2
Jordanhill La *KNTSWD* G13 ....39 D2
Jordan St *SCOT* G14....59 C1
Jordanvale Av *SCOT* G14....59 C1
Jowitt Av *CLYDBK* G81....21 D2
Jubilee Ct *CARD/HILL/MSPK* G52....57 C4
Jubilee Gdns *BSDN* G61....15 C3
Julian Av *KVD/HLHD* G12....41 D3
Julian La *KVD/HLHD* G12 ....41 D3
Juniper Pl *CAR/SHTL* G32 ....95 D3
Juniper Ter *CAR/SHTL* G32 ....95 C3
Jura Av *RNFRW* PA4....56 A2
Jura St *CARD/HILL/MSPK* G52....83 D2

K

Kaim Dr *PLK/PH/NH* G53....121 D1
Katewell Av *DRUM* G15....12 A3
Katewell Pl *DRUM* G15 ....12 A3
Katrine Av *BSHPBGS* G64 ....32 B2
Katrine Pl *BLTYR/CAMB* G72....132 B1
Kaystone Rd *DRUM* G15 ....23 C2
Kay St *SPRGB/BLRNK* G21....46 A3
Keal Av *DRUM* G15....23 D3
Keal Crs *DRUM* G15 ....23 C3
Keal Dr *DRUM* G15 ....23 C3
Keal Pl *DRUM* G15 ....23 C3
Kearn Av *DRUM* G15 ....23 D2
Kearn Pl *DRUM* G15....23 D2
Keir Dr *BSHPBGS* G64....31 D1
Keir St *PLKSD/SHW* G41....86 B4
Keir's Wk *BLTYR/CAMB* G72 ....132 B1
Keith Av *GIF/THBK* G46 ....124 B4
Keith Ct *PTCK* G11 ....61 D1
Keith St *PTCK* G11 ....61 D1
Kelbourne St *MRYH/FIRH* G20 ....42 B3
Kelburne Dr *PSLY* PA1 ....78 B2
Kelburne Gdns *BAIL/MDB/MHD* G69....96 A4
PSLY PA1 ....78 A2
Kelburne Ov *PSLY* PA1....78 A2
Kelhead Av *CARD/HILL/MSPK* G52....80 B3
Kelhead Dr *CARD/HILL/MSPK* G52 ....80 B2
Kelhead Pth *CARD/HILL/MSPK* G52....80 B2
Kelhead Pl *PSLY* PA1 ....80 B2
Kellas St *GOV/IBX* G51 ....60 B4
Kells Pl *DRUM* G15 ....12 A3
Kelso Av *RUTH* G73 ....110 A4
Kelso Pl *SCOT* G14 ....36 B1
Kelso St *KNTSWD* G13 ....22 B4
SCOT G14....36 B1
Kelton St *CAR/SHTL* G32 ....93 D3
Kelvin Av *CARD/HILL/MSPK* G52 ....57 D3
Kelvin Crs *BSDN* G61 ....25 D1
Kelvindale Gdns *MRYH/FIRH* G20 ....41 D1
Kelvindale Pl *MRYH/FIRH* G20 ....42 A1
Kelvindale Rd *KVD/HLHD* G12 ....41 D2
Kelvin Dr *BRHD/NEIL* G78 ....119 C4
BSHPBGS G64 ....32 A1
MRYH/FIRH G20 ....42 A3
Kelvingrove St *KVGV* G3 ....62 B3
Kelvinhaugh Ga *KVGV* G3 ....62 A3
Kelvinhaugh Pl *KVGV* G3 ....62 A3
Kelvinhaugh St *KVGV* G3....62 A3
Kelvin Rd *UD/BTH/TAN* G71 ....117 D4
Kelvinside Av *MRYH/FIRH* G20....42 B3
Kelvinside Dr *MRYH/FIRH* G20....43 C3
Kelvinside Gdns *MRYH/FIRH* G20 ....42 B3
Kelvinside Gdns East *MRYH/FIRH* G20 ....43 C3
Kelvinside Gardens La *MRYH/FIRH* G20 ..42 B4
Kelvinside Ter South *KVD/HLHD* G12 ....42 B4
Kelvinside Ter West *MRYH/FIRH* G20 ....42 B4
Kelvin Wy *KVGV* G3 ....62 A2
Kemp Av *PSLYN/LNWD* PA3 ....54 B2
Kempsthorn Crs *PLK/PH/NH* G53 ....100 B2
Kempsthorn Pl *PLK/PH/NH* G53 ....101 C2
Kempsthorn Rd *PLK/PH/NH* G53 ....100 B2
Kemp St *SPRGB/BLRNK* G21 ....45 D3
Kendal Av *GIF/THBK* G46....124 B4
KVD/HLHD G12 ....40 B1
Kendal Dr *KVD/HLHD* G12....40 B1
Kendoon Av *DRUM* G15 ....12 A4
Kenilworth Av *PLKSD/SHW* G41....105 C3
Kenilworth Crs *BSDN* G61....14 A1
Kenmar Gdns *UD/BTH/TAN* G71 ....117 D3
Kenmore Gdns *BSDN* G61....16 B2
Kenmore St *CAR/SHTL* G32....93 C2
Kenmuir Av *CAR/SHTL* G32....95 C4
Kenmuirhill Rd *CAR/SHTL* G32 ....114 A1
Kenmuir Rd *CAR/SHTL* G32....114 A3
Kenmuir St *CTBR* ML5 ....99 D3
Kenmure Av *BSHPBGS* G64....31 C2
Kenmure Crs *BSHPBGS* G64 ....31 D2
Kenmure Dr *BSHPBGS* G64....31 D2
Kenmure Gdns *BSHPBGS* G64 ....31 C2
Kenmure La *BSHPBGS* G64 ....31 D2
Kenmure St *PLKSD/SHW* G41 ....86 B4
Kenmure Wy *RUTH* G73 ....130 A4
Kennedar Dr *GOV/IBX* G51 ....59 D3
Kennedy St *COWCAD* G4 ....4 C3
Kennishead Av *GIF/THBK* G46 ....122 B2
Kennishead Pl *GIF/THBK* G46....122 B2
Kennishead Rd *GIF/THBK* G46 ....123 C3
PLK/PH/NH G53 ....121 D2
Kennisholm Av *GIF/THBK* G46 ....122 B2
Kennoway Dr *PTCK* G11 ....60 A1
Kennyhill Sq *DEN/PKHD* G31 ....67 C3
Kensington Dr *GIF/THBK* G46....137 D2
Kensington Ga *KVD/HLHD* G12 ....41 D3

Kensington Gate La *KVD/HLHD* G12 ....41 D3
Kensington Rd *KVD/HLHD* G12 ....41 D3
Kentallen Rd *STPS/GTHM/RID* G33 ....94 B1
Kent Dr *RUTH* G73 ....131 C2
Kentigern Ter *BSHPBGS* G64 ....32 A3
Kent Rd *KVGV* G3 ....62 B3
Kent St *CGLE* G1 ....9 D4
Keppel Dr *LNPK/KPK* G44 ....108 B4
Keppochhill Dr *SPRGB/BLRNK* G21 ....45 C4
Keppochhill Rd *PPK/MIL* G22 ....44 B4
SPRGB/BLRNK G21 ....45 D4
Keppoch St *SPRGB/BLRNK* G21 ....45 C4
Kerfield Pl *DRUM* G15 ....12 A3
Kerr Dr *DMNK/BRGTN* G40 ....89 D2
Kerrera Pl *STPS/GTHM/RID* G33 ....94 B1
Kerrera Rd *STPS/GTHM/RID* G33 ....94 B1
Kerr Pl *DMNK/BRGTN* G40 ....89 D2
Kerr St *DMNK/BRGTN* G40 ....89 D2
PSLYN/LNWD PA3 ....76 B2
Kerrycroy Av *GVH/MTFL* G42 ....108 A3
Kerrycroy Pl *GVH/MTFL* G42 ....108 A3
Kerrycroy St *GVH/MTFL* G42 ....108 A3
Kerrydale St *DMNK/BRGTN* G40 ....90 B3
Kerrylamont Av *GVH/MTFL* G42 ....108 B4
Kerry Pl *DRUM* G15 ....12 A4
Kersland Dr *MLNGV* G62 ....11 C1
Kersland La *KVD/HLHD* G12 ....42 A4
MLNGV G62 ....11 C1
Kersland St *KVD/HLHD* G12 ....42 A4
Kessington Dr *BSDN* G61 ....16 A3
Kessington Rd *BSDN* G61 ....16 B4
Kessington Sq *BSDN* G61 ....16 B4
Kessock Dr *PPK/MIL* G22 ....44 A4
Kessock Pl *PPK/MIL* G22 ....44 A4
Kestrel Rd *KNTSWD* G13 ....38 B1
Kew La *KVD/HLHD* G12 ....42 A4
Kew Ter *KVD/HLHD* G12 ....42 A3
Keystone Av *MLNGV* G62 ....10 B3
Keystone Qd *MLNGV* G62 ....10 A3
Keystone Rd *MLNGV* G62 ....10 B3
Kidston Ter *GBLS* G5 ....88 A3
Kilbarchan St *GBLS* G5* 87 D2
Kilbeg Ter *GIF/THBK* G46 ....122 A4
Kilberry St *SPRGB/BLRNK* G21 ....66 B2
Kilbirnie Pl *GBLS* G5 ....87 C3
Kilbirnie St *GBLS* G5 ....87 C3
Kilbowie Rd *CLYDBK* G81 ....20 B2
Kilbride St *GBLS* G5 ....108 A1
Kilburn Pl *KNTSWD* G13 ....38 A1
Kilchattan Dr *LNPK/KPK* G44 ....107 D4
Kilchoan Rd *STPS/GTHM/RID* G33 ....70 B1
Kilcloy Av *DRUM* G15 ....13 C3
Kildale Wy *RUTH* G73 ....109 C3
Kildary Av *LNPK/KPK* G44 ....126 B2
Kildary Rd *LNPK/KPK* G44 ....126 B2
Kildermorie Rd *ESTRH* G34 ....72 A3
Kildonan Dr *PTCK* G11 ....60 B1
Kildrostan St *PLKSD/SHW* G41 ....106 A1
Kilearn Rd *PSLYN/LNWD* PA3 ....55 C4
Kilearn Wy *PSLYN/LNWD* PA3 ....55 C4
Kilfinan St *PPK/MIL* G22 ....29 D4
Kilgarth St *CTBR* ML5 ....99 D3
Kilkerran Dr *STPS/GTHM/RID* G33 ....49 C1
Killearn Dr *PSLY* PA1 ....80 B3
Killearn St *PPK/MIL* G22 ....44 B3
Killermont Av *BSDN* G61 ....26 B1
Killermont Rd *BSDN* G61 ....15 D4
Killermont St *CGLE* G1 ....3 F4
Killermont Vw *MRYH/FIRH* G20 ....26 A1
Killiegrew Rd *PLKSD/SHW* G41 ....105 C1
Killin St *CAR/SHTL* G32 ....93 D4
Killoch Dr *BRHD/NEIL* G78 ....119 C4
KNTSWD G13 ....23 C4
Kilmailing Rd *LNPK/KPK* G44 ....127 C2
Kilmair Pl *MRYH/FIRH* G20 ....42 A2
Kilmaluag Ter *GIF/THBK* G46 ....122 A4
Kilmany Dr *CAR/SHTL* G32 ....92 B2
Kilmany Gdns *CAR/SHTL* G32 ....92 B2
Kilmardinny Av *BSDN* G61 ....15 D1
Kilmardinny Crs *BSDN* G61 ....16 A1
Kilmardinny Dr *BSDN* G61 ....15 D1
Kilmardinny Ga *BSDN* G61 ....15 D2
Kilmardinny Gv *BSDN* G61 ....15 D1
Kilmari Gdns *DRUM* G15 ....12 A3
Kilmarnock Rd *PLKSW/MSWD* G43 ....125 C1
Kilmartin Pl *GIF/THBK* G46 ....122 B3
Kilmaurs Dr *GIF/THBK* G46 ....125 D4
Kilmaurs St *GOV/IBX* G51 ....83 D1
Kilmore Crs *DRUM* G15 ....12 A3
Kilmorie Dr *RUTH* G73 ....108 B4
Kilmuir Crs *GIF/THBK* G46 ....122 A3
Kilmuir Dr *GIF/THBK* G46 ....122 B3
Kilmuir Rd *GIF/THBK* G46 ....122 A4
Kilmun St *MRYH/FIRH* G20 ....27 D4
Kilnside Rd *PSLY* PA1 ....77 D2
Kiloran St *GIF/THBK* G46 ....123 C3
Kilpatrick Dr *RNFRW* PA4 ....55 C3
STPS/GTHM/RID G33 ....51 D2
Kilpatrick Gdns *CRMNK/CLK/EAG* G76 ....137 D4
Kiltearn Rd *STPS/GTHM/RID* G33 ....72 A4
Kilvaxter Dr *GIF/THBK* G46 ....122 B4
Kinalty Rd *PLKSW/MSWD* G43 ....126 B2
Kinarvie Crs *PLK/PH/NH* G53 ....100 A4
Kinarvie Pl *PLK/PH/NH* G53 ....100 A4
Kinarvie Rd *PLK/PH/NH* G53 ....100 A4
Kinarvie Ter *PLK/PH/NH* G53 ....100 A4
Kinbuck St *PPK/MIL* G22 ....45 C3
Kincaid Gdns *BLTYR/CAMB* G72 ....132 B1
Kincardine Dr *BSHPBGS* G64 ....32 B3
Kincardine Pl *BSHPBGS* G64 ....33 C4
Kincardine Sq *STPS/GTHM/RID* G33 ....71 C2
Kincath Av *RUTH* G73 ....130 B4
Kinclaven Av *DRUM* G15 ....13 C4
Kinclaven Gdns *DRUM* G15 ....13 D4
Kinclaven Pl *DRUM* G15 ....13 D4
Kincraig St *GOV/IBX* G51 ....82 B1
Kinellan Rd *BSDN* G61 ....25 D2
Kinellar Dr *SCOT* G14 ....37 D1
Kinfauns Dr *DRUM* G15 ....12 B4
DRUM G15 ....14 A4
Kingarth La *GVH/MTFL* G42 ....106 B1
Kingarth St *PLKSD/SHW* G41 ....106 B1
King Edward La *KNTSWD* G13 ....40 A2
King Edward Rd *KNTSWD* G13 ....40 A2
Kingfisher Dr *KNTSWD* G13 ....22 B4
King George Ct *RNFRW* PA4 ....56 B2
King George Gdns *RNFRW* PA4 ....56 B1
King George Park Av *RNFRW* PA4 ....56 B2
King George Pl *RNFRW* PA4 ....56 B2
King George Wy *RNFRW* PA4 ....56 B2
Kinghorn Dr *LNPK/KPK* G44 ....127 D1
Kinglas Rd *BSDN* G61 ....24 A1
King Pl *BAIL/MDB/MHD* G69 ....99 C2
Kingsacre Rd *LNPK/KPK* G44 ....107 D4
RUTH G73 ....108 B4
Kingsbarns Dr *LNPK/KPK* G44 ....107 C4
Kingsborough Gdns *KVD/HLHD* G12 ....41 C3
Kingsborough Ga *KVD/HLHD* G12 ....41 C4
Kingsborough La *KVD/HLHD* G12 ....41 C4
Kingsborough La East *KVD/HLHD* G12 ....41 C4
Kingsbrae Av *LNPK/KPK* G44 ....107 D4
Kingsbridge Crs *LNPK/KPK* G44 ....128 A1
Kingsbridge Dr *LNPK/KPK* G44 ....127 D1
Kingsburgh Dr *PSLY* PA1 ....78 B2
Kingsburn Dr *RUTH* G73 ....129 D1
Kingsburn Gv *RUTH* G73 ....129 D1
Kingscliffe Av *LNPK/KPK* G44 ....107 D4
Kingscourt Av *LNPK/KPK* G44 ....108 A4
Kings Crs *BLTYR/CAMB* G72 ....133 C2
Kingsdale Av *LNPK/KPK* G44 ....107 D4
King's Dr *DMNK/BRGTN* G40 ....89 C3
Kingsdyke Av *LNPK/KPK* G44 ....108 A4
Kingsford Av *LNPK/KPK* G44 ....125 D3
Kingsheath Av *RUTH* G73 ....128 B1
Kingshill Dr *LNPK/KPK* G44 ....127 D1
Kingshouse Av *LNPK/KPK* G44 ....107 D4
Kingshurst Av *LNPK/KPK* G44 ....127 D1
King's Inch Rd *RNFRW* PA4 ....37 C3
Kingsknowe Dr *RUTH* G73 ....128 B1
Kingsland Dr *CARD/HILL/MSPK* G52 ....81 D1
Kingsley Av *GVH/MTFL* G42 ....107 C2
Kingslynn Dr *LNPK/KPK* G44 ....128 A1
King's Park Av *LNPK/KPK* G44 ....127 D1
RUTH G73 ....128 B1
King's Park Rd *GVH/MTFL* G42 ....107 C4
King's Pl *PPK/MIL* G22 ....44 A1
Kingston Br *GOV/IBX* G51 ....6 B3
Kingston St *GBLS* G5 ....6 C4
King St *CGLE* G1 ....8 A4
CLYDBK G81 ....21 D3
PSLY PA1 ....76 A2
RUTH G73 ....109 D3
King Street La *RUTH* G73 ....109 D3
Kingsway *SCOT* G14 ....38 A2
Kingsway Ct *SCOT* G14 ....37 D2
Kingswood Dr *LNPK/KPK* G44 ....127 D1
Kingussie Dr *LNPK/KPK* G44 ....127 D1
Kiniver Dr *DRUM* G15 ....23 C2
Kinloch Av *BLTYR/CAMB* G72 ....133 C3
Kinloch Rd *RNFRW* PA4 ....55 C2

Kinloch St *DMNK/BRGTN* G40 **91** C3
Kinmount Av *LNPK/KPK* G44 **107** C4
Kinnaird Crs *BSDN* G61 **16** B2
Kinnaird Pl *BSHPBGS* G64 **32** B3
Kinnear Rd *DMNK/BRGTN* G40 **90** B4
Kinnell Av *CARD/HILL/MSPK* G52 **82** A4
Kinnell Crs *CARD/HILL/MSPK* G52 **82** A4
Kinnell Pl *CARD/HILL/MSPK* G52 **82** B4
Kinning St *GBLS* G5 **6** A5
Kinnoul La *KVD/HLHD* G12 **41** D4
Kinpurnie Rd *PSLY* PA1 **79** D2
Kinross Av *CARD/HILL/MSPK* G52 **81** D3
Kinsail Dr *CARD/HILL/MSPK* G52 **80** B1
Kinstone Av *SCOT* G14 **37** D2
Kintessack Pl *BSHPBGS* G64 **33** D1
Kintillo Dr *KNTSWD* G13 **38** A1
Kintore Rd *PLKSW/MSWD* G43 **126** A1
Kintra St *GOV/IBX* G51 **84** B1
Kintyre St *SPRGB/BLRNK* G21 **66** B2
Kippen St *PPK/MIL* G22 **45** C1
Kippford St *CAR/SHTL* G32 **94** A3
Kirkaig Av *RNFRW* PA4 **57** C1
Kirkbean Av *RUTH* G73 **129** D3
Kirkbriggs Gdns *RUTH* G73 **130** A2
Kirkburn Av *BLTYR/CAMB* G72 **132** B3
Kirkcaldy Rd *PLKSD/SHW* G41 **105** C1
Kirkconnel Av *KNTSWD* G13 **37** C1
Kirkconnel Dr *RUTH* G73 **129** C2
Kirkdale Dr *CARD/HILL/MSPK* G52 **83** C3
Kirkhill Av *BLTYR/CAMB* G72 **132** B4
Kirkhill Dr *MRYH/FIRH* G20 **42** A2
Kirkhill Gdns *BLTYR/CAMB* G72 **132** B4
Kirkhill Gv *BLTYR/CAMB* G72 **132** B4
Kirkhill Pl *MRYH/FIRH* G20 **42** A2
Kirkhill Rd *UD/BTH/TAN* G71 **117** D3
Kirkhill Ter *BLTYR/CAMB* G72 **132** B4
Kirkhope Dr *DRUM* G15 **23** D1
Kirkinner Rd *CAR/SHTL* G32 **94** B4
Kirkintilloch Rd *BSHPBGS* G64 **31** D4
Kirklandneuk Rd *RNFRW* PA4 **34** B3
Kirkland St *MRYH/FIRH* G20 **43** C4
Kirk La *BSDN* G61 **15** C2
PLKSW/MSWD G43 **104** B4
Kirklee Circ *KVD/HLHD* G12 **42** A3
Kirklee Gdns *KVD/HLHD* G12 **41** D3
Kirklee Gardens La *KVD/HLHD* G12 **41** D3
Kirklee Pl *KVD/HLHD* G12 **42** A3
Kirklee Qd *KVD/HLHD* G12 **42** A3
Kirklee Quadrant La *KVD/HLHD* G12 **42** A3
Kirklee Rd *KVD/HLHD* G12 **41** D3
Kirklee Ter *KVD/HLHD* G12 **41** D3
Kirklee Terrace La *KVD/HLHD* G12 **42** A3
Kirklee Terrace Rd *KVD/HLHD* G12 **41** D3
Kirkliston St *CAR/SHTL* G32 **92** B1
Kirkmichael Av *PTCK* G11 **40** B4
Kirkmichael Gdns *PTCK* G11 **40** B4
Kirkmuir Dr *RUTH* G73 **130** A4
Kirknewton St *CAR/SHTL* G32 **93** C1
Kirkoswald Rd *PLKSW/MSWD* G43 **125** C1
Kirkpatrick St *DMNK/BRGTN* G40 **90** A2
Kirk Pl *BSDN* G61 **15** C2
Kirkriggs Av *RUTH* G73 **130** A2
Kirk Rd *BSDN* G61 **15** C2
Kirkstall Gdns *BSHPBGS* G64 **19** D3
Kirkton Av *BRHD/NEIL* G78 **118** A3
KNTSWD G13 **37** D1
Kirkton Crs *KNTSWD* G13 **37** D1
Kirkton Rd *BLTYR/CAMB* G72 **133** C2
Kirktonside *BRHD/NEIL* G78 **118** A4
Kirkview Gdns *UD/BTH/TAN* G71 **117** D3
Kirkville Pl *DRUM* G15 **23** D2
Kirkwell Rd *LNPK/KPK* G44 **127** C2
Kirkwood Av *CLYDBK* G81 **22** A2
Kirkwood St *GOV/IBX* G51 **85** C2
RUTH G73 **109** D3
Kirn St *MRYH/FIRH* G20 **27** C3
Kirriemuir Av *CARD/HILL/MSPK* G52 **82** A4
Kirriemuir Gdns *BSHPBGS* G64 **33** C1
Kirriemuir Pl *CARD/HILL/MSPK* G52 **82** A3
Kirriemuir Rd *BSHPBGS* G64 **33** C2
Kirtle Dr *RNFRW* PA4 **56** B1
Kishorn Pl *STPS/GTHM/RID* G33 **70** B2
Knapdale St *PPK/MIL* G22 **29** C4
Knightsbridge St *KNTSWD* G13 **39** C1
Knightscliffe Av *KNTSWD* G13 **24** B3
Knightswood Rd *KNTSWD* G13 **24** B4
Knockhall St *STPS/GTHM/RID* G33 **71** C1
Knockhill Dr *LNPK/KPK* G44 **107** C4
Knockhill Rd *RNFRW* PA4 **55** C2
Knollpark Dr *CRMNK/CLK/EAG* G76 **137** D4
Knowehead Gdns *PLKSD/SHW* G41 **86** B4
Knowehead Ter *PLKSD/SHW* G41 **86** A4
Knowe Rd *PSLYN/LNWD* PA3 **55** C4
Knowe St *MLNGV* G62 **10** A1
Knowetap St *MRYH/FIRH* G20 **28** A4
Kyleakin Rd *GIF/THBK* G46 **122** A4
Kyleakin Ter *GIF/THBK* G46 **122** A4
Kyle Dr *GIF/THBK* G46 **125** D4
Kylepark Crs *UD/BTH/TAN* G71 **117** C4
Kylepark Dr *UD/BTH/TAN* G71 **117** C4
Kylerhea Rd *GIF/THBK* G46 **122** A4
Kyle Sq *CSMK* G45 **129** C2
Kyle St *COWCAD* G4 **4** B3

L

La Belle Allee *KVGV* G3 **62** B2
La Belle Pl *KVGV* G3 **62** B2
Laburnum Av *BLTYR/CAMB* G72 **134** B4
Laburnum Rd *PLKSD/SHW* G41 **85** C3
Lacy St *PSLY* PA1 **78** A2
Lade Ter *CARD/HILL/MSPK* G52 **81** C3
Ladhope Pl *KNTSWD* G13 **22** A3
Ladybank Dr *CARD/HILL/MSPK* G52 **83** C3
Ladyburn St *PSLY* PA1 **78** A3
Ladyhill Dr *BAIL/MDB/MHD* G69 **96** A3
Ladykirk Crs *CARD/HILL/MSPK* G52 **81** D1
PSLYS PA2 **77** D4
Ladykirk Dr *CARD/HILL/MSPK* G52 **81** D1
Lady La *PSLY* PA1 **76** B3
Ladyloan Av *DRUM* G15 **12** B3
Ladyloan Ct *DRUM* G15 **12** A3
Ladyloan Gdns *DRUM* G15 **12** B3
Ladymuir Crs *PLK/PH/NH* G53 **101** D1
Ladywell St *COWCAD* G4 **9** E1
Ladywood *MLNGV* G62 **11** C1
Laggan Rd *BSHPBGS* G64 **32** B2
PLKSW/MSWD G43 **125** D2
Laggan Ter *RNFRW* PA4 **35** C3
Laidlaw St *GBLS* G5 **6** B5
Laighpark Vw *PSLYN/LNWD* PA3 **53** D4
Laird Pl *DMNK/BRGTN* G40 **89** D3
Lamberton Dr *CARD/HILL/MSPK* G52 **81** D1
Lambhill Qd *PLKSD/SHW* G41 **85** D2
Lambhill St *PLKSD/SHW* G41 **85** D2
Lamb St *PPK/MIL* G22 **44** A1
Lamington Rd *CARD/HILL/MSPK* G52 **81** D3
Lamlash Crs *STPS/GTHM/RID* G33 **70** A3
Lamlash Pl *STPS/GTHM/RID* G33 **70** A3
Lammermoor Av *CARD/HILL/MSPK* G52 **82** A4
Lamont Rd *SPRGB/BLRNK* G21 **47** C1
Lancaster Crs *KVD/HLHD* G12 **41** D3
Lancaster Crescent La *KVD/HLHD* G12 **41** D3
Lancaster Rd *BSHPBGS* G64 **19** D3
Lancefield Quay *KVGV* G3 **62** B4
Lancefield St *KVGV* G3 **63** C4
Landemer Dr *RUTH* G73 **129** C1
Landressy Pl *DMNK/BRGTN* G40 **89** D3
Landressy St *DMNK/BRGTN* G40 **89** D3
Lanfine Rd *PSLY* PA1 **79** C3
Langa St *MRYH/FIRH* G20 **28** A4
Lang Av *RNFRW* PA4 **56** A2
Langbar Crs *STPS/GTHM/RID* G33 **71** D4
Langcroft Dr *BLTYR/CAMB* G72 **133** D3
Langcroft Pl *GOV/IBX* G51 **58** B4
Langcroft Rd *GOV/IBX* G51 **59** C4
Langcroft Ter *GOV/IBX* G51 **59** C4
Langdale Av *STPS/GTHM/RID* G33 **48** B4
Langdale St *STPS/GTHM/RID* G33 **48** B4
Langfaulds Crs *CLYDBK* G81 **12** A1
Langford Dr *PLK/PH/NH* G53 **120** B4
Langford Pl *PLK/PH/NH* G53 **121** C4
Langhaul Rd *PLK/PH/NH* G53 **100** A2
Langlands Av *GOV/IBX* G51 **59** C4
Langlands Ct *GOV/IBX* G51 **60** A3
Langlands Dr *GOV/IBX* G51 **58** B3
Langlands Rd *GOV/IBX* G51 **59** C4
Langlea Av *BLTYR/CAMB* G72 **131** C3
Langlea Ct *BLTYR/CAMB* G72 **131** D3
Langlea Dr *BLTYR/CAMB* G72 **131** D2
Langlea Gdns *BLTYR/CAMB* G72 **131** D2
Langlea Gv *BLTYR/CAMB* G72 **131** D3
Langlea Rd *BLTYR/CAMB* G72 **131** D3
Langley Av *KNTSWD* G13 **23** D4
Langlook Rd *PLK/PH/NH* G53 **100** A2

Langmuir Rd *BAIL/MDB/MHD* G69 ....99 C2
Langmuir Wy *CTBR* ML5 ....99 C2
Langness Rd *STPS/GTHM/RID* G33 ....70 A3
Langrig Rd *SPRGB/BLRNK* G21 ....46 B3
Langshot St *GOV/IBX* G51 ....85 D2
Langside Av *PLKSD/SHW* G41 ....105 D2
Langside Dr *PLKSW/MSWD* G43 ....125 D1
Langside Gdns *GVH/MTFL* G42 ....106 B4
Langside La *GVH/MTFL* G42 ....106 B2
Langside Pl *PLKSD/SHW* G41 ....106 A3
Langside Rd *GVH/MTFL* G42 ....106 B1
Langstile Rd *CARD/HILL/MSPK* G52 ....80 B2
Lang St *PSLY* PA1 ....78 A3
Langton Crs *BRHD/NEIL* G78 ....119 C4
PLK/PH/NH G53 ....101 D2
Langton Gdns *BAIL/MDB/MHD* G69 ....95 D3
Langton Rd *PLK/PH/NH* G53 ....101 D3
Langtree Av *GIF/THBK* G46 ....136 A2
Lansbury Gdns *PSLYN/LNWD* PA3 ....53 C4
Lansdowne Crs *COWCAD* G4 ....63 C1
MRYH/FIRH G20 ....43 C4
Lansdowne Crescent La *COWCAD* G4 ....63 C1
Lanton Dr *CARD/HILL/MSPK* G52 ....81 D2
Lanton Rd *PLKSW/MSWD* G43 ....125 D2
Lappin St *CLYDBK* G81 ....21 D3
Larbert St *COWCAD* G4 ....3 E3
Larch Av *BSHPBGS* G64 ....32 B3
Larch Cl *BLTYR/CAMB* G72 ....134 B4
Larchfield Av *SCOT* G14 ....38 A3
Larchfield Dr *RUTH* G73 ....130 B3
Larchfield Pl *SCOT* G14 ....38 A3
Larchfield Rd *BSDN* G61 ....25 D2
Larchgrove Av *CAR/SHTL* G32 ....94 A1
Larchgrove Pl *CAR/SHTL* G32 ....70 B4
Larchgrove Rd *CAR/SHTL* G32 ....70 B4
Larch Rd *PLKSD/SHW* G41 ....84 B3
Larchwood Ter *BRHD/NEIL* G78 ....119 C4
Largie Rd *LNPK/KPK* G44 ....126 A2
Larkfield St *GVH/MTFL* G42 ....87 D4
Larkin Gdns *PSLYN/LNWD* PA3 ....53 C4
Lasswade St *SCOT* G14 ....36 B1
Latherton Dr *MRYH/FIRH* G20 ....42 A2
Latimer Gdns *CARD/HILL/MSPK* G52 ....81 C3
Lauderdale Gdns *PTCK* G11 ....41 C4
Lauderdale La *KVD/HLHD* G12 ....41 C4
Lauder Dr *RUTH* G73 ....111 C4
Laundry La *STPS/GTHM/RID* G33 ....50 B2
Laurelbank Rd *CAR/SHTL* G32 ....113 D3
Laurel La *BLTYR/CAMB* G72 ....134 B4
Laurel Park Gdns *KNTSWD* G13 ....38 B2
Laurel Pl *PTCK* G11 ....60 B1
Laurel St *PTCK* G11 ....60 B1
Laurel Wy *BRHD/NEIL* G78 ....118 A2
Laurel Wynd *BLTYR/CAMB* G72 ....135 C4
Laurence Ct *DRUM* G15 ....12 A4
Laurence Dr *BSDN* G61 ....14 B1
DRUM G15 ....12 A4
Laurence Gdns *DRUM* G15 ....12 A4
Laurieston Rd *GBLS* G5 ....88 A2
Laurieston Wy *RUTH* G73 ....129 D3
Laverockhall St *SPRGB/BLRNK* G21 ....46 A4
Lawers Rd *PLKSW/MSWD* G43 ....124 A2
RNFRW PA4 ....55 C2
Lawhill Av *CSMK* G45 ....128 A3
Lawmoor Av *GBLS* G5 ....88 A4
Lawmoor Pl *GBLS* G5 ....107 D1
Lawmoor Rd *GBLS* G5 ....88 A4
Lawmoor St *GBLS* G5 ....88 A4
Lawnmoor Rd *GBLS* G5 ....88 A4
Lawn Pk *MLNGV* G62 ....11 D2
Lawn St *PSLY* PA1 ....77 D2
Lawrence Av *GIF/THBK* G46 ....137 C2
Lawrence St *PTCK* G11 ....61 D1
Lawrie St *PTCK* G11 ....61 C1
Law St *DMNK/BRGTN* G40 ....90 A2
Laxford Av *LNPK/KPK* G44 ....126 B3
Leadburn Rd *SPRGB/BLRNK* G21 ....47 D3
Leadburn St *STPS/GTHM/RID* G33 ....68 B4
Leader St *STPS/GTHM/RID* G33 ....68 A2
Leander Crs *RNFRW* PA4 ....56 B1
Learmont Pl *MLNGV* G62 ....10 A1
Leckie St *PLKSD/SHW* G41 ....104 B3
Ledaig St *DEN/PKHD* G31 ....67 D4
Ledard Rd *GVH/MTFL* G42 ....106 A4
Ledcameroch Crs *BSDN* G61 ....14 B3
Ledcameroch Pk *BSDN* G61 ....14 B3
Ledcameroch Rd *BSDN* G61 ....14 B3
Ledgowan Pl *MRYH/FIRH* G20 ....27 D3
Ledi Rd *PLKSW/MSWD* G43 ....124 B2
Ledmore Dr *DRUM* G15 ....12 B3
Lednock Rd *CARD/HILL/MSPK* G52 ....81 C2
STPS/GTHM/RID G33 ....50 B2
Lee Av *STPS/GTHM/RID* G33 ....68 B2
Lee Crs *BSHPBGS* G64 ....31 D3
Leehill Rd *SPRGB/BLRNK* G21 ....31 C4
Leglen Wd *STPS/GTHM/RID* G33 ....48 A1
Leglen Wood Dr *STPS/GTHM/RID* G33 ....48 A1
Leglen Wood Rd *STPS/GTHM/RID* G33 ....48 A1
Leicester Av *KVD/HLHD* G12 ....41 C2
Leighton St *MRYH/FIRH* G20 ....42 B1
Leithland Av *PLK/PH/NH* G53 ....101 C2
Leithland Rd *PLK/PH/NH* G53 ....101 C2
Leith St *STPS/GTHM/RID* G33 ....68 A3
Lembert Dr *CRMNK/CLK/EAG* G76 ....137 D3
Lendale La *BSHPBGS* G64 ....19 C4
Lendel Pl *GOV/IBX* G51 ....85 D2
Lennox Av *MLNGV* G62 ....10 B2
SCOT G14 ....38 B4
Lennox Crs *BSHPBGS* G64 ....31 D3
Lennox Dr *BSDN* G61 ....15 D1
Lennox Gdns *SCOT* G14 ....39 C4
Lennox La East *SCOT* G14 ....39 C4
Lennox La West *SCOT* G14 ....39 C3
Lennox St *MRYH/FIRH* G20 ....27 C4
Lennox Ter *PSLYN/LNWD* PA3 ....54 B3
Lentran St *ESTRH* G34 ....74 A4
Leny St *MRYH/FIRH* G20 ....43 C3
Lenzie St *SPRGB/BLRNK* G21 ....46 A2
Lenzie Ter *SPRGB/BLRNK* G21 ....45 D1
Leslie Rd *PLKSD/SHW* G41 ....105 D1
Leslie St *PLKSD/SHW* G41 ....86 B4
Lesmuir Dr *SCOT* G14 ....37 D2
Lesmuir Pl *SCOT* G14 ....37 C2
Letham Ct *PLKSW/MSWD* G43 ....125 D2
Letham Dr *BSHPBGS* G64 ....33 C3
PLKSW/MSWD G43 ....125 D2
Lethamhill Pl *STPS/GTHM/RID* G33 ....68 B2
Lethamhill Rd *STPS/GTHM/RID* G33 ....68 B2
Letham Ov *BSHPBGS* G64 ....33 D3
Letherby Dr *LNPK/KPK* G44 ....107 C4
Lethington Av *PLKSD/SHW* G41 ....105 D3
Lethington Pl *PLKSD/SHW* G41 ....105 D3
Lethington Rd *GIF/THBK* G46 ....136 A4
Letterfearn Rd *SMSTN* G23 ....27 D1
Letterickhills Crs *BLTYR/CAMB* G72 ....134 B4
Lettoch St *GOV/IBX* G51 ....60 B4
Leven Av *BSHPBGS* G64 ....32 B2
Leven Dr *BSDN* G61 ....15 D3
Leven St *PLKSD/SHW* G41 ....86 B4
Levern Bridge Ct *PLK/PH/NH* G53 ....100 A4
Levern Bridge Gv *PLK/PH/NH* G53 ....100 A4
Levern Bridge Pl *PLK/PH/NH* G53 ....120 A1
Levern Bridge Wy *PLK/PH/NH* G53 ....120 A1
Levern Crs *BRHD/NEIL* G78 ....118 A4
Leverndale Ct *PLK/PH/NH* G53 ....100 A2
Leverndale Rd *PLK/PH/NH* G53 ....100 A2
Levern Gdns *BRHD/NEIL* G78 ....118 A2
Levernside Av *PLK/PH/NH* G53 ....101 D3
Levernside Crs *PLK/PH/NH* G53 ....101 C2
Levernside Rd *PLK/PH/NH* G53 ....101 C2
Lewis Av *RNFRW* PA4 ....56 A2
Lewis Gdns *BSDN* G61 ....13 D1
Lewiston Dr *SMSTN* G23 ....27 D2
Lewiston Pl *SMSTN* G23 ....27 D2
Lewiston Rd *SMSTN* G23 ....27 D2
Leyden Gdns *MRYH/FIRH* G20 ....42 B2
Leyden St *MRYH/FIRH* G20 ....42 B2
The Leys *BSHPBGS* G64 ....32 A2
Liberton St *STPS/GTHM/RID* G33 ....68 B3
Liberty Av *BAIL/MDB/MHD* G69 ....98 B2
Libo Av *PLK/PH/NH* G53 ....102 A2
Library Gdns *BLTYR/CAMB* G72 ....132 A1
Library La *GIF/THBK* G46 ....123 C4
Liddells Ct *BSHPBGS* G64 ....32 A4
Liddell St *CAR/SHTL* G32 ....113 D2
Liddesdale Pl *PPK/MIL* G22 ....31 C4
Liddesdale Rd *PPK/MIL* G22 ....30 A4
Liddesdale Sq *PPK/MIL* G22 ....31 C4
Liddesdale Ter *PPK/MIL* G22 ....31 C4
Liddoch Wy *RUTH* G73 ....109 C3
Liff Gdns *BSHPBGS* G64 ....33 D3
Liff Pl *ESTRH* G34 ....73 D2
Lightburn Pl *CAR/SHTL* G32 ....70 A4
Lightburn Rd *BLTYR/CAMB* G72 ....134 A3
DEN/PKHD G31 ....91 C1
Lilac Gdns *BSHPBGS* G64 ....32 B3
Lilac Wynd *BLTYR/CAMB* G72 ....134 B3
Lillyburn Pl *DRUM* G15 ....12 A3
Lilybank Av *BLTYR/CAMB* G72 ....133 C3
Lilybank Gdns *KVD/HLHD* G12 ....62 A1

Lilybank Gardens La *KVD/HLHD* G12 ......62 A1
Lilybank Ter *KVD/HLHD* G12 ......62 A1
Lilybank Terrace La *KVD/HLHD* G12 ......62 A1
Lily St *DMNK/BRGTN* G40 ......90 A4
Limeside Av *RUTH* G73 ......110 B4
Limeside Gdns *RUTH* G73 ......110 B4
Lime St *SCOT* G14 ......39 C4
Linacre Dr *CAR/SHTL* G32 ......94 A2
Linacre Gdns *CAR/SHTL* G32 ......94 B2
Linburn Pl *CARD/HILL/MSPK* G52 ......81 C1
Linburn Rd *CARD/HILL/MSPK* G52 ......57 C4
Lincoln Av *KNTSWD* G13 ......24 A4
Lincuan Av *GIF/THBK* G46 ......137 C3
Linden Pl *KNTSWD* G13 ......25 D4
Linden St *KNTSWD* G13 ......25 D4
Lindores Av *RUTH* G73 ......110 A4
Lindores St *GVH/MTFL* G42 ......107 C3
Lindrick Dr *SMSTN* G23 ......27 D2
Lindsay Dr *KVD/HLHD* G12 ......41 C1
Lindsay Pl *KVD/HLHD* G12 ......41 C1
Linfern Rd *KVD/HLHD* G12 ......41 D4
Linhead Dr *PLK/PH/NH* G53 ......121 D1
Links Rd *CAR/SHTL* G32 ......94 B4
Linkwood Av *DRUM* G15 ......12 B4
Linkwood Crs *DRUM* G15 ......13 C4
Linkwood Dr *DRUM* G15 ......12 B4
Linkwood Gdns *DRUM* G15 ......13 D4
Linkwood Pl *DRUM* G15 ......12 B4
Linlithgow Gdns *CAR/SHTL* G32 ......94 B2
Linn Dr *LNPK/KPK* G44 ......126 A4
Linnet Pl *KNTSWD* G13 ......22 B4
Linnhead Dr *PLK/PH/NH* G53 ......121 C2
Linnhead Pl *SCOT* G14 ......38 A3
Linnhe Av *BSHPBGS* G64 ......32 B2
LNPK/KPK G44 ......126 B3
Linn Valley Vw *CSMK* G45 ......128 A4
Linside Av *PSLY* PA1 ......78 A3
Linthaugh Rd *PLK/PH/NH* G53 ......81 D4
Linthaugh Ter *PLK/PH/NH* G53 ......102 A2
Linthouse Buildings *GOV/IBX* G51 ......59 D3
Linthouse Rd *GOV/IBX* G51 ......59 C2
Lintlaw Dr *CARD/HILL/MSPK* G52 ......81 D1
Linton St *STPS/GTHM/RID* G33 ......68 B3
Lismore Av *RNFRW* PA4 ......56 A2
Lismore Rd *KVD/HLHD* G12 ......41 C2
Lister Pl *CARD/HILL/MSPK* G52 ......57 D4
Lister Rd *CARD/HILL/MSPK* G52 ......57 D4
Lister St *COWCAD* G4 ......4 C3
Little Dovehill *COWCAD* G4 ......8 C3
Littlehill St *SPRGB/BLRNK* G21 ......46 B3
Littlemill Crs *PLK/PH/NH* G53 ......100 B3
Littlemill Dr *PLK/PH/NH* G53 ......100 B3
Littlemill Gdns *PLK/PH/NH* G53 ......100 B3
Little St *KVGV* G3 ......63 C4
Littleton St *MRYH/FIRH* G20 ......27 D2
Livingstone Av *CARD/HILL/MSPK* G52 ......57 D3
Livingstone St *CLYDBK* G81 ......21 D2
Lloyd Av *CAR/SHTL* G32 ......112 B1
Lloyd St *DEN/PKHD* G31 ......66 B3
RUTH G73 ......110 A2
Loanbank Pl *GOV/IBX* G51 ......60 B4
Loanbank Qd *GOV/IBX* G51 ......60 B4
Loancroft Av *BAIL/MDB/MHD* G69 ......97 C4
Loancroft Pl *BAIL/MDB/MHD* G69 ......96 B4
Loanfoot Av *KNTSWD* G13 ......23 C4
Loanhead Av *RNFRW* PA4 ......36 A4
Loanhead St *CAR/SHTL* G32 ......69 C4
The Loaning *GIF/THBK* G46 ......136 A4
Lobnitz Av *RNFRW* PA4 ......36 A4
Lochaber Dr *RUTH* G73 ......131 C3
Lochaber Rd *BSDN* G61 ......26 B1
Loch Achray St *CAR/SHTL* G32 ......94 A3
Lochaline Dr *LNPK/KPK* G44 ......126 B3
Lochar Crs *PLK/PH/NH* G53 ......102 A1
Lochay St *CAR/SHTL* G32 ......94 A3
Lochbrae Dr *RUTH* G73 ......131 C3
Lochbridge Rd *ESTRH* G34 ......72 B4
Lochburn Crs *MRYH/FIRH* G20 ......28 A4
Lochburn Pas *MRYH/FIRH* G20 ......28 A4
Lochburn Rd *MRYH/FIRH* G20 ......28 A4
Lochdochart Rd *ESTRH* G34 ......74 A3
Lochend Crs *BSDN* G61 ......14 B4
Lochend Dr *BSDN* G61 ......14 B4
Lochend Rd *BAIL/MDB/MHD* G69 ......75 D1
BSDN G61 ......15 C4
ESTRH G34 ......73 C2
Lochfauld Rd *SMSTN* G23 ......29 C1
Lochgilp St *MRYH/FIRH* G20 ......27 C4
Lochgoin Av *DRUM* G15 ......12 A3
Lochgreen St *STPS/GTHM/RID* G33 ......48 A4
Lochiel Rd *GIF/THBK* G46 ......123 C3
Lochinver Dr *LNPK/KPK* G44 ......126 B2
Lochinver Gv *BLTYR/CAMB* G72 ......133 C2
Loch Laidon St *CAR/SHTL* G32 ......94 B3
Lochlea Rd *PLKSW/MSWD* G43 ......125 C1
RUTH G73 ......129 C2
Lochleven La *GVH/MTFL* G42 ......106 B4
Lochleven Rd *GVH/MTFL* G42 ......106 B4
Lochlibo Av *KNTSWD* G13 ......37 C1
Lochmaben Rd *CARD/HILL/MSPK* G52 ......80 B3
Lochmaddy Av *LNPK/KPK* G44 ......126 B3
Lochore Av *PSLYN/LNWD* PA3 ......54 B4
Loch Rd *STPS/GTHM/RID* G33 ......51 C2
Lochside *BSDN* G61 ......15 D4
Lochside St *PLKSD/SHW* G41 ......105 D2
Lochview Crs *STPS/GTHM/RID* G33 ......49 C4
Lochview Dr *STPS/GTHM/RID* G33 ......49 C4
Lochview Gdns *STPS/GTHM/RID* G33 ......49 C4
Lochview Pl *STPS/GTHM/RID* G33 ......49 C4
Lochview Rd *BSDN* G61 ......15 C4
Loch Voil St *CAR/SHTL* G32 ......94 B3
Lochwood St *STPS/GTHM/RID* G33 ......68 B1
Lochy Av *RNFRW* PA4 ......57 C2
Lockerbie Av *PLKSW/MSWD* G43 ......126 A1
Lockhart Av *BLTYR/CAMB* G72 ......134 A1
Lockhart Dr *BLTYR/CAMB* G72 ......134 A1
Lockhart Pl *UD/BTH/TAN* G71 ......116 A1
Lockhart St *SPRGB/BLRNK* G21 ......67 C1
Locksley Av *KNTSWD* G13 ......24 A3
Logan Dr *PSLYN/LNWD* PA3 ......76 A1
Logan St *GBLS* G5 ......108 A1
Lomax St *STPS/GTHM/RID* G33 ......68 A3
Lomond Av *RNFRW* PA4 ......55 C2
Lomond Ct *BRHD/NEIL* G78 ......118 B3
Lomond Dr *BRHD/NEIL* G78 ......118 A1
BSHPBGS G64 ......18 B4
Lomond Pl *STPS/GTHM/RID* G33 ......51 C3
Lomond Rd *BSDN* G61 ......25 C1
Lomondside Av *CRMNK/CLK/EAG* G76 ......137 C3
Lomond St *PPK/MIL* G22 ......44 A2
London Rd *CAR/SHTL* G32 ......92 A4
DEN/PKHD G31 ......91 D4
DMNK/BRGTN G40 ......9 D4
London St *RNFRW* PA4 ......36 A2
Lonend *PSLY* PA1 ......77 D4
Longay Pl *PPK/MIL* G22 ......30 A3
Longay St *PPK/MIL* G22 ......30 A3
Longden St *CLYDBK* G81 ......21 D3
Longford St *STPS/GTHM/RID* G33 ......68 A3
Longlee *BAIL/MDB/MHD* G69 ......96 B3
Long Rw *BAIL/MDB/MHD* G69 ......97 C1
Longstone Rd *STPS/GTHM/RID* G33 ......70 A3
Lonmay Rd *STPS/GTHM/RID* G33 ......71 C3
Lonsdale Av *GIF/THBK* G46 ......124 B4
Lora Dr *CARD/HILL/MSPK* G52 ......83 C3
Loretto Pl *STPS/GTHM/RID* G33 ......69 C3
Loretto St *STPS/GTHM/RID* G33 ......69 C3
Lorne Crs *BSHPBGS* G64 ......33 D1
Lorne Rd *CARD/HILL/MSPK* G52 ......57 C3
Lorne St *GOV/IBX* G51 ......85 D1
Lorne Ter *BLTYR/CAMB* G72 ......132 A4
Lorraine Gdns *KVD/HLHD* G12 ......41 D3
Lorraine Gardens La *KVD/HLHD* G12 ......41 D3
Lorraine Rd *KVD/HLHD* G12 ......41 D3
Loskin Dr *PPK/MIL* G22 ......29 D4
Lossie Crs *RNFRW* PA4 ......57 C1
Lossie St *STPS/GTHM/RID* G33 ......68 A2
Lothian Dr *CRMNK/CLK/EAG* G76 ......137 D3
Lothian Gdns *MRYH/FIRH* G20 ......42 B4
Lothian St *CARD/HILL/MSPK* G52 ......56 B3
Louden Hill Pl *STPS/GTHM/RID* G33 * 48 B1
Louden Hill Rd *STPS/GTHM/RID* G33 ......48 B1
Loudon Rd *STPS/GTHM/RID* G33 ......50 A3
Lounsdale Pl *SCOT* G14 ......38 A3
Lourdes Av *CARD/HILL/MSPK* G52 ......82 B3
Lovat Pl *CARD/HILL/MSPK* G52 ......56 B4
RUTH G73 ......131 C3
Love St *PSLYN/LNWD* PA3 ......77 C1
Low Crs *CLYDBK* G81 ......22 A3
Lower Bourtree Dr *RUTH* G73 ......130 B3
Lowndes St *BRHD/NEIL* G78 ......118 B3
Low Rd *PSLYS* PA2 ......76 A4
Lowther Ter *KVD/HLHD* G12 ......41 D3
Loyne Dr *RNFRW* PA4 ......57 C1
Luath St *GOV/IBX* G51 ......60 B3
Lubas Av *GVH/MTFL* G42 ......108 A4
Lubas Pl *GVH/MTFL* G42 ......108 A4
Lubnaig Rd *PLKSW/MSWD* G43 ......125 D2
Lucy Brae *UD/BTH/TAN* G71 ......117 D3
Luffness Gdns *CAR/SHTL* G32 ......113 C1

Lugar Dr *CARD/HILL/MSPK* G52 ....83 C3
Lugar Pl *LNPK/KPK* G44 ....128 B2
Luggiebank Pl *BAIL/MDB/MHD* G69 ....99 C3
Luing Rd *CARD/HILL/MSPK* G52 ....83 C2
Luma Gdns *GOV/IBX* G51 ....58 B4
Lumloch St *SPRGB/BLRNK* G21 ....46 B3
Lumsden La *KVGV* G3 ....62 A2
Lumsden St *KVGV* G3 ....62 A3
Lunan Dr *BSHPBGS* G64 ....33 C3
Lunan Pl *GOV/IBX* G51 ....59 D4
Luncarty Pl *CAR/SHTL* G32 ....93 C4
Luncarty St *CAR/SHTL* G32 ....93 C4
Lunderston Dr *PLK/PH/NH* G53 ....100 B4
Lundie Gdns *BSHPBGS* G64 ....33 D3
Lundie St *CAR/SHTL* G32 ....92 A4
Lusshill Ter *UD/BTH/TAN* G71 ....116 A1
Luss Rd *GOV/IBX* G51 ....60 A4
Lymburn St *KVGV* G3 ....62 A2
Lyndale Pl *MRYH/FIRH* G20 ....27 D3
Lyndale Rd *MRYH/FIRH* G20 ....27 D3
Lyndhurst Gdns *MRYH/FIRH* G20 ....43 C4
Lyndhurst Gardens La *MRYH/FIRH* G20 ..42 B4
Lyne Cft *BSHPBGS* G64 ....19 C3
Lynedoch Crs *KVGV* G3 ....63 C2
Lynedoch Crescent La *KVGV* G3 ....63 C2
Lynedoch Pl *KVGV* G3 ....63 C2
Lynedoch St *KVGV* G3 ....63 C2
Lynedoch Ter *KVGV* G3 ....63 C2
Lynn Dr *MLNGV* G62 ....11 D1
Lynne Dr *SMSTN* G23 ....28 A2
Lynton Av *GIF/THBK* G46 ....136 A2
Lyoncross Av *BRHD/NEIL* G78 ....119 C3
Lyoncross Crs *BRHD/NEIL* G78 ....119 C2
Lyoncross Rd *PLK/PH/NH* G53 ....101 C1
Lytham Dr *SMSTN* G23 ....28 A2

M

Macarthur Wynd *BLTYR/CAMB* G72 ....133 D2
Macbeth Pl *DEN/PKHD* G31 ....91 D3
Macbeth St *DEN/PKHD* G31 ....91 D3
Maccallum Dr *BLTYR/CAMB* G72 ....133 D2
Macdonald St *RUTH* G73 ....109 D3
Macdougal Dr *BLTYR/CAMB* G72 ....133 D2
Macdougall St *PLKSW/MSWD* G43 ....104 B4
Macdowall St *PSLYN/LNWD* PA3 ....76 B1
Macduff Pl *DEN/PKHD* G31 ....91 D3
Macduff St *DEN/PKHD* G31 ....91 D3
Mace Rd *KNTSWD* G13 ....24 A2
Macfarlane Crs *BLTYR/CAMB* G72 ....133 D2
Macfarlane Rd *BSDN* G61 ....15 D4
Machrie Dr *CSMK* G45 ....129 C3
Machrie Rd *CSMK* G45 ....129 C3
Machrie St *CSMK* G45 ....129 C3
Macintyre St *KVGV* G3 ....6 A1
Mackean St *PSLYN/LNWD* PA3 ....76 A1
Mackeith St *DMNK/BRGTN* G40 ....89 D3
Mackinlay St *GBLS* G5 ....87 D3
Maclean Sq *GOV/IBX* G51 ....85 D1
Maclean St *CLYDBK* G81 ....22 A3
GOV/IBX G51 ....85 D1
Maclellan St *PLKSD/SHW* G41 ....85 D2
Macleod St *COWCAD* G4 ....9 D1
Macleod Wy *BLTYR/CAMB* G72 ....133 D2
Madison Av *LNPK/KPK* G44 ....127 C2
Madras St *DMNK/BRGTN* G40 ....89 D4
Mafeking St *GOV/IBX* G51 ....84 B1
Magnolia Dr *BLTYR/CAMB* G72 ....135 C4
Magnus Crs *LNPK/KPK* G44 ....127 C3
Maidland Rd *PLK/PH/NH* G53 ....101 D4
Mailing Av *BSHPBGS* G64 ....32 B1
Mainhill Av *BAIL/MDB/MHD* G69 ....97 D2
Mainhill Dr *BAIL/MDB/MHD* G69 ....97 C2
Mainhill Pl *BAIL/MDB/MHD* G69 ....97 C2
Mainhill Rd *BAIL/MDB/MHD* G69 ....98 B2
Main Rd *PSLYS* PA2 ....76 B4
Mains Av *GIF/THBK* G46 ....136 B2
Main St *BAIL/MDB/MHD* G69 ....97 C3
BLTYR/CAMB G72 ....132 A1
BRHD/NEIL G78 ....118 B3
BSDN G61 ....10 B4
DMNK/BRGTN G40 ....89 D4
GIF/THBK G46 ....123 C4
MLNGV G62 ....10 B2
RUTH G73 ....109 D3
Mair St *GOV/IBX* G51 ....86 A1
Maitland Pl *RNFRW* PA4 ....55 C1
Maitland St *COWCAD* G4 ....3 E2
Malborough La North *PTCK* G11 ....40 A4
Malborough La South *PTCK* G11 ....40 A4
Malin Pl *STPS/GTHM/RID* G33 ....69 C3
Mallaig Pl *GOV/IBX* G51 ....59 C4
Mallaig Rd *GOV/IBX* G51 ....59 C4
Malloch St *MRYH/FIRH* G20 ....42 B2
Maltbarns St *MRYH/FIRH* G20 ....43 D4
Mambeg Dr *GOV/IBX* G51 ....59 D3
Mamore Pl *PLKSW/MSWD* G43 ....124 B1
Mamore St *PLKSW/MSWD* G43 ....124 B1
Manchester Dr *KVD/HLHD* G12 ....40 B1
Mannering Ct *PLKSD/SHW* G41 ....104 B3
Mannering Rd *PLKSD/SHW* G41 ....104 B3
Mannofield *BSDN* G61 ....14 B3
Manor Rd *DRUM* G15 ....22 B2
SCOT G14 ....39 D3
Manor Wy *RUTH* G73 ....130 B3
Manresa Pl *COWCAD* G4 ....3 D1
Manse Av *BSDN* G61 ....15 D2
Manse Brae *LNPK/KPK* G44 ....127 C1
Manse Ct *BRHD/NEIL* G78 ....119 C2
Mansefield Av *BLTYR/CAMB* G72 ....132 B3
Mansel St *SPRGB/BLRNK* G21 ....46 A2
Manse Rd *BAIL/MDB/MHD* G69 ....98 A1
BSDN G61 ....15 D2
CAR/SHTL G32 ....94 B3
Manse St *RNFRW* PA4 ....36 A3
Mansewood Rd *GIF/THBK* G46 ....124 A3
Mansfield Rd *CARD/HILL/MSPK* G52 ....57 C4
Mansfield St *PTCK* G11 ....61 D1
Mansion Ct *BLTYR/CAMB* G72 ....132 B1
Mansionhouse Av *CAR/SHTL* G32 ....113 D3
Mansionhouse Dr *CAR/SHTL* G32 ....94 A1
Mansionhouse Gdns *PLKSD/SHW* G41 ..105 D4
Mansionhouse Gv *CAR/SHTL* G32 ....95 C4
Mansionhouse Rd *CAR/SHTL* G32 ....95 C3
PLKSD/SHW G41 ....105 D4
PSLY PA1 ....78 A2
Mansion St *BLTYR/CAMB* G72 ....132 B1
PPK/MIL G22 ....44 B2
Maple Crs *BLTYR/CAMB* G72 ....135 C4
Maple Rd *PLKSD/SHW* G41 ....84 B3
Marchbank Gdns *PSLY* PA1 ....79 D3
Marchfield Av *PSLYN/LNWD* PA3 ....53 C3
Marchglen Pl *GOV/IBX* G51 ....59 C4
Marchmont Gdns *BSHPBGS* G64 ....18 B4
Marchmont Ter *KVD/HLHD* G12 ....41 D4
March St *PLKSD/SHW* G41 ....106 A1
Mar Dr *BSDN* G61 ....10 A4
Maree Dr *CARD/HILL/MSPK* G52 ....83 C3
Maree Gdns *BSHPBGS* G64 ....32 B2
Marfield St *CAR/SHTL* G32 ....68 B4
Mar Gdns *RUTH* G73 ....131 C3
Marine Crs *GOV/IBX* G51 ....86 A1
Marine Gdns *GOV/IBX* G51 ....86 B1
Mariner Ct *CLYDBK* G81 ....20 A1
Mariscat Rd *PLKSD/SHW* G41 ....105 D1
Marjory Dr *PSLYN/LNWD* PA3 ....54 B4
Marjory Rd *RNFRW* PA4 ....54 B2
Markdow Av *PLK/PH/NH* G53 ....100 B2
Marlach Pl *PLK/PH/NH* G53 ....100 B3
Marlborough Av *PTCK* G11 ....40 A4
Marldon La *PTCK* G11 ....40 A4
Marlow St *PLKSD/SHW* G41 ....86 A3
Marlow Ter *PLKSD/SHW* G41 ....86 A3
Marne St *DEN/PKHD* G31 ....67 C4
Marshall's La *PSLY* PA1 ....77 C3
Martha St *CGLE* G1 ....4 A5
Martin Crs *BAIL/MDB/MHD* G69 ....97 C2
Martin St *DMNK/BRGTN* G40 ....89 D4
Mart St *CGLE* G1 ....8 A4
Martyrs Pl *BSHPBGS* G64 ....32 A3
Marwick St *DEN/PKHD* G31 ....67 C4
Maryhill Rd *BSDN* G61 ....26 A1
COWCAD G4 ....2 B2
MRYH/FIRH G20 ....43 C4
Maryland Dr *CARD/HILL/MSPK* G52 ....83 C2
Maryland Gdns *CARD/HILL/MSPK* G52 ....83 C2
Maryston St *STPS/GTHM/RID* G33 ....68 A1
Maryville Av *GIF/THBK* G46 ....137 C1
Maryville Gdns *GIF/THBK* G46 ....137 C1
Maryville Vw *UD/BTH/TAN* G71 ....117 C2
Marywood Sq *PLKSD/SHW* G41 ....106 A1
Masterton St *COWCAD* G4 ....44 B4
Mathieson Rd *RUTH* G73 ....110 B2
Mathieson St *PSLY* PA1 ....78 B2
Matilda Rd *PLKSD/SHW* G41 ....86 A4

Mauchline St *GBLS* G5 87 C3
Maukinfauld Ct *DEN/PKHD* G31 91 D4
Maukinfauld Rd *CAR/SHTL* G32 92 A4
Mauldslie St *DMNK/BRGTN* G40 90 B3
Maule Dr *PTCK* G11 60 B1
Mavis Bank *BSHPBGS* G64 31 D3
Mavisbank Gdns *GOV/IBX* G51 86 A1
Mavisbank Rd *GOV/IBX* G51 85 D1
Mavisbank Ter *PSLY* PA1 77 D4
Maxton Ter *BLTYR/CAMB* G72 132 A4
Maxwell Av *BAIL/MDB/MHD* G69 96 A3
BSDN G61 25 C1
PLKSD/SHW G41 86 A3
Maxwell Dr *BAIL/MDB/MHD* G69 95 D2
PLKSD/SHW G41 85 C3
Maxwell Gdns *PLKSD/SHW* G41 85 D3
Maxwell Gv *PLKSD/SHW* G41 85 D3
Maxwell La *PLKSD/SHW* G41 86 A3
Maxwell Pl *PLKSD/SHW* G41 87 C4
Maxwell Rd *PLKSD/SHW* G41 86 B3
Maxwell St *BAIL/MDB/MHD* G69 96 B3
CGLE G1 7 F3
PSLY PA1 77 C2
Maxwellton St *PSLYS* PA2 76 A4
Maxwelton Rd *STPS/GTHM/RID* G33 68 A1
Maybank La *GVH/MTFL* G42 106 B2
Maybank St *GVH/MTFL* G42 106 B2
Mayberry Crs *CAR/SHTL* G32 94 A2
Mayberry Gdns *CAR/SHTL* G32 94 B2
Mayberry Gv *CAR/SHTL* G32 94 B2
Maybole St *PLK/PH/NH* G53 120 A1
Mayfield St *MRYH/FIRH* G20 43 C1
May Ter *GIF/THBK* G46 124 B4
GVH/MTFL G42 107 C3
McAlpine St *KVGV* G3 6 B3
McArthur St *PLKSW/MSWD* G43 104 B4
McAslin Ct *COWCAD* G4 4 C4
McAslin St *COWCAD* G4 5 D4
McCallum Av *RUTH* G73 110 A4
McClue Av *RNFRW* PA4 35 C3
McClue Rd *RNFRW* PA4 35 C3
McCracken Av *RNFRW* PA4 55 C1
McCreery St *CLYDBK* G81 21 D3
McCulloch St *PLKSD/SHW* G41 86 B3
McDonald Crs *CLYDBK* G81 21 D3
McFarlane St *COWCAD* G4 9 D4
PSLYN/LNWD PA3 52 B4
McGown St *PSLYN/LNWD* PA3 76 B1
McGregor Av *RNFRW* PA4 55 C1
McGregor St *CLYDBK* G81 21 D3
GOV/IBX G51 83 D1
McIntosh St *DEN/PKHD* G31 9 F2
McIntyre Ter *BLTYR/CAMB* G72 132 B1
McIver St *BLTYR/CAMB* G72 134 A1
McKechnie St *GOV/IBX* G51 60 B3
McKenzie St *PSLYN/LNWD* PA3 76 A2
McKerrell St *PSLY* PA1 78 A2
McLaren Av *RNFRW* PA4 55 D2
McLaren Ct *GIF/THBK* G46 136 B2
McLaren Crs *MRYH/FIRH* G20 28 A4
McLaren Gdns *MRYH/FIRH* G20 28 A4
McLean Pl *PSLYN/LNWD* PA3 53 C4
McLennan St *GVH/MTFL* G42 106 B3
McNair St *CAR/SHTL* G32 93 C2
McNeil Av *CLYDBK* G81 22 A2
McNeil Gdns *GBLS* G5 88 B3
McNeil St *GBLS* G5 88 B3
McPhail St *DMNK/BRGTN* G40 89 C3
McPhater St *COWCAD* G4 3 E3
Meadowburn *BSHPBGS* G64 19 C3
Meadow La *RNFRW* PA4 36 A2
Meadowpark St *DEN/PKHD* G31 67 C4
Meadow Rd *PTCK* G11 60 B2
Meadowside St *PTCK* G11 60 B2
RNFRW PA4 36 A2
Meadowwell St *CAR/SHTL* G32 93 D2
Medwin St *BLTYR/CAMB* G72 134 A2
Medwyn St *SCOT* G14 39 C4
Meek Pl *BLTYR/CAMB* G72 133 C2
Meetinghouse La *PSLY* PA1 77 C2
Megan St *DMNK/BRGTN* G40 89 D3
Meikle Av *RNFRW* PA4 55 D1
Meiklerig Crs *PLK/PH/NH* G53 101 D1
Meikle Rd *PLK/PH/NH* G53 101 D3
Meiklewood Rd *GOV/IBX* G51 82 B1
Melbourne Ct *GIF/THBK* G46 125 C4
Melbourne St *DEN/PKHD* G31 9 F3
Meldon Pl *GOV/IBX* G51 59 C4
Meldrum Gdns *PLKSD/SHW* G41 105 C1
Meldrum St *CLYDBK* G81 21 D3
Melford Av *GIF/THBK* G46 137 D1
Melfort Av *PLKSD/SHW* G41 84 B3
Mellerstain Dr *SCOT* G14 36 B1
Melness Pl *GOV/IBX* G51 59 C4
Melrose Av *BAIL/MDB/MHD* G69 98 B2
RUTH G73 110 A4
Melrose Gdns *MRYH/FIRH* G20 43 C4
Melrose St *COWCAD* G4 2 A2
Melvaig Pl *MRYH/FIRH* G20 42 A2
Melvick Pl *GOV/IBX* G51 59 C4
Melville Ct *CGLE* G1 8 A3
Melville Gdns *BSHPBGS* G64 32 A1
Melville St *PLKSD/SHW* G41 86 B4
Memel St *PPK/MIL* G22 45 D2
Memus Av *CARD/HILL/MSPK* G52 82 A3
Mennock Dr *BSHPBGS* G64 19 C3
Menock Rd *LNPK/KPK* G44 127 D1
Menteith Av *BSHPBGS* G64 32 B2
Menzies Dr *SPRGB/BLRNK* G21 46 B2
Menzies Pl *SPRGB/BLRNK* G21 46 B2
Menzies Rd *SPRGB/BLRNK* G21 46 B2
Merchant La *CGLE* G1 8 A4
Merchiston St *CAR/SHTL* G32 68 B4
Merkland St *PTCK* G11 61 C1
Merlinford Av *RNFRW* PA4 36 B4
Merlinford Crs *RNFRW* PA4 36 B4
Merlinford Dr *RNFRW* PA4 36 B4
Merlinford Wy *RNFRW* PA4 36 B4
Merlin Wy *PSLYN/LNWD* PA3 55 C4
Merrick Gdns *GOV/IBX* G51 84 B2
Merrick Wy *RUTH* G73 130 A4
Merryburn Av *PLKSW/MSWD* G43 125 C3
Merrycrest Av *GIF/THBK* G46 125 C3
Merrycroft Av *GIF/THBK* G46 125 C3
Merryland Pl *GOV/IBX* G51 61 C4
Merryland St *GOV/IBX* G51 61 D4
Merrylee Crs *PLKSW/MSWD* G43 124 B2
Merrylee Pk *GIF/THBK* G46 124 B2
Merrylee Park Av *GIF/THBK* G46 125 C3
Merrylee Rd *PLKSW/MSWD* G43 125 D2
Merryton Av *DRUM* G15 13 D4
GIF/THBK G46 124 B3
Merryton Pl *DRUM* G15 13 D4
Merryvale Av *PLKSW/MSWD* G43 125 C3
Merryvale Pl *PLKSW/MSWD* G43 124 B2
Merton Dr *CARD/HILL/MSPK* G52 81 C2
Meryon Gdns *CAR/SHTL* G32 114 A1
Meryon Rd *CAR/SHTL* G32 94 B4
Methil St *SCOT* G14 38 B4
Methuen Rd *PSLYN/LNWD* PA3 54 A3
Methven Av *BSDN* G61 16 B2
Methven St *DEN/PKHD* G31 91 D4
Metropole La *CGLE* G1 7 F4
Mews La *PSLYN/LNWD* PA3 54 A4
Micklehouse Ov *BAIL/MDB/MHD* G69 96 B1
Micklehouse Pl *BAIL/MDB/MHD* G69 96 B1
Micklehouse Rd *BAIL/MDB/MHD* G69 96 B1
Micklehouse Wynd
BAIL/MDB/MHD G69 96 B1
Midcroft Av *LNPK/KPK* G44 128 B2
Middlesex Gdns *PLKSD/SHW* G41 86 A2
Middlesex St *PLKSD/SHW* G41 86 A2
Middleton Dr *MLNGV* G62 11 C1
Middleton St *GOV/IBX* G51 85 C1
Midfaulds Av *RNFRW* PA4 56 B1
Midland St *CGLE* G1 7 D2
Midlem Dr *CARD/HILL/MSPK* G52 82 A2
Midlem Ov *CARD/HILL/MSPK* G52 82 A2
Midlock St *GOV/IBX* G51 85 C2
Midlothian Dr *PLKSD/SHW* G41 105 C2
Midton St *SPRGB/BLRNK* G21 46 A4
Mid-Wharf St *COWCAD* G4 4 A1
Migvie Pl *MRYH/FIRH* G20 41 D2
Milford St *STPS/GTHM/RID* G33 69 D3
Millarbank St *SPRGB/BLRNK* G21 45 D3
Millar St *PSLY* PA1 77 D2
Millbeg Crs *STPS/GTHM/RID* G33 95 D2
Millbeg Pl *STPS/GTHM/RID* G33 95 C2
Millbrae Crs *GVH/MTFL* G42 105 D4
KNTSWD G13 21 D4
Millbrae Gdns *PLKSD/SHW* G41 106 A4
Millbrae Rd *GVH/MTFL* G42 105 D4
Millbrix Av *SCOT* G14 37 D2
Millburn Av *KNTSWD* G13 22 A3
RNFRW PA4 36 A4
RUTH G73 129 D1
Millburn Dr *RNFRW* PA4 36 B4
Millburn Rd *RNFRW* PA4 36 A4
Millburn St *SPRGB/BLRNK* G21 66 B2
Millburn Wy *RNFRW* PA4 36 B4

Mill Ct *RUTH* G73 .... **109** D3
Mill Crs *DMNK/BRGTN* G40 .... **89** D4
Millcroft Rd *RUTH* G73 .... **109** C1
Millennium Gdns *ESTRH* G34 .... **73** D4
Millerfield Pl *DMNK/BRGTN* G40 .... **90** B4
Millerfield Rd *DMNK/BRGTN* G40 .... **90** B4
Millersneuk Crs *STPS/GTHM/RID* G33 .... **49** D2
Millerston St *DMNK/BRGTN* G40 .... **90** A1
Miller St *BAIL/MDB/MHD* G69 .... **96** B3
CGLE G1 .... **7** F2
CLYDBK G81 .... **20** B2
Millholm Rd *LNPK/KPK* G44 .... **127** C3
Millhouse Crs *MRYH/FIRH* G20 .... **26** B4
Millhouse Dr *MRYH/FIRH* G20 .... **26** B4
Millichen Rd *SMSTN* G23 .... **17** D3
Millport Av *LNPK/KPK* G44 .... **107** D4
Mill Rd *BLTYR/CAMB* G72 .... **133** D1
KNTSWD G13 .... **21** D4
Millroad Dr *DMNK/BRGTN* G40 .... **9** E4
Millroad St *DMNK/BRGTN* G40 .... **9** E4
Millstream Ct *PSLY* PA1 .... **77** D3
Mill St *DMNK/BRGTN* G40 .... **89** D4
PSLY PA1 .... **77** D3
RUTH G73 .... **129** D1
Millview *BRHD/NEIL* G78 .... **119** C2
Millview Pl *PLK/PH/NH* G53 .... **121** C3
Millwood St *PLKSD/SHW* G41 .... **105** D3
Milnbank St *DEN/PKHD* G31 .... **66** B3
Milncroft Pl *STPS/GTHM/RID* G33 .... **69** D2
Milncroft Rd *STPS/GTHM/RID* G33 .... **69** D2
Milner La *KNTSWD* G13 .... **39** D2
Milner Rd *KNTSWD* G13 .... **39** D2
Milngavie Rd *BSDN* G61 .... **15** D4
Milnpark Gdns *GOV/IBX* G51 .... **85** D2
Milnpark St *PLKSD/SHW* G41 .... **86** A2
Milovaig Av *SMSTN* G23 .... **27** D1
Milovaig St *SMSTN* G23 .... **27** D2
Milrig Rd *RUTH* G73 .... **109** C4
Milton Av *BLTYR/CAMB* G72 .... **131** D2
Milton Dr *BSHPBGS* G64 .... **31** C4
Milton Gdns *UD/BTH/TAN* G71 .... **117** D3
Milton St *COWCAD* G4 .... **3** F3
Milverton Av *BSDN* G61 .... **14** A1
Milverton Rd *GIF/THBK* G46 .... **136** A2
Minard Rd *PLKSD/SHW* G41 .... **105** D2
Minerva St *KVGV* G3 .... **62** B3
Minerva Wy *KVGV* G3 .... **62** A3
Mingarry La *MRYH/FIRH* G20 .... **42** B3
Mingarry St *MRYH/FIRH* G20 .... **42** B3
Mingulay Crs *PPK/MIL* G22 .... **30** B3
Mingulay Pl *PPK/MIL* G22 .... **31** C3
Mingulay St *PPK/MIL* G22 .... **30** B3
Minmoir Rd *PLK/PH/NH* G53 .... **100** A4
Minstrel Rd *KNTSWD* G13 .... **24** B2
Minto Av *RUTH* G73 .... **131** C3
Minto Crs *CARD/HILL/MSPK* G52 .... **83** D2
Minto St *CARD/HILL/MSPK* G52 .... **83** D2
Mireton St *PPK/MIL* G22 .... **44** A2
Mirrlees Dr *KVD/HLHD* G12 .... **41** D3
Mirrlees La *KVD/HLHD* G12 .... **41** D3
Mitchell Av *BLTYR/CAMB* G72 .... **134** B1
RNFRW PA4 .... **55** C1
Mitchell Dr *MLNGV* G62 .... **11** D2
RUTH G73 .... **130** A1
Mitchell La *CGLE* G1 .... **7** E1
Mitchell St *CGLE* G1 .... **7** E2
CTBR ML5 .... **99** D2
Mitre Ct *PTCK* G11 .... **40** A4
Mitre La *SCOT* G14 .... **39** C3
Mitre La West *SCOT* G14 .... **39** C3
Mitre Rd *PTCK* G11 .... **40** A3
SCOT G14 .... **39** D3
Moat Av *KNTSWD* G13 .... **24** A4
Mochrum Rd *PLKSW/MSWD* G43 .... **125** D1
Moffat St *GBLS* G5 .... **88** B3
Moidart Av *RNFRW* PA4 .... **35** C3
Moidart Ct *BRHD/NEIL* G78 .... **118** A1
Moidart Crs *CARD/HILL/MSPK* G52 .... **83** C2
Moidart Pl *CARD/HILL/MSPK* G52 .... **83** C2
Moidart Rd *CARD/HILL/MSPK* G52 .... **83** C2
Moir St *CGLE* G1 .... **8** C4
Molendinar St *CGLE* G1 .... **8** C3
Mollinsburn St *SPRGB/BLRNK* G21 .... **45** D4
Monach Rd *STPS/GTHM/RID* G33 .... **70** B3
Monar Dr *PPK/MIL* G22 .... **44** A4
Monar St *PPK/MIL* G22 .... **44** A4
Monart Pl *MRYH/FIRH* G20 .... **43** C3
Moncrieff St *PSLY* PA1 .... **77** C2
Moncur St *DMNK/BRGTN* G40 .... **9** E4
Moness Dr *CARD/HILL/MSPK* G52 .... **83** C3
Monifieth Av *CARD/HILL/MSPK* G52 .... **82** B4
Monikie Gdns *BSHPBGS* G64 .... **33** D2
Monkcastle Dr *BLTYR/CAMB* G72 .... **132** B1
Monkland View Crs
BAIL/MDB/MHD G69 .... **99** C2
Monksbridge Av *KNTSWD* G13 .... **24** A2
Monkscroft Av *PTCK* G11 .... **40** B4
Monkscroft Ct *PTCK* G11 .... **60** B1
Monkton Dr *DRUM* G15 .... **23** D2
Monmouth Av *KVD/HLHD* G12 .... **40** B2
Monreith Av *BSDN* G61 .... **24** B1
Monreith Rd *PLKSW/MSWD* G43 .... **125** D1
Monreith Rd East *LNPK/KPK* G44 .... **126** B2
Montague La *KVD/HLHD* G12 .... **41** C3
Montague St *COWCAD* G4 .... **63** C1
Monteith Pl *DMNK/BRGTN* G40 .... **9** D5
Monteith Rw *CGLE* G1 .... **8** C4
DMNK/BRGTN G40 .... **9** D5
Montford Av *LNPK/KPK* G44 .... **108** A4
Montgomery Av *PSLYN/LNWD* PA3 .... **55** C3
Montgomery Dr *GIF/THBK* G46 .... **137** C2
Montgomery Rd *PSLYN/LNWD* PA3 .... **54** B3
Montgomery St *BLTYR/CAMB* G72 .... **134** A2
DMNK/BRGTN G40 .... **90** A3
Montraive St *RUTH* G73 .... **110** B2
Montrave St *CARD/HILL/MSPK* G52 .... **82** B3
Montrose Av *CAR/SHTL* G32 .... **113** C2
CARD/HILL/MSPK G52 .... **57** C4
Montrose St *CGLE* G1 .... **8** B2
CLYDBK G81 .... **20** B1
Montrose Ter *BSHPBGS* G64 .... **33** C4
Monymusk Gdns *BSHPBGS* G64 .... **33** D1
Monymusk Pl *CLYDBK* G81 .... **12** A2
Moodiesburn St *STPS/GTHM/RID* G33 .... **68** A1
Moorburn Av *GIF/THBK* G46 .... **124** A4
Moore Dr *BSDN* G61 .... **15** D4
Moore St *DMNK/BRGTN* G40 .... **9** F3
Moorfoot Av *GIF/THBK* G46 .... **123** D4
Moorfoot St *CAR/SHTL* G32 .... **92** A1
Moorhouse Av *KNTSWD* G13 .... **37** C1
Moorhouse St *BRHD/NEIL* G78 .... **118** B3
The Moorings *PSLY* PA1 .... **76** A4
Moorpark Av *CARD/HILL/MSPK* G52 .... **80** B1
Moorpark Dr *CARD/HILL/MSPK* G52 .... **81** C1
Moorpark Sq *RNFRW* PA4 .... **55** C1
Moor Rd *MLNGV* G62 .... **11** C1
Moraine Av *DRUM* G15 .... **23** D2
Moraine Circ *DRUM* G15 .... **23** C2
Moraine Dr *CRMNK/CLK/EAG* G76 .... **137** C3
DRUM G15 .... **23** C2
Moraine Pl *DRUM* G15 .... **23** D2
Morar Crs *BSHPBGS* G64 .... **31** D1
Morar Dr *BSDN* G61 .... **16** B4
RUTH G73 .... **130** A4
Morar Pl *RNFRW* PA4 .... **35** C3
Morar Rd *CARD/HILL/MSPK* G52 .... **83** C2
Morar Ter *RUTH* G73 .... **131** C4
Moray Pl *BSHPBGS* G64 .... **33** C2
PLKSD/SHW G41 .... **105** D1
Mordaunt St *DMNK/BRGTN* G40 .... **90** A4
Moredun Crs *CAR/SHTL* G32 .... **70** B4
Moredun St *CAR/SHTL* G32 .... **70** B4
Morefield Rd *GOV/IBX* G51 .... **59** C4
Morgan Ms *GVH/MTFL* G42 .... **87** D4
Morina Gdns *PLK/PH/NH* G53 .... **121** D4
Morion Rd *KNTSWD* G13 .... **24** B3
Morley St *GVH/MTFL* G42 .... **106** B4
Morna La *SCOT* G14 .... **59** D1
Morningside St *STPS/GTHM/RID* G33 .... **68** A3
Morrin St *SPRGB/BLRNK* G21 .... **45** D4
Morrison Qd *CLYDBK* G81 .... **22** A2
Morrison St *GBLS* G5 .... **6** B4
Morriston Crs *RNFRW* PA4 .... **57** C2
Morriston Park Dr *BLTYR/CAMB* G72 .... **112** B4
Morriston St *BLTYR/CAMB* G72 .... **132** B1
Morton Gdns *PLKSD/SHW* G41 .... **104** B2
Morven Av *BSHPBGS* G64 .... **33** C2
Morven Dr *CRMNK/CLK/EAG* G76 .... **137** D3
Morven Rd *BLTYR/CAMB* G72 .... **132** A4
BSDN G61 .... **15** C1
Morven St *CARD/HILL/MSPK* G52 .... **83** C2
Mosesfield St *SPRGB/BLRNK* G21 .... **46** A2
Mosque Av *GBLS* G5 .... **7** F5
Mossbank Av *STPS/GTHM/RID* G33 .... **49** C3
Mossbank Dr *STPS/GTHM/RID* G33 .... **49** C3
Mosscastle Rd *STPS/GTHM/RID* G33 .... **70** B1
Mossend La *STPS/GTHM/RID* G33 .... **71** C3
Mossend St *STPS/GTHM/RID* G33 .... **71** C4
Mossgiel Av *RUTH* G73 .... **129** D2
Mossgiel Gdns *UD/BTH/TAN* G71 .... **117** D3

Mossgiel Pl *RUTH* G73 ....129 D2
Mossgiel Rd *PLKSW/MSWD* G43....105 C4
Mosshead Rd *BSDN* G61 ....10 A4
Moss Heights Av *CARD/HILL/MSPK* G52 ..82 B2
Mossland Rd *CARD/HILL/MSPK* G52 ....56 A3
Mosslands Rd *PSLYN/LNWD* PA3 ....53 C4
Mosspark Av *CARD/HILL/MSPK* G52 ....83 D4
Mosspark Bvd *CARD/HILL/MSPK* G52 ....83 D4
Mosspark Dr *CARD/HILL/MSPK* G52 ....82 A4
Mosspark Ov *CARD/HILL/MSPK* G52 ....83 C4
Mosspark Sq *CARD/HILL/MSPK* G52 ....83 C4
Moss Rd *GOV/IBX* G51 ....59 C3
Moss-Side Rd *PLKSD/SHW* G41 ....105 D2
Moss St *PSLY* PA1 ....77 C2
Mossvale La *PSLYN/LNWD* PA3 ....76 B1
Mossvale Rd *STPS/GTHM/RID* G33 ....70 B1
Mossvale Sq *STPS/GTHM/RID* G33....70 A1
Mossvale St *PSLYN/LNWD* PA3....53 C4
Mossview La *CARD/HILL/MSPK* G52 ....82 A2
Mossview Qd *CARD/HILL/MSPK* G52....82 B2
Mossview Rd *STPS/GTHM/RID* G33....51 D2
Motehill Rd *PSLYN/LNWD* PA3 ....55 C4
Mote Hill Rd *PSLYN/LNWD* PA3 ....78 A1
Moulin Circ *CARD/HILL/MSPK* G52....81 D3
Moulin Pl *CARD/HILL/MSPK* G52 ....81 C3
Moulin Rd *CARD/HILL/MSPK* G52....81 C3
Moulin Ter *CARD/HILL/MSPK* G52 ....81 C4
Mountainblue St *DMNK/BRGTN* G40....90 A2
Mount Annan Dr *LNPK/KPK* G44 ....107 C4
Mountgarrie Rd *GOV/IBX* G51 ....59 C4
Mount Harriet Av *STPS/GTHM/RID* G33 ..51 D1
Mount Harriet Dr *STPS/GTHM/RID* G33 ..51 C1
Mount Lockhart *UD/BTH/TAN* G71 ....116 A1
Mount St *MRYH/FIRH* G20 ....43 C4
Mount Stuart St *PLKSD/SHW* G41 ....105 D3
Mount Vernon Av *CAR/SHTL* G32 ....95 C4
Moyne Rd *PLK/PH/NH* G53....100 B1
Mugdock Rd *MLNGV* G62 ....10 B1
Muirbank Av *RUTH* G73....109 C4
Muirbank Gdns *RUTH* G73 ....109 C4
Muirbrae Rd *RUTH* G73 ....130 A3
Muirbrae Wy *RUTH* G73 ....130 A3
Muirdrum Av *CARD/HILL/MSPK* G52 ....82 B4
Muirdykes Av *CARD/HILL/MSPK* G52....81 C2
Muirdykes Rd *CARD/HILL/MSPK* G52 ....81 C2
Muiredge Ter *BAIL/MDB/MHD* G69 ....96 B3
Muirend Av *LNPK/KPK* G44....126 A2
Muirend Rd *LNPK/KPK* G44....125 D3
Muirfield Ct *LNPK/KPK* G44 ....126 A3
Muirfield Crs *SMSTN* G23 ....28 A2
Muirhead Gdns *BAIL/MDB/MHD* G69 ....97 C3
Muirhead Gv *BAIL/MDB/MHD* G69 ....97 C3
Muirhead Rd *BAIL/MDB/MHD* G69 ....96 B4
Muirhead Wy *BSHPBGS* G64....33 D2
Muirhill Av *LNPK/KPK* G44 ....125 D3
Muirhill Crs *KNTSWD* G13 ....22 B4
Muirhouse St *PLKSD/SHW* G41 ....87 C4
Muirkirk Dr *KNTSWD* G13 ....25 D4
Muirpark Av *RNFRW* PA4 ....55 D1
Muirpark Dr *BSHPBGS* G64....32 A3
Muirpark St *PTCK* G11 ....61 C1
Muirpark Ter *BSHPBGS* G64 ....32 A3
Muirshiel Crs *PLK/PH/NH* G53 ....121 D1
Muirside Av *CAR/SHTL* G32....95 C4
Muirside Rd *BAIL/MDB/MHD* G69 ....96 B3
Muirside St *BAIL/MDB/MHD* G69....96 B3
Muirskeith Crs *PLKSW/MSWD* G43 ....126 A1
Muirskeith Pl *PLKSW/MSWD* G43 ....126 A1
Muirskeith Rd *PLKSW/MSWD* G43....126 A1
Muir St *BSHPBGS* G64 ....32 A2
RNFRW PA4....36 A3
Muir Ter *PSLYN/LNWD* PA3 ....54 B4
Muirton Dr *BSHPBGS* G64 ....18 B4
Muiryfauld Dr *CAR/SHTL* G32 ....92 A3
Mulben Crs *PLK/PH/NH* G53....100 A4
Mulben Pl *PLK/PH/NH* G53....100 A4
Mulben Ter *PLK/PH/NH* G53....100 A4
Mulberry Rd *PLKSW/MSWD* G43 ....125 C2
Mulberry Wynd *BLTYR/CAMB* G72 ....135 C4
Mullardoch St *SMSTN* G23 ....27 D2
Mull Av *RNFRW* PA4....55 D2
Mull St *SPRGB/BLRNK* G21 ....67 C1
Munlochy Rd *GOV/IBX* G51....59 C4
Munro La *KNTSWD* G13 ....39 D2
Munro La East *KNTSWD* G13 ....39 D2
Munro Pl *KNTSWD* G13 ....25 C4
Munro Rd *KNTSWD* G13....39 D2
Murano St *MRYH/FIRH* G20 ....43 C3
Murchison *KVD/HLHD* G12 ....40 B1
Muriel La *BRHD/NEIL* G78 ....118 B2
Muriel St *BRHD/NEIL* G78 ....118 B2
Murrayfield Dr *BSDN* G61 ....25 C2
Murrayfield St *CAR/SHTL* G32 ....68 B4
Murray Pl *BRHD/NEIL* G78 ....119 C1
Murray St *PSLYN/LNWD* PA3 ....76 A1
RNFRW PA4....35 D4
Murrin Av *BSHPBGS* G64 ....33 D2
Murroes Rd *GOV/IBX* G51 ....59 C4
Muslin St *DMNK/BRGTN* G40 ....89 D3
Mybster Pl *GOV/IBX* G51 ....59 C4
Myreside Pl *CAR/SHTL* G32 ....91 D1
Myreside St *CAR/SHTL* G32....92 A1
Myres Rd *PLK/PH/NH* G53 ....102 A3
Myrie Gdns *BSHPBGS* G64....32 B1
Myrtle Hill La *GVH/MTFL* G42 ....107 D3
Myrtle Pk *GVH/MTFL* G42 ....107 C2
Myrtle Pl *GVH/MTFL* G42....107 D3
Myrtle Sq *BSHPBGS* G64 ....32 A3
Myrtle View Rd *GVH/MTFL* G42 ....107 D3
Myrtle Wk *BLTYR/CAMB* G72 ....132 A1

N

Naburn Ga *GBLS* G5 ....88 A3
Nairnside Rd *SPRGB/BLRNK* G21 ....33 C4
Nairn St *KVGV* G3 ....62 A2
Naismith St *CAR/SHTL* G32....113 D3
Nansen St *MRYH/FIRH* G20....43 D4
Napier Dr *GOV/IBX* G51 ....61 C3
Napier Pl *GOV/IBX* G51 ....61 C3
Napier Rd *CARD/HILL/MSPK* G52 ....57 C2
GOV/IBX G51....61 C3
Napiershall La *COWCAD* G4....63 C1
Napiershall Pl *MRYH/FIRH* G20 ....63 C1
Napiershall St *COWCAD* G4....63 C1
MRYH/FIRH G20 ....43 C4
Napier St *CLYDBK* G81 ....21 C4
GOV/IBX G51 ....61 C3
Napier Ter *GOV/IBX* G51 ....61 C3
Naseby Av *PTCK* G11 ....40 A4
Naseby La *PTCK* G11 ....40 A4
Nasmyth Rd *CARD/HILL/MSPK* G52....57 D4
Nasmyth Rd North
CARD/HILL/MSPK G52 ....57 D4
Nasmyth Rd South
CARD/HILL/MSPK G52 ....57 D4
National Bank La *CGLE* G1 ....7 E1
Naver St *STPS/GTHM/RID* G33 ....68 B2
Neidpath Rd West *NMRNS* G77 ....136 A4
Neilsland Ov *PLK/PH/NH* G53....102 A3
Neilsland Sq *PLK/PH/NH* G53 ....102 A2
Neilston Av *PLK/PH/NH* G53....121 D2
Neil St *RNFRW* PA4....36 A2
Neilvaig Dr *RUTH* G73 ....130 B4
Neistpoint Dr *STPS/GTHM/RID* G33....69 D3
Nelson Mandela Pl *CGLW* G2 ....3 F5
Nelson Pl *BAIL/MDB/MHD* G69 ....96 B3
Nelson St *BAIL/MDB/MHD* G69 ....96 B3
GBLS G5 ....6 C4
Neptune St *GOV/IBX* G51 ....61 C4
Ness Gdns *BSHPBGS* G64....32 B2
Ness Rd *RNFRW* PA4 ....35 C3
Ness St *STPS/GTHM/RID* G33 ....68 B2
Nether Auldhouse Rd
PLKSW/MSWD G43....124 B1
Netherby Dr *PLKSD/SHW* G41 ....85 D3
Nethercairn Rd *GIF/THBK* G46 ....124 B3
Netherdale Dr *PSLY* PA1 ....80 B4
Netherfield St *DEN/PKHD* G31 ....91 C1
Nethergreen Crs *RNFRW* PA4 ....35 C4
Nethergreen Wynd *RNFRW* PA4 ....35 C4
Netherhill Crs *PSLYN/LNWD* PA3 ....78 A1
Netherhill Rd *PSLYN/LNWD* PA3 ....77 D1
Netherhouse Pl *BAIL/MDB/MHD* G69....74 B3
Netherhouse Rd *BAIL/MDB/MHD* G69 ....74 B4
Netherlee Pl *LNPK/KPK* G44 ....126 B3
Netherlee Rd *LNPK/KPK* G44 ....126 B3
Nethermains Rd *MLNGV* G62 ....10 B3
Netherplace Crs *PLK/PH/NH* G53 ....101 C3
Netherplace Rd *PLK/PH/NH* G53....101 C3
Netherton Av *KNTSWD* G13 ....25 C4
Netherton Dr *BRHD/NEIL* G78 ....119 C3
Netherton Rd *KNTSWD* G13 ....25 D4
Netherton St *KNTSWD* G13....25 D4
Nevis Ct *BRHD/NEIL* G78 ....118 B4

Nevis Rd PLKSW/MSWD G43 124 A2
RNFRW PA4 55 C2
Nevis Wy PSLYN/LNWD PA3 53 D2
Newark Dr PLKSD/SHW G41 86 A4
Newbank Ct DEN/PKHD G31 92 A3
Newbank Gdns DEN/PKHD G31 91 D3
Newbank Rd DEN/PKHD G31 91 D3
Newbattle Ct CAR/SHTL G32 113 C1
Newbattle Gdns CAR/SHTL G32 113 C1
Newbattle Pl CAR/SHTL G32 113 C1
Newbattle Rd CAR/SHTL G32 112 B2
Newbold Av SPRGB/BLRNK G21 31 C4
Newburgh St PLKSW/MSWD G43 105 C4
Newcastleton Dr SMSTN G23 28 A2
New City Rd COWCAD G4 2 C2
Newcroft Dr LNPK/KPK G44 128 A2
New Edinburgh Rd UD/BTH/TAN G71 117 D4
Newfield Pl RUTH G73 108 B4
Newfield Sq PLK/PH/NH G53 120 B1
Newhall St DMNK/BRGTN G40 89 C4
Newhaven Rd STPS/GTHM/RID G33 70 A3
Newhaven St CAR/SHTL G32 69 D4
Newhills Rd STPS/GTHM/RID G33 71 D4
New Inchinnan Rd PSLYN/LNWD PA3 53 D4
Newington St CAR/SHTL G32 92 B1
New Kirk Rd BSDN G61 15 C2
Newlandsfield Rd PLKSW/MSWD G43 105 C4
Newlands Rd PLKSW/MSWD G43 125 D1
New Luce Dr CAR/SHTL G32 94 B4
Newmains Rd RNFRW PA4 55 D2
Newmill Rd SPRGB/BLRNK G21 47 D2
Newnham Rd PSLY PA1 79 D3
Newpark Crs BLTYR/CAMB G72 112 B4
New Rd BLTYR/CAMB G72 134 B3
New Sneddon St PSLY PA1 77 C2
Newstead Gdns SMSTN G23 28 A2
New St PSLY PA1 77 C3
Newton Av BLTYR/CAMB G72 134 A1
Newton Brae BLTYR/CAMB G72 135 C2
Newton Farm Rd BLTYR/CAMB G72 115 C4
Newtongrange Av CAR/SHTL G32 113 C1
Newtongrange Gdns CAR/SHTL G32 113 C1
Newton St CGLW G2 2 A4
Newton Station Rd BLTYR/CAMB G72 134 B3
Newton St PSLY PA1 76 A3
Newton Terrace La KVGV G3 63 C3
Newtyle Dr PLK/PH/NH G53 100 A2
Newtyle Pl BSHPBGS G64 33 D2
PLK/PH/NH G53 100 A2
Newtyle Rd PSLY PA1 79 C3
New Wynd CGLE G1 8 A3
Nicholas St CGLE G1 8 C1
Nicholson St GBLS G5 7 E5
Nicolson Ct STPS/GTHM/RID G33 51 C2
Niddrie Rd GVH/MTFL G42 106 A1
Niddrie Sq GVH/MTFL G42 106 A2
Niddry St PSLYN/LNWD PA3 77 C2
Nigel Gdns PLKSD/SHW G41 105 C2
Nigg Pl ESTRH G34 72 B3
Nimmo Dr GOV/IBX G51 59 D4
Nisbet St DEN/PKHD G31 91 D2
Nissen Pl PLK/PH/NH G53 100 A2
Nith Dr RNFRW PA4 56 B1
Nithsdale Crs BSDN G61 14 A1
Nithsdale Dr PLKSD/SHW G41 106 A1
Nithsdale Pl PLKSD/SHW G41 86 B4
Nithsdale Rd PLKSD/SHW G41 84 B3
PLKSD/SHW G41 106 A1
Nithsdale St PLKSD/SHW G41 106 A1
Nith St STPS/GTHM/RID G33 68 A2
Nitshill Rd PLK/PH/NH G53 120 B2
PLK/PH/NH G53 121 D4
Niven St MRYH/FIRH G20 41 D1
Noldrum Av CAR/SHTL G32 113 D3
Noldrum Gdns CAR/SHTL G32 113 D3
Norbreck Dr GIF/THBK G46 124 B3
Norby Rd PTCK G11 40 A4
Norfield Dr LNPK/KPK G44 107 C4
Norfolk Ct GBLS G5 7 E5
Norfolk Crs BSHPBGS G64 18 A4
Norfolk St GBLS G5 7 E5
Norham St PLKSD/SHW G41 105 D2
Norman St DMNK/BRGTN G40 89 D4
Norse La North SCOT G14 38 B3
Norse La South SCOT G14 38 B3
Norse Pl SCOT G14 38 B3
Norse Rd SCOT G14 38 B3
Northampton Dr KVD/HLHD G12 41 C1
North Av BLTYR/CAMB G72 132 A1
CLYDBK G81 20 A1
Northbank Av BLTYR/CAMB G72 134 A1
North Bank Pl CLYDBK G81 21 C3
Northbank St BLTYR/CAMB G72 134 A1
North Bank St CLYDBK G81 21 C3
Northbrae Pl KNTSWD G13 38 A1
North Calder Pl UD/BTH/TAN G71 116 A1
North Campbell Av MLNGV G62 10 A2
North Canal Bank COWCAD G4 4 A1
North Canal Bank St COWCAD G4 3 F1
North Claremont La MLNGV G62 10 B1
North Claremont St KVGV G3 62 B2
North Ct CGLE G1 7 F1
North Court La CGLE G1 7 F1
North Croft St PSLYN/LNWD PA3 77 C2
North Douglas St CLYDBK G81 21 C3
North Dumgoyne Av MLNGV G62 10 A1
North Elgin Pl CLYDBK G81 21 C4
North Elgin St CLYDBK G81 21 D3
North Erskine Pk BSDN G61 14 B2
North Frederick St CGLE G1 8 A1
North Gardner St PTCK G11 61 C1
Northgate Qd SPRGB/BLRNK G21 47 D1
Northgate Rd SPRGB/BLRNK G21 33 C4
North Gower St GOV/IBX G51 85 C2
North Grange Rd BSDN G61 15 C1
North Hanover St CGLE G1 4 A5
Northinch St SCOT G14 59 C1
Northland Av SCOT G14 38 B2
Northland Dr SCOT G14 38 B3
Northland Gdns SCOT G14 38 B3
Northland La SCOT G14 38 B3
North Lodge Rd RNFRW PA4 35 D3
Northmuir Rd DRUM G15 13 D3
North Park Av BRHD/NEIL G78 118 A2
GIF/THBK G46 123 C3
Northpark St MRYH/FIRH G20 43 C3
North Portland St COWCAD G4 8 B1
North St CGLW G2 2 A5
PSLYN/LNWD PA3 77 C1
Northumberland St MRYH/FIRH G20 42 B3
North Vw BSDN G61 24 B1
North Wallace St COWCAD G4 4 B3
North Woodside Rd COWCAD G4 63 C1
MRYH/FIRH G20 43 C4
Norval St PTCK G11 60 B1
Norwich Dr KVD/HLHD G12 41 C2
Norwood Dr GIF/THBK G46 136 A2
Norwood Pk BSDN G61 15 D4
Nottingham Av KVD/HLHD G12 41 C1
Nottingham La KVD/HLHD G12 41 C1
Novar Dr KVD/HLHD G12 40 B3
Novar Gdns BSHPBGS G64 31 C2
Nuneaton St DMNK/BRGTN G40 90 A4
Nurseries Rd BAIL/MDB/MHD G69 95 D1
Nursery La PLKSD/SHW G41 106 A1
Nursery St PLKSD/SHW G41 87 C4
Nutberry Ct GVH/MTFL G42 107 C2

O

Oak Av BSDN G61 10 A4
Oakburn Av MLNGV G62 10 A2
Oakburn Crs MLNGV G62 10 A2
Oak Crs BAIL/MDB/MHD G69 96 A3
Oak Dr BLTYR/CAMB G72 133 D3
Oakfield Av KVD/HLHD G12 42 B4
Oakfield La KVD/HLHD G12 62 B1
Oakhill Av CAR/SHTL G32 95 D4
Oakley Dr LNPK/KPK G44 126 A4
Oakley Ter DEN/PKHD G31 66 A4
Oak Pk BSHPBGS G64 32 B2
Oakridge Rd CTBR ML5 99 D1
Oakshaw Brae PSLY PA1 76 B2
Oakshaw St East PSLY PA1 76 B2
Oakshaw St West PSLY PA1 76 B2
Oak St CGLW G2 6 B1
Oaktree Gdns CSMK G45 129 C3
Oak Wynd BLTYR/CAMB G72 135 C4
Oatfield St SPRGB/BLRNK G21 47 C3
Oban Dr MRYH/FIRH G20 42 B3
Oban La MRYH/FIRH G20 42 B3
Obiston Gdns CAR/SHTL G32 93 C2
Observatory Rd KVD/HLHD G12 41 D4
Ochil Dr BRHD/NEIL G78 118 A4
Ochil Pl CAR/SHTL G32 93 C3

Ochil Rd *BSHPBGS* G64 ....**33** C2
RNFRW PA4 ....**55** C2
Ochil St *CAR/SHTL* G32 ....**93** C3
Ochiltree Av *KNTSWD* G13 ....**25** D4
Ogilvie Pl *DEN/PKHD* G31 ....**91** D3
Ogilvie St *DEN/PKHD* G31 ....**91** D3
Old Castle Gdns *LNPK/KPK* G44 ....**127** C1
Old Castle Rd *LNPK/KPK* G44 ....**126** B1
Old Church Gdns *BAIL/MDB/MHD* G69 ....**99** C2
Old Dalmarnock Rd *DMNK/BRGTN* G40 ....**89** D3
Old Dumbarton Rd *KVGV* G3 ....**61** D2
Old Edinburgh Rd *UD/BTH/TAN* G71 ....**117** D2
Old Glasgow Rd *UD/BTH/TAN* G71 ....**117** C3
Old Govan Rd *RNFRW* PA4 ....**37** C4
Oldhall Rd *PSLY* PA1 ....**79** D2
Old Manse Rd *CAR/SHTL* G32 ....**94** B3
Old Mill Rd *BLTYR/CAMB* G72 ....**134** A2
Old Renfrew Rd *RNFRW* PA4 ....**57** D1
Old Rutherglen Rd *GBLS* G5 ....**88** B3
Old Shettleston Rd *CAR/SHTL* G32 ....**93** C2
Old Sneddon St *PSLY* PA1 ....**77** C2
Old Wood Rd *BAIL/MDB/MHD* G69 ....**96** A4
Old Wynd *CGLE* G1 ....**8** A3
Olive St *STPS/GTHM/RID* G33 ....**48** A3
Olympia St *DMNK/BRGTN* G40 ....**89** D2
O'Neill Av *BSHPBGS* G64 ....**32** B3
Onslow Dr *DEN/PKHD* G31 ....**66** B4
Onslow Rd *CLYDBK* G81 ....**21** C1
Onslow Sq *DEN/PKHD* G31 ....**66** B4
Oran Gdns *MRYH/FIRH* G20 ....**42** B2
Oran Ga *MRYH/FIRH* G20 ....**42** B2
Oran Pl *MRYH/FIRH* G20 ....**42** B3
Oran St *MRYH/FIRH* G20 ....**42** B3
Orcades Dr *LNPK/KPK* G44 ....**127** C3
Orchard Ct *CAR/SHTL* G32 ....**113** C3
GIF/THBK G46 ....**123** D4
Orchard Dr *GIF/THBK* G46 ....**124** A4
RUTH G73 ....**109** C3
Orchard Gv *GIF/THBK* G46 ....**124** A3
Orchard Pk *GIF/THBK* G46 ....**124** B4
Orchard Park Av *GIF/THBK* G46 ....**123** D3
Orchard St *BAIL/MDB/MHD* G69 ....**95** D4
PSLY PA1 ....**77** C3
RNFRW PA4 ....**36** A3
Orchy Crs *BSDN* G61 ....**24** B2
Orchy St *LNPK/KPK* G44 ....**126** B1
Oregon Pl *GBLS* G5 ....**88** A3
Orion Wy *BLTYR/CAMB* G72 ....**132** B1
Orkney Pl *GOV/IBX* G51 ....**61** C4
Orkney St *GOV/IBX* G51 ....**61** C4
Orleans Av *SCOT* G14 ....**39** D4
Orleans La *SCOT* G14 ....**39** D4
Ormiston Av *SCOT* G14 ....**38** B3
Ormiston La *SCOT* G14 ....**38** B3
Ormiston La North *SCOT* G14 ....**38** B3
Ormiston La South *SCOT* G14 ....**38** B3
Ormonde Av *LNPK/KPK* G44 ....**126** A4
Ormonde Ct *LNPK/KPK* G44 ....**125** D4
Ormonde Crs *LNPK/KPK* G44 ....**126** A4
Ormonde Dr *LNPK/KPK* G44 ....**126** A4
Ornsay St *PPK/MIL* G22 ....**30** B4
Oronsay Crs *BSDN* G61 ....**16** B4
Orr Sq *PSLY* PA1 ....**77** C2
Orr St *DMNK/BRGTN* G40 ....**89** D2
PSLY PA1 ....**76** B2
PSLYS PA2 ....**77** C4
Orton Pl *GOV/IBX* G51 ....**84** A1
Osborne St *CGLE* G1 ....**7** F3
Ossian Av *PSLY* PA1 ....**80** B2
Ossian Rd *PLKSW/MSWD* G43 ....**125** D1
Oswald St *CGLE* G1 ....**7** D3
Oswald Wk *MLNGV* G62 ....**11** D3
Otago La *KVD/HLHD* G12 ....**62** B1
Otago St *KVD/HLHD* G12 ....**62** B1
Otterburn Dr *GIF/THBK* G46 ....**137** C1
Otterswick Pl *STPS/GTHM/RID* G33 ....**70** B1
Overbrae Gdns *DRUM* G15 ....**12** B3
Overbrae Pl *DRUM* G15 ....**12** B2
Overdale Av *GVH/MTFL* G42 ....**106** A3
Overdale Gdns *GVH/MTFL* G42 ....**106** A3
Overdale St *GVH/MTFL* G42 ....**106** A3
Overlea Av *RUTH* G73 ....**131** C1
Overnewton Pl *KVGV* G3 ....**62** A3
Overnewton Sq *KVGV* G3 ....**62** A2
Overnewton St *KVGV* G3 ....**62** A2
Overton Rd *BLTYR/CAMB* G72 ....**134** B3
Overton St *BLTYR/CAMB* G72 ....**134** A3
Overtoun Dr *RUTH* G73 ....**109** D4
Overtown Av *PLK/PH/NH* G53 ....**120** B1
Overtown St *DEN/PKHD* G31 ....**90** A2
Overwood Dr *LNPK/KPK* G44 ....**127** D1
Oxford La *GBLS* G5 ....**7** E5
RNFRW PA4 ....**35** D4
Oxford Rd *RNFRW* PA4 ....**35** D4
Oxford St *GBLS* G5 ....**7** E4
Oxton Dr *CARD/HILL/MSPK* G52 ....**81** D2

P

Paisley Rd *BRHD/NEIL* G78 ....**118** A1
GBLS G5 ....**6** B4
GOV/IBX G51 ....**86** A1
RNFRW PA4 ....**55** C2
Paisley Rd West *CARD/HILL/MSPK* G52 ....**81** C3
GOV/IBX G51 ....**85** C2
Paladin Av *KNTSWD* G13 ....**23** D3
Palladium Pl *SCOT* G14 ....**39** C4
Palmer Av *KNTSWD* G13 ....**24** B2
Palmerston Pl *KVGV* G3 ....**62** A3
Panmure Pl *MRYH/FIRH* G20 ....**43** D2
Panmure St *MRYH/FIRH* G20 ....**43** D3
Park Av *BRHD/NEIL* G78 ....**118** A4
BSHPBGS G64 ....**19** C4
KVGV G3 ....**63** C1
MLNGV G62 ....**10** B2
Parkbrae Dr *MRYH/FIRH* G20 ....**43** D1
Parkbrae Gdns *MRYH/FIRH* G20 ....**43** D1
Parkbrae La *MRYH/FIRH* G20 ....**43** D1
Park Circ *KVGV* G3 ....**62** B2
Park Circus La *KVGV* G3 ....**62** B2
Park Circus Pl *KVGV* G3 ....**63** C2
Park Ct *BSHPBGS* G64 ....**19** D4
GIF/THBK G46 ....**124** A4
Park Crs *BSDN* G61 ....**14** A2
BSHPBGS G64 ....**19** C4
Park Dr *KVGV* G3 ....**62** B1
RUTH G73 ....**109** D4
Park Gdns *KVGV* G3 ....**62** B2
Park Ga *KVGV* G3 ....**62** B2
Parkgrove Av *GIF/THBK* G46 ....**125** C4
Parkgrove Ter *KVGV* G3 ....**62** B2
Parkgrove Terrace La *KVGV* G3 ....**62** B2
Parkhill Dr *RUTH* G73 ....**109** D4
Parkhill Rd *PLKSW/MSWD* G43 ....**104** B3
Parkholm La *GBLS* G5 ....**86** B1
Parkhouse Rd *PLK/PH/NH* G53 ....**120** A3
Parklands Rd *LNPK/KPK* G44 ....**126** A4
Parklands Vw *PLK/PH/NH* G53 ....**100** A1
Park La *DMNK/BRGTN* G40 ....**89** D2
Parkneuk Rd *PLKSW/MSWD* G43 ....**124** B3
Park Qd *KVGV* G3 ....**62** B2
Park Rd *BAIL/MDB/MHD* G69 ....**98** B2
BSHPBGS G64 ....**32** A1
CAR/SHTL G32 ....**113** D3
GIF/THBK G46 ....**137** C1
KVGV G3 ....**62** B1
MLNGV G62 ....**10** B2
Parkside Gdns *MRYH/FIRH* G20 ....**43** D1
Parkside Pl *MRYH/FIRH* G20 ....**43** D1
Park St South *KVGV* G3 ....**62** B2
Park Ter *KVGV* G3 ....**62** B2
Park Terrace East La *KVGV* G3 ....**62** B2
Park Terrace La *KVGV* G3 ....**62** B2
Parkview Dr *STPS/GTHM/RID* G33 ....**51** D1
Parnie St *CGLE* G1 ....**8** B3
Parsonage Rw *COWCAD* G4 ....**8** C2
Parsonage Sq *COWCAD* G4 ....**8** C2
Partick Bridge St *KVGV* G3 ....**61** D2
Partickhill Av *PTCK* G11 ....**61** C1
Partickhill Rd *PTCK* G11 ....**61** C1
Paterson St *GBLS* G5 ....**6** B5
Pathhead Gdns *STPS/GTHM/RID* G33 ....**49** C1
Patna St *DMNK/BRGTN* G40 ....**90** B4
Paton St *DEN/PKHD* G31 ....**67** C4
Patrick St *PSLYS* PA2 ....**77** D4
Patterton Dr *BRHD/NEIL* G78 ....**119** C4
Payne St *COWCAD* G4 ....**3** F2
Pearce La *GOV/IBX* G51 ....**60** B3
Pearce St *GOV/IBX* G51 ....**60** B3
Pearson Dr *RNFRW* PA4 ....**56** A1
Peathill St *SPRGB/BLRNK* G21 ....**44** B4
Peat Rd *PLK/PH/NH* G53 ....**120** B1
Peebles Dr *RUTH* G73 ....**111** C4
Peel Glen Gdns *DRUM* G15 ....**13** C2
Peel Glen Rd *BSDN* G61 ....**13** C1

Peel La PTCK G11 60 B1
Peel St PTCK G11 61 C1
Pembroke St KVGV G3 63 C3
Pencaitland Dr CAR/SHTL G32 93 C4
Pencaitland Gv CAR/SHTL G32 112 B1
Pencaitland Pl SMSTN G23 28 A2
Pendale Ri CSMK G45 128 A4
Pendeen Crs STPS/GTHM/RID G33 95 C2
Pendeen Pl STPS/GTHM/RID G33 95 D1
Pendeen Rd STPS/GTHM/RID G33 95 D2
Pendicle Crs BSDN G61 14 B4
Pendicle Rd BSDN G61 14 B4
Penilee Rd PSLYN/LNWD PA3 56 A3
Penilee Ter CARD/HILL/MSPK G52 56 B4
Peninver Dr GOV/IBX G51 59 C3
Penman Av RUTH G73 109 C3
Pennan Pl SCOT G14 37 D2
Penneld Rd CARD/HILL/MSPK G52 80 B2
Penrith Av GIF/THBK G46 137 C1
Penrith Dr KVD/HLHD G12 40 B1
Penryn Gdns CAR/SHTL G32 94 B4
Penston Rd STPS/GTHM/RID G33 71 C3
Pentland Dr BRHD/NEIL G78 118 A4
BSHPBGS G64 33 D1
RNFRW PA4 55 C3
Pentland Rd PLKSW/MSWD G43 124 B2
Percy Dr GIF/THBK G46 137 C2
Percy Rd PSLYN/LNWD PA3 54 B3
Percy St GOV/IBX G51 85 C2
Perth St KVGV G3 6 A1
Petershill Dr SPRGB/BLRNK G21 47 C3
Petershill Pl SPRGB/BLRNK G21 47 C3
Petershill Rd SPRGB/BLRNK G21 46 B4
Peterson Dr KNTSWD G13 22 A3
Peterson Gdns KNTSWD G13 22 A3
Pettigrew St CAR/SHTL G32 93 C2
Peveril Av PLKSD/SHW G41 105 C2
RUTH G73 130 B2
Pharonhill St DEN/PKHD G31 92 A2
Piccadilly St KVGV G3 6 A2
Piershill St CAR/SHTL G32 69 C4
Pikeman Rd KNTSWD G13 24 A4
Pilmuir Av LNPK/KPK G44 126 A3
Pilrig St CAR/SHTL G32 68 B4
Pilton Rd DRUM G15 13 C4
Pine Av BLTYR/CAMB G72 135 C4
Pine Gv CTBR ML5 99 C1
Pine Pl GBLS G5 88 A3
Pinkerton Av RUTH G73 109 C3
Pinkerton La RNFRW PA4 56 A2
Pinkston Dr SPRGB/BLRNK G21 5 D1
Pinkston Rd SPRGB/BLRNK G21 65 C1
Pinmore Pl PLK/PH/NH G53 120 A2
Pinmore St PLK/PH/NH G53 120 A2
Pinwherry Dr STPS/GTHM/RID G33 49 C1
Pitcairn St DEN/PKHD G31 92 A3
Pitcaple Dr PLKSW/MSWD G43 124 A1
Pitlochry Dr CARD/HILL/MSPK G52 81 D3
Pitmedden Rd BSHPBGS G64 33 D1
Pitmilly Rd DRUM G15 14 A3
Pitreavie Pl STPS/GTHM/RID G33 70 B1
Pitt St CGLW G2 2 C5
Pladda Rd RNFRW PA4 56 A2
Plantation Park Gdns GOV/IBX G51 85 D2
Plantation Sq GOV/IBX G51 86 A1
Plant St DEN/PKHD G31 91 C1
Playfair St DMNK/BRGTN G40 90 A4
Plean St SCOT G14 37 D2
Pleasance St PLKSW/MSWD G43 104 B3
Pointhouse Rd KVGV G3 61 D3
Pollock Rd BSDN G61 16 A4
Pollok Dr BSHPBGS G64 31 C2
Pollokshaws Rd PLKSD/SHW G41 87 D3
PLKSD/SHW G41 105 D2
PLKSW/MSWD G43 104 A4
Pollokshields Sq PLKSD/SHW G41 105 D1
Polmadie Av GBLS G5 108 A1
Polmadie Rd GBLS G5 89 C4
GVH/MTFL G42 107 D2
Polmadie St GVH/MTFL G42 107 D2
Polnoon Av KNTSWD G13 37 D1
Polquhap Ct PLK/PH/NH G53 100 B3
Polquhap Gdns PLK/PH/NH G53 100 B3
Polquhap Pl PLK/PH/NH G53 100 B3
Polquhap Rd PLK/PH/NH G53 100 B3
Polwarth La KVD/HLHD G12 41 C4
Polwarth St KVD/HLHD G12 41 C4
Poplar Av PTCK G11 40 A3
Poplar Wy BLTYR/CAMB G72 135 C4
Poplin St DMNK/BRGTN G40 89 D4
Porchester St STPS/GTHM/RID G33 71 C1
Portal Rd KNTSWD G13 24 A3
Port Dundas Pl COWCAD G4 3 F4
Port Dundas Rd COWCAD G4 3 E2
Porterfield Rd RNFRW PA4 35 C4
Porter St GOV/IBX G51 85 C2
Portland Rd PSLYS PA2 78 B4
Portman St PLKSD/SHW G41 86 A2
Portmarnock Dr SMSTN G23 28 A3
Portree Pl DRUM G15 12 A3
Portsoy Av KNTSWD G13 22 A3
Portsoy Pl KNTSWD G13 22 B3
Port St KVGV G3 63 C4
Portugal St GBLS G5 87 D2
Possil Rd COWCAD G4 44 A4
Potter Cl CAR/SHTL G32 92 A4
Potter Gv CAR/SHTL G32 92 A4
Potterhill Rd PLK/PH/NH G53 100 B1
Potter Pl CAR/SHTL G32 92 A4
Potter St CAR/SHTL G32 92 A4
Powburn Crs UD/BTH/TAN G71 117 C4
Powfoot St DEN/PKHD G31 91 D2
Powrie St STPS/GTHM/RID G33 50 B4
Preston Pl GVH/MTFL G42 107 C1
Preston St GVH/MTFL G42 107 C1
Prestwick St PLK/PH/NH G53 120 B1
Priesthill Av PLK/PH/NH G53 121 D1
Priesthill Crs PLK/PH/NH G53 121 D1
Priesthill Rd PLK/PH/NH G53 121 C1
Primrose St SCOT G14 38 B4
Prince Albert Rd KVD/HLHD G12 41 C4
Prince Edward St GVH/MTFL G42 106 B1
Prince of Wales Gdns MRYH/FIRH G20 27 C3
Prince's Gdns KVD/HLHD G12 41 C4
Princes Ga RUTH G73 109 D3
Prince's Pl KVD/HLHD G12 41 D4
Princess Crs PSLY PA1 78 B1
Princess Dr BAIL/MDB/MHD G69 99 C2
Princes Sq BRHD/NEIL G78 118 B2
Princes St RUTH G73 109 D3
Prince's Ter KVD/HLHD G12 41 D4
Princes Terrace La KVD/HLHD G12 41 D4
Priorwood Pl KNTSWD G13 39 C1
Priory Av PSLYN/LNWD PA3 54 B4
Priory Dr UD/BTH/TAN G71 117 C4
Priory Pl KNTSWD G13 24 B4
Priory Rd KNTSWD G13 24 B4
Prosen St CAR/SHTL G32 92 A4
Prospect Av BLTYR/CAMB G72 132 A1
Prospecthill Circ GVH/MTFL G42 108 B2
Prospecthill Crs GVH/MTFL G42 108 B3
Prospecthill Dr GVH/MTFL G42 107 D3
Prospecthill Pl RUTH G73 108 B3
Prospecthill Rd GVH/MTFL G42 107 C3
Prospecthill Sq GVH/MTFL G42 108 A3
Prospect Rd PLKSD/SHW G41 105 C3
Provand Hall Crs BAIL/MDB/MHD G69 96 B4
Provanhill St SPRGB/BLRNK G21 5 F2
Provanmill Rd STPS/GTHM/RID G33 48 A4
Provan Rd DEN/PKHD G31 67 D2
Provost Driver Ct RNFRW PA4 56 A2
Purdon St PTCK G11 61 C1

Q

Quadrant Rd PLKSW/MSWD G43 125 D2
Quarry Av BLTYR/CAMB G72 134 A4
Quarrybrae Av CRMNK/CLK/EAG G76 137 D4
Quarrybrae St DEN/PKHD G31 92 A2
Quarryknowe RUTH G73 109 C4
Quarryknowe Gdns DEN/PKHD G31 92 A2
Quarryknowe St DEN/PKHD G31 92 A2
Quarry Pl BLTYR/CAMB G72 131 D1
Quarry Rd BRHD/NEIL G78 118 A1
Quarrywood Av SPRGB/BLRNK G21 47 D3
Quarrywood Rd SPRGB/BLRNK G21 48 A3
Quay Rd RUTH G73 109 D3
Quay Rd North RUTH G73 109 D2
Quebec Wynd CAR/SHTL G32 113 D3
Queen Elizabeth Av
CARD/HILL/MSPK G52 56 B4
Queen Margaret Dr KVD/HLHD G12 42 A4
Queen Margaret Rd MRYH/FIRH G20 42 B3
Queen Mary Av CLYDBK G81 21 D1

GVH/MTFL G42 107 C2
Queen Mary St *DMNK/BRGTN* G40 90 A3
Queen's Av *BLTYR/CAMB* G72 133 C1
Queensborough Gdns *KVD/HLHD* G12 40 B3
Queensby Av *BAIL/MDB/MHD* G69 96 B2
Queensby Pl *BAIL/MDB/MHD* G69 97 C1
Queensby Rd *BAIL/MDB/MHD* G69 96 B1
Queen's Ct *MLNGV* G62 10 B3
Queen's Crs *BAIL/MDB/MHD* G69 98 B2
COWCAD G4 2 A1
Queen's Dr *GVH/MTFL* G42 106 B2
Queen's Drive La *GVH/MTFL* G42 106 B2
Queensferry St *GBLS* G5 108 B1
Queen's Gdns *KVD/HLHD* G12 41 D4
Queensland Dr *CARD/HILL/MSPK* G52 82 A1
Queensland Gdns
CARD/HILL/MSPK G52 82 A1
Queensland La East
CARD/HILL/MSPK G52 82 A2
Queensland La West
CARD/HILL/MSPK G52 82 A1
Queenslie St *STPS/GTHM/RID* G33 68 A1
Queen's Park Av *GVH/MTFL* G42 107 C2
Queen's Pl *KVD/HLHD* G12 41 D4
Queen Sq *PLKSD/SHW* G41 106 A1
Queen St *CGLE* G1 7 F2
PSLY PA1 76 A3
RNFRW PA4 36 A4
RUTH G73 109 D3
Queen Victoria Dr *SCOT* G14 38 B3
Queen Victoria Ga *KNTSWD* G13 38 B2
Quendale Dr *CAR/SHTL* G32 92 B4
Quentin St *PLKSD/SHW* G41 105 D2
Quinton Gdns *BAIL/MDB/MHD* G69 96 A2

R

Raasay St *PPK/MIL* G22 30 A3
Rachan St *ESTRH* G34 74 A2
Raeberry St *MRYH/FIRH* G20 43 C4
Raeburn Av *PSLY* PA1 78 A3
Raeswood Dr *PLK/PH/NH* G53 100 A3
Raeswood Rd *PLK/PH/NH* G53 100 A3
Rafford St *GOV/IBX* G51 60 B4
Raglan St *COWCAD* G4 2 C1
Raith Av *CSMK* G45 128 A3
Raithburn Av *CSMK* G45 127 D3
Raithburn Rd *CSMK* G45 127 D4
Ralston Av *CARD/HILL/MSPK* G52 80 B3
Ralston Ct *CARD/HILL/MSPK* G52 80 B3
Ralston Dr *CARD/HILL/MSPK* G52 80 B3
Ralston Pl *CARD/HILL/MSPK* G52 80 B3
Ralston Rd *BRHD/NEIL* G78 118 B3
BSDN G61 15 C2
Ralston St *PSLY* PA1 78 A3
Rampart Av *KNTSWD* G13 23 C3
Ram St *CAR/SHTL* G32 92 B2
Ranald Gdns *RUTH* G73 131 C4
Randolph La *PTCK* G11 40 A4
Randolph Rd *PTCK* G11 40 A4
Ranfurly Rd *CARD/HILL/MSPK* G52 80 B2
Rannoch Av *BSHPBGS* G64 32 B2
Rannoch Dr *BSDN* G61 26 A1
RNFRW PA4 35 D3
Rannoch Pl *PSLYS* PA2 78 A4
Rannoch Rd *UD/BTH/TAN* G71 117 D2
Rannoch St *LNPK/KPK* G44 126 B1
Raploch Av *SCOT* G14 38 A3
Raploch La *SCOT* G14 38 A3
Rathlin St *GOV/IBX* G51 60 B3
Ratho Dr *SPRGB/BLRNK* G21 45 D3
Rattray St *CAR/SHTL* G32 92 A4
Ravel Rw *DEN/PKHD* G31 91 D2
Ravelston Rd *BSDN* G61 25 C1
Ravelston St *CAR/SHTL* G32 91 D1
Ravenscliffe Dr *GIF/THBK* G46 124 A4
Ravenscraig Dr *PLK/PH/NH* G53 121 C1
Ravenscraig Ter *PLK/PH/NH* G53 121 D2
Ravenshall Rd *PLKSD/SHW* G41 104 B3
Ravenstone Dr *GIF/THBK* G46 124 B2
Ravenswood Dr *PLKSD/SHW* G41 105 C2
Ravenswood Rd *BAIL/MDB/MHD* G69 97 C3
Rayne Pl *DRUM* G15 13 D3
Redan St *DMNK/BRGTN* G40 89 D2
Redburn Av *GIF/THBK* G46 136 B3
Redcastle Sq *STPS/GTHM/RID* G33 71 C2
Redford St *STPS/GTHM/RID* G33 68 A3
Redgate Pl *SCOT* G14 38 A3
Redlands La *KVD/HLHD* G12 41 D3
Redlands Rd *KVD/HLHD* G12 41 D3
Redlands Ter *KVD/HLHD* G12 41 D3
Redlands Terrace La *KVD/HLHD* G12 41 D3
Redlawood Pl *BLTYR/CAMB* G72 135 D1
Redlawood Rd *BLTYR/CAMB* G72 135 D1
Redmoss St *MRYH/FIRH* G20 44 A2
Rednock St *PPK/MIL* G22 44 B3
Redpath Dr *CARD/HILL/MSPK* G52 81 D1
Red Rd *SPRGB/BLRNK* G21 47 C3
Red Road Ct *SPRGB/BLRNK* G21 47 C4
Redwood Crs *BLTYR/CAMB* G72 135 C3
Redwood Dr *SPRGB/BLRNK* G21 46 B4
Redwood Wy *BLTYR/CAMB* G72 135 C4
Reelick Av *KNTSWD* G13 22 A3
Reelick Qd *KNTSWD* G13 22 A3
Regent Dr *RUTH* G73 109 D3
Regent Moray St *KVGV* G3 62 A2
Regent Park Sq *PLKSD/SHW* G41 106 A1
Regent St *PSLY* PA1 78 B2
Regwood St *PLKSD/SHW* G41 105 C3
Reid Av *BSDN* G61 16 A1
Reid Pl *DMNK/BRGTN* G40 89 D3
Reid St *DMNK/BRGTN* G40 89 D4
RUTH G73 110 A3
Reidvale St *DEN/PKHD* G31 89 D1
Renfield La *CGLW* G2 7 E1
Renfield St *CGLW* G2 3 E4
RNFRW PA4 36 A3
Renfrew Ct *CGLW* G2 3 F4
Renfrew Rd *GOV/IBX* G51 58 B2
PSLYN/LNWD PA3 77 D2
RNFRW PA4 57 D2
Renfrew St *KVGV* G3 2 C3
Renshaw Dr *CARD/HILL/MSPK* G52 81 D1
Renton St *COWCAD* G4 3 F2
Resipol Rd *STPS/GTHM/RID* G33 51 D2
Reston Dr *CARD/HILL/MSPK* G52 81 D1
Reuther Av *RUTH* G73 110 A4
Revoch Dr *KNTSWD* G13 23 C4
Rhannan Rd *LNPK/KPK* G44 126 B2
Rhannan Ter *LNPK/KPK* G44 126 B2
Rhindhouse Pl *BAIL/MDB/MHD* G69 97 D2
Rhindhouse Rd *BAIL/MDB/MHD* G69 97 D2
Rhindmuir Av *BAIL/MDB/MHD* G69 97 C2
Rhindmuir Ct *BAIL/MDB/MHD* G69 97 C1
Rhindmuir Crs *BAIL/MDB/MHD* G69 97 C1
Rhindmuir Dr *BAIL/MDB/MHD* G69 97 C1
Rhindmuir Gdns *BAIL/MDB/MHD* G69 97 C1
Rhindmuir Pth *BAIL/MDB/MHD* G69 97 D1
Rhindmuir Pl *BAIL/MDB/MHD* G69 97 D1
Rhindmuir Rd *BAIL/MDB/MHD* G69 97 C1
Rhindmuir Wynd *BAIL/MDB/MHD* G69 97 D1
Rhindsdale Crs *BAIL/MDB/MHD* G69 97 C2
Rhinds St *CTBR* ML5 99 D3
Rhymer St *SPRGB/BLRNK* G21 5 E3
Rhymie Rd *CAR/SHTL* G32 94 B4
Rhynie Dr *GOV/IBX* G51 84 B2
Riccarton St *GVH/MTFL* G42 107 D1
Riccartsbar Av *PSLYS* PA2 76 B4
Richmond Ct *RUTH* G73 110 B3
Richmond Dr *BLTYR/CAMB* G72 131 D2
RUTH G73 111 C4
Richmond Gv *RUTH* G73 110 B4
Richmond Pl *RUTH* G73 110 B3
Richmond Rd *RUTH* G73 111 C4
Richmond St *CLYDBK* G81 21 C2
COWCAD G4 8 B1
Riddon Av *KNTSWD* G13 22 A3
Riddon Pl *KNTSWD* G13 22 A3
Riddrie Crs *STPS/GTHM/RID* G33 68 B3
Riddrie Knowes *STPS/GTHM/RID* G33 68 B3
Riddrievale Ct *STPS/GTHM/RID* G33 68 B2
Riddrievale St *STPS/GTHM/RID* G33 68 B2
Rigby St *CAR/SHTL* G32 91 D1
Riggside Rd *STPS/GTHM/RID* G33 70 B1
Riglaw Pl *KNTSWD* G13 23 C4
Rimsdale St *DMNK/BRGTN* G40 90 A2
Ringford St *SPRGB/BLRNK* G21 46 A4
Ripon Dr *KVD/HLHD* G12 40 B1
Ritchie St *GBLS* G5 87 C3
Riverbank St *PLKSW/MSWD* G43 104 B4
Riverford Rd *PLKSW/MSWD* G43 104 B4
RUTH G73 110 B2
River Rd *CAR/SHTL* G32 113 C4
Riversdale La *SCOT* G14 37 D2
Riverside *MLNGV* G62 10 B1

Riverside Pl *BLTYR/CAMB* G72 ....**134** B1
Riverside Rd *PLKSW/MSWD* G43 ....**105** D4
Riverview Dr *GBLS* G5 ....**6** B3
Riverview Gdns *KVGV* G3 ....**6** C3
Riverview Pl *GBLS* G5 ....**6** B3
Robert Dr *GOV/IBX* G51 ....**60** B4
Roberton Av *PLKSD/SHW* G41 ....**104** B1
Robertson Av *RNFRW* PA4 ....**35** C4
Robertson Cl *RNFRW* PA4 ....**35** C4
Robertson Dr *RNFRW* PA4 ....**35** C4
Robertson La *CGLW* G2 ....**6** C2
Robertson St *BRHD/NEIL* G78 ....**118** A2
KVGV G3 ....**7** D3
Robert St *GOV/IBX* G51 ....**60** B4
Robert Templeton Dr
BLTYR/CAMB G72 ....**133** C2
Robroyston Av *STPS/GTHM/RID* G33 ....**48** B4
Robroyston Rd *STPS/GTHM/RID* G33 ....**48** A4
Robslee Crs *GIF/THBK* G46 ....**123** D4
Robslee Dr *GIF/THBK* G46 ....**124** A4
Robslee Rd *GIF/THBK* G46 ....**123** D4
Robson Gv *GVH/MTFL* G42 ....**107** C1
Rockall Dr *LNPK/KPK* G44 ....**127** C3
Rockbank Pl *DMNK/BRGTN* G40 ....**90** A2
Rockbank St *DMNK/BRGTN* G40 ....**90** A2
Rockburn Dr *CRMNK/CLK/EAG* G76 ....**137** C3
Rockcliffe St *DMNK/BRGTN* G40 ....**89** D4
Rockfield Pl *SPRGB/BLRNK* G21 ....**47** D2
Rockfield Rd *SPRGB/BLRNK* G21 ....**47** D2
Rockmount Av *BRHD/NEIL* G78 ....**119** C4
GIF/THBK G46 ....**123** D4
Rock St *COWCAD* G4 ....**44** A4
Rodger Dr *RUTH* G73 ....**129** D1
Rodger Pl *RUTH* G73 ....**129** D1
Rodil Av *LNPK/KPK* G44 ....**127** D3
Rodney St *COWCAD* G4 ....**44** A4
Roebank Dr *BRHD/NEIL* G78 ....**118** B4
Roebank St *DEN/PKHD* G31 ....**67** C3
Roffey Park Rd *PSLY* PA1 ....**79** D2
Rogart St *DMNK/BRGTN* G40 ....**89** D2
Rogerfield Rd *BAIL/MDB/MHD* G69 ....**73** D4
Roman Av *BSDN* G61 ....**15** D2
DRUM G15 ....**23** C2
Roman Ct *BSDN* G61 ....**15** C2
Roman Dr *BSDN* G61 ....**15** D2
Roman Gdns *BSDN* G61 ....**15** D2
Roman Rd *BSDN* G61 ....**15** D2
Romney Av *LNPK/KPK* G44 ....**127** D2
Ronaldsay Dr *BSHPBGS* G64 ....**33** D1
Ronaldsay St *PPK/MIL* G22 ....**30** B4
Rona St *SPRGB/BLRNK* G21 ....**67** C1
Rona Ter *BLTYR/CAMB* G72 ....**132** A4
Ronay St *PPK/MIL* G22 ....**30** B4
Ropework La *CGLE* G1 ....**7** F4
Rosebank Dr *BLTYR/CAMB* G72 ....**133** D3
Rosebank Gdns *UD/BTH/TAN* G71 ....**116** A1
Rosebank Ter *BAIL/MDB/MHD* G69 ....**98** B3
Roseberry St *GBLS* G5 ....**108** B1
Rose Dl *BSHPBGS* G64 ....**32** B3
Rosedale Dr *BAIL/MDB/MHD* G69 ....**96** A3
Rosedale Gdns *MRYH/FIRH* G20 ....**27** C3
Rosefield Gdns *UD/BTH/TAN* G71 ....**117** D4
Rose Knowe Rd *GVH/MTFL* G42 ....**108** A3
Roselea Gdns *KNTSWD* G13 ....**25** D4
Roselea Rd *UD/BTH/TAN* G71 ....**117** D3
Rosemount St *SPRGB/BLRNK* G21 ....**66** B3
Roseness Pl *STPS/GTHM/RID* G33 ....**69** D3
Rose St *KVGV* G3 ....**3** D4
Rosevale Rd *BSDN* G61 ....**15** C3
Rosevale St *PTCK* G11 ....**60** B1
Rosewood St *KNTSWD* G13 ....**25** C4
Roslea Dr *DEN/PKHD* G31 ....**66** B4
Roslyn Dr *BAIL/MDB/MHD* G69 ....**98** B2
Rosneath St *GOV/IBX* G51 ....**60** B3
Ross Av *RNFRW* PA4 ....**54** B2
Rossendale Ct *PLKSD/SHW* G41 ....**104** B3
Rossendale Rd *PLKSD/SHW* G41 ....**104** B3
Rosshall Av *PSLY* PA1 ....**79** C3
Ross Hall Pl *RNFRW* PA4 ....**36** A4
Rosshill Av *CARD/HILL/MSPK* G52 ....**80** B2
Rosshill Rd *CARD/HILL/MSPK* G52 ....**80** B2
Rossie Crs *BSHPBGS* G64 ....**33** C3
Rosslea Dr *GIF/THBK* G46 ....**137** C1
Rosslyn Av *RUTH* G73 ....**110** B4
Rosslyn Rd *BSDN* G61 ....**13** D1
Rosslyn Ter *KVD/HLHD* G12 ....**41** D3
Ross Pl *RUTH* G73 ....**131** C3
Ross St *CGLE* G1 ....**8** C4
PSLY PA1 ....**78** A4
Rostan Rd *PLKSW/MSWD* G43 ....**124** B2
Rosyth Rd *GBLS* G5 ....**108** B1
Rosyth St *GBLS* G5 ....**108** B1
Rotherwick Dr *PSLY* PA1 ....**80** A3
Rotherwood Av *KNTSWD* G13 ....**24** A2
Rotherwood La *KNTSWD* G13 ....**24** A1
Rotherwood Pl *KNTSWD* G13 ....**24** B3
Rothes Dr *SMSTN* G23 ....**27** D3
Rothes Pl *MRYH/FIRH* G20 ....**27** C2
Rottenrow *COWCAD* G4 ....**4** B5
Rottenrow East *COWCAD* G4 ....**8** C1
Roukenburn St *GIF/THBK* G46 ....**122** B3
Rouken Glen Rd *GIF/THBK* G46 ....**136** A2
Roundknowe Rd *UD/BTH/TAN* G71 ....**116** B2
Rowallan Gdns *PTCK* G11 ....**40** A4
Rowallan La *PTCK* G11 ....**40** A4
Rowallan La East *PTCK* G11 ....**40** B4
Rowallan Ter *STPS/GTHM/RID* G33 ....**50** A3
Rowan Av *RNFRW* PA4 ....**35** D3
Rowandale Av *BAIL/MDB/MHD* G69 ....**96** A3
Rowand Av *GIF/THBK* G46 ....**137** C1
Rowan Dr *BSDN* G61 ....**10** A4
Rowan Gdns *PLKSD/SHW* G41 ....**84** B3
Rowanlea Dr *GIF/THBK* G46 ....**125** C3
Rowan Pl *BLTYR/CAMB* G72 ....**133** D1
Rowan Rd *PLKSD/SHW* G41 ....**84** B3
The Rowans *BSHPBGS* G64 ....**31** D1
Rowantree Av *RUTH* G73 ....**130** A3
Rowena Av *KNTSWD* G13 ....**24** B2
Roxburgh St *KVD/HLHD* G12 ....**42** A4
Royal Crs *KVGV* G3 ....**62** B3
Royal Exchange Ct *CGLE* G1 ....**7** F1
Royal Exchange Sq *CGLE* G1 ....**7** F1
Royal Inch Ter *RNFRW* PA4 ....**36** A2
Royal Ter *KVGV* G3 ....**62** B2
Royal Terrace La *KVGV* G3 ....**62** B2
Roystonhill *SPRGB/BLRNK* G21 ....**5** F3
Royston Rd *SPRGB/BLRNK* G21 ....**5** E3
STPS/GTHM/RID G33 ....**48** B4
Royston Sq *SPRGB/BLRNK* G21 ....**5** E2
Roy St *SPRGB/BLRNK* G21 ....**45** C4
Rozelle Av *DRUM* G15 ....**13** D4
Rubislaw Dr *BSDN* G61 ....**15** C4
Ruby St *DMNK/BRGTN* G40 ....**90** A3
Ruchazie Pl *STPS/GTHM/RID* G33 ....**69** C3
Ruchazie Rd *STPS/GTHM/RID* G33 ....**69** C3
Ruchill Pl *MRYH/FIRH* G20 ....**43** C2
Ruchill St *MRYH/FIRH* G20 ....**42** B2
Ruel St *LNPK/KPK* G44 ....**106** B4
Rufflees Av *BRHD/NEIL* G78 ....**119** C2
Rugby Av *KNTSWD* G13 ....**23** D3
Rullion Pl *STPS/GTHM/RID* G33 ....**69** C3
Rumford St *DMNK/BRGTN* G40 ....**89** D4
Rupert St *COWCAD* G4 ....**2** A1
Rushyhill St *SPRGB/BLRNK* G21 ....**46** B3
Ruskin La *KVD/HLHD* G12 ....**42** B4
Ruskin Ter *KVD/HLHD* G12 ....**42** B4
Russell Dr *BSDN* G61 ....**15** D1
Russell St *PSLYN/LNWD* PA3 ....**53** C4
Rutherford Ct *CLYDBK* G81 ....**20** A1
Rutherglen Rd *GBLS* G5 ....**89** C4
Ruthven Av *GIF/THBK* G46 ....**137** D2
Ruthven La *KVD/HLHD* G12 ....**41** D4
Ruthven Pl *BSHPBGS* G64 ....**33** C3
Ruthven St *KVD/HLHD* G12 ....**41** D4
Rutland Crs *GOV/IBX* G51 ....**86** A1
Rutland Pl *GOV/IBX* G51 ....**86** A1
Ryan Rd *BSHPBGS* G64 ....**32** B2
Ryan Wy *RUTH* G73 ....**130** B4
Rye Crs *SPRGB/BLRNK* G21 ....**47** C2
Ryecroft Dr *BAIL/MDB/MHD* G69 ....**96** B2
Ryedale Pl *DRUM* G15 ....**13** C3
Ryefield Rd *SPRGB/BLRNK* G21 ....**47** C2
Ryehill Pl *SPRGB/BLRNK* G21 ....**47** D2
Ryehill Rd *SPRGB/BLRNK* G21 ....**47** D2
Ryemount Rd *SPRGB/BLRNK* G21 ....**47** D2
Rye Rd *SPRGB/BLRNK* G21 ....**47** C2
Ryeside Rd *SPRGB/BLRNK* G21 ....**47** C3
Rylands Dr *CAR/SHTL* G32 ....**94** B3
Rylands Gdns *CAR/SHTL* G32 ....**95** C3
Rylees Crs *CARD/HILL/MSPK* G52 ....**56** B4
Rylees Rd *CARD/HILL/MSPK* G52 ....**80** A1
Ryvra Rd *KNTSWD* G13 ....**39** C1

S

Sackville Av KNTSWD G13 40 A2
Sackville La KNTSWD G13 40 A2
Saddell Rd DRUM G15 13 D3
St Andrew's Av BSHPBGS G64 31 C1
St Andrews Crs PLKSD/SHW G41 86 A3
PSLYN/LNWD PA3 52 B2
St Andrew's Dr PLKSD/SHW G41 104 B1
PSLYN/LNWD PA3 53 D2
St Andrew's Dr West PSLYN/LNWD PA3 52 B3
St Andrew's La CGLE G1 8 B3
St Andrew's Rd PLKSD/SHW G41 86 B3
RNFRW PA4 35 D4
St Andrew's Sq CGLE G1 8 B4
St Andrew's St CGLE G1 8 B3
St Ann's Dr GIF/THBK G46 137 C1
St Blane's Dr RUTH G73 128 B1
St Bride's Rd PLKSW/MSWD G43 125 C1
St Catherine's Rd GIF/THBK G46 137 C1
St Clair Av GIF/THBK G46 124 B4
St Clair St MRYH/FIRH G20 63 C1
St Cyrus Gdns BSHPBGS G64 33 C2
St Cyrus Rd BSHPBGS G64 33 C2
St Enoch Pl CGLE G1 7 E3
St Fillans Rd STPS/GTHM/RID G33 50 B2
St George's Rd COWCAD G4 2 B1
KVGV G3 2 A3
St Germains BSDN G61 15 C3
St James Av PSLYN/LNWD PA3 52 A4
St James Rd COWCAD G4 4 C5
St James' St PSLYN/LNWD PA3 77 C2
St John's Ct PLKSD/SHW G41 86 A3
St John's Qd PLKSD/SHW G41 86 A3
St John's Rd PLKSD/SHW G41 85 D4
St Joseph's Ct SPRGB/BLRNK G21 66 A2
St Joseph's Vw SPRGB/BLRNK G21 66 A2
St Kenneth Dr GOV/IBX G51 59 C3
St Kilda Dr SCOT G14 39 D3
St Leonard's Dr GIF/THBK G46 124 B4
St Lukes Pl GBLS G5 88 A2
St Lukes Ter GBLS G5 88 A2
St Margaret's Ct PSLYN/LNWD PA3 77 D1
St Margaret's Pl CGLE G1 8 A4
St Mark Gdns CAR/SHTL G32 92 B2
St Mark St CAR/SHTL G32 92 A2
St Marnock St DMNK/BRGTN G40 90 A2
St Mary's Crs BRHD/NEIL G78 118 B3
St Marys Gdns BRHD/NEIL G78 118 B3
St Mary's La CGLW G2 7 E1
St Mary's Rd BSHPBGS G64 31 C1
St Mirren St PSLY PA1 77 C3
St Monance St SPRGB/BLRNK G21 46 A2
St Mungo Av COWCAD G4 4 A4
St Mungo Pl COWCAD G4 4 C4
St Mungo St BSHPBGS G64 31 D3
St Ninian Ter GBLS G5 88 A2
St Peter's La CGLW G2 6 C1
St Ronan's Dr PLKSD/SHW G41 105 C2
RUTH G73 130 B2
St Stephens Av RUTH G73 130 B4
St Stephen's Crs RUTH G73 131 C4
St Vincent Crs KVGV G3 62 A3
St Vincent Crescent La KVGV G3 62 A3
St Vincent La CGLW G2 2 C5
St Vincent Pl CGLE G1 7 F1
St Vincent St CGLW G2 2 C5
KVGV G3 63 C3
St Vincent Ter KVGV G3 2 A5
Salamanca St DEN/PKHD G31 91 D2
Salasaig Ct STPS/GTHM/RID G33 69 D4
Salen St CARD/HILL/MSPK G52 83 D2
Salisbury St GBLS G5 87 D3
Salkeld St GBLS G5 87 C3
Salmona St PPK/MIL G22 44 A3
Saltmarket CGLE G1 8 A4
Saltmarket Pl CGLE G1 * 8 A4
Saltoun La KVD/HLHD G12 42 A4
Saltoun St KVD/HLHD G12 42 A4
Salvia St BLTYR/CAMB G72 131 D1
Sandaig Rd STPS/GTHM/RID G33 95 C2
Sanda St MRYH/FIRH G20 42 B3
Sandbank Av MRYH/FIRH G20 27 D4
Sandbank Crs MRYH/FIRH G20 42 A1
Sandbank Dr MRYH/FIRH G20 27 D4
Sandbank St MRYH/FIRH G20 42 A1
Sandbank Ter MRYH/FIRH G20 27 D4
Sandend Rd PLK/PH/NH G53 100 B4
Sanderling Rd PSLYN/LNWD PA3 53 C3
Sandfield St MRYH/FIRH G20 42 B2
Sandgate Av CAR/SHTL G32 94 B4
Sandhaven Pl PLK/PH/NH G53 100 B4
Sandhaven Rd PLK/PH/NH G53 100 B4
Sandholes St PSLY PA1 76 A3
Sandholm Pl SCOT G14 37 C2
Sandholm Ter SCOT G14 37 C2
Sandiefield Rd GBLS G5 88 A3
Sandilands St CAR/SHTL G32 93 D2
Sandmill St SPRGB/BLRNK G21 66 B2
Sandra Rd BSHPBGS G64 33 C1
Sandringham La KVD/HLHD G12 42 A4
Sandwood Rd CARD/HILL/MSPK G52 81 C1
Sandyfaulds Sq GBLS G5 88 A3
Sandyfaulds St GBLS G5 88 B3
Sandyford Place La KVGV G3 62 B3
Sandyford Rd PSLYN/LNWD PA3 54 A3
Sandyford St KVGV G3 61 D3
Sandyhills Crs CAR/SHTL G32 93 D4
Sandyhills Dr CAR/SHTL G32 93 D4
Sandyhills Gv CAR/SHTL G32 113 D1
Sandyhills Pl CAR/SHTL G32 93 D4
Sandyhills Rd CAR/SHTL G32 93 D4
Sandy Rd PTCK G11 60 B2
RNFRW PA4 55 D2
Sannox Gdns DEN/PKHD G31 67 C3
Sanquhar Dr PLK/PH/NH G53 100 B3
Sanquhar Gdns PLK/PH/NH G53 100 B3
Sanquhar Pl PLK/PH/NH G53 100 B3
Sanquhar Rd PLK/PH/NH G53 100 B3
Saracen Head Rd COWCAD G4 9 D3
Saracen St PPK/MIL G22 44 B3
Sardinia La KVD/HLHD G12 42 A4
Saucel Hill Ter PSLYS PA2 77 C4
Saucel St PSLY PA1 77 D3
Sauchiehall La CGLW G2 2 B4
Sauchiehall St KVGV G3 2 B4
Saughs Av STPS/GTHM/RID G33 49 C1
Saughs Dr STPS/GTHM/RID G33 49 C1
Saughs Ga STPS/GTHM/RID G33 49 C1
Saughs Pl STPS/GTHM/RID G33 49 C1
Saughs Rd STPS/GTHM/RID G33 49 D1
Saughton St CAR/SHTL G32 68 B4
Savoy St DMNK/BRGTN G40 89 D3
Sawmillfield St COWCAD G4 64 A1
Saxon Rd KNTSWD G13 24 B4
Scalpay Pl PPK/MIL G22 30 B4
Scalpay St PPK/MIL G22 30 B4
Scapa St SMSTN G23 28 A3
Scaraway Dr PPK/MIL G22 30 B3
Scaraway Pl PPK/MIL G22 30 B3
Scaraway St PPK/MIL G22 30 A3
Scaraway Ter PPK/MIL G22 30 B3
Scarba Dr PLKSW/MSWD G43 124 A1
Scarrel Dr CSMK G45 129 D3
Scarrel Rd CSMK G45 129 D3
Scarrel Ter CSMK G45 129 D3
Scavaig Crs DRUM G15 12 A3
Schaw Dr BSDN G61 15 C1
Schaw Rd PSLYN/LNWD PA3 78 A1
School Av BLTYR/CAMB G72 133 C2
School La BLTYR/CAMB G72 134 B3
School Rd PSLY PA1 80 A2
STPS/GTHM/RID G33 51 D1
School Wynd PSLY PA1 77 C2
Scioncroft Av RUTH G73 110 B4
Scone St PPK/MIL G22 44 B4
Sconser St SMSTN G23 28 A2
Scorton Gdns CAR/SHTL G32 95 D3
Scotland St GBLS G5 86 B2
Scotland St West GOV/IBX G51 85 D2
Scotsburn Rd SPRGB/BLRNK G21 47 D3
Scotstoun St SCOT G14 38 B4
Scott Dr BSDN G61 14 A1
Scott Rd CARD/HILL/MSPK G52 57 C3
Scott's Rd PSLYS PA2 79 C4
Scott St BAIL/MDB/MHD G69 96 B3
KVGV G3 2 C3
Seafield Av BSDN G61 10 A4
Seafield Dr RUTH G73 131 C4
Seaforth Rd CARD/HILL/MSPK G52 57 D4
CLYDBK G81 20 B2
Seaforth Rd North
CARD/HILL/MSPK G52 57 D4
Seaforth Rd South
CARD/HILL/MSPK G52 57 D4
Seagrove St CAR/SHTL G32 91 D1
Seamill St PLK/PH/NH G53 120 A2

Seamore St *MRYH/FIRH* G20 **63** C1
Seath Rd *RUTH* G73 **109** D2
Seath St *GVH/MTFL* G42 **107** D1
Seaward La *PLKSD/SHW* G41 **86** A1
Seaward Pl *PLKSD/SHW* G41 **86** B2
Seaward St *GOV/IBX* G51 **86** B1
PLKSD/SHW G41 **86** A3
Second Av *BSDN* G61 **16** A4
LNPK/KPK G44 **127** C1
RNFRW PA4 **55** D2
STPS/GTHM/RID G33 **50** A2
UD/BTH/TAN G71 **117** D2
Second Gdns *PLKSD/SHW* G41 **84** A3
Seedhill *PSLY* PA1 **77** D3
Seedhill Rd *PSLY* PA1 **77** D3
Seggielea La *KNTSWD* G13 **39** C1
Seggielea Rd *KNTSWD* G13 **39** C1
Seil Dr *LNPK/KPK* G44 **127** C3
Selborne Pl *KNTSWD* G13 **39** D2
Selborne Place La *KNTSWD* G13 **39** D2
Selborne Rd *KNTSWD* G13 **39** D2
Selby Gdns *CAR/SHTL* G32 **94** B2
Selkirk Av *CARD/HILL/MSPK* G52 **82** A3
Selkirk Dr *RUTH* G73 **110** B4
Sella Rd *BSHPBGS* G64 **33** D1
Selvieland Rd *CARD/HILL/MSPK* G52 **80** A2
Seres Rd *CRMNK/CLK/EAG* G76 **137** D3
Seton Ter *DEN/PKHD* G31 **66** A4
Settle Gdns *BAIL/MDB/MHD* G69 **95** D3
Seyton Av *GIF/THBK* G46 **137** C2
Shaftesbury St *KVGV* G3 **2** A5
Shafton Pl *KNTSWD* G13 **25** C3
Shafton Rd *KNTSWD* G13 **25** C3
Shakespeare St *MRYH/FIRH* G20 **42** B2
Shamrock St *COWCAD* G4 **2** C2
Shandwick St *ESTRH* G34 **72** B3
Shanks Av *BRHD/NEIL* G78 **118** B3
Shanks St *MRYH/FIRH* G20 **42** B2
Shannon St *MRYH/FIRH* G20 **43** C2
Shapinsay St *PPK/MIL* G22 **30** B3
Shawbridge St *PLKSW/MSWD* G43 **104** B4
Shawfield Dr *GBLS* G5 **108** B1
Shawfield Rd *GBLS* G5 **89** D4
Shawhill Ct *PLKSD/SHW* G41 **105** C3
Shawhill Rd *PLKSW/MSWD* G43 **105** C3
Shawholm Crs *PLKSW/MSWD* G43 **104** A4
Shawmoss Rd *PLKSD/SHW* G41 **104** B2
Shawpark St *MRYH/FIRH* G20 **42** B1
Shaw Rd *MLNGV* G62 **10** B3
Shaw St *GOV/IBX* G51 **60** B3
Sheddens Pl *CAR/SHTL* G32 **92** B1
Sheepburn Rd *UD/BTH/TAN* G71 **117** D4
Sheila St *STPS/GTHM/RID* G33 **48** B3
Sheldaig Rd *PPK/MIL* G22 **30** A3
Shelley Rd *KVD/HLHD* G12 **40** A2
Sherbrooke Av *PLKSD/SHW* G41 **85** C4
Sherbrooke Dr *PLKSD/SHW* G41 **85** C3
Sherbrooke Gdns *PLKSD/SHW* G41 **85** C4
Sherburn Gdns *CAR/SHTL* G32 **95** D3
Sheriff Park Av *RUTH* G73 **109** D4
Sherwood Av *PSLY* PA1 **78** A1
Sherwood Dr *GIF/THBK* G46 **123** D4
Sherwood Pl *DRUM* G15 **13** D4
Shetland Dr *LNPK/KPK* G44 **127** C3
Shettleston Rd *DEN/PKHD* G31 **92** A2
Shielbridge Gdns *SMSTN* G23 **28** A2
Shieldaig Dr *RUTH* G73 **130** A3
Shieldburn Rd *GOV/IBX* G51 **82** A1
Shieldhall Gdns *GOV/IBX* G51 **58** B4
Shieldhall Rd *GOV/IBX* G51 **58** B4
Shields Rd *PLKSD/SHW* G41 **86** B2
Shiel Rd *BSHPBGS* G64 **32** B2
Shilford Av *KNTSWD* G13 **23** C4
Shillay St *PPK/MIL* G22 **31** C3
Shilton Dr *PLK/PH/NH* G53 **121** D2
Shinwell Av *CLYDBK* G81 **21** D2
Shiskine Dr *MRYH/FIRH* G20 **27** C3
Shiskine Pl *MRYH/FIRH* G20 **27** C3
Shiskine St *MRYH/FIRH* G20 **27** C3
Shore St *DMNK/BRGTN* G40 **109** C1
Shortridge St *MRYH/FIRH* G20 **42** B2
Shortroods Av *PSLYN/LNWD* PA3 **53** C4
Shortroods Crs *PSLYN/LNWD* PA3 **53** C4
Shortroods Rd *PSLYN/LNWD* PA3 **53** C4
Shotts St *STPS/GTHM/RID* G33 **71** C3
Shuna Gdns *MRYH/FIRH* G20 **42** B2
Shuna Pl *MRYH/FIRH* G20 **42** B2
Shuna St *MRYH/FIRH* G20 **42** B1
Shuttle St *CGLE* G1 **8** C1
PSLY PA1 **77** C3
Sidland Rd *SPRGB/BLRNK* G21 **47** D2
Sidlaw Av *BRHD/NEIL* G78 **118** B4
Sidlaw Rd *BSDN* G61 **13** D1
Sielga Pl *ESTRH* G34 **72** B3
Siemens Pl *SPRGB/BLRNK* G21 **67** C1
Siemens St *SPRGB/BLRNK* G21 **66** B1
Sievewright St *RUTH* G73 **110** B2
Silkin Av *CLYDBK* G81 **21** D2
Silk St *PSLY* PA1 **77** D2
Silver Birch Dr *GOV/IBX* G51 **59** C4
Silver Birch Gdns *GOV/IBX* G51 **59** C4
Silverburn St *STPS/GTHM/RID* G33 **68** B3
Silverdale St *DEN/PKHD* G31 **91** C3
Silverfir St *GBLS* G5 **88** B4
Silvergrove St *DMNK/BRGTN* G40 **89** C3
Simons Crs *RNFRW* PA4 **36** A2
Simpson Ct *CLYDBK* G81 **20** A1
Simpson St *MRYH/FIRH* G20 **43** C4
Simshill Rd *LNPK/KPK* G44 **127** C4
Sinclair Av *BSDN* G61 **15** C1
Sinclair Dr *GVH/MTFL* G42 **106** A4
Sinclair Gdns *BSHPBGS* G64 **32** B3
Sinclair St *CLYDBK* G81 **21** D3
MLNGV G62 **10** B1
Sir Michael Pl *PSLY* PA1 **76** B3
Sixth Av *RNFRW* PA4 **55** D2
Sixth St *UD/BTH/TAN* G71 **117** D2
Skaethorn Rd *MRYH/FIRH* G20 **26** B4
Skaterigg La *KNTSWD* G13 **39** D2
Skelbo Pl *ESTRH* G34 **74** A2
Skene Rd *GOV/IBX* G51 **84** A2
Skerray Qd *PPK/MIL* G22 **30** A3
Skerray St *PPK/MIL* G22 **30** A3
Skerryvore Pl *STPS/GTHM/RID* G33 **70** A3
Skerryvore Rd *STPS/GTHM/RID* G33 **70** A3
Skipness Dr *GOV/IBX* G51 **59** C3
Skirsa Ct *SMSTN* G23 **29** C3
Skirsa Pl *SMSTN* G23 **28** B4
Skirsa Sq *SMSTN* G23 **29** C4
Skirsa St *SMSTN* G23 **28** B3
Skirving St *PLKSD/SHW* G41 **105** D3
Skye Av *RNFRW* PA4 **55** D2
Skye Gdns *BSDN* G61 **13** D1
Skye Rd *RUTH* G73 **131** C4
Slatefield St *DEN/PKHD* G31 **90** A1
Slenavon Av *RUTH* G73 **131** C4
Sloy St *PPK/MIL* G22 **45** C3
Smeaton Dr *BSHPBGS* G64 **19** C3
Smeaton Gv *MRYH/FIRH* G20 **43** C1
Smeaton St *MRYH/FIRH* G20 **43** C1
Smithhills St *PSLY* PA1 **77** C2
Smith's La *PSLYN/LNWD* PA3 **77** C1
Smith St *SCOT* G14 **59** D1
Smithycroft Rd *STPS/GTHM/RID* G33 **68** B2
Snaefell Av *RUTH* G73 **130** B3
Snaefell Crs *RUTH* G73 **130** B2
Snowdon St *GBLS* G5 **88** B3
Snuff Mill Rd *LNPK/KPK* G44 **126** B2
Society St *DEN/PKHD* G31 **90** B2
Sollas Pl *KNTSWD* G13 **22** A3
Solway Rd *BSHPBGS* G64 **33** D1
Solway St *DMNK/BRGTN* G40 **109** C1
Somerford Rd *BSDN* G61 **25** D2
Somerled Av *PSLYN/LNWD* PA3 **54** A2
Somerset Pl *KVGV* G3 **63** C2
Somerset Place Ms *KVGV* G3 **63** C2
Somervell St *BLTYR/CAMB* G72 **132** A1
Somerville Dr *GVH/MTFL* G42 **107** C3
Sorby St *DEN/PKHD* G31 **91** D2
Sorley St *PTCK* G11 **60** A1
Sorn St *DMNK/BRGTN* G40 **90** B4
Southampton Dr *KVD/HLHD* G12 **41** C1
Southampton La *KVD/HLHD* G12 **41** C1
South Annandale St *GVH/MTFL* G42 **107** C1
South Av *CLYDBK* G81 **20** A1
RNFRW PA4 **36** A4
South Bank St *CLYDBK* G81 **21** C4
Southbank St *DEN/PKHD* G31 **91** D2
Southbar Av *KNTSWD* G13 **23** C4
Southbrae Dr *KNTSWD* G13 **39** C3
Southbrae La *KNTSWD* G13 **39** D2
South Campbell St *PSLYS* PA2 **77** C4
South Chester St *CAR/SHTL* G32 **93** C2
South Claremont La *MLNGV* G62 **10** B2
Southcroft Rd *RUTH* G73 **108** B2
Southcroft St *GOV/IBX* G51 **61** C4
South Crosshill Rd *BSHPBGS* G64 **32** A2
Southdeen Av *DRUM* G15 **13** D4
Southdeen Rd *DRUM* G15 **13** C4
South Douglas St *CLYDBK* G81 **21** C3

South Elgin Pl *CLYDBK* G81 **21** C4
South Elgin St *CLYDBK* G81 **21** C4
Southern Av *RUTH* G73 **130** A2
South Erskine Pk *BSDN* G61 **14** B2
Southesk Av *BSHPBGS* G64 **18** B4
South Exchange Ct *CGLE* G1 **7** F2
Southfield Crs *PLK/PH/NH* G53 **101** D3
South Frederick St *CGLE* G1 **8** A2
Southgate *MLNGV* G62 **10** B2
South Glassford St *MLNGV* G62 **11** C2
Southhill Av *RUTH* G73 **130** B2
Southinch Av *KNTSWD* G13 **36** B1
Southinch La *SCOT* G14 **36** B1
Southlea Av *GIF/THBK* G46 **123** D4
Southloch Gdns *SPRGB/BLRNK* G21 **46** A4
Southloch St *SPRGB/BLRNK* G21 **46** A4
South Mains Rd *MLNGV* G62 **10** A2
Southmuir Pl *MRYH/FIRH* G20 **42** A2
South Park Av *BRHD/NEIL* G78 **118** A2
Southpark Av *KVD/HLHD* G12 **42** B4
Southpark La *KVD/HLHD* G12 **62** B1
South Portland St *GBLS* G5 **7** E5
South Scott St *BAIL/MDB/MHD* G69 **96** B3
Southside Crs *GBLS* G5 **87** D3
South St *SCOT* G14 **37** D3
SCOT G14 **59** C1
South Vesalius St *CAR/SHTL* G32 **93** C2
Southview *BSDN* G61 **14** A2
Southview Ct *SPRGB/BLRNK* G21 **31** D4
Southview Ter *SPRGB/BLRNK* G21 **31** D4
Southwold Rd *PSLY* PA1 **80** A2
Southwood Dr *LNPK/KPK* G44 **127** D2
South Woodside Rd *COWCAD* G4 **62** B1
MRYH/FIRH G20 **43** C4
Soutra Pl *STPS/GTHM/RID* G33 **70** A3
Spean St *LNPK/KPK* G44 **106** B4
Speirsfield Gdns *PSLYS* PA2 **77** C4
Speirshall Cl *SCOT* G14 **37** C2
Speirshall Ter *SCOT* G14 **36** B1
Speirs Rd *BSDN* G61 **16** A4
Spencer St *KNTSWD* G13 **25** D4
Spence St *MRYH/FIRH* G20 **27** C3
Spey Dr *RNFRW* PA4 **56** B1
Spey Rd *BSDN* G61 **24** A1
Spey St *STPS/GTHM/RID* G33 **69** C3
Spiersbridge Av *GIF/THBK* G46 **123** C4
Spiersbridge La *GIF/THBK* G46 **122** B4
Spiersbridge Ter *GIF/THBK* G46 **122** B4
Spiers Gv *GIF/THBK* G46 **123** C4
Spittal Rd *CSMK* G45 **129** D2
Spoutmouth *CGLE* G1 **8** C3
Springbank Rd *PSLYN/LNWD* PA3 **53** C4
Springbank St *MRYH/FIRH* G20 **43** C3
Springbank Ter *PSLYN/LNWD* PA3 **53** C4
Springboig Av *CAR/SHTL* G32 **94** A1
Springboig Rd *CAR/SHTL* G32 **70** B4
Springburn Rd *SPRGB/BLRNK* G21 **5** E2
SPRGB/BLRNK G21 **45** D1
Springburn Wy *SPRGB/BLRNK* G21 **45** D3
Springcroft Av *BAIL/MDB/MHD* G69 **96** B1
Springcroft Crs *BAIL/MDB/MHD* G69 **96** B1
Springcroft Dr *BAIL/MDB/MHD* G69 **96** A1
Springcroft Gdns *BAIL/MDB/MHD* G69 **97** C1
Springcroft Gv *BAIL/MDB/MHD* G69 **96** B1
Springcroft Rd *BAIL/MDB/MHD* G69 **96** B1
Springcroft Wynd *BAIL/MDB/MHD* G69 **96** B1
Springfield Av *BSHPBGS* G64 **32** A3
PSLY PA1 **78** B3
Springfield Ct *CGLE* G1 **7** F2
Springfield Crs *BSHPBGS* G64 **32** A3
Springfield Dr *BRHD/NEIL* G78 **119** D4
Springfield Park Rd *RUTH* G73 **130** B1
Springfield Quay *GOV/IBX* G51 **6** A3
Springfield Rd *BSHPBGS* G64 **32** A2
DEN/PKHD G31 **91** C3
DMNK/BRGTN G40 **90** B4
Springfield Sq *BSHPBGS* G64 **32** A3
Springhill Dr South
BAIL/MDB/MHD G69 **96** A1
Springhill Farm Gv
BAIL/MDB/MHD G69 **96** A1
Springhill Farm Pl
BAIL/MDB/MHD G69 **96** A1
Springhill Farm Rd
BAIL/MDB/MHD G69 **96** A1
Springhill Farm Wy
BAIL/MDB/MHD G69 **96** A1
Springhill Gdns *PLKSD/SHW* G41 **105** D2
Springhill Pkwy *BAIL/MDB/MHD* G69 **96** A1
Springhill Rd *BAIL/MDB/MHD* G69 **95** D2
Springkell Av *PLKSD/SHW* G41 **84** B4
Springkell Dr *PLKSD/SHW* G41 **104** A1
Springkell Gdns *PLKSD/SHW* G41 **104** B1
Springkell Ga *PLKSD/SHW* G41 **105** C1
Springside Gdns *DRUM* G15 **13** C2
Springside Pl *DRUM* G15 **13** C3
Springvale Ter *SPRGB/BLRNK* G21 **45** D3
Spruce Dr *BLTYR/CAMB* G72 **135** C3
Spruce St *PPK/MIL* G22 **45** C2
Spruce Wy *BLTYR/CAMB* G72 **135** C3
Squire St *SCOT* G14 **59** C1
Staffa Av *RNFRW* PA4 **55** D2
Staffa Rd *BLTYR/CAMB* G72 **132** A4
Staffa St *DEN/PKHD* G31 **67** C3
Staffin Dr *SMSTN* G23 **27** D2
Staffin St *SMSTN* G23 **28** A2
Stafford St *COWCAD* G4 **4** B3
Stag St *GOV/IBX* G51 **61** C4
Stamford St *DEN/PKHD* G31 **90** B2
Stanalane St *GIF/THBK* G46 **123** C3
Standburn Rd *SPRGB/BLRNK* G21 **47** D1
Stanford St *CLYDBK* G81 **21** C2
Stanhope Dr *RUTH* G73 **131** C2
Stanley Dr *BSHPBGS* G64 **32** B1
Stanley St *PLKSD/SHW* G41 **86** A2
Stanley Street La *PLKSD/SHW* G41 **86** A2
Stanmore Rd *GVH/MTFL* G42 **107** C3
Startpoint St *STPS/GTHM/RID* G33 **69** D3
Station Crs *RNFRW* PA4 **36** B3
Station Pk *BAIL/MDB/MHD* G69 **97** C3
Station Rd *BAIL/MDB/MHD* G69 **97** C3
BSDN G61 **14** B3
GIF/THBK G46 **124** B4
MLNGV G62 **10** B1
MRYH/FIRH G20 **27** C3
RNFRW PA4 **36** A3
STPS/GTHM/RID G33 **49** D2
Staybrae Dr *PLK/PH/NH* G53 **100** A2
Staybrae Gv *PLK/PH/NH* G53 **100** A2
Steel St *CGLE* G1 **8** B4
Stenton St *CAR/SHTL* G32 **68** B4
Stepford Pl *STPS/GTHM/RID* G33 **72** A4
Stepford Rd *STPS/GTHM/RID* G33 **72** A4
Stephen Crs *BAIL/MDB/MHD* G69 **95** D2
Stephenson St *CARD/HILL/MSPK* G52 **56** B3
Stepps Rd *STPS/GTHM/RID* G33 **70** B3
Stevenson St *DMNK/BRGTN* G40 **9** E5
PSLYS PA2 **77** C4
Stewart Av *RNFRW* PA4 **54** B2
Stewart Ct *BRHD/NEIL* G78 **118** B1
Stewart Crs *BRHD/NEIL* G78 **119** C1
Stewart Dr *CRMNK/CLK/EAG* G76 **137** D3
CTBR ML5 **99** D1
Stewarton Dr *BLTYR/CAMB* G72 **131** D2
Stewart Pl *BRHD/NEIL* G78 **119** C1
Stewart St *BRHD/NEIL* G78 **119** C1
COWCAD G4 **3** E2
MLNGV G62 **10** B2
Stewartville St *PTCK* G11 **61** C1
Stirling Av *BSDN* G61 **25** C1
Stirling Dr *BSDN* G61 **14** A1
BSHPBGS G64 **18** A4
RUTH G73 **130** A2
Stirlingfauld Pl *GBLS* G5 **87** D3
Stirling Gdns *BSHPBGS* G64 **18** A4
Stirling Rd *COWCAD* G4 **4** C5
Stirrat St *MRYH/FIRH* G20 **41** D1
PSLYN/LNWD PA3 **52** A4
Stobcross Rd *KVGV* G3 **61** D3
Stobcross Wynd *KVGV* G3 **61** D3
Stobhill Rd *SPRGB/BLRNK* G21 **31** D4
Stobs Dr *BRHD/NEIL* G78 **118** A1
Stockholm Crs *PSLYS* PA2 **77** C4
Stockwell Pl *CGLE* G1 **7** F3
Stockwell St *CGLE* G1 **8** A4
Stonedyke Gv *DRUM* G15 **23** D1
Stonefield Av *KVD/HLHD* G12 **41** C1
Stonefield Crs *CRMNK/CLK/EAG* G76 **137** C3
Stonelaw Dr *RUTH* G73 **110** A4
Stonelaw Rd *RUTH* G73 **110** A4
Stoneside Dr *PLKSW/MSWD* G43 **124** A1
Stoneside Sq *PLKSW/MSWD* G43 **123** D1
Stoney Brae *PSLYN/LNWD* PA3 **77** C2
Stonyhurst St *PPK/MIL* G22 **44** B3
Storie St *PSLY* PA1 **77** C3
Stormyland Wy *BRHD/NEIL* G78 **118** B3
Stornoway St *PPK/MIL* G22 **30** A3
Stow Brae *PSLY* PA1 **77** C4
Stow St *PSLY* PA1 **77** C3
Strachur St *PPK/MIL* G22 **29** C4

Straiton St *STPS/GTHM/RID* G33 **68** B4
Stranka Av *PSLYS* PA2 **76** A4
Stranraer Dr *DRUM* G15 **24** A1
Stratford St *MRYH/FIRH* G20 **42** A2
Strathallon Pl *RUTH* G73 **131** C4
Strathblane Gdns *KNTSWD* G13 **25** D3
Strathblane Rd *MLNGV* G62 **11** C1
Strathbran St *DEN/PKHD* G31 **91** D3
Strathcarron Pl *MRYH/FIRH* G20 **42** A2
Strathclyde Dr *RUTH* G73 **109** D4
Strathclyde St *DMNK/BRGTN* G40 **109** D1
Strathcona Dr *KNTSWD* G13 **25** D4
Strathcona Gdns *MRYH/FIRH* G20 **26** A4
Strathcona Pl *RUTH* G73 **131** C3
Strathcona St *KNTSWD* G13 **40** A1
Strathendrick Dr *PLKSW/MSWD* G43 **125** D3
Strathkelvin Av *SPRGB/BLRNK* G21 **31** D4
Strathmore Av *PSLY* PA1 **79** D3
Strathmore Gdns *RUTH* G73 **131** C3
Strathmore Rd *PPK/MIL* G22 **29** D4
Strathord St *CAR/SHTL* G32 **93** C4
Strathyre Gdns *BSDN* G61 **16** B2
Strathyre St *PLKSD/SHW* G41 **105** D3
Stratton Dr *GIF/THBK* G46 **136** B1
Strauss Av *CLYDBK* G81 **22** A2
Streamfield Ga *STPS/GTHM/RID* G33 **33** D4
Strenabey Av *RUTH* G73 **131** C3
Striven Gdns *MRYH/FIRH* G20 **43** C4
Stroma St *SPRGB/BLRNK* G21 **67** C1
Stromness St *GBLS* G5 **87** C3
Stronend St *PPK/MIL* G22 **44** A2
Strone Rd *STPS/GTHM/RID* G33 **70** A4
Stronsay St *SPRGB/BLRNK* G21 **67** C1
Stronvar Dr *SCOT* G14 **38** A3
Strowan Crs *CAR/SHTL* G32 **93** D3
Strowan St *CAR/SHTL* G32 **93** D3
Struan Av *GIF/THBK* G46 **124** A4
Struan Gdns *LNPK/KPK* G44 **126** B2
Struan Rd *LNPK/KPK* G44 **126** B2
Struie St *ESTRH* G34 **72** B3
Struma Dr *CRMNK/CLK/EAG* G76 **137** C3
Stuart Av *RUTH* G73 **130** A2
Stuart Dr *BSHPBGS* G64 **31** C3
Succoth St *KNTSWD* G13 **25** D4
Suffolk St *CGLE* G1 **8** C4
Sugworth Av *BAIL/MDB/MHD* G69 **96** B2
Sumburgh St *STPS/GTHM/RID* G33 **69** C4
Summerfield St *DMNK/BRGTN* G40 **110** A1
Summerhill Dr *DRUM* G15 **13** D3
Summerhill Gdns *DRUM* G15 **13** D3
Summerhill Pl *DRUM* G15 **13** D3
Summerhill Rd *DRUM* G15 **13** D3
Summerlea Rd *GIF/THBK* G46 **123** C3
Summerlee St *STPS/GTHM/RID* G33 **70** B3
Summer St *DMNK/BRGTN* G40 **89** D2
Summertown Rd *GOV/IBX* G51 **61** C4
Sunart Av *RNFRW* PA4 **35** C3
Sunart Gdns *BSHPBGS* G64 **33** C2
Sunart Rd *BSHPBGS* G64 **33** C2
CARD/HILL/MSPK G52 **83** C2
Sunbury Av *CRMNK/CLK/EAG* G76 **137** C4
Sunningdale Rd *SMSTN* G23 **27** D3
Sunnylaw St *PPK/MIL* G22 **44** A3
Sunnyside Dr *BAIL/MDB/MHD* G69 **98** B2
CRMNK/CLK/EAG G76 **137** D3
DRUM G15 **23** C2
Sunnyside Pl *BRHD/NEIL* G78 **118** A3
DRUM G15 **23** C2
Surrey La *GBLS* G5 **87** D3
Surrey St *GBLS* G5 **87** D3
Sussex St *PLKSD/SHW* G41 **86** A2
Sutcliffe Ct *KNTSWD* G13 **25** C4
Sutcliffe Rd *KNTSWD* G13 **25** D4
Sutherland Av *PLKSD/SHW* G41 **85** C4
Sutherland Dr *GIF/THBK* G46 **137** D2
Sutherland La *PTCK* G11 **61** D1
Sutherland Rd *CLYDBK* G81 **20** B1
Sutherland St *PSLY* PA1 **76** B2
Sutherness Dr *STPS/GTHM/RID* G33 **69** D4
Swallow Gdns *KNTSWD* G13 **22** B4
Swanston St *DMNK/BRGTN* G40 **109** D1
Swan St *COWCAD* G4 **4** A2
Sween Av *LNPK/KPK* G44 **126** B3
Swift Crs *KNTSWD* G13 **22** B4
Swinton Av *BAIL/MDB/MHD* G69 **97** D2
Swinton Crs *BAIL/MDB/MHD* G69 **97** C2
CTBR ML5 **99** D3
Swinton Dr *CARD/HILL/MSPK* G52 **81** D2
Swinton Gdns *BAIL/MDB/MHD* G69 **97** D2
Swinton Pth *BAIL/MDB/MHD* G69 **97** D2
Swinton Pl *CARD/HILL/MSPK* G52 **81** D2
Swinton Rd *BAIL/MDB/MHD* G69 **97** C2
Swinton Vw *BAIL/MDB/MHD* G69 **97** C2
Switchback Rd *BSDN* G61 **25** D2
Swordale Pl *ESTRH* G34 **72** B3
Sword St *DEN/PKHD* G31 **89** D1
Sycamore Wy *BLTYR/CAMB* G72 **135** C3
Sydenham Rd *KVD/HLHD* G12 **41** D4
Sydney St *DEN/PKHD* G31 **9** E3
Symington Dr *CLYDBK* G81 **20** A1
Syriam Pl *SPRGB/BLRNK* G21 **46** A3
Syriam St *SPRGB/BLRNK* G21 **46** A2

T

Tabard Pl *KNTSWD* G13 **24** A3
Tabard Rd *KNTSWD* G13 **24** A3
Tabernacle La *BLTYR/CAMB* G72 **132** B2
Tabernacle St *BLTYR/CAMB* G72 **132** B2
Tait Av *BRHD/NEIL* G78 **119** C1
Talbot Ct *KNTSWD* G13 **38** A2
Talbot Dr *KNTSWD* G13 **38** A2
Talbot Pl *SCOT* G14 **38** A2
Talbot Ter *SCOT* G14 **38** A2
UD/BTH/TAN G71 **117** D3
Talisman Rd *KNTSWD* G13 **38** B1
Tallant Rd *DRUM* G15 **13** D4
Tallant Ter *DRUM* G15 **14** A4
Talla Rd *CARD/HILL/MSPK* G52 **81** D2
Tambowie Av *MLNGV* G62 **10** A1
Tambowie Crs *MLNGV* G62 **10** A1
Tambowie St *KNTSWD* G13 **25** C4
Tamshill St *MRYH/FIRH* G20 **43** C1
Tanar Av *RNFRW* PA4 **57** C2
Tanera Av *LNPK/KPK* G44 **127** D2
Tanfield Pl *CAR/SHTL* G32 **70** B4
Tanfield St *CAR/SHTL* G32 **70** B4
Tankerland Rd *PLKSW/MSWD* G43 **126** B1
Tannadice Av *CARD/HILL/MSPK* G52 **82** A4
Tanna Dr *CARD/HILL/MSPK* G52 **83** D4
Tannahill Rd *PLKSW/MSWD* G43 **125** D1
Tannock St *PPK/MIL* G22 **44** A3
Tantallon Rd *BAIL/MDB/MHD* G69 **96** A4
PLKSD/SHW G41 **105** D4
Tanzieknowe Av *BLTYR/CAMB* G72 **133** C3
Tanzieknowe Dr *BLTYR/CAMB* G72 **133** C4
Tanzieknowe Pl *BLTYR/CAMB* G72 **132** B4
Tanzieknowe Rd *BLTYR/CAMB* G72 **133** C4
Taransay St *GOV/IBX* G51 **60** A3
Tarbolton Rd *PLKSW/MSWD* G43 **125** C1
Tarfside Av *CARD/HILL/MSPK* G52 **82** B3
Tarfside Gdns *CARD/HILL/MSPK* G52 **82** B3
Tarfside Ov *CARD/HILL/MSPK* G52 **82** B4
Tarland St *GOV/IBX* G51 **83** D1
Tarras Dr *RNFRW* PA4 **56** B2
Tassie St *PLKSD/SHW* G41 **105** C3
Tattershall Rd *STPS/GTHM/RID* G33 **70** B1
Tavistock Dr *PLKSW/MSWD* G43 **125** C2
Tay Av *RNFRW* PA4 **36** B4
Tay Crs *BSHPBGS* G64 **32** B2
STPS/GTHM/RID G33 **68** B2
Taylor Pl *COWCAD* G4 **4** C5
Taylor St *CLYDBK* G81 **21** C3
COWCAD G4 **8** C1
Taymouth St *CAR/SHTL* G32 **93** D4
Taynish Dr *LNPK/KPK* G44 **127** C3
Tay Rd *BSDN* G61 **24** B1
BSHPBGS G64 **32** B2
Teal Dr *KNTSWD* G13 **23** C4
Tealing Av *CARD/HILL/MSPK* G52 **82** A3
Tealing Crs *CARD/HILL/MSPK* G52 **82** A3
Teasel Av *PLK/PH/NH* G53 **121** C4
Teith Av *RNFRW* PA4 **57** C1
Teith Dr *BSDN* G61 **14** A4
Teith St *STPS/GTHM/RID* G33 **68** B2
Telephone La *KVD/HLHD* G12 **61** D1
Templar Av *KNTSWD* G13 **24** B3
Temple Gdns *KNTSWD* G13 **25** D4
Templeland Rd *PLK/PH/NH* G53 **101** D1
Temple Locks Ct *KNTSWD* G13 **25** D4
Temple Locks Pl *KNTSWD* G13 **25** D4
Temple Rd *MRYH/FIRH* G20 **26** A4
Templeton St *DMNK/BRGTN* G40 **89** C2
Tennant St *RNFRW* PA4 **36** A3
Tennyson Dr *DEN/PKHD* G31 **92** A3

Terregles Av *PLKSD/SHW* G41 ....**104** B1
Terregles Crs *PLKSD/SHW* G41 ....**104** A1
Terregles Dr *PLKSD/SHW* G41 ....**104** B1
Teviot Av *BSHPBGS* G64 ....**19** C4
Teviot Crs *BSDN* G61 ....**24** B1
Teviot St *KVGV* G3 ....**61** D3
Thane Rd *KNTSWD* G13 ....**38** B1
Tharsis St *SPRGB/BLRNK* G21 ....**66** A2
Third Av *LNPK/KPK* G44 ....**107** C4
RNFRW PA4 ....**55** D1
STPS/GTHM/RID G33 ....**50** A2
Third Gdns *PLKSD/SHW* G41 ....**84** A3
Thirdpart Crs *KNTSWD* G13 ....**22** A4
Thistle St *GBLS* G5 ....**7** F5
Thistle Ter *GBLS* G5 ....**87** D3
Thomas Muir Av *BSHPBGS* G64 ....**32** A3
Thompson St *DEN/PKHD* G31 ....**90** A1
Thomson Dr *BSDN* G61 ....**15** D1
Thomson Gv *BLTYR/CAMB* G72 ....**112** B4
Thomson St *RNFRW* PA4 ....**55** D1
Thornbank St *KVGV* G3 ....**61** D3
Thornbridge Av *BAIL/MDB/MHD* G69 ....**96** B2
KVD/HLHD G12 ....**41** D2
Thornbridge Gdns
BAIL/MDB/MHD G69 ....**96** A2
Thornbridge Rd *BAIL/MDB/MHD* G69 ....**96** A2
Thorncliffe Gdns *PLKSD/SHW* G41 ....**105** D1
Thorncroft Dr *LNPK/KPK* G44 ....**128** A3
Thornden La *SCOT* G14 ....**37** D3
Thorn Dr *BSDN* G61 ....**14** B2
RUTH G73 ....**130** B3
Thornlea Dr *GIF/THBK* G46 ....**125** C3
Thornley Av *KNTSWD* G13 ....**38** A1
Thornliebank Rd *GIF/THBK* G46 ....**123** D3
Thorn Rd *BSDN* G61 ....**14** A2
Thornton La *MRYH/FIRH* G20 ....**28** A4
Thornton St *MRYH/FIRH* G20 ....**27** D4
Thornwood Av *PTCK* G11 ....**60** B1
Thornwood Crs *PTCK* G11 ....**40** A4
Thornwood Dr *PTCK* G11 ....**60** A1
Thornwood Gdns *PTCK* G11 ....**60** A1
Thornwood Pl *PTCK* G11 ....**40** A4
Thornwood Rd *PTCK* G11 ....**60** A1
Thornwood Ter *PTCK* G11 ....**60** A1
Thornyburn Dr *BAIL/MDB/MHD* G69 ....**97** D3
Thornyburn Pl *BAIL/MDB/MHD* G69 ....**97** C3
Threestonehill Av *CAR/SHTL* G32 ....**93** D1
Thrums Av *BSHPBGS* G64 ....**33** C2
Thurso St *PTCK* G11 ....**61** D2
Thurston Rd *CARD/HILL/MSPK* G52 ....**81** C2
Tibbermore Rd *PTCK* G11 ....**40** B4
Tillet Ov *PSLYN/LNWD* PA3 ....**53** C4
Tillie St *MRYH/FIRH* G20 ....**43** C4
Tillycairn Dr *STPS/GTHM/RID* G33 ....**71** C1
Tillycairn Rd *STPS/GTHM/RID* G33 ....**71** C1
Tillycairn St *STPS/GTHM/RID* G33 ....**71** D1
Tilt St *STPS/GTHM/RID* G33 ....**68** B1
Tinto Rd *BSDN* G61 ....**13** D1
CTBR ML5 ....**99** D1
PLKSW/MSWD G43 ....**124** B2
Tinwald Pth *CARD/HILL/MSPK* G52 ....**81** C2
Tiree Av *RNFRW* PA4 ....**55** D3
Tiree Gdns *BSDN* G61 ....**13** D1
Tiree St *SPRGB/BLRNK* G21 ....**67** D1
Tirry Av *RNFRW* PA4 ....**57** C1
Titwood Rd *PLKSD/SHW* G41 ....**104** B1
Tiverton Av *CAR/SHTL* G32 ....**94** B4
Tobago Pl *DMNK/BRGTN* G40 ....**9** F5
Tobago St *DMNK/BRGTN* G40 ....**9** E5
Tobermory Rd *RUTH* G73 ....**131** C4
Todd St *DEN/PKHD* G31 ....**67** D4
Tofthill Av *BSHPBGS* G64 ....**31** D1
Tofthill Gdns *BSHPBGS* G64 ....**31** C1
Tollcross Park Gdns *CAR/SHTL* G32 ....**92** A4
Tollcross Park Gv *CAR/SHTL* G32 ....**92** B4
Tollcross Park Vw *CAR/SHTL* G32 ....**92** B4
Tollcross Rd *CAR/SHTL* G32 ....**93** D4
DEN/PKHD G31 ....**91** D2
Toll La *GOV/IBX* G51 ....**86** A1
Tolsta St *SMSTN* G23 ....**28** A2
Tontine La *CGLE* G1 ....**8** B3
Tontine Pl *RUTH* G73 ....**131** D3
Torbreck St *CARD/HILL/MSPK* G52 ....**83** D2
Torburn Av *GIF/THBK* G46 ....**124** A3
Torgyle St *SMSTN* G23 ....**27** D2
Tormore St *GOV/IBX* G51 ....**82** B1
Tormusk Dr *CSMK* G45 ....**129** D3
Tormusk Gdns *CSMK* G45 ....**129** D3
Tormusk Gv *CSMK* G45 ....**129** D3
Tormusk Rd *CSMK* G45 ....**129** D4
Torness St *PTCK* G11 ....**61** D1
Torogay Pl *PPK/MIL* G22 ....**31** C3
Torogay St *PPK/MIL* G22 ....**30** A4
Torogay Ter *PPK/MIL* G22 ....**30** A3
Torphin Crs *CAR/SHTL* G32 ....**69** D4
Torphin Wk *CAR/SHTL* G32 ....**70** A4
Torrance St *SPRGB/BLRNK* G21 ....**46** A3
Torran Rd *STPS/GTHM/RID* G33 ....**72** A4
Torridon Av *PLKSD/SHW* G41 ....**84** B4
Torrington Av *GIF/THBK* G46 ....**136** A3
Torrington Crs *CAR/SHTL* G32 ....**94** B4
Torrin Rd *SMSTN* G23 ....**27** D2
Torrisdale St *GVH/MTFL* G42 ....**106** A1
Torr Rd *BSHPBGS* G64 ....**33** D2
Torr St *PPK/MIL* G22 ....**45** C3
Torryburn Rd *SPRGB/BLRNK* G21 ....**47** D3
Toryglen Rd *RUTH* G73 ....**108** B3
Toryglen St *GBLS* G5 ....**108** B1
Toward Rd *STPS/GTHM/RID* G33 ....**70** B4
Tower Av *BRHD/NEIL* G78 ....**119** C1
Tower Crs *RNFRW* PA4 ....**55** C1
Tower Dr *RNFRW* PA4 ....**55** C1
Towerhill Rd *KNTSWD* G13 ....**24** A2
Tower Pl *MLNGV* G62 ....**11** C1
Towerside Crs *PLK/PH/NH* G53 ....**100** B1
Towerside Rd *PLK/PH/NH* G53 ....**100** B1
Tower St *PLKSD/SHW* G41 ....**86** A2
Tower Ter *PSLY* PA1 ....**76** B3
Townhead Rd *CTBR* ML5 ....**75** D2
Townhead Ter *PSLY* PA1 ....**76** B3
Townmill Rd *DEN/PKHD* G31 ....**66** B3
Townsend St *COWCAD* G4 ....**3** F2
Tradeston St *GBLS* G5 ....**6** C5
Trafalgar St *DMNK/BRGTN* G40 ....**89** D4
Trainard Av *CAR/SHTL* G32 ....**92** B3
Tranent Pl *STPS/GTHM/RID* G33 ....**68** B3
Traquair Dr *CARD/HILL/MSPK* G52 ....**81** D3
Treeburn Av *GIF/THBK* G46 ....**124** A4
Treemain Rd *GIF/THBK* G46 ....**136** A3
Trees Park Av *BRHD/NEIL* G78 ....**118** A1
Trefoil Av *PLKSD/SHW* G41 ....**105** C3
Tresta Rd *SMSTN* G23 ....**28** B3
Trinity Av *CARD/HILL/MSPK* G52 ....**82** A3
Trinity Dr *BLTYR/CAMB* G72 ....**133** D4
Trinley Rd *KNTSWD* G13 ....**24** B2
Trondra Pth *ESTRH* G34 ....**72** A3
Trondra Pl *ESTRH* G34 ....**72** A3
Trongate *CGLE* G1 ....**8** B3
Troon St *DMNK/BRGTN* G40 ....**90** B4
Trossachs Ct *MRYH/FIRH* G20 ....**43** D4
Trossachs St *MRYH/FIRH* G20 ....**43** D4
Truce Rd *KNTSWD* G13 ....**23** D3
Tudor La South *SCOT* G14 ....**39** D4
Tudor Rd *SCOT* G14 ....**39** D4
Tudor St *BAIL/MDB/MHD* G69 ....**95** D4
Tullis St *DMNK/BRGTN* G40 ....**89** C3
Tulloch-Ard Pl *RUTH* G73 ....**131** C4
Tulloch St *LNPK/KPK* G44 ....**126** B1
Tummel St *STPS/GTHM/RID* G33 ....**68** B2
Tunnel St *KVGV* G3 ....**62** B4
Turnberry Av *KVD/HLHD* G12 ....**41** C4
Turnberry Dr *RUTH* G73 ....**129** C3
Turnberry Pl *RUTH* G73 ....**129** C2
Turnberry Rd *PTCK* G11 ....**40** B4
Turnbull St *CGLE* G1 ....**8** B4
Turner Rd *PSLYN/LNWD* PA3 ....**54** A3
Turnlaw St *GBLS* G5 ....**88** B3
Turret Crs *KNTSWD* G13 ....**24** A3
Turret Rd *KNTSWD* G13 ....**24** A3
Turriff St *GBLS* G5 ....**87** D3
Tweed Crs *RNFRW* PA4 ....**56** B1
STPS/GTHM/RID G33 ....**68** A2
Tweed Dr *BSDN* G61 ....**14** B4
Tweedsmuir *BSHPBGS* G64 ....**33** C1
Tweedsmuir Rd *CARD/HILL/MSPK* G52 ....**81** D3
Tweedvale Av *SCOT* G14 ....**36** B1
Tweedvale Pl *SCOT* G14 ....**36** B1
Twinlaw St *ESTRH* G34 ....**74** A2
Tylney Rd *PSLY* PA1 ....**79** D2
Tyndrum Rd *BSDN* G61 ....**16** B2
Tyndrum St *COWCAD* G4 ....**3** F2
Tynecastle Crs *CAR/SHTL* G32 ....**70** A4
Tynecastle Pl *CAR/SHTL* G32 ....**70** A4
Tynecastle St *CAR/SHTL* G32 ....**70** A4
Tynwald Av *RUTH* G73 ....**130** B3

U

Uig Pl *STPS/GTHM/RID* G33 ....95 C1
Uist Crs *STPS/GTHM/RID* G33 ....51 D3
Uist St *GOV/IBX* G51 ....60 A4
Ulva St *CARD/HILL/MSPK* G52 ....83 D2
Underwood La *PSLY* PA1 ....76 B2
Underwood Rd *PSLY* PA1 ....76 A2
RUTH G73 ....130 B1
Underwood St *PLKSD/SHW* G41 ....105 D3
Union Pl *CGLE* G1 ....7 E1
Union St *CGLE* G1 ....7 E2
Unity Pl *COWCAD* G4 ....2 C1
University Av *KVD/HLHD* G12 ....62 A1
University Gdns *KVD/HLHD* G12 ....62 A1
University Pl *KVD/HLHD* G12 ....62 A1
PTCK G11 ....61 D1
Unsted Pl *PSLY* PA1 ....78 A3
Uphall Pl *STPS/GTHM/RID* G33 ....68 B3
Upland La *SCOT* G14 ....38 B3
Upland Rd *SCOT* G14 ....38 B3
Upper Bourtree Ct *RUTH* G73 ....130 B3
Upper Bourtree Dr *RUTH* G73 ....130 A3
Upper Glenburn Rd *BSDN* G61 ....14 B2
Urquhart Crs *RNFRW* PA4 ....55 D1
Urrdale Rd *PLKSD/SHW* G41 ....84 B2
Usmore Pl *STPS/GTHM/RID* G33 ....95 C2

V

Vaila St *SMSTN* G23 ....28 B4
Valeview Ter *GVH/MTFL* G42 ....106 B3
Vallay St *PPK/MIL* G22 ....30 B3
Valleyfield St *SPRGB/BLRNK* G21 ....45 D4
Valley Vw *BLTYR/CAMB* G72 ....133 D1
Vancouver La *SCOT* G14 ....38 B3
Vancouver Rd *SCOT* G14 ....38 B4
Vanguard St *CLYDBK* G81 ....21 D1
Vardar Av *CRMNK/CLK/EAG* G76 ....137 C3
Varna La *SCOT* G14 ....39 D4
Varna Rd *SCOT* G14 ....39 D3
Vassart Pl *MRYH/FIRH* G20 ....43 C2
Vennacher Rd *RNFRW* PA4 ....34 B3
Vennard Gdns *PLKSD/SHW* G41 ....106 A1
Vermont Av *RUTH* G73 ....109 D4
Vermont St *PLKSD/SHW* G41 ....86 A2
Verona Av *SCOT* G14 ....38 B3
Verona Gdns *SCOT* G14 ....38 B3
Verona La *SCOT* G14 ....38 B3
Vesalius St *CAR/SHTL* G32 ....93 C2
Vicarfield St *GOV/IBX* G51 ....61 C4
Vicarland Rd *BLTYR/CAMB* G72 ....132 B2
Vicars Wk *BLTYR/CAMB* G72 ....133 C2
Victoria Av *BRHD/NEIL* G78 ....118 A1
Victoria Br *GBLS* G5 ....7 F4
Victoria Circ *KVD/HLHD* G12 ....41 D4
Victoria Crs *BRHD/NEIL* G78 ....118 A1
Victoria Crescent La *KVD/HLHD* G12 ....41 D4
Victoria Crescent Pl *KVD/HLHD* G12 ....41 D4
Victoria Crescent Rd *KVD/HLHD* G12 ....41 D4
Victoria Dr *BRHD/NEIL* G78 ....118 A1
Victoria Dr East *RNFRW* PA4 ....55 D1
Victoria Dr West *RNFRW* PA4 ....35 C4
Victoria Gdns *BRHD/NEIL* G78 ....118 A1
Victoria Gv *BRHD/NEIL* G78 ....118 A1
Victoria Park Cnr *SCOT* G14 ....39 C3
Victoria Park Dr North *SCOT* G14 ....39 D4
Victoria Park Dr South *SCOT* G14 ....39 C4
Victoria Park Gdns North *PTCK* G11 ....40 A4
Victoria Park Gdns South *PTCK* G11 ....40 A4
Victoria Park La South *SCOT* G14 ....39 C4
Victoria Park St *SCOT* G14 ....39 C4
Victoria Pl *BRHD/NEIL* G78 ....118 A1
MLNGV G62 ....11 C2
Victoria Rd *BRHD/NEIL* G78 ....118 A1
GVH/MTFL G42 ....87 C4
RUTH G73 ....130 A1
STPS/GTHM/RID G33 ....51 C2
Victoria St *RUTH* G73 ....109 D3
Viewbank *GIF/THBK* G46 ....123 D4
Viewfield Av *BAIL/MDB/MHD* G69 ....95 D2
BSHPBGS G64 ....31 C3
Viewfield Dr *BAIL/MDB/MHD* G69 ....95 C2
Viewfield La *KVD/HLHD* G12 ....62 B1
Viewfield Rd *BSHPBGS* G64 ....31 C3
Viewmount Dr *MRYH/FIRH* G20 ....27 D4
Viewpark Av *DEN/PKHD* G31 ....67 C3
Viewpark Dr *RUTH* G73 ....130 A1
Viewpark Gdns *RNFRW* PA4 ....55 C1
Viewpoint Rd *SPRGB/BLRNK* G21 ....46 A1
Viking Wy *GIF/THBK* G46 ....123 C2
Villafield Av *BSHPBGS* G64 ....19 C4
Villafield Dr *BSHPBGS* G64 ....19 C4
Village Rd *BLTYR/CAMB* G72 ....134 B2
Vine St *PTCK* G11 ....61 C1
Vinicombe La *KVD/HLHD* G12 ....42 A4
Vinicombe St *KVD/HLHD* G12 ....42 A4
Vintner St *COWCAD* G4 ....64 B1
Violet St *PSLY* PA1 ....78 A3
Virginia Ct *CGLE* G1 ....7 F2
Virginia Gdns *MLNGV* G62 ....11 D3
Virginia Pl *CGLE* G1 ....8 A2
Virginia St *CGLE* G1 ....8 A2
Viscount Av *RNFRW* PA4 ....55 D2
Vivian Av *MLNGV* G62 ....10 A2
Voil Dr *LNPK/KPK* G44 ....126 B3
Vorlich Ct *BRHD/NEIL* G78 ....118 B4
Vulcan St *SPRGB/BLRNK* G21 ....45 D3

W

Waddell St *GBLS* G5 ....88 B3
Waldemar Rd *KNTSWD* G13 ....24 A4
Waldo St *KNTSWD* G13 ....25 D4
Walkerburn Rd *CARD/HILL/MSPK* G52 ....81 D3
Walker Ct *PTCK* G11 ....61 C2
Walker St *PSLY* PA1 ....76 B3
PTCK G11 ....61 C2
Walkinshaw St *DMNK/BRGTN* G40 ....90 A3
Wallace Ga *BSHPBGS* G64 ....33 D3
Wallace Rd *RNFRW* PA4 ....54 B2
Wallace St *CLYDBK* G81 ....20 B3
GBLS G5 ....6 C5
PSLYN/LNWD PA3 ....77 C1
RUTH G73 ....109 D4
Wallacewell Crs *SPRGB/BLRNK* G21 ....47 C2
Wallacewell Pl *SPRGB/BLRNK* G21 ....47 C2
Wallacewell Qd *SPRGB/BLRNK* G21 ....47 D1
Wallacewell Rd *SPRGB/BLRNK* G21 ....47 D1
Wallneuk *PSLY* PA1 ....77 D2
Wallneuk Rd *PSLYN/LNWD* PA3 ....77 D2
Walls St *CGLE* G1 ....8 B2
Walmer Crs *GOV/IBX* G51 ....85 C2
Walnut Crs *PPK/MIL* G22 ....45 C2
Walnut Ga *BLTYR/CAMB* G72 ....135 C3
Walnut Rd *PPK/MIL* G22 ....44 B2
Walter St *DEN/PKHD* G31 ....67 C4
Walton St *BRHD/NEIL* G78 ....118 B2
PLKSD/SHW G41 ....105 D3
Wamba Av *KNTSWD* G13 ....25 C3
Wandilla Av *CLYDBK* G81 ....21 D1
Wanlock St *GOV/IBX* G51 ....60 B2
Warden Rd *KNTSWD* G13 ....24 B4
Wardhill Rd *SPRGB/BLRNK* G21 ....47 C2
Wardie Pl *STPS/GTHM/RID* G33 ....72 A4
Wardie Rd *BAIL/MDB/MHD* G69 ....72 B4
Wardlaw Av *RUTH* G73 ....110 A4
Wardlaw Dr *RUTH* G73 ....110 A3
Wardlaw Rd *BSDN* G61 ....25 D2
Wardrop St *GOV/IBX* G51 ....60 B3
PSLY PA1 ....77 C3
Ware Rd *STPS/GTHM/RID* G33 ....72 A4
Warilda Av *CLYDBK* G81 ....21 C1
Warnock St *COWCAD* G4 ....5 E5
Warren St *GVH/MTFL* G42 ....107 C2
Warriston Crs *STPS/GTHM/RID* G33 ....68 B3
Warriston Pl *CAR/SHTL* G32 ....70 A4
Warriston St *STPS/GTHM/RID* G33 ....68 A3
Warroch St *KVGV* G3 ....6 A2
Washington Rd *PSLYN/LNWD* PA3 ....54 A3
Washington St *KVGV* G3 ....6 B3
Waterfoot Av *PLK/PH/NH* G53 ....101 D3
Waterfoot Ter *PLK/PH/NH* G53 ....101 D3
Waterford Rd *GIF/THBK* G46 ....124 A4
Waterhaughs Gdns
STPS/GTHM/RID G33 ....33 D4
Waterhaughs Gv *SPRGB/BLRNK* G21 ....33 D4

Waterloo La *CGLW* G2 ....7 D1
Waterloo St *CGLW* G2 ....6 C1
Water Rd *BRHD/NEIL* G78 ....118 B2
Water Rw *GOV/IBX* G51 ....60 B3
Waterside St *GBLS* G5 ....88 B3
Watling St *UD/BTH/TAN* G71 ....117 D2
Watson Av *RUTH* G73 ....109 C4
Watson St *CGLE* G1 ....8 B3
Watt Low Av *RUTH* G73 ....129 D1
Watt Rd *CARD/HILL/MSPK* G52 ....57 D4
Watt St *GBLS* G5 ....86 B2
Waukglen Crs *PLK/PH/NH* G53 ....121 D4
Waukglen Dr *PLK/PH/NH* G53 ....121 C4
Waukglen Gdns *PLK/PH/NH* G53 ....121 C4
Waukglen Pth *PLK/PH/NH* G53 ....121 C4
Waukglen Pl *PLK/PH/NH* G53 ....121 C4
Waukglen Rd *PLK/PH/NH* G53 ....121 C4
Waulkmill Av *BRHD/NEIL* G78 ....118 B1
Waulkmill St *GIF/THBK* G46 ....122 B3
Waulkmill Wy *BRHD/NEIL* G78 ....119 C1
Waverley Dr *RUTH* G73 ....110 B4
Waverley Gdns *PLKSD/SHW* G41 ....105 D2
Waverley St *PLKSD/SHW* G41 ....105 D2
Weardale La *STPS/GTHM/RID* G33 ....70 B3
Weardale St *STPS/GTHM/RID* G33 ....70 B3
Weaver St *COWCAD* G4 ....8 C1
Weaver Ter *PSLYS* PA2 ....78 A4
Webster St *DMNK/BRGTN* G40 ....90 A4
KNTSWD G13 ....22 A3
Wedderlea Dr *CARD/HILL/MSPK* G52 ....81 D2
Weensmoor Rd *PLK/PH/NH* G53 ....120 B2
Weighhouse Cl *PSLY* PA1 ....77 C3
Weir Av *BRHD/NEIL* G78 ....118 B3
Weir St *PSLY* PA1 ....77 C2
Weirwood Av *BAIL/MDB/MHD* G69 ....95 D3
Weirwood Gdns *BAIL/MDB/MHD* G69 ....95 D2
Welbeck Rd *PLK/PH/NH* G53 ....121 C2
Welfare Av *BLTYR/CAMB* G72 ....134 A3
Wellcroft Pl *GBLS* G5 ....87 D3
Wellfield Av *GIF/THBK* G46 ....124 A4
Wellfield St *SPRGB/BLRNK* G21 ....46 A3
Well Gn *PLKSW/MSWD* G43 ....104 B3
Wellhouse Crs *STPS/GTHM/RID* G33 ....71 D4
Wellhouse Gdns *STPS/GTHM/RID* G33 ....72 A4
Wellhouse Rd *STPS/GTHM/RID* G33 ....72 A3
Wellington La *CGLW* G2 ....6 C1
Wellington Rd *BSHPBGS* G64 ....19 D3
Wellington St *CGLW* G2 ....7 D1
PSLYN/LNWD PA3 ....76 B2
Wellmeadow Rd *PLKSW/MSWD* G43 ....123 D1
Wellmeadow St *PSLY* PA1 ....76 B3
Wellpark St *COWCAD* G4 ....9 E2
Wellshot Dr *BLTYR/CAMB* G72 ....132 A2
Wellshot Rd *CAR/SHTL* G32 ....92 B3
Wellside Dr *BLTYR/CAMB* G72 ....133 D3
Well St *PSLY* PA1 ....76 A2
Wemyss Gdns *BAIL/MDB/MHD* G69 ....96 A4
Wentworth Dr *SMSTN* G23 ....28 A2
West Av *RNFRW* PA4 ....35 D4
STPS/GTHM/RID G33 ....51 C2
Westbank La *KVD/HLHD* G12 ....62 B1
Westbank Qd *KVD/HLHD* G12 ....62 B1
Westbourne Crs *BSDN* G61 ....14 A2
Westbourne Dr *BSDN* G61 ....14 A2
Westbourne Gardens La
KVD/HLHD G12 ....41 C3
Westbourne Gdns South
KVD/HLHD G12 ....41 D3
Westbourne Gdns West
KVD/HLHD G12 ....41 D3
Westbourne Rd *KVD/HLHD* G12 ....41 C3
Westbourne Terrace La North
KVD/HLHD G12 ....41 C3
Westbourne Terrace La South
KVD/HLHD G12 ....41 C3
West Brae *PSLY* PA1 ....76 B3
Westbrae Dr *KNTSWD* G13 ....39 D3
Westburn Av *BLTYR/CAMB* G72 ....134 A1
Westburn Crs *RUTH* G73 ....109 C4
Westburn Farm Rd *BLTYR/CAMB* G72 ....133 C1
Westburn Rd *BLTYR/CAMB* G72 ....133 C1
West Campbell St *CGLW* G2 ....6 C2
Westcastle Ct *CSMK* G45 ....128 A4
Westcastle Crs *CSMK* G45 ....128 A4
Westcastle Gdns *CSMK* G45 ....128 A4
Westcastle Gv *CSMK* G45 ....128 A4
West Chapelton Av *BSDN* G61 ....15 D3
West Chapelton Crs *BSDN* G61 ....15 D3
West Chapelton Dr *BSDN* G61 ....15 D3
Westclyffe St *PLKSD/SHW* G41 ....105 D2
West Coats Rd *BLTYR/CAMB* G72 ....132 A3
Westend Park St *COWCAD* G4 ....2 A2
Westerburn St *CAR/SHTL* G32 ....92 B1
Wester Cleddens Rd *BSHPBGS* G64 ....32 A1
Wester Common Dr *PPK/MIL* G22 ....43 D3
Wester Common Rd *PPK/MIL* G22 ....43 D3
Westercraigs *DEN/PKHD* G31 ....66 A4
Westerhill Rd *BSHPBGS* G64 ....19 D3
Westerhouse Rd *ESTRH* G34 ....72 B3
Westerkirk Dr *SMSTN* G23 ....28 A2
Westerlands *KVD/HLHD* G12 ....40 A1
Western Av *RUTH* G73 ....109 C3
Western Rd *BLTYR/CAMB* G72 ....132 A4
Wester Rd *CAR/SHTL* G32 ....94 B4
Westerton Av *KNTSWD* G13 ....25 D3
Westfield Av *RUTH* G73 ....109 C4
Westfield Crs *BSDN* G61 ....25 C1
Westfield Dr *BSDN* G61 ....25 C1
CARD/HILL/MSPK G52 ....81 C2
Westfield Rd *GIF/THBK* G46 ....136 A1
Westfields *BSHPBGS* G64 ....18 A4
West George La *CGLW* G2 ....2 C5
West George St *CGLE* G1 ....7 F1
CGLW G2 ....2 B5
West Graham St *COWCAD* G4 ....2 C3
West Greenhill Pl *KVGV* G3 ....62 B3
Westhorn Dr *CAR/SHTL* G32 ....112 B2
Westhouse Av *RUTH* G73 ....108 B4
Westhouse Gdns *RUTH* G73 ....108 B4
Westland Dr *SCOT* G14 ....39 C4
West Lodge Rd *RNFRW* PA4 ....35 C3
Westmoreland St *GVH/MTFL* G42 ....106 B1
Westmuir Pl *RUTH* G73 ....108 B3
Westmuir St *DEN/PKHD* G31 ....91 D2
West Nile St *CGLE* G1 ....7 E1
West Prince's La *COWCAD* G4 ....62 B1
West Prince's St *COWCAD* G4 ....2 A1
Westray Circ *PPK/MIL* G22 ....44 B1
Westray Pl *PPK/MIL* G22 ....30 B4
Westray Sq *PPK/MIL* G22 ....30 A4
Westray St *PPK/MIL* G22 ....30 A4
West Regent La *CGLW* G2 ....3 D5
West Regent St *CGLW* G2 ....2 C4
West St *CLYDBK* G81 ....22 A3
GBLS G5 ....6 C5
PSLY PA1 ....76 A3
West Whitby St *DEN/PKHD* G31 ....91 C3
Westwood Av *GIF/THBK* G46 ....124 A4
Westwood Qd *CLYDBK* G81 ....21 D2
Westwood Rd *PLKSW/MSWD* G43 ....124 A1
Weymouth Dr *KVD/HLHD* G12 ....40 B1
Whamflet Av *BAIL/MDB/MHD* G69 ....73 D4
Wheatfield Rd *BSDN* G61 ....14 B4
Wheatley Ct *CAR/SHTL* G32 ....93 C2
Wheatley Dr *CAR/SHTL* G32 ....93 C2
Wheatley Loan *BSHPBGS* G64 ....33 C3
Wheatley Pl *CAR/SHTL* G32 ....93 C2
Whinfield Rd *PLK/PH/NH* G53 ....120 B3
Whinhill Rd *PLK/PH/NH* G53 ....81 C4
Whins Rd *PLKSD/SHW* G41 ....104 B2
Whirlow Gdns *BAIL/MDB/MHD* G69 ....96 A2
Whirlow Rd *BAIL/MDB/MHD* G69 ....96 A2
Whistlefield Ct *BSDN* G61 ....15 C4
Whitacres Rd *PLK/PH/NH* G53 ....120 A3
Whitburn St *CAR/SHTL* G32 ....69 C4
White Cart Rd *PSLYN/LNWD* PA3 ....53 D3
Whitecraigs Pl *SMSTN* G23 ....28 A3
Whitecrook St *CLYDBK* G81 ....21 C3
Whitefield Av *BLTYR/CAMB* G72 ....132 B3
Whitefield Rd *GOV/IBX* G51 ....85 C1
Whitehall St *KVGV* G3 ....6 A2
Whitehaugh Av *PSLY* PA1 ....78 B2
Whitehaugh Crs *PLK/PH/NH* G53 ....120 B3
Whitehaugh Dr *PSLY* PA1 ....78 B2
Whitehaugh Rd *PLK/PH/NH* G53 ....120 B3
Whitehill Av *STPS/GTHM/RID* G33 ....51 C1
Whitehill Farm Rd
STPS/GTHM/RID G33 ....51 C1
Whitehill Gdns *DEN/PKHD* G31 ....66 B4
Whitehill Rd *BSDN* G61 ....14 B3
Whitehill St *DEN/PKHD* G31 ....66 B4
Whitehill Street La *DEN/PKHD* G31 ....66 B4
Whitehurst *BSDN* G61 ....14 A1
Whitekirk Pl *DRUM* G15 ....23 C1
Whitelaw St *MRYH/FIRH* G20 ....27 C4
Whitemoss Av *LNPK/KPK* G44 ....126 A3
White St *CLYDBK* G81 ....21 D4
PTCK G11 ....61 C1
Whitevale St *DEN/PKHD* G31 ....66 B4
Whithope Rd *PLK/PH/NH* G53 ....120 A2

Whitlawburn Av *BLTYR/CAMB* G72 ....**131** D3
Whitlawburn Rd *BLTYR/CAMB* G72........**131** D3
Whitlawburn Ter *BLTYR/CAMB* G72 ......**131** D3
Whitriggs Rd *PLK/PH/NH* G53 ....**120** A3
Whitslade Pl *ESTRH* G34 ....**72** B2
Whitslade St *ESTRH* G34 ....**72** B2
Whittingehame Dr *KVD/HLHD* G12..........**40** A2
Whittingehame La *KNTSWD* G13..............**40** A2
Whittlemuir Av *LNPK/KPK* G44 ....**126** A3
Whitton Dr *GIF/THBK* G46..........................**125** C3
Whitton St *MRYH/FIRH* G20 ....**27** C3
Whitworth Dr *CLYDBK* G81..........................**20** A1
MRYH/FIRH G20 ....**43** D1
Whitworth Gdns *MRYH/FIRH* G20...........**43** D1
Whyte Av *BLTYR/CAMB* G72 ....**131** D1
The Wickets *PSLY* PA1 ....**78** A4
Wilfred Av *KNTSWD* G13 ....**24** B4
Williamsburgh Ter *PSLY* PA1 ....**78** A2
Williamson St *DMNK/BRGTN* G40 ....**91** C3
William St *KVGV* G3 ....**2** A5
PSLY PA1 ....**76** A2
William Ure Pl *BSHPBGS* G64 ....**19** D2
Willock Pl *MRYH/FIRH* G20 ....**28** A4
Willoughby Dr *KNTSWD* G13 ....**40** A1
Willoughby La *KNTSWD* G13........................**40** A1
Willow Av *BSHPBGS* G64 ....**32** A3
Willowbank Crs *KVGV* G3 ....**63** C1
Willowbank St *KVGV* G3 ....**63** C2
Willowdale Crs *BAIL/MDB/MHD* G69 ......**96** A3
Willowdale Gdns *BAIL/MDB/MHD* G69.....**96** A3
Willowford Rd *PLK/PH/NH* G53..............**120** A3
Willow La *CAR/SHTL* G32.........................**113** C1
Willow St *KNTSWD* G13 ....**25** D4
Wilmot Rd *KNTSWD* G13 ....**39** C1
Wilson St *CGLE* G1 ....**8** A2
RNFRW PA4...**36** A3
Wiltonburn Rd *PLK/PH/NH* G53 ....**120** B3
Wilton Crescent La *MRYH/FIRH* G20........**43** C4
Wilton Dr *MRYH/FIRH* G20 ....**43** C4
Wilton St *MRYH/FIRH* G20 ....**42** B4
Wilverton Rd *KNTSWD* G13.........................**25** C3
Winchester Dr *KVD/HLHD* G12.....................**41** C1
Windhill Crs *PLKSW/MSWD* G43.............**124** A2
Windhill Rd *PLKSW/MSWD* G43 ....**124** A2
Windlaw Gdns *LNPK/KPK* G44 ....**126** A3
Windlaw Park Gdns *GIF/THBK* G46 ....**126** A3
Windsor Crs *PSLY* PA1 ....**78** A1
Windsor Rd *RNFRW* PA4 ....**55** D1
Windsor St *MRYH/FIRH* G20.........................**63** D1
Windsor Ter *MRYH/FIRH* G20.......................**63** D1
Windyedge Crs *KNTSWD* G13.......................**38** B2
Windyedge Pl *KNTSWD* G13.........................**38** B2
Winfield Av *BLTYR/CAMB* G72 ....**111** D4
Winifred St *STPS/GTHM/RID* G33 ....**48** A3
Winning Rw *DEN/PKHD* G31 ....**91** D2
Winton Av *GIF/THBK* G46 ....**137** C1
Winton Dr *KVD/HLHD* G12 ....**41** D2
Winton La *KVD/HLHD* G12 ....**41** D2
Wirran Pl *KNTSWD* G13 ....**22** A3
Wishart St *DEN/PKHD* G31 ....**5** E5
Wisner Ct *GIF/THBK* G46 ....**123** C3
Wiston St *BLTYR/CAMB* G72 ....**134** A2
Woddrop St *DMNK/BRGTN* G40..............**110** A1
Wolseley St *GBLS* G5 ....**88** B4
Woodburn Rd *PLKSW/MSWD* G43..........**125** C2
Woodburn Wy *MLNGV* G62..........................**10** B2
Woodcroft Av *PTCK* G11.................................**40** A3
Woodend Ct *CAR/SHTL* G32 ....**114** B1
Woodend Dr *KNTSWD* G13 ....**39** D2
PSLY PA1 ....**79** D3
Woodend Gdns *CAR/SHTL* G32 ....**114** A1
Woodend La *KNTSWD* G13 ....**39** D2
Woodend Rd *CAR/SHTL* G32......................**114** A1
RUTH G73 ....**130** A3
Wood Farm Rd *GIF/THBK* G46 ....**136** A2
Woodfield Av *BSHPBGS* G64.........................**32** B3
Woodfoot Pl *PLK/PH/NH* G53 ....**120** B3
Woodfoot Qd *PLK/PH/NH* G53 ....**121** C3
Woodfoot Rd *PLK/PH/NH* G53 ....**120** B3
Woodford St *PLKSW/MSWD* G43............**105** C4
Woodgreen Av *LNPK/KPK* G44.................**127** C1
Woodhall St *DMNK/BRGTN* G40...............**109** D1
Woodhead Rd *PLK/PH/NH* G53 ....**120** A2
Woodhill Rd *BSHPBGS* G64..........................**33** C3
SPRGB/BLRNK G21..**47** C1
Woodholm Av *LNPK/KPK* G44 ....**127** D1
Woodhouse St *KNTSWD* G13 ....**25** C4
Woodland Crs *BLTYR/CAMB* G72 ....**133** C3
Woodlands Crs *GIF/THBK* G46 ....**123** C4
Woodlands Dr *COWCAD* G4 ....**63** C1
Woodlands Ga *GIF/THBK* G46....................**123** C4
KVGV G3 ....**63** C2
Woodlands Rd *KVGV* G3 ....**63** C1
Woodlands St *MLNGV* G62 ....**10** B1
Woodlands Ter *KVGV* G3 ....**62** B2
Woodlea Dr *GIF/THBK* G46 ....**125** C3
Woodlinn Av *LNPK/KPK* G44......................**127** C2
Woodneuk Rd *PLK/PH/NH* G53 ....**121** C3
Wood Qd *CLYDBK* G81 ....**22** A3
Woodrow Circ *PLKSD/SHW* G41.................**85** D3
Woodrow Pl *PLKSD/SHW* G41 ....**85** C3
Woodrow Rd *PLKSD/SHW* G41 ....**85** D3
Woodside Av *GIF/THBK* G46.......................**123** D4
RUTH G73 ....**110** B4
Woodside Crs *BRHD/NEIL* G78 ....**119** C3
KVGV G3..**2** A3
PSLY PA1 ....**76** A3
Woodside Gdns *CRMNK/CLK/EAG* G76 ..**137** D4
Woodside Pl *KVGV* G3 ....**63** C2
Woodside Place La *KVGV* G3 ....**63** C2
Woodside Ter *KVGV* G3 ....**63** C2
Woodside Terrace La *KVGV* G3 ....**63** C2
Woodside Gv *RUTH* G73 ....**110** B4
Woodstock Av *PLKSD/SHW* G41 ....**105** C3
Wood St *DEN/PKHD* G31 ....**67** C3
PSLYS PA2 ....**78** B4
Woodvale Av *BSDN* G61 ....**26** B1
GIF/THBK G46 ....**136** B3
Woodville Pk *GOV/IBX* G51..........................**84** B1
Woodville St *GOV/IBX* G51 ....**84** B1
Wraes Av *BRHD/NEIL* G78 ....**119** C1
Wright St *RNFRW* PA4 ....**54** A2
Wykeham Pl *KNTSWD* G13 ....**38** B1
Wykeham Rd *KNTSWD* G13 ....**38** B1
Wyndford Dr *MRYH/FIRH* G20......................**42** A2
Wyndford Pl *MRYH/FIRH* G20 ....**42** A2
Wyndford Rd *MRYH/FIRH* G20 ....**41** D2
Wyndham Ct *KVD/HLHD* G12 ....**42** A3
Wyndham St *KVD/HLHD* G12 ....**42** A3
Wyper Pl *DMNK/BRGTN* G40 ....**90** A1
Wyvil Av *KNTSWD* G13.................................**25** C2
Wyvis Av *KNTSWD* G13 ....**22** A3
Wyvis Pl *KNTSWD* G13 ....**22** B3
Wyvis Qd *KNTSWD* G13 ....**22** B3

Y

Yair Dr *CARD/HILL/MSPK* G52.....................**81** C1
Yarrow Gdns *MRYH/FIRH* G20 ....**43** C4
Yarrow Gardens La *MRYH/FIRH* G20 ......**43** C4
Yarrow Rd *BSHPBGS* G64 ....**19** C3
Yate St *DEN/PKHD* G31 ....**90** B2
Yetholm St *SCOT* G14 ....**36** B1
Yew Dr *SPRGB/BLRNK* G21 ....**46** B4
Yokerburn Pl *KNTSWD* G13...........................**22** A4
Yokerburn Ter *CLYDBK* G81 ....**21** D4
Yoker Ferry Rd *SCOT* G14..............................**36** B1
Yoker Mill Gdns *KNTSWD* G13 ....**22** A4
Yoker Mill Rd *KNTSWD* G13..........................**22** A4
York Dr *RUTH* G73 ....**131** C2
Yorkhill Pde *KVGV* G3 ....**61** D2
Yorkhill St *KVGV* G3 ....**62** A3
York St *CGLW* G2 ....**6** C2
CLYDBK G81...**21** D1
Young Ter *SPRGB/BLRNK* G21 ....**46** B3

Z

Zena Crs *STPS/GTHM/RID* G33 ....**47** D3
Zena Pl *STPS/GTHM/RID* G33 ....**48** A3
Zena St *STPS/GTHM/RID* G33 ....**48** A3
Zetland Rd *CARD/HILL/MSPK* G52 ....**57** C3

Abbey Mill Business Centre
PSLY PA1 ....77 D3
Abercorn Industrial Estate
PSLYN/LNWD PA3 ....53 D4
PSLYN/LNWD PA3 ....77 D1
Abercorn School
COWCAD G4 ....3 D1
Air Link Industrial Estate
PSLYN/LNWD PA3 ....53 D3
Aiton Primary School
BLTYR/CAMB G72 ....132 B1
Albert Primary School
SPRGB/BLRNK G21 ....46 A2
Alexandra Golf Club
DEN/PKHD G31 ....67 C3
Alexandra Parade Primary School
DEN/PKHD G31 ....66 B4
Allandar Sports Centre
BSDN G61 ....11 C4
All Saints Secondary School
SPRGB/BLRNK G21 ....47 D2
The Anderson Doe Podiatry Clinic
SCOT G14 ....40 A3
Anderson Primary School
KVGV G3 ....63 C3
Anderston Medical Centre
KVGV G3 ....62 B3
Annette Street Primary School
GVH/MTFL G42 ....106 B1
Annfield Medical Centre
DEN/PKHD G31 ....66 B4
Anniesland College
KVD/HLHD G12 ....40 B2
Anniesland College of Further Education
PTCK G11 ....60 A1
Anniesland Industrial Estate
KNTSWD G13 ....25 C3
Antonine Wall: Bearsden Bath-House
BSDN G61 ....15 D3
Arcadia Business Centre
CLYDBK G81 ....20 A2
Arches Theatre
CGLE G1 ....7 D3
Arden Primary School
GIF/THBK G46 ....122 A3
Ardoch Medical Centre
BLTYR/CAMB G72 ....132 A1
Argo Sports Centre
DRUM G15 ....12 A4
Argyle Indoor Market
CGLE G1 ....7 F2
Arkleston Primary School
RNFRW PA4 ....56 A2
Ashcraig School
STPS/GTHM/RID G33 ....50 A4
Ashfield Medical Practice
MLNGV G62 ....10 B2
Auchenback Primary School
BRHD/NEIL G78 ....119 C4
Auchinairn Primary School
BSHPBGS G64 ....32 B3
Auldhouse Retail Park
PLKSW/MSWD G43 ....124 B1
Baillieston FC
BAIL/MDB/MHD G69 ....97 C3
Baillieston Health Centre
BAIL/MDB/MHD G69 ....96 B3
Balmuildy Primary School
BSHPBGS G64 ....18 A4
Balornock Primary School
SPRGB/BLRNK G21 ....47 C3
Bankhead Primary School
KNTSWD G13 ....37 D1
RUTH G73 ....109 C4
Bannerman High School
BAIL/MDB/MHD G69 ....96 A3
Bargeddie Primary School
CTBR ML5 ....99 C1
Barlanark Primary School
STPS/GTHM/RID G33 ....95 C1
Barmulloch Primary School
SPRGB/BLRNK G21 ....47 D3
Barras Market
DMNK/BRGTN G40 ....9 D4
Barratt Trading Estate
COWCAD G4 ....3 D1
Barrhead Bowling Club
BRHD/NEIL G78 ....118 B2
Barrhead High School
BRHD/NEIL G78 ....119 C2
Barrhead Sports Centre
BRHD/NEIL G78 ....118 B2
Barrowfield Primary School
DMNK/BRGTN G40 ....90 B3
Battlefield Primary School
GVH/MTFL G42 ....106 A4
Bearsden Academy
BSDN G61 ....15 C1
Bearsden Golf Club
BSDN G61 ....14 A2
Bearsden Primary School
BSDN G61 ....15 C2
Bellahouston Academy
PLKSD/SHW G41 ....85 C2
Bellahouston Leisure Centre
CARD/HILL/MSPK G52 ....83 D3
Bellahouston Primary School
GOV/IBX G51 ....85 C1
Benburb FC
GOV/IBX G51 ....83 C1
Birkenshaw Industrial Estate
UD/BTH/TAN G71 ....117 D2
Bishopbriggs Golf Club
BSHPBGS G64 ....31 D1
Bishopbriggs High School
BSHPBGS G64 ....32 A2
Bishopbriggs Sports Centre
BSHPBGS G64 ....18 A3
Bishoploch Primary School
ESTRH G34 ....73 D2
Blackfriars Primary School
GBLS G5 ....88 A3
Blairbeth Golf Club
CSMK G45 ....129 D4
Blairdardie Primary School
DRUM G15 ....23 D2
Blairtummock Primary School
ESTRH G34 ....73 C3
Blawarthill Hospital
KNTSWD G13 ....37 D1
Blythswood Estate
RNFRW PA4 ....35 C3
Boclair Academy
BSDN G61 ....17 C3
Bonnyholm Primary School
PLK/PH/NH G53 ....81 C4
Bowling Alley
CLYDBK G81 ....21 C2
KVGV G3 ....63 C4
PSLYN/LNWD PA3 ....77 D1
Braehead Arena
RNFRW PA4 ....37 C3
Braehead Business Park
RNFRW PA4 ....37 C4
Braehead Retail Park
RNFRW PA4 ....58 A1
Braehead Shopping Centre
RNFRW PA4 ....37 D4
Braeside Primary School
CSMK G45 ....129 C3
Braidbar Primary School
GIF/THBK G46 ....125 C4
Braidcraft Medical Centre
PLK/PH/NH G53 ....101 D2
Braidfield High School
CLYDBK G81 ....21 C1
Bridgeton Business Centre
DMNK/BRGTN G40 ....9 F5
Bridgeton Health Centre
DMNK/BRGTN G40 ....9 F5
Broomhill Primary School
PTCK G11 ....40 A3
Broomlea School
PTCK G11 ....60 A1
Buchanan Bus Station
COWCAD G4 ....3 F4
Buchanan Galleries & Shopping Centre
CGLE G1 ....3 F5
Burgh Primary School
RUTH G73 ....109 D3
Burmah Doctors Surgery
PTCK G11 ....61 C1
Burnbrae Primary School
PLK/PH/NH G53 ....122 A2
Burnhill Sports Centre
RUTH G73 ....109 C3

Burnside Primary School
RUTH G73 ....130 A2
Burrell Collection
PLKSD/SHW G41 ....104 A2
Butterbiggins Medical Centre
GVH/MTFL G42 ....87 D4
Byres Road Market
PTCK G11 ....61 D1
Cadder Primary School
SMSTN G23 ....28 B4
Cairnbrook Industrial Estate
ESTRH G34 ....73 C3
Cairns Primary School
BLTYR/CAMB G72 ....133 D3
Calderbraes Golf Club
UD/BTH/TAN G71 ....116 B2
Caldercuilt Primary School
SMSTN G23 ....28 A2
Calderwood Lodge
Jewish Primary School
PLKSW/MSWD G43 ....125 D2
Calderwood Primary School
RUTH G73 ....130 B1
Caledonian University
CGLW G2 ....3 E4
Caledonia Primary School
BAIL/MDB/MHD G69 ....96 B4
Callander Street Clinic
MRYH/FIRH G20 ....43 D4
Cambuslang Avory Club
BLTYR/CAMB G72 ....132 B3
Cambuslang College
BLTYR/CAMB G72 ....133 C2
Cambuslang Golf Club
BLTYR/CAMB G72 ....113 C4
Cambuslang Rangers FC
BLTYR/CAMB G72 ....132 A1
Cambuslang Recreation Centre
BLTYR/CAMB G72 ....134 A2
Cambuslang RFC
BLTYR/CAMB G72 ....131 C2
Canniesburn Hospital
BSDN G61 ....25 C1
Cardonald Clinic
CARD/HILL/MSPK G52 ....82 A2
Cardonald College
CARD/HILL/MSPK G52 ....82 B4
Cardonald Primary School
CARD/HILL/MSPK G52 ....81 D3
Carlibar Primary School
BRHD/NEIL G78 ....118 B2
Carmichael Hall
GIF/THBK G46 ....136 B1
Carmyle Medical Centre
CAR/SHTL G32 ....113 C3
Carmyle Primary School
CAR/SHTL G32 ....113 D2
Carntyne Primary School
STPS/GTHM/RID G33 ....68 A3
Carnwadric Primary School
GIF/THBK G46 ....123 C3
Cartvale School
GOV/IBX G51 ....61 C4
Castlebank Industrial Estate
PTCK G11 ....60 B2
Castlehead High School
PSLYS PA2 ....76 B4
Castlehill Primary School
BSDN G61 ....13 D1
Castlemilk Health Centre
CSMK G45 ....128 B4
Castlemilk Pool
CSMK G45 ....128 B4
Castlemilk Sports Centre
CSMK G45 ....128 B4
Castleton Primary School
CSMK G45 ....127 D4
Cathcart Castle Golf Club
CRMNK/CLK/EAG G76 ....137 C4
Cathkin High School
BLTYR/CAMB G72 ....131 D3
Cathkin Primary School
RUTH G73 ....131 C4
Cawder Golf Club
BSHPBGS G64 ....18 B1
Celtic FC (Celtic Park)
DEN/PKHD G31 ....90 B2
Central College of Commerce
COWCAD G4 ....4 B5
Chapel Street Industrial Estate
MRYH/FIRH G20 ....42 B1
Charing Cross Clinic
KVGV G3 ....2 A3
The Charleston Surgery
PSLYS PA2 ....77 C4
Child Health Clinic
PLKSW/MSWD G43 ....104 B3
Chirnsyde Primary School
PPK/MIL G22 ....45 C1
City Chambers
CGLE G1 ....8 A1
City Halls
CGLE G1 ....8 B2
Cleveden Secondary School
KVD/HLHD G12 ....41 C2
MRYH/FIRH G20 ....42 B3
Clyde Auditorium
KVGV G3 ....62 A4
Clydebank Business Centre
CLYDBK G81 ....21 C3
Clydebank Town Hall
CLYDBK G81 ....20 A2
Clydebuilt
RNFRW PA4 ....37 D4
Clyde Industrial Estate
RUTH G73 ....111 C3
Clydesdale Cricket Club
PLKSD/SHW G41 ....105 C1
Clyde Tunnel
GOV/IBX G51 ....59 D2
Clydeway Business Centre
KVGV G3 ....62 B4
Coats Observatory
PSLY PA1 ....76 B2
College of Building & Printing
CGLE G1 ....4 A5
College of Food & Technology
CGLE G1 ....4 A5
Colquhoun Park Primary School
BSDN G61 ....14 A4
Commonhead Primary School
ESTRH G34 ....74 A3
Copeland Primary School
GOV/IBX G51 ....61 C4
Corpus Christi Primary School
KNTSWD G13 ....38 B1
Corus Hotel
CGLW G2 ....6 C2
Cotton Street Business Park
DMNK/BRGTN G40 ....109 D1
Cowglen Golf Club
PLKSW/MSWD G43 ....103 C4
Cowglen Hospital
PLK/PH/NH G53 ....102 A4
Craigdhu Primary School
MLNGV G62 ....10 A3
Craigholme School
PLKSD/SHW G41 ....85 C4
Craigton Crematorium
CARD/HILL/MSPK G52 ....82 B2
Craigton Primary School
CARD/HILL/MSPK G52 ....83 C2
Croftcroighn School
STPS/GTHM/RID G33 ....71 C2
Crookston Castle NTS
PLK/PH/NH G53 ....101 C1
Crowngate Business Centre
DMNK/BRGTN G40 ....89 D2
Crownpoint Sports Complex
DMNK/BRGTN G40 ....89 D1
Cunard Primary School
CLYDBK G81 ....21 C2
Cuthbertson Primary School
PLKSD/SHW G41 ....87 C4
Daily Record & Sunday Mail Offices
KVGV G3 ....63 C4
Dairsie House School
PLKSW/MSWD G43 ....125 D1
Daldowie Crematorium
UD/BTH/TAN G71 ....116 A3
Dalmarnock Industrial Estate
RUTH G73 ....110 A1
Dalmarnock Primary School
DMNK/BRGTN G40 ....90 A3
Dalmarnock Trading Estate
RUTH G73 ....109 D2
Dalsholm Industrial Estate
MRYH/FIRH G20 ....26 B4

Darnley Primary School
PLK/PH/NH G53 ....122 A3
David Dale College
DMNK/BRGTN G40 ....89 D2
David Lloyd Sports Centre
PSLYN/LNWD PA3 ....54 B3
Dean Park Hotel
RNFRW PA4 ....56 B1
Dental Hospital & School
KVGV G3 ....2 C4
Donald Dewar Leisure Centre
DRUM G15 ....23 C1
Douglas Inch Centre
KVGV G3 ....2 A3
Douglas Park Golf Club
BSDN G61 ....16 A2
Dowanhill Primary School
PTCK G11 ....61 D1
Drumchapel Health Centre
DRUM G15 ....12 B4
Drumchapel High School
DRUM G15 ....13 C3
Drumchapel Hospital
DRUM G15 ....23 C1
Drumchapel Pool
DRUM G15 ....22 B1
Drummore School
DRUM G15 ....14 A3
Drumoyne Industrial Estate
GOV/IBX G51 ....83 C1
Drumoyne Primary School
GOV/IBX G51 ....59 D4
Drumpark Special School
CTBR ML5 ....99 D1
Drumpellier Country Park Visitor Centre
CTBR ML5 ....75 D2
Drumry Primary School
DRUM G15 ....22 A1
Duchess Industrial Estate
RUTH G73 ....110 B2
Dunard Primary School
MRYH/FIRH G20 ....43 C3
Dundas Business Centre
COWCAD G4 ....3 D2
Eastbank Academy
CAR/SHTL G32 ....93 D3
Eastbank Primary School
CAR/SHTL G32 ....94 A2
Easterhouse Pool
ESTRH G34 ....72 B3
Easterhouse Sports Centre
ESTRH G34 ....72 A2
Easthall Primary School
STPS/GTHM/RID G33 ....72 A4
Eastmuir Special School
STPS/GTHM/RID G33 ....94 B1
East Park Home School
MRYH/FIRH G20 ....42 B2
Eastwood Recreation Centre
GIF/THBK G46 ....136 B1
Eastwood Theatre
GIF/THBK G46 ....136 B1
Elderpark Clinic
GOV/IBX G51 ....60 A4
Elder Park Primary School
GOV/IBX G51 ....59 D3
Elmvale Primary School
PPK/MIL G22 ....45 D2
The Ewington Hotel
GVH/MTFL G42 ....106 A2
Express by Holiday Inn
CGLE G1 ....8 A3
COWCAD G4 ....3 F4
Family Planning Clinic
KVGV G3 ....63 C2
Farm Castle Industrial Estate
RUTH G73 ....110 B3
Farmeloan Industrial Estate
RUTH G73 ....110 A3
Ferguslie Cricket Club
PSLYS PA2 ....76 A4
Fernhill School
RUTH G73 ....130 B4
Festival Business Centre
GOV/IBX G51 ....85 C1
Film Theatre
KVGV G3 ....3 D4
Firhill Business Centre
MRYH/FIRH G20 ....43 D3
Flemington Industrial Estate
BLTYR/CAMB G72 ....134 B3
Florence Street Clinic
GBLS G5 ....8 A5
Forge Shopping Centre
DEN/PKHD G31 ....91 C1
The Fort Theatre
BSHPBGS G64 ....31 D2
French Street Industrial Estate
RNFRW PA4 ....55 C1
Gadburn Special School
SPRGB/BLRNK G21 ....47 D2
Gallery of Modern Art
CGLE G1 ....7 F1
Gallowgate Market
CGLE G1 ....8 C4
Gallowhill Primary School
PSLYN/LNWD PA3 ....55 C4
Garnetbank Primary School
KVGV G3 ....2 B3
Garrowhill Primary School
BAIL/MDB/MHD G69 ....96 A2
Garscadden Primary School
KNTSWD G13 ....22 B4
Garthamlock Primary School
STPS/GTHM/RID G33 ....70 B2
Garthamlock Secondary School
STPS/GTHM/RID G33 ....71 C1
Gartnavel General Hospital
KVD/HLHD G12 ....40 B3
Gartnavel Royal Hospital
KVD/HLHD G12 ....40 B3
Gask House School
BSHPBGS G64 ....31 D4
GHK RFC
KNTSWD G13 ....40 A1
Giffnock Primary School
GIF/THBK G46 ....124 B4
The Glasgow Academy
KVD/HLHD G12 ....42 B4
Glasgow Airport
PSLYN/LNWD PA3 ....53 C2
Glasgow Botanic Gardens
KVD/HLHD G12 ....42 A3
Glasgow Caledonian University
COWCAD G4 ....4 A3
KVD/HLHD G12 ....40 B1
KVGV G3 ....62 B1
Glasgow Cathedral
COWCAD G4 ....5 D5
Glasgow College of Nautical Studies
CGLE G1 ....8 A5
Glasgow Cross
CGLE G1 ....8 B3
Glasgow Gaelic School
COWCAD G4 ....2 A2
Glasgow Golf Club
BSDN G61 ....27 C1
Glasgow Marriott Hotel
KVGV G3 ....6 B1
Glasgow Moat House
KVGV G3 ....62 A4
Glasgow Museums Resource Centre (The Open Museum)
PLK/PH/NH G53 ....120 A2
Glasgow Necropolis
COWCAD G4 ....9 E1
Glasgow Nuffield Hospital
KVD/HLHD G12 ....41 C2
Glasgow Royal Infirmary
COWCAD G4 ....5 D4
Glasgow School of Art
COWCAD G4 ....3 D3
Glasgow Science Centre & IMAX
GOV/IBX G51 ....62 A4
Glasgow Steiner School
KVGV G3 ....62 A3
Glasgow Tower
GOV/IBX G51 ....61 D4
Glasgow Zoopark
UD/BTH/TAN G71 ....116 A1
Glendale Primary School
PLKSD/SHW G41 ....86 B3
Glenduffhill Cemetery
CAR/SHTL G32 ....94 B1
Glen Family Centre
GIF/THBK G46 ....136 A1
Glenpark Industrial Estate
DEN/PKHD G31 ....90 B1

Glenvale FC
PSLY PA1 ....76 A3
Glenwood Business Centre
CSMK G45 ....128 B4
Glenwood Business Park
CSMK G45 ....128 B4
Glynhill Hotel
RNFRW PA4 ....55 C2
Golfhill Primary School
DEN/PKHD G31 ....5 F5
Gorbals Health Centre
GBLS G5 ....88 A3
Gorbals Leisure Centre
GBLS G5 ....8 B5
Govan Health Centre
GOV/IBX G51 ....59 D3
Govan High School
GOV/IBX G51 ....59 D4
Govanhill Health Centre
GVH/MTFL G42 ....107 C1
Gowanbank Primary School
PLK/PH/NH G53 ....120 B1
Greenfield Primary School
GOV/IBX G51 ....60 A4
Greenview School
PPK/MIL G22 ....45 C1
Haggs Castle Golf Club
PLKSW/MSWD G43 ....84 A4
Haghill Primary School
DEN/PKHD G31 ....67 C4
Hallside Primary School
BLTYR/CAMB G72 ....134 B3
Hamiltonhill Industrial Estate
PPK/MIL G22 ....44 A3
Hampden Park
GVH/MTFL G42 ....107 D3
Hampden Special School
GVH/MTFL G42 ....108 A3
The Harvest Clinic
COWCAD G4 ....2 B2
Hawkhead Cemetery
PSLYS PA2 ....79 C4
Heatherbank Museum of Social Work Trust
KVD/HLHD G12 ....62 B1
High School of Glasgow
BSDN G61 ....14 B3
The High School of Glasgow
KNTSWD G13 ....39 D1
Hillhead High School
KVD/HLHD G12 ....62 B1
Hillhead Primary School
KVD/HLHD G12 ....42 B4
Hillhead RFC
KVD/HLHD G12 ....41 C3
Hillington Industrial Estate
CARD/HILL/MSPK G52 ....57 C4
Hillington Park Retail & Amenities Centre
CARD/HILL/MSPK G52 ....57 D3
Hillington Primary School
CARD/HILL/MSPK G52 ....81 C1
Hillpark Secondary School
PLKSW/MSWD G43 ....124 B2
Hill's Trust Primary School
GOV/IBX G51 ....60 A3
HM Prison Barlinnie
STPS/GTHM/RID G33 ....69 C2
Holiday Inn
CGLW G2 ....6 C1
PSLYN/LNWD PA3 ....53 C2
Hollybrook Special School
GVH/MTFL G42 ....107 C1
Holmlea Primary School
LNPK/KPK G44 ....126 B1
Holmwood House NTS
LNPK/KPK G44 ....127 C3
Holy Cross Primary School
GVH/MTFL G42 ....107 C1
Holyrood Secondary School & Sports Centre
GVH/MTFL G42 ....107 D2
Hotel Ibis
CGLW G2 ....2 C4
House for an Art Lover
CARD/HILL/MSPK G52 ....84 A3
Househillmuir Primary School
PLK/PH/NH G53 ....121 C2
Howford Special School
PLK/PH/NH G53 ....100 B1
Hunterhill Tutorial Centre
PSLYS PA2 ....78 A4
Hunterian Museum
KVD/HLHD G12 ....62 A1
Hutchesons Grammar Junior School
KVD/HLHD G12 ....62 A1
Hutchesons Grammar Prep School
GVH/MTFL G42 ....106 B1
Hutchesons Grammar School
PLKSD/SHW G41 ....105 D1
Hutchesons' Hall
CGLE G1 ....8 A2
Hutchesons St Aloysians RFC
GIF/THBK G46 ....123 D2
Hyndland Primary School
PTCK G11 ....61 C1
Hyndland Secondary School
KVD/HLHD G12 ....40 B4
Ibrox Industrial Estate
GOV/IBX G51 ....84 B1
Ibrox Primary School
GOV/IBX G51 ....84 A2
International Christian College
COWCAD G4 ....4 C5
IQRA Academy
GOV/IBX G51 ....85 C2
Isobel Mair School
CRMNK/CLK/EAG G76 ....137 D2
Italian Centre
CGLE G1 ....8 A2
John Hillhouse Industrial Estate
BLTYR/CAMB G72 ....111 C4
John Paul Academy
SMSTN G23 ....27 C2
John Wheatley College
CAR/SHTL G32 ....93 D2
ESTRH G34 ....73 C2
Jordanhill School
KNTSWD G13 ....39 D2
Jurys Hotel
KVD/HLHD G12 ....40 B2
Kelbourne School
MRYH/FIRH G20 ....42 B2
Kelburne Cricket Club
PSLY PA1 ....78 A2
Kelvindale Primary School
KVD/HLHD G12 ....40 B2
Kelvingrove Art Gallery & Museum
KVD/HLHD G12 ....62 A2
Kelvin Hall International Sports Arena
KVGV G3 ....61 D2
Kelvinhaugh Primary School
KVGV G3 ....61 D3
The Kelvin Park Lorne Hotel
KVGV G3 ....62 B2
Kelvin School
KVGV G3 ....61 D2
The Kelvinside Academy
KVD/HLHD G12 ....42 A2
Kennyhill School
DEN/PKHD G31 ....67 D3
Kibble Education & Care Centre
PSLYN/LNWD PA3 ....52 B3
Kilbowie Cemetery
CLYDBK G81 ....21 C1
Kilbowie Retail Park
CLYDBK G81 ....21 C1
Killermont Primary School
BSDN G61 ....16 A3
Kings Park Secondary School
LNPK/KPK G44 ....127 D2
Kings Theatre
CGLW G2 ....2 B4
Kinning Park Medical Centre
PLKSD/SHW G41 ....86 A1
Kirkhill Golf Club
BLTYR/CAMB G72 ....132 B4
Kirklandneuk Primary School
RNFRW PA4 ....35 C4
Kirk Lane Cemetery
PLKSW/MSWD G43 ....104 B4
Kirkriggs School
CSMK G45 ....129 D2
Knightswood Community Centre
KNTSWD G13 ....38 A1
Knightswood Golf Club
KNTSWD G13 ....23 D4
Knightswood Primary School
KNTSWD G13 ....25 C4

Knightswood Secondary School
KNTSWD G13 ....39 C1
Knockburn Primary School
SPRGB/BLRNK G21 ....33 C4
Ladywell School
SCOT G14 ....59 C1
Laird Business Park
DMNK/BRGTN G40 ....109 D1
Lambhill Cemetery
SMSTN G23 ....28 B2
Lamlash Primary School
STPS/GTHM/RID G33 ....70 A3
Langfaulds Primary School
DRUM G15 ....12 B3
Langlands School
GOV/IBX G51 ....59 D4
Langs Hotel
CGLE G1 ....3 F4
Langside College
CSMK G45 ....129 C4
GVH/MTFL G42 ....106 B3
Langside Primary School
PLKSD/SHW G41 ....105 C3
Lansdowne Clinic
KVD/HLHD G12 ....40 B2
Leithland Primary School
PLK/PH/NH G53 ....101 C3
Lethamhill Golf Club
STPS/GTHM/RID G33 ....49 C4
Leverndale Hospital
PLK/PH/NH G53 ....100 A1
Lightburn Hospital
CAR/SHTL G32 ....70 A4
The Lighthouse
CGLE G1 ....7 E2
Linburn Special School
CARD/HILL/MSPK G52 ....80 B1
Linn Park Gardens
LNPK/KPK G44 ....126 B4
Linn Park Golf Club
LNPK/KPK G44 ....127 C3
Linnpark Industrial Estate
CSMK G45 ....127 D4
Linnvale Primary School
CLYDBK G81 ....21 D2
Littlehill Golf Club
BSHPBGS G64 ....32 A4
Littlehill Primary School
STPS/GTHM/RID G33 ....48 A4
Lochend Community High School
ESTRH G34 ....73 D3
Lochend Secondary School
ESTRH G34 ....73 D3
Lochgoin Primary School
DRUM G15 ....12 B3
Lochinch Playing Fields & Sports Club
PLKSW/MSWD G43 ....103 C2
Loch Primary School
RUTH G73 ....131 C3
London Road Primary School
DMNK/BRGTN G40 ....90 B3
Lorne Street Primary School
GOV/IBX G51 ....85 D1
Lourdes Primary School
CARD/HILL/MSPK G52 ....82 A3
Lourdes Secondary School
CARD/HILL/MSPK G52 ....82 B3
M8 Trading Estate
PLKSD/SHW G41 ....86 A2
Madhok Medical Centre
GVH/MTFL G42 ....106 B4
Malmaison Hotel
CGLW G2 ....2 C5
Maryhill Crematorium
SMSTN G23 ....28 A3
Maryhill FC
MRYH/FIRH G20 ....42 B1
Maryhill Health Centre
MRYH/FIRH G20 ....42 B1
Maryhill Primary School
MRYH/FIRH G20 ....27 D4
McGill Primary School
PLK/PH/NH G53 ....101 D1
Mclellan Galleries
KVGV G3 ....2 C4
Meadowburn Primary School
BSHPBGS G64 ....19 C4
Meadowside Industrial Estate
RNFRW PA4 ....36 A1
Merrylee Primary School
PLKSW/MSWD G43 ....126 A2
Middlefield Residential School
PTCK G11 ....61 C1
Midlock Medical Centre
GOV/IBX G51 ....84 B2
Millennium Hotel
CGLE G1 ....7 F1
Milncroft Primary School
STPS/GTHM/RID G33 ....70 B3
Milngavie Business Centre
MLNGV G62 ....10 B2
Milngavie Primary School
MLNGV G62 ....10 B1
Miltonbank Primary School
PPK/MIL G22 ....30 A3
Milton Clinic
PPK/MIL G22 ....30 A4
Milton School
PPK/MIL G22 ....31 C4
Mitchell Theatre & Library
KVGV G3 ....2 A4
Moorpark Primary School
RNFRW PA4 ....55 C1
Mosspark Primary School
CARD/HILL/MSPK G52 ....83 C4
Mossvale Primary School
PSLYN/LNWD PA3 ....53 C4
Mount Florida Medical Centre
GVH/MTFL G42 ....106 B3
Mount Florida Primary School
GVH/MTFL G42 ....107 C4
Mount Manor Business Park
KVGV G3 ....62 A3
Mount Vernon Primary School
CAR/SHTL G32 ....94 B4
Munro Business Centre
KNTSWD G13 ....25 C4
Murano Medical Centre
MRYH/FIRH G20 ....43 C3
Museum of Scottish Football
GVH/MTFL G42 ....107 C4
Museum of Transport
PTCK G11 ....61 D2
National Piping Centre
COWCAD G4 ....3 F3
National Swimming Centre at Tollcross Leisure Centre
CAR/SHTL G32 ....92 B3
Nethercommon Industrial Estate
PSLYN/LNWD PA3 ....53 D4
Nethercraigs Sports Centre
PLK/PH/NH G53 ....102 A1
New Albion Industrial Estate
KNTSWD G13 ....22 A4
Newhills School
STPS/GTHM/RID G33 ....71 D4
Newmains Primary School
RNFRW PA4 ....55 D2
Newspaper Offices
CGLE G1 ....8 B1
Nitshill Primary School
PLK/PH/NH G53 ....120 B3
North Glasgow College
SPRGB/BLRNK G21 ....46 A3
North Woodside Swimming Pool
COWCAD G4 ....2 C1
Notre Dame High School
KVD/HLHD G12 ....41 D4
Notre Dame Primary School
KVD/HLHD G12 ....41 D4
Novotel
CGLW G2 ....2 C4
Nuneaton Industrial Estate
DMNK/BRGTN G40 ....90 A4
Oakbank Industrial Estate
COWCAD G4 ....64 A1
MRYH/FIRH G20 ....43 D4
Oakgrove Primary School
COWCAD G4 ....2 C1
Odeon Cinema
CGLW G2 ....3 E5
GOV/IBX G51 ....86 B1
Ogilvie Primary School
STPS/GTHM/RID G33 ....72 A4
One Devonshire Gardens Hotel
KVD/HLHD G12 ....41 C3
Optimax Laser Eye Clinic
KVGV G3 ....2 A3

Our Holy Redeemers Primary School *CLYDBK* G81 ....21 D4
Our Lady of the Annunciation Primary School *PLKSW/MSWD* G43 ....125 D2
Our Lady of the Assumption Primary School *MRYH/FIRH* G20 ....43 D2
Our Lady of the Missions Primary School *GIF/THBK* G46 ....136 A1
Our Lady of the Rosary Primary School *CARD/HILL/MSPK* G52 ....82 B3
Outdoor Recreation Centre *BSHPBGS* G64 ....31 D3
Paisley Abbey *PSLY* PA1 ....77 D2
Paisley Crematorium *PSLY* PA1 ....76 A2
Paisley Grammar School *PSLY* PA1 ....78 A2
Paisley Museum & Art Galleries *PSLY* PA1 ....76 B3
Parkhead Hospital *DEN/PKHD* G31 ....91 D2
Parkview Business Centre *KVGV* G3 ....2 A3
Parkview Primary School *SMSTN* G23 ....27 D3
Partick Market *PTCK* G11 ....61 D1
Partick Thistle FC (Firhill Stadium) *MRYH/FIRH* G20 ....43 D3
The Pavilion Theatre *CGLW* G2 ....3 E4
Penilee Secondary School *CARD/HILL/MSPK* G52 ....80 B1
Pentagon Business Centre *CGLW* G2 ....6 B2
People's Palace *DMNK/BRGTN* G40 ....8 C5
Petershill FC *SPRGB/BLRNK* G21 ....46 A4
Petershill Recreation Centre *SPRGB/BLRNK* G21 ....47 C4
Phoenix Industrial Estate *PSLYN/LNWD* PA3 ....53 D4
Pinewood Primary School *DRUM* G15 ....14 A4
The Play Drome *CLYDBK* G81 ....20 B2
Pollok Country Park *PLKSD/SHW* G41 ....103 D2
Pollok Golf Club *PLKSW/MSWD* G43 ....103 D4
Pollok House *PLK/PH/NH* G53 ....103 C3
Pollok Leisure Centre *PLK/PH/NH* G53 ....101 D4
Pollok Shopping Centre *PLK/PH/NH* G53 ....101 D4
Pollokshields Primary School *PLKSD/SHW* G41 ....86 B4
Possil Loch Nature Reserve *SMSTN* G23 ....29 D3
Possilpark Health Centre *PPK/MIL* G22 ....44 B3
Premier Lodge *CGLW* G2 ....2 B4
Prince's Square Shopping Centre *CGLE* G1 ....7 E2
Provand's Lordship *COWCAD* G4 ....4 C5
Provan Hall NTS *ESTRH* G34 ....72 A2
Provanhall Primary School *ESTRH* G34 ....72 B2
Quality Hotel *CGLW* G2 ....7 D1
Quarry Brae Primary School *DEN/PKHD* G31 ....92 A2
Queenslie Industrial Estate *STPS/GTHM/RID* G33 ....71 D3
Queen's Park FC (Hampden Park) *GVH/MTFL* G42 ....107 D3
Radisson SAS Glasgow *CGLW* G2 ....7 D2
Ralston Golf Club *PSLY* PA1 ....79 D3
Ralston Primary School *PSLY* PA1 ....80 A2
Ramoy Business Centre *PSLY* PA1 ....76 A3
Ramshorn Theatre *CGLE* G1 ....8 B1
Rangers FC (Ibrox) *GOV/IBX* G51 ....84 A1
Regency Medical Clinic *KVGV* G3 ....62 B2
Reid Kerr College *PSLYN/LNWD* PA3 ....77 D1
Renfrew Golf Club *RNFRW* PA4 ....35 C2
Renfrew Health Centre *RNFRW* PA4 ....55 D1
Renfrew High School *RNFRW* PA4 ....56 A1
Renfrew-Paisley Lagoon Ice Rink *PSLY* PA1 ....77 D3
Richmond Doctors Surgery *PTCK* G11 ....60 B1
Richmond Park School *GBLS* G5 ....88 B4
Riddrie Park Cemetery *STPS/GTHM/RID* G33 ....48 B4
Robslee Primary School *GIF/THBK* G46 ....136 B1
Rogerfield Primary School *ESTRH* G34 ....73 D3
Rosevale School *PPK/MIL* G22 ....30 B4
Rosshall Academy *CARD/HILL/MSPK* G52 ....81 C3
Ross Hall Hospital *CARD/HILL/MSPK* G52 ....81 C4
Royal College of Nursing *KVGV* G3 ....63 C2
Royal Concert Hall *CGLE* G1 ....3 F5
Royal Highland Fusilliers Museum *KVGV* G3 ....2 B3
Royal Hospital for Sick Children & Maternity Hospital *KVGV* G3 ....61 D2
Royal Maternity Hospital *COWCAD* G4 ....8 B1
Royston Primary School *SPRGB/BLRNK* G21 ....5 F3
Royal Scottish Academy of Music and Drama *CGLW* G2 ....3 D4
Ruchazie Primary School *STPS/GTHM/RID* G33 ....69 D2
Ruchill Primary School *MRYH/FIRH* G20 ....43 C1
Rutherglen Cemetery *RUTH* G73 ....129 D1
Rutherglen Health Centre *RUTH* G73 ....110 A4
Rutherglen High School *RUTH* G73 ....110 A3
Rutherglen Swimming Pool *RUTH* G73 ....109 D4
Sacred Heart Primary School *DMNK/BRGTN* G40 ....89 D3
SAE Technology College *PLKSD/SHW* G41 ....86 A2
St Agnes Primary School *SMSTN* G23 ....28 A3
St Aidans Special School *CAR/SHTL* G32 ....68 A4
St Alberts Primary School *PLKSD/SHW* G41 ....85 D3
St Aloysius College *KVGV* G3 ....2 C3
St Aloysius Preparatory School *KVGV* G3 ....2 C3
St Aloysius Primary School *SPRGB/BLRNK* G21 ....45 D2
St Andrews Cathedral *CGLE* G1 ....7 E3
St Andrews Clinics for Children *KVD/HLHD* G12 ....42 A4
St Andrews High School *CLYDBK* G81 ....21 C3
St Andrews Primary School *BSDN* G61 ....14 A1
St Andrews RC Secondary School *CAR/SHTL* G32 ....69 D4

St Angelas Primary School
PLK/PH/NH G53 ....121 D4
St Annes Primary School
DMNK/BRGTN G40 ....90 A1
St Anthonys FC
GOV/IBX G51 ....84 A1
St Anthonys Primary School
GOV/IBX G51 ....60 A3
RUTH G73 ....130 B3
St Augustine's Primary School
PPK/MIL G22 ....30 A4
St Bartholomews Primary School
CSMK G45 ....129 C3
St Benedict's Primary School
ESTRH G34 ....72 B2
St Bernards Primary School
PLK/PH/NH G53 ....120 A2
St Blanes Primary School
SMSTN G23 ....27 D2
St Brendan's Primary School
KNTSWD G13 ....22 A4
St Bride's Primary School
BLTYR/CAMB G72 ....132 B2
GVH/MTFL G42 ....106 B1
St Bridgets Primary School
BAIL/MDB/MHD G69 ....96 B2
St Brigid's Primary School
GVH/MTFL G42 ....108 A3
St Cadoc's Primary School
BLTYR/CAMB G72 ....133 D3
St Catherine's Primary School
PSLYN/LNWD PA3 ....77 D1
St Catherines Primary School
SPRGB/BLRNK G21 ....47 D2
St Charles Primary School
BLTYR/CAMB G72 ....135 C1
MRYH/FIRH G20 ....43 C3
St Clare's Primary School
DRUM G15 ....13 C3
St Clares Primary School
ESTRH G34 ....74 A3
St Columbkilles Primary School
RUTH G73 ....109 D4
St Convals Primary School
PLKSW/MSWD G43 ....105 C3
St Cuthberts Primary School
PPK/MIL G22 ....44 A3
St Denis Primary School
DEN/PKHD G31 ....67 C4
St Edmunds Primary School
PLK/PH/NH G53 ....102 A2
St Elizabeth Seton Primary School
STPS/GTHM/RID G33 ....70 A3
St Enoch Business Centre
CGLE G1 ....7 E3
St Enoch Shopping Centre
CGLE G1 ....7 F3
St Eunans Primary School
CLYDBK G81 ....21 C1
St Fillans Primary School
LNPK/KPK G44 ....127 C1
St Francis of Assisi Primary School
BAIL/MDB/MHD G69 ....95 D4
St Francis Primary School
GBLS G5 ....88 B3
St Georges Medical Centre
COWCAD G4 ....2 A2
St Georges Primary School
CARD/HILL/MSPK G52 ....80 B2
St Georges School
CARD/HILL/MSPK G52 ....81 C2
St Gerard's Secondary School
GOV/IBX G51 ....61 C4
St Gilberts Primary School
SPRGB/BLRNK G21 ....47 D4
St Gregorys Primary School
MRYH/FIRH G20 ....42 A2
St Helens Primary School
BSHPBGS G64 ....33 C1
St James Primary School
DMNK/BRGTN G40 ....9 D5
St James's Primary School
RNFRW PA4 ....35 C4
St James's RC Primary School
PSLYN/LNWD PA3 ....53 C4
St James Street Health Centre
PSLY PA1 ....76 B2
St Jerome's Primary School
GOV/IBX G51 ....59 D4
St Joachims RC Primary School
CAR/SHTL G32 ....113 D2
St Joan of Arc Secondary School
PPK/MIL G22 ....29 D4
St John Ogilvie Primary School
PSLY PA1 ....78 B3
St Johns Approved School
CAR/SHTL G32 ....71 C4
St John's Primary School
BRHD/NEIL G78 ....118 B1
St Johns Primary School
GBLS G5 ....7 E5
St Josephs Primary School
COWCAD G4 ....2 C1
COWCAD G4 ....63 D1
MLNGV G62 ....10 A2
STPS/GTHM/RID G33 ....51 D2
St Judes Primary School
STPS/GTHM/RID G33 ....95 C1
St Julies Primary School
LNPK/KPK G44 ....128 A3
St Kevins's Primary School
BAIL/MDB/MHD G69 ....99 C2
St Kevins Special School
SPRGB/BLRNK G21 ....5 D1
St Louise Primary School
GIF/THBK G46 ....122 A3
St Mark's Primary School
BRHD/NEIL G78 ....118 B4
CAR/SHTL G32 ....92 A2
St Marks Primary School
RUTH G73 ....130 A2
St Marnock's Primary School
PLK/PH/NH G53 ....101 D2
St Marthas RC Primary School
SPRGB/BLRNK G21 ....47 C2
St Marys Cathedral
COWCAD G4 ....63 C1
St Mary's Kenmure School
BSHPBGS G64 ....31 C2
St Marys (Maryhill) Primary School
MRYH/FIRH G20 ....27 C4
St Marys Primary School
PSLY PA1 ....76 A3
St Matthews Primary School
BSHPBGS G64 ....32 B1
St Michael's Primary School
DEN/PKHD G31 ....91 C2
St Mirins Primary School
LNPK/KPK G44 ....127 D2
St Mirren FC (St Mirren Park)
PSLYN/LNWD PA3 ....77 C1
St Modans Primary School
STPS/GTHM/RID G33 ....69 D3
St Monicas Primary School
PLK/PH/NH G53 ....100 B2
St Mungo Museum of
Religious Life & Art
COWCAD G4 ....5 D5
St Mungo's Academy
DMNK/BRGTN G40 ....90 A1
St Mungos Primary School
COWCAD G4 ....4 C4
St Ninian's Primary School
KNTSWD G13 ....24 A2
St Oswald's School
LNPK/KPK G44 ....126 B2
St Patricks Primary School
KVGV G3 ....2 A5
St Paul's High School
PLK/PH/NH G53 ....102 A3
St Paul's Primary School
CAR/SHTL G32 ....93 C4
St Pauls Primary School
SCOT G14 ....38 B4
St Peter's Primary School
PTCK G11 ....61 D1
St Philip's Primary School
STPS/GTHM/RID G33 ....69 D2
St Philomena's Primary School
STPS/GTHM/RID G33 ....48 A4
St Pius Primary School
DRUM G15 ....13 C3
St Robert's Primary School
PLK/PH/NH G53 ....121 D1
St Rochs Primary School
SPRGB/BLRNK G21 ....66 A1
St Rochs Secondary School
SPRGB/BLRNK G21 ....5 E3

St Rose of Lima Primary School
STPS/GTHM/RID G33 ....70 A1
St Saviour's Primary School
GOV/IBX G51 ....61 C4
St Stephen's Primary School
SPRGB/BLRNK G21 ....5 D1
St Teresa's Primary School
PPK/MIL G22 ....44 B4
St Thomas Aquinas RC Secondary School
SCOT G14 ....39 D3
St Thomas Primary School
STPS/GTHM/RID G33 ....68 B2
St Timothys Primary School
CAR/SHTL G32 ....69 D4
St Vincent's Primary School
GIF/THBK G46 ....122 B3
St Vincents School Tollcross
CAR/SHTL G32 ....112 B1
Sandaig Primary School
STPS/GTHM/RID G33 ....95 C1
Sandwood Primary School
CARD/HILL/MSPK G52 ....81 C2
Saracen Health Centre
PPK/MIL G22 ....44 A3
Saracen Primary Annexe
PPK/MIL G22 ....44 B4
Saracen Primary School
PPK/MIL G22 ....44 A3
Scotland Street School Museum
GBLS G5 ....86 B2
Scotstoun Leisure Centre
SCOT G14 ....39 C3
Scotstoun Primary School
SCOT G14 ....38 B3
Scotstoun Stadium
SCOT G14 ....38 B3
Scottish Enterprises
CGLW G2 ....6 B1
Scottish Exhibition & Conference Centre
KVGV G3 ....62 A4
Scottish TV
CGLW G2 ....3 E4
Scottish Youth Theatre
CGLE G1 ....7 E1
Scotus College
BSDN G61 ....14 A3
Shawbridge Industrial Estate
PLKSW/MSWD G43 ....104 B4
Shawlands Academy
PLKSD/SHW G41 ....105 C2
Shawlands Primary School
PLKSD/SHW G41 ....105 C2
Shawlands Surgery
PLKSD/SHW G41 ....105 C3
Sheriff Court
GBLS G5 ....7 F4
Shettleston Day Hospital
CAR/SHTL G32 ....92 B3
Shettleston Health Centre
CAR/SHTL G32 ....93 C2
Showcase Cinema
BAIL/MDB/MHD G69 ....99 D3
Sighthill Cemetery
SPRGB/BLRNK G21 ....45 D4
Sighthill Primary School
SPRGB/BLRNK G21 ....45 C4
Simshill Primary School
LNPK/KPK G44 ....127 C3
Sir John Maxwell Primary School
PLKSW/MSWD G43 ....104 B4
Smithycroft Secondary School
STPS/GTHM/RID G33 ....68 B2
Somerset Eye Clinic
KVGV G3 ....62 B3
Southern General Hospital NHS Trust
GOV/IBX G51 ....59 C3
Spectrum Business Centre
RUTH G73 ....109 D3
Spiersbridge Business Park
GIF/THBK G46 ....122 B4
Spittal Primary School
RUTH G73 ....129 C2
Springburn Academy
SPRGB/BLRNK G21 ....46 A2
Springburn Health Centre
SPRGB/BLRNK G21 ....46 A3
Springburn Sports Centre
SPRGB/BLRNK G21 ....46 A3
Springfield Primary School
DMNK/BRGTN G40 ....110 A1
Springhill Primary School
BRHD/NEIL G78 ....118 A4
Stepps Primary School
STPS/GTHM/RID G33 ....51 D1
Stirling's Library
CGLE G1 ....7 F2
Stobhill General Hospital
SPRGB/BLRNK G21 ....46 B1
Stonedyke Primary School
DRUM G15 ....23 D1
Stonelaw High School
RUTH G73 ....110 A4
Stow College
COWCAD G4 ....2 C2
Strathclyde Art Centre
KVGV G3 ....6 B2
Strathclyde Business Centre
GOV/IBX G51 ....85 D1
PLKSD/SHW G41 ....86 A2
Strathkelvin Retail Park
BSHPBGS G64 ....19 D3
Summerhill Primary School
DRUM G15 ....13 D3
Sunnyside Primary School
STPS/GTHM/RID G33 ....50 A4
Swinton Primary School
BAIL/MDB/MHD G69 ....97 D1
The Tall Ship at Glasgow Harbour
GOV/IBX G51 ....61 D3
Temple Primary School
KNTSWD G13 ....25 D4
Templeton Business Centre
DMNK/BRGTN G40 ....89 C2
Tenement House
KVGV G3 ....2 B3
Tennant Caledonian Breweries & St Mungo Heritage Centre
COWCAD G4 ....9 E2
Thames Open College
CGLW G2 ....7 D1
Theatre Royal
COWCAD G4 ....3 E3
Thomas Muir High School
BSHPBGS G64 ....33 D2
Thornliebank Health Centre
GIF/THBK G46 ....123 C3
Thornliebank Industrial Estate
GIF/THBK G46 ....122 B4
Thornliebank Primary School
GIF/THBK G46 ....123 D3
Thorntree Primary School
CAR/SHTL G32 ....93 C1
Thornwood Primary School
PTCK G11 ....60 A1
Tinto Primary School
PLKSW/MSWD G43 ....124 B1
Tolbooth Steeple
CGLE G1 ....8 B3
Tollcross Industrial Estate
CAR/SHTL G32 ....93 C4
Toonspeak Young Peoples Theatre
SPRGB/BLRNK G21 ....66 A1
Tormusk Primary School
CSMK G45 ....129 D4
Toryglen Primary School
GVH/MTFL G42 ....108 B3
Townhead Health Centre
COWCAD G4 ....5 E4
Travel Inn
CGLE G1 ....8 B1
PSLYN/LNWD PA3 ....53 D3
UD/BTH/TAN G71 ....116 A2
Travelodge
CGLW G2 ....3 D3
GBLS G5 ....6 A4
The Triangle Shopping Centre
BSHPBGS G64 ....32 A2
Trinity High School
BLTYR/CAMB G72 ....111 D4
RNFRW PA4 ....36 A3
Tron Steeple
CGLE G1 ....8 A3
Tron Theatre
CGLE G1 ....8 B3
Turnbull High School
BSHPBGS G64 ....31 C1
UCI Cinemas
CLYDBK G81 ....20 B1

UGC Cinema
CGLW G2 .... **3** F4
DEN/PKHD G31 .... **91** C2
University of Glasgow
BSDN G61 .... **26** A3
PTCK G11 .... **61** D1
University of Glasgow Visitor Centre
KVD/HLHD G12 .... **62** A1
University of Paisley
PSLY PA1 .... **77** C2
PSLYS PA2 .... **76** B4
University of Strathclyde
COWCAD G4 .... **4** B5
KNTSWD G13 .... **39** C2
University of Strathclyde RFC
STPS/GTHM/RID G33 .... **50** A3
Victoria Buildings Business Centre
PSLY PA1 .... **78** A3
Victoria Infirmary
PLKSD/SHW G41 .... **106** A3
Victoria Primary School
GVH/MTFL G42 .... **107** C1
Victory Baths
RNFRW PA4 .... **36** A3
Walker Clinic
KVGV G3 .... **63** C3
Wellgreen Health Centre
PLKSW/MSWD G43 .... **104** B3
Wellhouse Primary School
STPS/GTHM/RID G33 .... **71** D4
Wellshot Primary School
CAR/SHTL G32 .... **92** B3
Westburn Cemetery
BLTYR/CAMB G72 .... **133** D1
West Coats Primary School
BLTYR/CAMB G72 .... **132** A2
Wester Cleddens Primary School
BSHPBGS G64 .... **32** A1
Westercommon Primary School
PPK/MIL G22 .... **43** D3
Western Infirmary Accident & Emergency
PTCK G11 .... **61** D1
Westerton Primary School
BSDN G61 .... **24** B1
Westfield Health Clinic
CARD/HILL/MSPK G52 .... **81** C2
Westmuir Medical Centre
DEN/PKHD G31 .... **91** D2
West of Scotland Cricket Club
PTCK G11 .... **61** C1
West of Scotland Science Park
MRYH/FIRH G20 .... **26** A2
West Primary School
PSLY PA1 .... **76** A3
Westwood Business Centre
ESTRH G34 .... **73** C3
Whitecrook Business Centre
CLYDBK G81 .... **21** C2
Whitecrook Primary School
CLYDBK G81 .... **21** C2
Whitehill Pool
DEN/PKHD G31 .... **67** C4
Whitehill Secondary School
DEN/PKHD G31 .... **67** C4
Whiteinch Business Park
SCOT G14 .... **59** C1
Whiteinch Indoor Bowling Stadium
SCOT G14 .... **59** D1
Whiteinch Primary School
SCOT G14 .... **39** D4
Whitlawburn Shopping Centre
BLTYR/CAMB G72 .... **131** D4
Williamsburgh Primary School
PSLY PA1 .... **78** A2
William Street Clinic
KVGV G3 .... **2** A5
Williamwood High School
CRMNK/CLK/EAG G76 .... **137** D3
Williamwood Medical Centre
CRMNK/CLK/EAG G76 .... **137** D3
Willowbank Primary School
COWCAD G4 .... **63** C1
Woodfarm High School
GIF/THBK G46 .... **123** D4
Woodhill Primary School
BSHPBGS G64 .... **33** C1
Woodside Place Business Centre
KVGV G3 .... **2** A3
Woodville Park Industrial Estate
GOV/IBX G51 .... **60** B4
Wyndford Primary School
MRYH/FIRH G20 .... **42** A1
Wyndford Recreation Centre
KVD/HLHD G12 .... **42** A2
Yoker Primary School
SCOT G14 .... **37** C1
Yoker Sports Centre
SCOT G14 .... **37** C1

Acknowledgements

The Post Office is a registered trademark of Post Office Ltd. in the UK and other countries.

Schools address data provided by Education Direct.

Petrol station information supplied by Johnsons

One-way street data provided by © Tele Atlas N.V. Tele Atlas

Garden centre information provided by

Garden Centre Association Britains best garden centres

Notes

QUESTIONNAIRE

Dear Atlas User
Your comments, opinions and recommendations are very important to us. So please help us to improve our street atlases by taking a few minutes to complete this simple questionnaire.

You do NOT need a stamp (unless posted outside the UK). If you do not want to remove this page from your street atlas, then photocopy it or write your answers on a plain sheet of paper.

Send to: The Editor, AA Street by Street, FREEPOST SCE 4598, Basingstoke RG21 4GY

ABOUT THE ATLAS...

Which city/town/county did you buy?

Are there any features of the atlas or mapping that you find particularly useful?

Is there anything we could have done better?

Why did you choose an AA Street by Street atlas?

Did it meet your expectations?

Exceeded ☐ **Met all** ☐ **Met most** ☐ **Fell below** ☐

Please give your reasons

MN069z

continued overleaf

Where did you buy it?

For what purpose? (please tick all applicable)

To use in your own local area ☐ **To use on business or at work** ☐

Visiting a strange place ☐ **In the car** ☐ **On foot** ☐

Other (please state)

LOCAL KNOWLEDGE...

Local knowledge is invaluable. Whilst every attempt has been made to make the information contained in this atlas as accurate as possible, should you notice any inaccuracies, please detail them below (if necessary, use a blank piece of paper) or e-mail us at *streetbystreet@theAA.com*

ABOUT YOU...

Name (Mr/Mrs/Ms)

Address

Postcode

Daytime tel no

E-mail address

Which age group are you in?

Under 25 ☐ **25-34** ☐ **35-44** ☐ **45-54** ☐ **55-64** ☐ **65+** ☐

Are you an AA member? **YES** ☐ **NO** ☐

Do you have Internet access? **YES** ☐ **NO** ☐

Thank you for taking the time to complete this questionnaire. Please send it to us as soon as possible, and remember, you do not need a stamp (unless posted outside the UK).

We may want to contact you about other products and services provided by us, or our partners (by mail, telephone) but please tick the box if you DO NOT wish to hear about such products and services from us by mail or telephone. ☐